UNFINISHED BUSINESS

Michael Jackson, Detroit,
and the Figural Economy
of American Deindustrialization

Judith Hamera

OXFORD
UNIVERSITY PRESS

OXFORD
UNIVERSITY PRESS

Oxford University Press is a department of the University of Oxford. It furthers
the University's objective of excellence in research, scholarship, and education
by publishing worldwide. Oxford is a registered trade mark of Oxford University
Press in the UK and certain other countries.

Published in the United States of America by Oxford University Press
198 Madison Avenue, New York, NY 10016, United States of America.

Library of Congress Cataloging-in-Publication Data
Names: Hamera, Judith.
Title: Unfinished business : Michael Jackson, Detroit, and the figural
economy of American deindustrialization / Judith Hamera.
Description: New York, NY : Oxford University Press, [2017] |
Includes bibliographical references and index.
Identifiers: LCCN 2017005799 | ISBN 9780199348596 (pbk. : alk. paper) |
ISBN 9780199348589 (cloth : alk. paper) | ISBN 9780199348619 (oxford scholarship online)
Subjects: LCSH: Jackson, Michael, 1958–2009—Criticism and interpretation. |
Deindustrialization—Social aspects—United States. |
Detroit (Mich.)—Economic conditions.
Classification: LCC ML420.J175 H36 2017 | DDC 306.3/408996073—dc23
LC record available at https://lccn.loc.gov/2017005799

9 8 7 6 5 4 3 2 1

Paperback printed by Webcom, Inc., Canada
Hardback printed by Bridgeport National Bindery, Inc., United States of America

For Alfred Bendixen, as ever,
and in loving memory of Joan Nowak (1903–1989)

CONTENTS

LIST OF PHOTOGRAPHS

PREFACE

I began thinking about the central question of this book on Tuesday night, November 4, 1980. I was working on presidential election coverage in the newsroom of WDET-FM, Detroit's public radio station. It had been a rough year for WDET. Listeners' financial contributions, a significant source of its funding, were declining as unemployment in Detroit and vicinity rose; plants were closing, and the local economy was clearly contracting. Station staff were leaving: laid off or seeing the writing on the wall. Wayne State University, the station's license holder, was facing budget challenges.

Even early that evening it was clear to all of us in the newsroom that conservative Republican Ronald Reagan would defeat Democratic incumbent Jimmy Carter in a landslide powered by "Reagan Democrats," including white, working-class ethnics from Macomb County that abutted Detroit. As the night wore on, one by one the giants of the Democratic Party progressive establishment were toppled. When it was announced that Birch Bayh, liberal incumbent Democratic senator from Indiana, lost his re-election bid, there was silence for a moment in the newsroom except for the tat-tat of the newswires. We knew then that we were witnessing the start of a profound political economic shift; someone—I don't remember who—said as much. We also knew from the demographics of the Reagan Democrats, and from Reagan's highly racialized rhetoric during the campaign, that race and racism were inextricable parts of it. It seemed in that moment that nothing had changed yet everything had changed, though I suspect none of us could have fully articulated what "everything" was. Deindustrialization did not begin with the election of Ronald Reagan, but for many of us in the newsroom that night, our awareness of the deindustrial as a racialized period of structural economic change did.

How can we study the ways structural economic change looks, feels, and operates at the level of public culture? In the final hours of November 4, 1980, I thought about this question with an emerging awareness of myself as a deindustrial subject at what felt like the spatiotemporal epicenter of a cultural, political, and economic shift. To me, the question felt personal.

Later I returned to this question as a scholar of performance studies. Performance studies offers the ideal critical tools for this inquiry. This is, in part, because performance makes structural economic change go: staging normative and aberrant relationships to capital in the new regime; narratizing memories of and nostalgia for the old one; animating rhetoric that touts or challenges the benefits or dangers of shifting modes of production; drawing on existing tropes and templates to imagine capitalism as benevolent, evolutionary, and racially neutral though, at the same time, highly racialized; dramatizing and resisting predatory impulses and practices. Performance is highly affective and affecting: both reflecting and shaping the ways liminal periods in capitalism feel at the level of the body and in the public sphere.

In this book I propose that *figural economies* of such tropes, performances, and narratives shape the ways US deindustrialization looked and felt between the mid-1980s and 2016. Figural economies combine the material conditions and details of individuals or places with their rhetorical, exemplary, and metaphoric potential. Figural economies circulate within political and libidinal economies: shaping desires, designating deserving and undeserving economic subjects. Figural economies operate through the dancing body, through stories, plays, public spectacles like trials, films, installations, and fantasies of urban redevelopment circulating in public discourse. Figural economies are deeply racialized, relying upon tropes of nineteenth-century race melodramas and blackface minstrelsy, African American performance, visual culture, and dance to construct and resist racial(-ist) representations of the social lives and work of capital.

In the United States, periods of structural economic change cannot be analyzed apart from issues of race and racial(-ist) hierarchies. Slavery was central to the emergence and consolidation of American capitalism. The Great Migration of African Americans to northern and Midwestern cities fueled American industrial expansion. It is my argument that US deindustrialization and the figural economies representing and shaping it are highly racialized: from the putatively normative deindustrial subject—the white ethnic Reagan Democrat—to Detroit, the majority African American city that is the period's most widely depicted cautionary tale. Images of and by African Americans operate within figural economies of American deindustrialization to shape hopes for social mobility in a changing economy, represent and assert black economic authority, generate fictions of black predatory agents responsible for deindustrial decline, and challenge the contemporary neoliberal dogmas of an intrinsically just, rational finance capitalism and public sector contraction. Representations of Michael Jackson and Detroit exemplify these operations, sometimes obviously, sometimes in ways that hide in plain sight.

I draw upon archival and ethnographic materials as data for this book. In anthropologist Carol J. Greenhouse's generative definition, "Ethnography, in contemporary usage, does not always involve 'fieldwork' in the conventional sense, but it always involves experience-based inquiry into the interpretive, institutional, and relational makings of the present."[1] In the case of *Unfinished Business*, this has meant repeated viewings of Michael Jackson's performances and repeated visits to key sites in Detroit, sometimes over almost thirty years. I rely on the critical skills developed in a humanities, and specifically a performance studies, education: attention to history and to allusions, resemblances, and mise en scène; close readings of texts and of bodies in motion; theoretically informed analyses of material culture, public discourse, and spectacle; and a critical focus on the rhetoric and operations of power.

Books about Detroit, especially though not exclusively first-person reportage, almost always begin by presenting the authors' local bona fides: their connections to the city past or present. As an ethnographer, I understand and appreciate these acts of self-situating, but in this context, I am also suspicious of them. In some cases, they read like anticipatory defensiveness or thinly veiled apologies for the authors' status as comparatively privileged white suburbanites or cosmopolitans writing about a poor black city. In others they seem like assertions of unproblematic ethnographic or moral authority. Yet I am also suspicious of my own suspicion. Given how frequently and disparagingly Detroit has been represented in the national media, why shouldn't those with a personal or purely intellectual investment in the city make clear that they are not the same as those opportunistic ruins porn producing, sensationalizing, and scopophilic others whose "curator's exhibitionism" contributes to the city's image as atavist no man's land or blank slate?[2]

Here I write about Detroit as an outsider and one-time insider: a status that gives me no special or inherent ethnographic, interpretative, or moral authority beyond a familiarity with history-in-place. I was born in Detroit to a family that was first-generation Polish American and became third-generation auto industry; mine was the first generation out of the factory. I grew up in East Detroit, a white, ethnic, working-class first-ring suburb that changed its name to "Eastpointe" in 1992: as if discursively expunging "Detroit" and replacing it with "pointe" would somehow align it with the affluent Grosse Pointes where auto industry elites—the Fords and the Dodges—lived in sprawling lakefront estates. The center of my early universe was my maternal grandmother Joan Nowak's white wood frame home in Detroit's Poletown neighborhood, one of the few racially mixed areas of the city. It seemed to me a warm, even magical place; I was too young to realize the area was ramshackle and increasingly poor. When Wayne State University, located in what was then called the "Cass Corridor"—Detroit's skid row now known as "Midtown"—offered me a full merit scholarship, I eagerly accepted, eventually finding a job at WDET-FM working alongside a diverse group of journalists, artists, and activists, most of whom were deeply committed to a just and expansive vision of the city. My family still lives in the Detroit metropolitan area.

. The auto industry provided for my family's material well-being; I learned very early that this well-being was won through struggle and that the union—the mighty United Auto Workers—was the hero of that struggle. But the industrial Detroit of my childhood and adolescence holds no nostalgia for me. Work in auto plant drop forges on the massive steam hammers destroyed my paternal grandfather's hearing. It affected my father's too, but he worked his way through law school while laboring in auto plants with the help of my mother, who also worked in the industry as an executive secretary for suppliers Detroit Diesel and Gear Grinding. Racism and sexism were overt and ubiquitous. My first substantial political memory was of segregationist George Wallace winning a Michigan presidential primary in 1972.

Intellectual or artistic ambitions were routinely dismissed, even by some of my closest friends who shared these ambitions, as frivolous at best. I left as soon as I could, not long after that night in the newsroom. My first significant solo performance was an elegy for Poletown, which was razed, then covered over by a General Motors plant, in 1981.

Unfinished Business did not start out as a book about Detroit but about Michael Jackson, and specifically about how and why Jackson matters as an exemplar of the promises and perils of postwar structural economic change. With Jackson too I am both an insider and an outsider in terms of fandom. As a child, I was devoted to the Jackson 5: their music, moves, and clothes. My brother and I howled appreciatively at their Saturday morning cartoon show. I bopped to Michael's cover of "Rockin' Robin" in Grace Thomas's tiny, tile-floored Detroit studio during jazz dance class. Jackson was roughly my age, and I felt—with wholly uncritical racial naiveté—that we were two of a kind: talented kids from working-class neighborhoods who loved to dance and were determined to move on to something better. I continued to follow his work, though not with the ardor of a true fan; while I was always captivated by his dancing, I found his post-1980s music superior to that of his *Thriller* heyday. By the time tabloids were devoting pages to accounts of his bizarre behavior, I had read Richard Sennett and Jonathan Cobb's book *The Hidden Injuries of Class* as well as critical race studies literature detailing the hidden and obvious injuries of racism. Given the brutality of Jackson's childhood in the steel town of Gary, Indiana, and his decades of labor both back and front stage in the entertainment industry, I figured he had earned the right to be strange.

How can we study the ways structural economic change looks, feels, and operates at the level of public culture? I returned to this question yet again during the recovery from the recent US Great Recession: a crisis reminding us that transitional periods within capitalism are treacherous times for all but the most highly privileged. Michael Jackson died during this long, slow recovery period in the midst of an attempted recovery of his own; Detroit went into and ultimately emerged from Chapter 9 bankruptcy. During this same period, the humanities in higher education were also in crisis: increasingly derided and dismissed as frivolous luxuries with a venom, reductive and instrumentalist thinking, and hostility to multiple dimensions of difference that made the anti-intellectualism I encountered as a smart, angry girl in Detroit seem positively enlightened by comparison. In positing figural economies as a way to track and analyze the affective, aesthetic, rhetorical, and above all racial dynamics shaping and powering the ways we experience deindustrialization, I unabashedly advocate for the critical humanities, and performance studies in particular, as analytical infrastructure crucial to understanding the cultural lives and work of capitalism. In times of structural economic change, though not only then, these lives and this work are too slippery and too consequential to be left only to economists.

ACKNOWLEDGMENTS

At times, during the course of this five-year project, "unfinished business" was simultaneously its title, a goad to keep at it, and possibly a prophecy about its ultimate fate. I am so grateful for dear friends and colleagues who kept me going throughout: buoying me with their optimism for this work; offering bibliography, keen insights, and memorable phrases; reading drafts; and reassuring me that the manuscript could be put aside as life repeatedly intruded.

My early research for *Unfinished Business* was supported by Texas A&M University's Melbern G. Glasscock Faculty Research Fellowship and by an Academy of Visual and Performing Arts Arts Research Enhancement Grant. I am very grateful to Texas A&M for providing these crucial resources.

D. Soyini Madison, my dear friend of more than thirty years, influenced every bit of this project. Her unerring political economic compass, her razor-sharp theorizing, and her passion for the critical potential of performance in theory and as practice are an ongoing inspiration.

Early in the writing of this book, I moved from Texas A&M to Princeton University. Jill Dolan and Stacy Wolf not only welcomed me with a depth and breadth of generosity that I can never repay but also read numerous drafts of key chapters and made invaluable suggestions for revisions. I am so grateful to both of them for their friendship, brilliance, and care.

Thank you to my colleagues and friends who read or heard drafts and provided insightful feedback during multiple phases of this project: Robin Bernstein, Anne Cheng, Micaela di Leonardo, Jill Dolan, Carol Greenhouse, Regina Kunzel, D. Soyini Madison, Susan Manning, Susan Vaneta Mason, Sally Ness, and Stacy Wolf. Thanks, too, to the generous interlocutors who made this project better by asking bracing questions, providing bibliography or an apt formulation that crystallized deeper insights, helping me hash out crucial points, and providing encouragement when it was needed most: Danielle Aubert, Jayson Beaster-Jones, Wendy Belcher, Harris M. Berger, Bettina Brandl-Risi, Gabriele Brandstetter, Karen Collias, Fred Corey, Clare Croft, Thomas De Frantz, Sherill Dodds, Michael Eric Dyson, Andrea Edwards, Kai van Eikels, Jennifer Erdely, Susan Leigh Foster, Mark Franko, Ed Greene, Cynthia Jackson, Claire Katz, Joseph Jewell, Amber Johnson, Hae

Kyung Lee, Marc Maxey, Kiri Miller, Kirsten Pullen, James Rosenheim, Toneisha Taylor, and Tamson Wolf.

My graduate and undergraduate students in performance studies at Texas A&M University were vital interlocutors during the early stages of this project. Special thanks to Yunina Barbour-Payne, Cymone Davis, Joshua Hardcastle, Ania Kalashnikova, Liz Livingston, Miguel Maymi, Elizabeth Melton, Andreaa Micu, Gary Powell, David Roby, Dani Sather, Dana Sayre, Alex Simpson, and Amber Wicks.

Portions of this project were presented at "In Bodies We Trust: Performance, Affect, and Political Economy," the Northwestern University Performance Studies Graduate Student Conference; the American Society for Theatre Research annual conference; the Davies Forum Lecture at the University of San Fancisco; the Colloquium for Doctoral Students in the Department of Dance, Texas Woman's University; the Center for Oral History and Performance as Social Action, Northwestern University; and the Temple University Dance Studies Colloquium. I am very grateful to audiences and questioners at these events for moving this work forward.

I did not anticipate that Simon Gikandi would become my Princeton colleague when he published the first installment of what would become part I of *Unfinished Business*, devoted to Michael Jackson, in *PMLA*. He was an exemplary editor in every way, and his insights defined this project in its most formative period.

In my second year at Princeton, and my third year with this project, I had the enormous good fortune to design and co-teach an extraordinary course with two wonderful colleagues and a group of students whose impact on this book has been transformative. "The Arts of Urban Transition," supported by the Princeton Mellon Initiative in Architecture, Urbanism, and the Humanities, allowed me to refine my thinking about Detroit in important ways. I could not have done so without my co-teachers Aaron Landsman and Aaron Shkuda. Our now two years of conversations about deindustrial cities and performance, and our two visits to Detroit, provided crucial conceptual infrastructure, and equally crucial inspiration, for part II of this book. Our students in the inaugural offering of the course were so engaged, so inspiring, so rigorous and creative in their thinking that they merit mention by name. Thank you Elie Albarran, Zachariah De Giulio, Sharim Estevez, Ryan Gedrich, Amelia Goldrup, Jacob Hamel, Emma Kaeser, William Lathrop, Spencer Parts, Alex Quetell, Loully Saney, Paige Shaw, Soumya Sudhakar, Maranatha Teferi, Oge Ude, Lauren Wodarski, Glenna Yu, and Lawrence Zietz. I can't tell you how much I enjoyed doing this work with you.

Princeton students Alex Quetell '17 and Sophie Andreassi '16 were as exemplary in providing research assistance as they are in their work as artists and intellectuals. I am very grateful for their help.

My Princeton Lewis Center and Dance Program colleagues Michael Cadden, Tina Fehlandt, Rebecca Lazier, Susan Marshall, Cindy Rosenfeld, and Aynsley Vandenbroucke have been supportive in every way since I first arrived on campus and have patiently borne my saying that I'd join them in New York for performances more often as soon as the book was done.

Tyree Guyton, creator of the *Heidelberg Project*, has been an inspiration since I first saw his work on Heidelberg Street almost thirty years ago. Jenenne Whitfield, the project's executive director, has been warm and generous in granting me access to the project's archives. Programming manager Margaret Grace and executive assistant Toni Nunn have been invaluable in helping me secure permissions for the images of the project in these pages.

I am grateful to Detroit interlocutors Halima Cassels (Detroit Narrative Agency), Amy Corle and Augusta Morrison (Museum of Contemporary Art Detroit), Maurice Cox (Detroit's planning director), Wayne Curtis and Richard Feldman (James and Grace Lee Boggs Center to Nurture Community Leadership), Erik Howard (the Alley Project), Invincible (ill) Weaver and Wesley Taylor (Complex Movements), William LeFevre (Walter P. Reuther Library, Wayne State University), Faina Lerman (Popp's Packing), George Jacobson (Kresge Foundation), and Amanda Sansoterra (Heidelberg Project). Thanks, too, to Karen Jania, Head of Access and Reference Services at the Bentley Historical Library, University of Michigan; Wendy Norris of the Theatre on Film and Tape Archive, New York Public Library; and Barbara McLaughlin, Princeton Library, for their assistance with the research and production of this manuscript. Thanks also to Ty Jones, Producing Artistic Director of the Classical Theatre of Harlem, and Michael Borowski of The Publicity Office for their assistance in securing production photographs of *Detroit '67* and *Detroit*, respectively.

Oxford University Press editor Norm Hirschy believed in this project from its earliest incarnation as a conference paper. I am grateful beyond measure for his support, his patience, and his insights. He is everything I could wish for and more in an editor. Thanks to Lauralee Yeary for her editorial assistance, and to the production staff at Oxford University Press.

An early version of chapter 1 of this book appeared in *PMLA* (October 2012) as "The Labors of Michael Jackson: Virtuosity, Deindustrialization, and Dancing 'Work.' "

My father died suddenly at the beginning of this project. My mother died at its conclusion after a long battle with a debilitating illness. They were, both of them, exemplary industrial subjects in every way: hard-working, firm believers in education as the only fulfilling route to a better life, and self-sacrificing so their children could enjoy and attain that life. I am forever grateful for their love and support.

Alfred Bendixen has been my most stalwart supporter in this enterprise, as in so many that have come before in our twenty years together. He has pulled me through when the going seemed insurmountable. This book, like all those before it, is for him. It is also written in memory of my beloved grandmother, Joan Nowak, who more than anyone else in my life inspired me to think deeply and clearhead-edly about Detroit with warm feelings but without nostalgia.

Introduction

"Never Can Say Goodbye":

US Deindustrialization as Unfinished Business

What are the ideas, symbols, and images that shape our conceptions of the "postindustrial"—
indeed that undergird the very way we think about our work lives?

> Jefferson Cowie and Joseph Heathcott, "Introduction,"
> *Beyond the Ruins: The Meanings of Deindustrialization*[1]

Michael Jackson and Detroit have more in common than Motown. Both were superstars with reputations for hard work: the King of Pop and the "arsenal of democracy."[2] Both are sensational racial and racialized subjects: Jackson the black icon who proudly asserted his racial identity and advanced an affective, affecting vision of the postracial in his music and charitable work, and Detroit, now a majority African American city that was a locus of black hope for economic opportunity in the Great Migrations of the early twentieth century and a site of interracial conflagration since the 1830s.[3] Both have been hypermediated spectacles. Each has been dismissed as an abject deviant deserving of public scorn. Both have been characterized as profligate spenders and prodigious debtors. Both fell on hard times; both offered promises of impending comebacks just around the corner. Both have been repeatedly declared dead, yet each stubbornly refuses to actually go away.

Jackson was as much a barely coherent set of representations and projections as he was a flesh-and-blood human being, even when he was alive. His body and public image operated as palimpsests: partial erasures with landscapes, performances, scandals, balance sheets, and faces layered one over another, earlier versions still barely discernible beneath the subsequent layers. Since his death he has been resurrected as a hologram, performatively reincarnated with each flash mob reproduction of *Thriller* and each subsequent recirculation on YouTube, and conjured as collateral to secure investment in never-quite-realized theme parks or museums, particularly in Gary, Indiana, the city of his birth.

Jackson's life and work have received surprisingly little scholarly attention given his global stature.[4] Further, his cultural ubiquity as a spectacle has obscured a crucial part of his legacy. At the height of his career, Michael Jackson very publicly exemplified the promise of working-class social mobility in the postwar US industrial moment. He was, as he himself observed, "by blood . . . as much crane operator as singer."[5] The discipline beaten into him by his crane operator father, coupled with his extraordinary artistry and legendary perfectionism, contributed to spectacular performances enabling his and his family's equally spectacular escape from the rigors and privations of their working-class life in Gary. That escape began when Jackson and his brothers signed with Motown, whose corporate DNA and production model were intimately linked to the auto industry via founder Berry Gordy's history on the Ford Motor Company assembly line.[6] Yet later in his career in the new millennium, as this very industrial infrastructure and its attendant promise of social mobility were increasingly, visibly imperiled, Jackson came to exemplify both the excesses of consumerism and financialization and, later, the demands of austerity readjustment. He spent too much, remade his face too much, borrowed too much, and appeared, or claimed to be, too frail to withstand the physical and emotional rigors of performance even as he embraced them. Over the arc of his career, Jackson embodied the promise and illustrated the perils of the shifting economic regimes that produced him.

Detroit's status as an urban cautionary tale, a ruin, and a blank slate, and its transformation from industrial solidity to putative no man's land to new creative class frontier, is well known and copiously documented.[7] Its potential as a political economic signifier is far more obvious than Jackson's despite the lack of consensus on the lessons to be drawn from its example. Images of Detroit's crumbling industrial, civic, and residential infrastructure circulate online, on film and on television, and as photo essays in expensive coffee-table books: ubiquitous disaster imagery feeding curiosity and voyeuristic fascination with scenes of racialized underclass decay.[8] Indeed, Detroit's persistence as/in representation—whether as ruin, synecdoche for a vanished Fordism, or urban dystopia—seemed at times inversely proportional to its persistence as an actual city as successive mayors have considered shrinking its physical footprint and its elected government was superseded by an appointed emergency manager from March 2013, to December 2014. Yet these very images of decay also informed the emergence of Detroit as a brand, particularly between 2011 and 2016. In this period, advertisements by Chrysler, Shinola, and Apple linked the city's deterioration to a "can-do" rhetoric of renewal, dependent on prior figurations of it as a rugged dystopia, blank slate, or new frontier. The city has been increasingly touted as the new SoHo, the new Brooklyn, or the new Berlin, where cheap real estate and a seemingly self-evident "realness" offer affordability, inspiration, potential community, and bohemian authenticity. Detroit-as-brand is now a gritty, creative national not-quite-comeback story.

Jackson and Detroit hit it big as a direct consequence of America's industrial heyday, but their fates and afterlives are also inextricably intertwined with its aftermath, including the long, slow, and wildly uneven emergence from the Great Recession of 2007–9, one which, almost a decade later, looks less like a "recovery" than the return of a new gilded age characterized by increasing income inequality, wage stagnation, and racial polarization. Jackson died on June 25, 2009, in the midst of his own attempt at fiscal repair: the fifty "This Is It" comeback concerts that would have helped settle his debts. At the time of his death, he owed between $400 and $500 million to creditors. Physician Dr. Conrad Murray was ultimately found criminally liable for Jackson's death from an overdose of the general anesthetic propofol, which Murray administered to Jackson, at the singer's request, to enable him to sleep. Jackson's physical and mental fitness to undertake the grueling regime of work in rehearsals required for the shows was a central issue in Murray's trial in 2011 and Jackson's mother's subsequent suit against his concert promoters, AEG Live, in 2013.

Also in 2013, in what was widely seen as an inevitable second act following the state's imposition of Kevyn Orr as emergency manager that same year, Detroit filed for Chapter 9 bankruptcy protection on July 18, the largest municipality to do so in United States history. At the time of the filing, the city had debts of between $18 and $20 billion. Work, fitness, and attempts at fiscal recovery were issues in the legal proceedings that followed, just as they were in the Murray trial and AEG lawsuit: evident in creditors' efforts to gut union protections for city workers and pensions for retired city employees, in the privatization of city assets and services, and in the city's unemployment rate: 9.7 percent in 2013, more than two full percentage points higher than for the country as a whole and more than one full percentage point higher than at earlier points in the US economic recovery.[9]

Ultimately, Jackson proved more profitable dead than alive. Six years after his death, his estate had earned an estimated $2 billion.[10] On Detroit the jury is still out. The city emerged from bankruptcy on December 10, 2014. Mayor Mike Duggan is proceeding with a redevelopment plan, the latest in a long series of such efforts stretching back decades.

This book is about what Michael Jackson and Detroit have in common: the spectacular coupling of race and work within an arc that took both from epic productivity through equally epic debt and contraction to efforts at fiscal and reputational recovery. What can this artist and this city tell us about how we conceptualize and imagine the times and political economies that produced them?

Unfinished Business argues that Michael Jackson and Detroit, both as material entities with specific histories and as representations with uncanny persistence, have something valuable to teach us about three decades of structural economic transition in the United States, and particularly about the changing nature of work and capitalism between the mid-1980s and 2016. They teach us about the racialization and aesthetics of these changes; about how they operate as structures of feeling and representational repertoires as well as shifts in the dominant mode of production; about how the industrial era has been—and is being—reimagined in light of present precarity; and about how its successor mode, financialization, uses imagery both very similar to and very different from its predecessor.[11] Specifically, *Unfinished Business* advances three major points:

- Figural economies of tropes, dance and theater conventions, and actual performances shape and reflect the ways structural change in dominant modes of production in the United States between the mid-1980s and 2016 congeal into public spectacles, circulate through a wide variety of media, and offer "lessons" to be learned about normative and aberrant relations to capital in transitional times.
- Michael Jackson and Detroit illuminate the operations of these figural economies with special clarity.
- Jackson's and Detroit's utility—their figural potential—resides in their capacities to both complicate and bring fictive coherence to the intertwining of race, work, and capital in this period.

"Deindustrialization" is the name most often given to this structural change in modes of production. I present a definition of deindustrialization in the next section of this introduction and discuss the specific trajectories of the US steel and auto industries in the chapters that follow. In line with current work on the subject, *Unfinished Business* presumes that what we call "deindustrialization" is uneven, locally inflected, multifaceted, and still in process: both a change in the dominant mode of production and a "struggle over meaning and collective memory."[12] Yet in addition to "deindustrialization" or "deindustrialized," I also employ the designation "the deindustrial" to characterize the specific transitional period from the mid-1980s to the present when, as historian Judith Stein pithily observes, the United States was increasingly shifting from "factories to finance."[13]

Whereas "deindustrialization" names the political economic processes of capital flight and the dissolution of the Fordist labor-management compact that led to workers' increasing economic precarity, crushing middle- and working-class debt, and wage stagnation, "the deindustrial" is both the temporal designation for the transitional period in which these shifts became acutely visible and the "historical sensorium," representational repertoires, and affects produced by these processes.[14] We now live within the deindustrial, and with all the anxiety and "cruel optimism" that characterizes such liminal periods of capitalism.[15] Some of this cruel optimism arises from rhetoric glamorizing contemporary contingent labor as flexible and entrepreneurial, but some also derives from an attachment to the Fordist labor-management compact made retrospectively more appealing in light of its retraction. The deindustrial thus includes both a repudiation of and a nostalgic fondness for elements of the US industrial imaginary. Further, characterizing this moment as "the deindustrial" underscores that deindustrialization itself is unfinished social, affective, and cultural business. Industrial infrastructure is not gone; the United States is still a leading global manufacturer even as union protections that defined this sphere have been whittled away, evaded, or dismantled.[16] Finally, the deindustrial as a period, a repertoire, and a structure of feeling both reflects and perpetuates the United States' unique intertwining of race, work, and capital: from chattel slavery through Jim Crow, the Great Migration and the segregated cities and interracial confrontations in the mid-twentieth-century industrial North, to the decline of the "Rust Belt," contraction of the social safety net, and the emergence of entrepreneurial "creative class" placemaking in the new millennium. This complex history of race, work, and capital is at the very heart of both Jackson's and Detroit's figural potential.

Because my focus is on the deindustrial as a liminal period within capitalism rather than on deindustrialization per se, *Unfinished Business* begins well after most histories of the latter. In the auto industry, for example, deindustrialization began as early as the 1950s in some accounts and escalated sharply in the "pivotal decade" of the 1970s.[17] While elements of this history are included in *Unfinished Business*, I focus on two other defining periods of the deindustrial in which the fraught nature of structural economic change was especially obvious: the mid-1980s, when the contraction of heavy industry and resulting unemployment became increasingly visible as a national problem, and the first sixteen years of the new millennium when the US consumer credit and real estate bubbles, and the subsequent global financial collapse, revealed that the transition from factories to finance was not the smooth, rational, evolutionary process elite economic institutions had postulated.

The period I examine here is loosely characterized as the "post–civil rights era" bracketed by the election of Ronald Reagan in chapter 1 and by the final years of Barack Obama's presidency in chapter 4. In this period, African Americans' public battles to desegregate schools, neighborhoods, and the industrial workplace in the 1950s, 1960s, and 1970s were widely viewed as both successful and past. Both Detroit and Gary, Indiana, had African American mayors for much of this time; Mike Duggan, Detroit's first white mayor in more than forty years, took office in 2014. Yet the period was also one of profound white racial(-ist) retrenchment and black resistance as two examples from opposite ends of the temporal arc covered here attest. Ronald Reagan secured support of blue-collar white "Reagan Democrats" in part through use of racist imagery like that of the profligate welfare queen living large on the public dime. Almost forty years later the Black Lives Matter movement organized during the putatively "postracial" years of Obama's presidency to combat an epidemic of police violence against African Americans.[18] *Unfinished Business* posits race and racial hierarchies as defining elements of the deindustrial and the figural economies that represent and shape it: from cross-racial identification with the virtuosic Michael Jackson of the mid-1980s through racist characterizations of black subprime debtors as scammers or hapless fools and the thirty-year efforts of Detroit artist Tyree Guyton to call attention to the civic abandonment and resilience of his African American neighborhood with his installation the *Heidelberg Project*.

The book begins with what I see as the formative years of the deindustrial: the mid-1980s, when Michael Jackson's career was at its height and Ronald Reagan was completing his first presidential term. Rising unemployment in heavy industry and the slow, visible death of so-called Rust Belt manufacturing centers characterized this period. An increasing number of political and economic analyses of deindustrialization per se evidenced the growing awareness that factory shutdowns were not momentary aberrations but symptoms of a structural change. Of course, by this point, the impacts of these changes had long been obvious to working-class families and communities. In Detroit, artist Tyree Guyton began to work on what would become the *Heidelberg Project* at this time (1986); the project is one of the subjects of chapter 4.

But the deindustrial also includes the consolidation and increasing visibility of the mode of production that came next: financialization, the "importance of financial markets, financial motives, financial institutions, and financial elites in the operation of the economy and its governing institutions, both at the national and at the international level."[19] Financialization generated its own crises, most acutely the consumer credit and real estate bubbles of the mid-2000s and the subsequent recession of 2007–9. In this same time frame, Michael Jackson became better known for his consumerist excesses and his debts than for his creative work. During the uneven US economic recovery that followed, artists actively reconsidered elements of the US postwar industrial legacy, including Dominique Morisseau's and Berry Gordy's plays set in the Detroit of the Motown era and Lisa D'Amour's use of "not necessarily" Detroit to dramatize contemporary middle-class precarity, as well as Mike Kelley's staging a reversal of white flight from the city in his large-scale Detroit installation *Mobile Homestead*.

Unfinished Business is not a cultural history of either deindustrialization or the deindustrial, nor is it a comprehensive survey of Michael Jackson's career or representations of Detroit over the past thirty years. It is, rather, a selective study of how two highly visible exemplars—one hiding in plain sight and the other glaringly obvious—both shape and reflect the ways the deindustrial looks and feels at the level of public culture. It probes what we talk about when we talk about living within changing modes of contemporary capitalism, including contracting structures of opportunity, debt, the nature of home and community, and, especially, the way race and racism shape our understanding of all these elements. It does so by examining how these issues emerge in Jackson's art, in coverage of his life, in works about Detroit and how they then circulate onstage, on the page, in the neighborhood, and in the museum. Though the book includes discussions of Jackson's and Detroit's histories prior to the 1980s—sometimes lengthy ones—it also focuses on how their figural work has operated over the past two decades of the new millennium.

In examining Jackson and Detroit, I focus on performances—dancing, theatrical productions, interactive installations, and media spectacle—and use performance as a critical tool to examine trials and historical events replete with theatricality. Performance is a particularly useful critical tool for examining structural economic change, and not only because, as noted in chapter 3, sometimes these transitions and their aftereffects are literally staged. Popular performance has long been a vehicle for articulating and imagining relations between bodies, work, and capital. Dance, theater, and public spectacle contributed significantly to the industrial imaginary. For example, chorus girls sexualized the value of precision and the atomization of the body in kick lines.[20] Strikes and labor theater challenged images of the nation's industrial infrastructure as intrinsically rational and unassailably monumental by exposing its material and psychic demands on workers and actively resisting its predations.[21] As the solidity of this mid-twentieth-century industrial infrastructure began to crumble, performers were cast as the paradigmatic immaterial, affective laborers of post-Fordism and "performance" became a new metric for assessing their efficiency as formulations like "performance-based management" indicate.[22]

Unfinished Business uses the theories and vocabulary of dance, performance, and theater studies to analyze some defining performances of the deindustrial, including those that gesture backward to the heyday of the industrial age. In so doing, it embraces "an activist project of culture-making" in which, as theater scholar Jill Dolan has argued, "we're called collectively to see what and who is stunningly, repeatedly evident and what and who is devastatingly invisible in the art and popular culture we regularly consume for edification and entertainment."[23]

African Americans are both repeatedly evident and often invisible in figural economies of the deindustrial. In the case of Detroit, though not only there, the city's majority black population has been implicitly linked to, and sometimes explicitly indicted for, its decrepitude.[24] Yet at the same time African Americans are so comparatively publicly invisible as creative agents within the deindustrial that Michael Jackson's status as an icon of the period must be vigorously asserted despite its seeming self-evidence given the artist's explicit references to his industrial roots, the prominence of Gary and Detroit in his celebrity narrative, and the often obvious deindustrial imagery in his video masterpieces. Instead, the deindustrial is typically bracketed cinematically by John Travolta in *Saturday Night Fever* (1977) at its seeming beginning and by Clint Eastwood in *Gran Torino* (2008), shot in Detroit, in its doldrums: the hard-working if disaffected white industrial heroes left out or left behind by structural economic change. In this repertoire, white men alone possessed the industrial era pedigree of hard work, discipline, and sacrifice that would render their deindustriality sufficiently alienating or tragic. Women as creative agents are almost entirely absent. As anthropologist Micaela di Leonardo has persuasively argued, deindustrialization's "folk model is the white American blue collar male."[25]

This folk model reflects the structural racism and sexism of US industrialization. The racial(-ist) politics of Gary's steel mills and Detroit's auto industry are emblematic; I discuss aspects of the racial history of each industry in chapters 1 and 3, respectively. But this folk model also has a darker history, one originating much earlier in the development of the US industrial imaginary. Historians David Roediger and Eric Lott assert that figures of African Americans were crucial to the consolidation of white masculinity within an emerging US "industrial morality" in the early nineteenth century.[26] The internalization of this new regime of discipline—"punctuality, regularity, and habits of sacrifice"—was fraught with anxiety alleviated by projection onto African Americans. Lott persuasively argues that US blackface minstrelsy in the early to mid-1840s especially materialized these projections:

> The blackface body figured the traditional "preindustrial" joys that social and economic pressures had begun to marginalize. The tortured and racist form of this pleasure indicates the ambivalent attitudes toward enjoyment itself that industrial morality encouraged.[27]

Roediger concludes that industrialization created a "new sense of whiteness by creating a new sense of blackness" through such figurations.[28]

More than a century later, deindustrialization too created a "new sense of whiteness," as it generated an increasing sense of precarity and anxiety that the Fordist good life, sustained by work in the plant, would soon be a thing of the past. Figurations of African Americans were central to this shift in modes of production as well. Perhaps the most striking example comes from the so-called Reagan Democrats, exemplified by white working-class ethnics living in suburban Detroit; by 1980, this group was facing increasing economic uncertainty due to plant closures and layoffs. Yet African Americans, not structural economic change or the predations of corporate elites or the indifference of elected officials, were blamed. As political scientist Stanley B. Greenberg noted, these white Reagan Democrats "expressed a profound distaste for black Americans, a sentiment that pervaded almost everything they thought about government and politics. Blacks constituted the explanation for their vulnerability and for almost everything that had gone wrong in their lives; not being black was what constituted being middle class."[29]

The deindustrial also relies on figurations of African Americans to ease white anxieties around, and provide scapegoats for, industrial decline; to maintain the racial status quo; and to provide "fetishistic escape" from its strictures.[30] These figurations also offer potential for cross-racial identification while providing projective compensation for challenges to the normative white patriarchal industrial subject from the civil rights, feminist, and LGBTQ movements. Images of post-industrial Detroit as a racialized ruin are obvious examples: "Look what *they* did to *our* city."[31] African American artists, including Michael Jackson, Dominique Morisseau, and Tyree Guyton, actively challenge such racist figurations.

In the chapters that follow, I examine the ways the deindustrial becomes visible and affectively palpable in works that explicitly link race and the changing nature of US capitalism from installations in specific neighborhoods of Detroit to coverage of Michael Jackson's child molestation trial in which his finances played a surprisingly prominent role. In so doing, I hope to expose both the racialized representational continuities linking the industrial to the deindustrial and the figural and affective ruptures between them. In the remainder of this introduction, I briefly review the definition of and literature about US deindustrialization, offer a definition of "figural economy," outline two typical tropes circulating within discourses about the deindustrial, and introduce the chapters that follow.

DEFINING DEINDUSTRIALIZATION

In 2011, comedian Tina Fey noted, almost as a throwaway, that "technology doesn't move backward. No society has ever de-industrialized."[32] She meant her assertion of the impossibility of technological atavism sarcastically. It's a joke: one that turns on three interrelated presumptions. First, it is presumably collectively obvious that the United States *has* in fact deindustrialized: past tense, a done deal. Second, this process is obviously unnatural, indeed, laughably regressive—a violation of the very immutable laws of progress that define technological modernity itself. Third, like all atavisms, deindustrialization is obviously a source of some anxiety, here both recalled and relieved by Fey's humor that enables us to chuckle, or wince, at the absurdity of it all.

"Deindustrialization" is itself a figuration: a representational and rhetorical shorthand subsuming a wide range of periods, places, industries, imagery, and discourses from popular and specialist sources, which then circulate as a putative whole. My characterization of the transitional period from the mid-1980s to the present, and the ethos of that period, as "the deindustrial" follows political economists Barry Bluestone and Bennett Harrison's classic definition of deindustrialization as the

> widespread, systematic disinvestment in the nation's basic productive capacity. Controversial as it may be, the essential problem with the U.S. can be traced to the way capital—in the form of financial resources and of real plant and equipment—has been diverted from productive investment in our basic national infrastructure into unproductive speculation, mergers and acquisitions, and foreign investment.[33]

This definition emphasizes the active diversion of capital from factories to finance, underscoring deindustrialization's inextricability from financialization and highlighting the intentionality of the process.

In contrast, elite economic institutions present the definition and causes of deindustrialization in quasi-evolutionary, generally positive terms. For example, the International Monetary Fund's *Economic Issues* paper "Deindustrialization—Its Causes and Implications" asserts: "Deindustrialization is simply the natural outcome of successful economic development and is generally associated with rising living standards."[34] This "natural" process is agentless; the service sector is simply replacing manufacturing "just as the earlier shift to manufacturing took place at the expense of the agricultural sector." Further, "deindustrialization is principally the result of higher productivity in manufacturing than in services" accompanied by a "pattern of trade specialization."[35] The specific natures of both "higher productivity" and "pattern[s] of trade specialization" are not explained; there is no mention of domestic outsourcing and relocation of semiskilled factory jobs and infrastructure to low-wage, nonunion regions or countries with lax regulatory environments: a process often incentivized with tax advantages for corporations. The consequences of this rise in productivity and pattern of trade specialization for workers' wages and communities are not mentioned at all. In this view, the process is not only "natural" but also both inevitable and unstoppable. Therefore, "as deindustrialization continues, the overall growth of productivity will depend more and more on growth of productivity in services."[36]

IMF definition aside, the agentiality implicit in the "de" ("undoing") of "deindustrialization" marks an important distinction from related, though not fully synonymous, formulations.[37] "Post-industrial" is one example. According to sociologist Daniel Bell, in *The Coming of Post-industrial Society*, "post-industrial" describes the alterations to social organization, including changing flows of power and expertise between multiple political economic sectors, that arise as a consequence of the declining importance of manufacturing.[38] "Post-Fordism," ironically the most specific-sounding of these terms, is perhaps the most elastic. For some, it signals the emergence and dominance of a flexible production/contingent workforce model over against the mass production/stable employment modes of a Fordist model, along with the abandonment of the Fordist wage labor–management compact mediated by unions and the state.[39] Others include the dismantling of the Keynesian welfare state under the rubric of post-Fordism.[40] Social theorist Paolo Virno offers an especially useful definition that aligns well with the idea of the deindustrial as a transitional period marked by both the persistence and the transformation of the industrial imaginary. According to Virno, while post-Fordism marks changing modes of production, it also signals the instantiation of the logics of production and the metrics of productivity within the most intimate aspects of social and personal life: "For the post-Fordist multitude, every qualitative difference between labour time and non-labour time falls short."[41]

Yet whether it precedes "Fordist" or "industrial," the use of "post" in and of itself suggests a succession that is purely temporal: an orientation to this structural change that is shared by elite economic actors and institutions. When I use "post-industrial" in the chapters that follow, I am specifically signaling this perspective. In the quasi-evolutionary view implicit in "post," industrial attachments, neighborhoods, and workers will simply be retrained and/or reabsorbed, consigned to extinction, persist invisibly and inconsequentially like vestigial tails, or some combination, if they are considered at all. In contrast, "de" serves as a continual reminder of the political economic decision-making that drove, and continues to drive, this process in the United States. In so doing, "de" more explicitly marks the social ruptures of the deindustrial as something other than inevitable and unavoidable given the natural logic of capital.

Further, along with its quasi-evolutionary connotations, "post" suggests a discrete successor stage, as if the industrial moment has now vanished as surely as the Mesozoic. US industrial infrastructure in multiple senses of the term may be diminished, but it is not gone. Moreover, "post-industrial" suggests the obsolescence of union and social service protections that sustained working- and middle-class life rather than the active dismantling of these protections. For example, Michigan's Republican governor and legislative majority succeeded in making the state, home of the once mighty United Auto Workers Union, a so-called right-to-work state in a lame-duck session in December 2012.[42] "Right-to-work" laws prohibit unions and employers from negotiating union security clauses, making organizing and financing of union activities and thus their protections of workers' interests difficult by design. Finally, although Virno's analyses will prove particularly useful in the following chapters, "post-Fordism" is semantically and figurally limited despite its eclectic roster of interpreters. In addition to the problematic elements of "post," "Fordism" adds its own complications. It conjures both a very specific production model and a fictively rationalized, routinized moment in the history of capital governed by the mutual self-interests of labor and management. While the pairing of the body and the routinization of the assembly line are central to the figural economies of both industrialization and deindustrialization, so too are violence, racism, irrationality, and dismemberment: important correctives against industrial nostalgia that "post-Fordism" tends to obscure. In addition, Virno's definition of post-Fordism overlooks the ways Henry Ford himself actively "Fordized" the private lives of his workers, a history discussed in chapter 3.

There is no single US deindustrialization and no single "deindustrial" site despite the common causes of disinvestment and capital flight. The consequences of closing New England textile mills in the early decades of the twentieth century are both similar to and fundamentally different from heavy industry's exodus from SoHo in the late 1950s and 1960s, the contraction of the steel industry in Gary in the late 1970s and early 1980s, and the auto plant shutdowns in Detroit that accelerated through the same period. *Unfinished Business* focuses on the so-called Midwest Rust Belt with particular attention to the auto and steel industries that birthed Detroit and Michael Jackson. In this I adhere to the "folk model" of deindustrialization outlined by di Leonardo even as I challenge that model's racial and gender blindness. I want to probe precisely how Detroit, this "folk model's" most recognizable exemplar, and Michael Jackson, the Rust Belt's most spectacular success story whose deindustriality is wholly unrecognized, operate as pedagogical tools and cautionary tales.

Literature on US deindustrialization is multidisciplinary. Works by economists and labor historians focus on global and domestic policy aspects, historical contexts, and demographic dimensions.[43] Ethnographic accounts and oral histories of deindustrializing areas and industries emphasize the fiscal and psychic costs to individuals and communities.[44] The cultural and representational aspects of deindustrialization have also attracted scholarly attention.[45] Some of this work examines efforts to musealize industrial relics as heritage.[46] Other studies analyze images of and encounters with decaying industrial infrastructure: "The cultural meaning of deindustrialization is embedded in . . . universalized images of falling smokestacks and imploding factories."[47] Some of these accounts theorize a " 'deindustrial sublime': a sense of being swept away by the beauty and terror of economic change."[48] While there is some truth in such arguments, it is important to note that deindustrialization is also palpably and affectively manifest in optimistic attachments, however cruel, to Michael Jackson's spectacular social mobility as the period's Horatio Alger story, and in the intimate scenes of domestic detritus—worn shoes, piles of discarded stuffed animals, old LPs nailed to an abandoned home— that constitute the *Heidelberg Project*.

Though scholars have eloquently called for moving "beyond the ruins" when examining the "mental and cultural frameworks of deindustrialization," there is surprisingly little attention to how such frameworks are generated on a national scale, and to the role of race within them.[49] While performance studies scholars and urban historians have explored the arts in deindustrial contexts, including analyses of specific works, there is little discussion of how such works might function in the public sphere as normative or aberrant scenarios of weathering structural change.[50] Finally, with a few exceptions, relatively little attention is devoted to representations of deindustrialization as an ongoing process, as if its cultural meanings end when the last unused smokestacks fall. A focus on the deindustrial as a transitional period that links factories to finance offers a more expansive representational repertoire of structural economic change.

Financialization, industrialization's successor mode of production, has also received considerable interdisciplinary popular and scholarly attention, much of it informed by critical cultural theory. Critical scholars have produced a wide range of popular and scholarly texts detailing its presumptions, operations, and effects.[51] Many have paid particular attention to the ways financialization operates as both a racialized discourse and a deeply unequal set of practices and effects.[52] Yet there has been relatively little attention paid to how financialization circulates as sets of images, narratives, and performances in the public sphere.[53] Indeed, its products and operations—high-frequency trading, derivatives, credit default swaps—are characterized using rhetoric that suggests they are simultaneously iterations of the mathematico-scientific Real and "ethereal, ephemeral, epiphenomenal, immaterial."[54] Yet "this chimera called finance" materializes with spectacular theatricality in public financial travails like those of Michael Jackson. As I discuss in chapter 2, key moments in the last decade of Jackson's life expose routine operations of financialization as neither rational nor immaterial but rather as a contemporary iteration of the highly affective racialized melodrama that has continuously staged relations between virtue and capital since the mid-nineteenth century. *Unfinished Business* insists that race(-ism) and financialization are inextricable from the mental and cultural frameworks we use to make sense of the deindustrial. Further, it also theorizes how such frameworks are produced: through figural economies of compelling images and performances that define normative, aberrant, and resistant orientations to changing modes of production, often by reshaping and redeploying elements from the industrial past.

FIGURAL ECONOMY

"Figure" is remarkably capacious: both a noun and a verb, each with an impressive array of possible definitions. For the noun, the *Oxford English Dictionary* offers twenty-four options that can be broadly categorized as formal ("outline, shape; of a living being, appearance"); representational ("image, likeness, or representation of something material or immaterial; an emblem, type"); and rhetorical ("figure of speech").[55] The same general categories characterize its use as a verb. "To figure" is "to bring into shape," "to portray or represent," or "to express by a metaphor or image."[56] In arguing that Michael Jackson and Detroit "figure" the deindustrial, I draw on this capaciousness. Throughout *Unfinished Business*, Jackson and the city are simultaneously material and historical entities whose fame or notoriety makes them subjects of intense interest; exemplars whose public dramas give form to the deindustrial as a period, a sensorium, and structure of feeling; and highly mediated representations whose specific qualities imbue them with rhetorical potential, particularly as racialized cautionary tales.[57]

"The figural" is both the adjectival form of "figure" and an interpretive strategy for identifying the simultaneously material/historical, exemplary, and representational qualities of an object of analysis. As Eric Auerbach states in his classic study, *Mimesis*:

> A figural schema permits both its poles—the figure and its fulfillment—to retain the characteristics of concrete historical reality, in contradistinction to what obtains with symbolic or allegorical personifications, so that figure and fulfillment—although one "signifies" the other—have a significance which is not incompatible with their being real. An event taken as a figure preserves its literal and historical meaning. It remains an event, does not become a mere sign.[58]

Building on Auerbach's analysis, historian Hayden White has argued that all descriptions of historical objects are figural.[59]

In opting for this interpretive strategy to theorize two exemplars of the deindustrial, I am neither reducing Jackson's and Detroit's materiality and history to mere metaphors nor denying the rhetorical, metaphoric potential that permeates representations of their conditions. Rather, by examining their specific circumstances over against key political economic moments of the deindustrial, I hope to chart their significance to the cultural frameworks we deploy or resist when making sense of this transitional period.

My use of "figural" in "figural economy" is also informed by, though not a direct application of, philosopher Jean-François Lyotard's theory of "the figural" in *Discourse, Figure*, and by D. N. Rodowick's and Kiff Bamford's adaptations of this theory to televisual and digital media and to performance art, respectively. While Auerbach and White characterize figural interpretation as attentiveness to the interplay of the real and the rhetorical-representational, Lyotard, Rodowick, and Bamford locate the figural object in the interplay of the discursive, the pictorial, and, in Bamford's case, the kinesthetic.

To simplify mightily, Lyotard posited that the opposition between linguistic and pictorial representations breaks down at the level of the letter, which is both; in the most basic sense, the discursive and the visual are inextricably entangled in the figural.[60] Rodowick expands on Lyotard's argument, noting that the figural enables the recognition that "discourse encompasses expression and affect, as well as signification and rationality" even as "the image has ceased to refer *to* things by becoming *a* thing of a particular order."[61] This view of the figural supports my argument that even the most seemingly dispassionate discourses of deindustrialization and financialization are partnered by, and circulate within, a field of affect-saturated images, performances, and texts that inspire optimistic attachments, industrial nostalgia, and deindustrial melancholy. It also establishes the materiality of Jackson's and Detroit's images—things in themselves—operating alongside if not necessarily in tandem with the "real" artist and city.

In Rodowick's theorizing, the figural and the deindustrial are contemporaries: the "figural is less a thing than a concept, designed to characterize the social physiognomics of postindustrial capitalism and the information society" characterized by televisual and digital communication.[62] The "social physiognomics" of the deindustrial that circulate through both these media and "live" forms of the theater and the installation are the focus of this book. Sometimes these are actual faces—like Michael Jackson's; sometimes they are representations of Detroit. But the figural is not limited to an "audiovisual archive."[63] For Kiff Bamford, Lyotard's emphasis on the perceptual dynamics of encountering representation—"the spatial and thus the bodily realm of gestures, movement and matter which are brought together in the realm of the figural"—makes the concept especially useful for examining performance art.[64] Following Bamford's line of reasoning, I posit Jackson's dancing, performance dynamics in three plays featuring Detroit, and movement through Detroit's *Heidelberg Project* and *Mobile Homestead* as figural kineses of the deindustrial.

"Figural economy" appears, undefined, in scriptural exegeses and theories of representation.[65] As I use it here, the term refers to the circulation of Michael Jackson and Detroit as material/historical entities, exemplars, and representations throughout the public sphere: sometimes constituting a representational commons, especially in Jackson's case, and sometimes serving as local and site-specific nodes in larger networks of deindustrial imagery. Figural economies are inextricable from libidinal and political ones, and the figural economy of the deindustrial is no exception. All are permeated and powered by desire and money and are thus both intrapsychic and highly commodified.

In positing and examining figural economies of the deindustrial, I do not adopt Frankfurt School theorists Theodor Adorno and Max Horkheimer's "culture industry" critique wherein a "ruthless unity" of media products unrelentingly reinforces the impossibility of ever escaping from capitalism.[66] Some of the works I probe here explicitly expose and resist deindustrialization's racialized predations. But I do not insist on a work's obvious resistance to deindustrial capitalism as a prerequisite for critical or figural worth. Insistence on resistance in particular seems to reinvigorate a Romantic view of the artist as a fully autonomous subject who must somehow always triumph over or trick back on commodification to merit consideration as a worthy political economic agent.

Michael Jackson is an excellent example of how simplistic binaries that oppose the resistant/subversive to the complicit blind us to the complex ways figural economies of the deindustrial actually operate. Jackson eagerly embraced—indeed became a face of—global capitalism.[67] He created spectacles on a global scale with himself at the center and was successful almost beyond measure. But he was also a "defiant compliant": actively asserting his racial identity and challenging racist modes of production, both resisting and submitting to industry strictures and the financial exigencies that dominated the last decade of his life.[68] Therein lies his figural potential. As an emblematic entrepreneurial subject who, despite surpluses of agency and artistry, could not outdance the operations of financialization in which he was fully enmeshed while he was alive (and, indeed, even after his death), Jackson demonstrates, among other things, the melodramatic peripety intrinsic to this mode of production, in sharp contrast to characterizations of its operations as abstract and rational. Thus, he functions as both a symptom and a representation of deindustrial financialized precarity as well as an agent within it.

Some of the artists whose works I examine here have impeccable subversion-resistance credentials. For example, Tyree Guyton has persevered through repeated city demolitions of his work on the *Heidelberg Project*, and recently through repeated arsons, to dramatize the civic and capital abandonment of his neighborhood, and hopes for its rebirth. Others are, in queer theorist Eve Kosofsky Sedgwick's memorable phrase, "kinda subversive, kinda hegemonic."[69] Still others produce works with profoundly problematic, even regressive, politics. But in all cases, these works reveal something crucial about how the deindustrial looks and feels, how race operates within it, how we imagine transitional moments in capitalism through the deindustrial's most visible and least obvious exemplars, and the ways elements of the industrial age—corporeal repertoires, melodrama as a genre, historical particulars—persist unexamined even after the factories close.

The Individual and the Ruin

Deindustrialization is typically figured at opposite ends of a representational scale: as intimate portraits of individuals whose lives have been devastated by plant closures or as images of blighted urban neighborhoods and ruined industrial infra-structure in which the sheer size of the devastation conveys the magnitude of a community's social and economic losses. In *Unfinished Business*, I both adhere to and depart from this convention. Jackson is certainly an individual, and Detroit has been described, albeit ironically, as "a contemporary Pompeii."[70] Yet, while Jackson is sui generis—certainly no typical deindustrial subject—he exemplifies a famil-iar US postwar baby boom generation trajectory, albeit in spectacular fashion. His blue-collar parents, and particularly his father's unrelenting focus on his children's careers, ensured that he would never have to toil in an auto plant or steel mill. He became an enthusiastic participant in the consumer economy, an investor, and a charitable donor. He managed the physical and psychic tolls of his service labors with varying degrees of success, and when he stopped working, he fell into debt and faced foreclosure. When he was fifty, he returned to work to stave off financial exigency, though the potential monetary gains were less than what he had been accustomed to decades earlier at the height of his success. Jackson's figural potential lies neither in his typicality nor in his exceptionalism but in the pairing of both: the latter making the former figurally, publicly visible and available. Through Jackson we see both the transcendence of collapsing blue-collar life in the Midwest—a col-lapse disproportionately affecting African American workers—and the melodrama of financialization, also deeply racialized, play out as aspirational success story, cau-tionary tale, and valiant attempt at redemption.

While Detroit may not be "the most representative city in America," as Jerry Herron asserted in 1993, it is certainly one of the most represented. Synonymous with deindustrial collapse, it offers a wealth of ruins imagery circulating in multiple media.[71] But, though the trope of Detroit-as-ruin undergirds some of the works I examine here, and the city's current fiscal challenges are important to chapter 4 in particular, I do not analyze this ruins iconography. Instead, I am most interested in the periods well before and shortly after "the ruins": in the ways the city's early Fordist history and racial politics inform its use as a figure of contemporary dystopia during the recovery from the Great Recession and the city's 2013–14 bankruptcy period, and in current rhetoric depicting the city as an up-and-coming artists' col-ony. Moreover, I examine this convergence of race(-ism), history, changing modes of production, and creative class utopian rhetoric in pieces about or sited in/as, the home: no tumbling-down Packard Plant, no windowless Michigan Central Depot, no other charismatic megafauna of Detroit ruins photojournalism. *Unfinished Business* uses Michael Jackson and Detroit separately to investigate racialized figural economies of the deindustrial at two distinct scales, though not those where the alignment seems obvious. Here, the individual figures deindustrial spectacle and *shadenfreude* while the city figures the period's intimate losses, not the other way around.

The book is divided into two parts of two chapters each. The first two chapters, devoted to Michael Jackson, cover the sweep of the deindustrial—from its increas-ing visibility as a seismic structural shift in the mid-1980s through the early years of recovery from the Great Recession—as well as the arc of his career from his success with *Thriller* and subsequent visit to the Reagan White House in 1984 to his death and posthumous release of his final performances, the rehearsals for *This Is It*, in 2009. My goal in this part is to analyze Jackson's figural work as the deindustrial's most spectacular, public, and popular subject.

In chapter 1, I establish Jackson's deindustriality. I argue that he is the period's exemplary transitional subject whose racial assertiveness and virtuosic dancing marked his own extraordinary social mobility while conjuring an industrial imaginary that was both fictively racially inclusive and apparently in the process of collapsing. He simultaneously incarnated the trope of the human motor—one of the defining figures of industrial modernity—and offered a compelling, cruelly optimistic spectacle of the exceptional individual's ability to glide away from this collapse with pleasure, precision, and hard work. In this chapter I also theorize virtuosity as a relational process linking performers to audiences and, in Jackson's case, accounting for his status as an icon of deindustrial mobility.

Chapter 2 discusses Jackson's fiscal travails from 2002 through his child molestation trial and the release of *This Is It* in 2009, reading coverage of his consumption, debt, and attempts at recovery as racialized public melodrama. This melodrama was especially figurally arresting and resonant given Jackson's earlier status as an exemplary virtuosic, entrepreneurial subject. His capitalist virtues of hard work and business savvy were not sufficient to sustain him through a series of crises that paralleled those of ordinary consumers and, indeed, of the US financial system itself in the same period. This is a long chapter because it is impossible to disentangle consumer spending from consumer debt, near economic collapse, and subsequent austerity regimens either in Jackson's case or in the US economy during the period covered here.

The chapter begins with a scene of Jackson shopping at the Regis Galerie in Las Vegas taken from Martin Bashir's documentary *Living with Michael Jackson*, viewed through both the emerging consumer credit bubble and William Smith's temperance melodrama *The Drunkard*. The film frames Jackson, and particularly his consumption, as aberrant and out of control: reinforcing racist caricatures of African Americans' relationship to consumer culture that were to reverberate both across his child molestation trial and in the subprime mortgage crisis. Next I examine the ways testimony about Jackson's finances, particularly his debts, played a pivotal role in his child molestation trial: reproducing a financialized version of Leslie Fiedler's and Linda Williams's Tom/anti-Tom melodramatic racial dialectic that would emerge again in the subprime crisis using the very same tropes. The chapter concludes by examining the parallels between accounts of Jackson's physical wasting on the set of *This Is It*, that of the compulsively dancing child in Hans Christian Andersen's melodramatic tale "The Red Shoes," and increasingly strident calls for a US austerity "diet." Jackson's reported wasting and the tale of "The Red Shoes" represent the process of disciplining past excesses through redemptive contraction at the same time US austerity rhetoric was reaching a crescendo.

The second part of the book is devoted to Detroit, and specifically to works centered on the city as home. In these works, the deindustrial is intimate business, inextricable from a shifting political economy and the seemingly intractable racial polarization of the place. In chapter 3, I discuss the ways the city as both an image and an actual place spatializes and racializes the affective fallout of deindustrialization in three plays whose New York runs coincided with both its impending bankruptcy and the anemic recovery from the Great Recession: *Detroit* by Lisa D'Amour, *Detroit '67* by Dominique Morisseau, and *Motown the Musical* by Berry Gordy. Each play uses Detroit to explore the interpersonal consequences of opportunities and crises in racialized capitalism. Each offers audiences intimate visions of the Fordist bargain in its seeming heyday: particularly compelling in a period of lackluster economic recovery. In this chapter, I introduce the formulations "re-siting" and "re-citing" to describe the ways in which elements of Detroit's incendiary history of interracial confrontations are redeployed to support images of a capitalist work ethic transcending or succumbing to racist violence, and to link the city to a seemingly race-neutral contemporary precarity.

Finally, chapter 4 examines Detroit as capital's putative post-industrial phoenix between 2011 and 2016: both a blank slate and an emerging comeback story. This chapter analyzes the ways national and local figurations of Detroit's widely touted arts- and artist-led renaissance *kunst*-wash the structural inequities and racialized austerity imperatives of some current redevelopment initiatives. Two Detroit installations, Tyree Guyton's *Heidelberg Project* and Mike Kelley's *Mobile Homestead*, challenge these *kunst*-washed figurations. Both draw their potency from their status as homes in a period when homes in the city were facing threats of tax foreclosure, water shutoffs, new versions of redlining, and proposed civic abandonment. I examine both works using Bertolt Brecht's concept of the *gest*: arguing that they stage essential critical confrontations with the racialization, debility, melancholy, and uncanniness of deindustriality itself.

US deindustrialization might have ignited a bracing national conversation about rethinking work: about the possibilities for replacing benumbing, dangerous, environmentally disastrous jobs with those offering dignity, sustainability, racial and gender equity, and a wage to purchase a good life. This conversation could have been a global model. This did not happen due to failures of political will and failures of imagination. Some of the racialized figural economies of the period discussed here contributed to, and continue to contribute to, those failures, but others insist that deindustriality can unfold otherwise. Critical attention to all of these figural economies will teach us something about our political economic history—real and imagined—about how the economy takes shape and takes flight in its public cultural lives, about how structural change feels at the level of collective culture, and above all, about the ways race(-ism) continues to profoundly shape our understanding and expectations of capitalism's operations and crises in transitional times.

PART I

Michael Jackson's Spectacular Deindustriality

CHAPTER 1

The Labors of Michael Jackson

Transitional Deindustriality, Dance,

and Virtuous(o) Work

If you just went by blood, I'd have as much crane operator in me as singer.
Michael Jackson, *Moonwalk*[1]

Neverland could never have happened without Gary [Indiana].
Denise Jordan Walker, cofounder and tour guide,
"The King of Pop Hometown Tour"[2]

Automatic, systematic
Full of color, self-contained
Tuned and gentle to your vibe
The Jackson 5, *"Dancing Machine"*[3]

B y all accounts, Michael Jackson's May 14, 1984, visit to the Reagan White
House was very strange (figure 1). Jackson's biographer J. Randy Taraborrelli
describes it as a mutually exploitative bit of theater from its inception. The administration, gearing up for re-election in November, wanted Jackson's song "Beat
It" as background for an anti–drunk driving public service announcement, and
Jackson would agree only if he both received a humanitarian award from, and
shared podium time with, the president and also met Nancy Reagan. During the
award ceremony, Jackson reportedly uttered a mere thirteen words.[4] A subsequent
private meeting with the first couple went badly after Jackson, who had been told
that only the Reagans and some staff members' children would be present, instead
encountered a room full of adults, fled, and hid in a nearby bathroom, refusing to
leave until the requisite children were produced.[5] Nancy Reagan, speculating on
Jackson's even then considerable cosmetic surgeries, reportedly observed: "It's all

Figure 1: Michael Jackson with Ronald and Nancy Reagan at the White House, May 14, 1984. White House Photographic Collection, 1/20/1981–1/20/1989. National Archives Identifier 198548. United States National Archives.

so peculiar, really. A boy who looks just like a girl, who whispers when he speaks, wears a glove on one hand and sunglasses all the time. I just don't know what to make of it."[6] Following the observation by a Jackson aide that she didn't know the half of it, she reportedly replied sharply, "Well, he *is* talented . . . and I would think that's all *you* should be concerned about." Ronald Reagan mentioned the meeting in his presidential diary, praising Jackson as a role model for being "totally opposed to drugs & alcohol & using his popularity to influence young people against them. I was surprised at how shy he is."[7] Jackson's only references to the visit in his autobiography, *Moonwalk*, are two photographs: one with him striding alongside the president, his gold-trimmed jacket, epaulets, and sash suggesting a visiting military dignitary, and another of him seated at a massive piano, seemingly alone in an unidentified multichandeliered hall. The two images share a single terse caption, a suitable bookend to Jackson's brief remarks on the day: "A visit to the White House."[8]

The Jackson-Reagan encounter offers an embarrassment of potential interpretive riches. It can be read against the iconic 1970 meeting of Elvis Presley, who suggested he be made a "Federal Agent at Large" in the Bureau of Narcotics and Dangerous Drugs, and Richard Nixon, who declared a "war on drugs" the following year.[9] Given that both Presley and Jackson died of drug overdoses, it can be read retrospectively as replete with irony: a repudiation of both that war and its interpersonal front, Nancy Reagan's "Just Say No" campaign. The meeting certainly offers the opportunity to reflect on the dawning of an age of self-evidently hypermediatized stagecraft of statecraft exemplified by two performers whose well-known charisma was morphing into popular caricature and critique.[10] But this meeting is also remarkable as the moment where the x-, y-, and z-axes of performance, race, and the changing nature of American work converge at a point of optimal iconic potential. Jackson and Reagan's meeting exemplifies the United States' ongoing and deeply conflicted racial-industrial imaginary. A young black man from Gary, Indiana—a child of both the civil rights movement and the steel industry, well on his way to becoming the most successful popular performer in the world—posed alongside an elderly white actor, now leader of the free world, who had extolled states' rights a few miles from where civil rights workers James Chaney, Andrew Goodman, and Michael Schwerner were murdered two decades earlier; figured the "welfare queen" as the black succubus afflicting the white workingman; and fractured the New Deal race-labor coalition by drawing votes of those very workingmen, particularly those from the Rust Belt, as the rust was just beginning to form.

Ronald Reagan's status as an industrial icon played out as publicly as his later role in deindustrialization. In 1954, thirty years before this odd and iconic meeting with Michael Jackson, Reagan humanized an evolving US industrial imaginary as the spokesperson for General Electric, most notably the host of television's *General Electric Theatre*; Fordism was at its apogee as Reagan's performance career seemed at its nadir.[11] By 1984, those trajectories had completely reversed. Though Reagan did not initiate the United States' deindustrial decline, in his first term he accelerated it exponentially, bringing the same affability to this operation as he did to humanizing General Electric. The steel industry, the main employer in Michael Jackson's hometown, was particularly imperiled in this period. Employment in the industry decreased by more than half from 1979 to 1986.[12] Reeling from the effects of free trade, big steel lost more than $2.5 billion in 1982 and more than $3 billion in 1983 alone.[13] In September 1984, Reagan refused to impose tariffs or quotas on imports of foreign steel that might have mitigated those effects. His administration's attitude toward the industry and, by extension its workers, was perhaps best expressed by his trade representative, Clayton Yeutter, who announced that domestic steel production was likely marked for extinction because "not everyone can survive [in the United States]."[14] In 1984, Jackson's relationship to both the steel industry and its unraveling seemed much more opaque, particularly in light of the stunning success of his *Thriller* album. Nancy Reagan was right about one thing: he was talented. And that was all his legions of fans were concerned about.

By any objective criteria, Michael Jackson was the closest thing to a consensual virtuoso performer that late twentieth-century popular culture has produced. Sales figures, fans' devotion, the acclaim of virtuosic peers, the foundational contributions and innovations for which he is credited—all attest to his command of that central paradox intrinsic to popular virtuosity: the ability to appear pathbreakingly original in a way that is collectively obvious. Yet, if all virtuosity can be described as "precarious excellence," Jackson's was more precarious than most: veering spectacularly from an indefinably pleasurable surplus (more talented, more charismatic, more "something" than his brothers) to equally indefinable and untoward excesses (too many strange stunts, too many surgeries and antics with boys, too much of too much).[15] His virtuosity was both produced by and entangled in multiple overlapping narratives of difference including raced and gendered histories of American popular performance, the possibilities and limits of the mutable self, the bedrock or millstone of family, the pleasures and perils of spectacle, and the permissions and constraints of celebrity. These have been picked apart in the popular press and, to a lesser degree, in the academy while another issue remains largely unexamined: the relationship between his virtuosity and the changing political economy of American work. Scholars have commented on Jackson's discomfiting ability to straddle multiple binaries: man/woman, gay/straight, black/white, child/man.[16] Yet one underlying binary remains unremarked except, as the first epigraph to this chapter indicates, by those in his hometown: that of Gary/Neverland—the seeming fixity of industrialization versus the "neither here nor there" fluidity of the financialization and globalization that came later. Jackson personified the shift from one end of this binary to the other at the precise moment deindustrialization became painfully visible as a national problem. Michael Jackson is biographically, culturally, aesthetically, and figurally deindustrial, and his virtuosity cannot be understood apart from these conditions even as it powerfully illuminates and comments on them.

In this chapter I argue that, in the middle to late 1980s, at the height of his career, Michael Jackson was indeed a role model of a very specific kind: a "transitional subject" who did crucial figural work mediating between an attachment to "Gary," a vanishing US industrial moment as it was and never was on the one hand and, on the other, a fraught hope for "neverland," the rising anxiety and "cruel optimism" about what was coming next.[17] His literal and figural agility in this role was enabled by his virtuosity and activated by his specific technical facility. The "transitional subject" is a variant on object relations psychoanalyst D. W. Winnicott's "transitional object," the phenomenon that produces subjectivity by bridging the gap between the nascent self and the other, operating simultaneously as "me" and "not me" and thereby establishing both positions.[18] Winnicott's transitional phenomena are both material and illusory. They are figurally, cathetically, and developmentally effective because they contain this paradoxical doubleness—material/illusory, "me"/"not me"—without resolving it. As Winnicott observes, "We will never ask [the deployer of the transitional phenomenon] the question 'Did you conceive of this or was it presented to you from without?' The important point is that no decision on this point is expected."[19] Performance theorist Richard Schechner links the productive doubleness of transitional phenomena to the foundational condition of theatrical performance itself, including the actor's ability to simultaneously embody the "not-me" and the "not-not-me."[20] Sociologist Jeffrey Alexander frames iconic celebrity performers in similar terms, which are particularly congenial to my reading of Michael Jackson. Such figures are, in Alexander's words:

> transitional objects for adults, mediating between internal and external reality, between the deepest emotional needs and contingent possibilities for their satisfaction. Yet, while saturated with emotion, the celebrity object carries a thoroughly cultural effect. The magnetic attraction of its material-aesthetic surface allows its depth-significance to be subjectified, to be taken into the heart and flesh.[21]

While it is certainly the case that Jackson mediates between the individual "internal and external realities" of his legions of fans, he also operates as a transitional subject on the public stage. Here he is both a public figure embodying and thus enabling collective fantasies of the deindustrial moment and an object for personal identification and cathexis. He exemplifies the intimate connections between the social and the intrapersonal operations of celebrity, and of both of these to fantasies of spectacular social mobility.[22] Further, in contrast to Alexander's examples—Greta Garbo's face, Gwyneth Paltrow's hair—Jackson's "magnetic attraction" was not simply a function of his physiognomy. Indeed, as Nancy Reagan's observations demonstrated, his appearance could be as distancing as fascinating; one "didn't know what to make of it." I believe his transitional figural potential—both as an object of attachment and as a vector through which attachment to a cruelly optimistic deindustrial imaginary circulates—resides in his virtuosity in performance, and the performative stability that virtuosity acquired through repetition. He is a transitional "subject" because, in these virtuosic enactments, he both exemplifies and produces the spectacular agential self replete with figural and cathectical potential that was especially potent during this period when Fordist subjectivity became increasingly unsettled.

One specific element of Jackson's virtuosity—his dancing—exposes his figural and affective potency as a deindustrial transitional subject with a clarity all the more remarkable for his invisibility within the pantheon of the period's most acclaimed popular performers. In the crucial deindustrial period of the early to mid-1980s, when the fraught solidity promised by manufacturing work was increasingly melting into air, his dancing body enabled audiences to imagine that this dematerialization of labor within the Fordist model of industrial production and its rematerialization in service production was both a smooth—if also laborious—process and an agential one.[23] Jackson's virtuosity as a dancing transitional subject at the height of his career activates both nostalgia for a vanishing industrial past and fantasies of an effortless transcendence of that past in ways best understood through the trope of the human motor. The trope operates through a pairing of kinesis—his movement vocabulary and exemplary execution in performance—and his personal narrative, particularly in *Moonwalk*. Yet this compelling partnership of motion and narration only barely contains the multiple contradictions and exclusions endemic to the US industrial modernist project, especially those around race. And here Jackson does more than mediate the key ambivalences of the deindustrial moment; he is not simply a neutral conduit. On the contrary, he forcefully poses a critique of its presumptive whiteness through a polyracial and polycorporeal dance vocabulary as well as pointed rhetoric that repudiates stereotypes of the black popular dancer.

This chapter examines Jackson's transitional deindustrial subjectivity as it emerges in selected performances from 1983 to 1988, the pinnacle of his dance career: the short films (he preferred the term to "video") *Thriller* and *Smooth Criminal*, and his performance at the *Motown 25: Yesterday, Today, Forever* anniversary celebration, as well as his autobiography, which serves as the rhetorical underpinning of his virtuoso narrative. I begin by probing Jackson's invisibility within the unofficial canon of deindustrial performers: itself a symptom of both the continuing misrecognition of dance's figural potential on the public stage and the United States' unfinished business around racializing work, including industrial labor and deindustriality. Next, I discuss three key factors that positioned Jackson as such a potent transitional figure during the consolidation of the deindustrial imaginary in the middle to late 1980s: a relational economy of virtuosity leading to affective investment in the exceptional performer; the figural potential of dance to illuminate other forms of labor coupled with Jackson's exceptional ability to model an agential industrial laboring subject; and the complex intersections of race, performance, and industrial modernity that prefigured him while persisting in his repertoire. From this theoretical and historical background, I turn to analyses of Jackson's dances and movement vocabulary.

"YOU MAY LOOK THE *OTHER* WAY": MICHAEL JACKSON AS DEINDUSTRIAL OTHER

If the United States' deindustrial imaginary condensed into one popular performer, the consensus among cultural historians is that the performer would be rocker Bruce Springsteen, though hip-hop pioneer DJ Kool Herc should also be a contender.[24] Springsteen, "America's foremost working-class hero," embodies the white, obviously heteronormative "superhero" masculinity that conjured the ideal Fordist working man.[25] Because he fit this consensual bill, he seems the logical figure to simultaneously decry the economic displacements shaking Fordist subjectivity to the core and reassure audiences of its persistence, if only as a set of fading ideals, in a new era of diminished expectations across the decades that followed.

In the early 1980s, Kool Herc's creative repurposing of the discarded technologies of the industrial age and syncopated Afro-Caribbean rhythms produced hip-hop affect in/as communal embodied practice: fury at the quickening pace of deindustrialization's predations—as unequally distributed as industrialization's rewards—coupled with insistent resilience. As American studies scholar Tricia Rose writes: "In hip hop, these abandoned parts, people, and social institutions were welded then spliced together, not only as a source of survival but also as a source of pleasure."[26]

With his high tenor voice, dancer-lean physique, polished routines, and enormous commercial appeal, Jackson had neither Springsteen's seemingly obvious Fordist conflation of vocal and corporeal muscularity nor hip-hop's seemingly obvious oppositionality, though his Fordist genealogy was an explicit part of his autobiography and despite the hip-hop vocabularies circulating throughout his vocal and physical repertoire. Jackson's unimpeachable Rust Belt labor pedigree, to which he regularly referred, was not sufficient for him to register as "deindustrial," or as a vector through which deindustriality publicly circulates, because he seemed insufficiently "industrial" to begin with.[27]

One way to further probe Jackson's centrality to, yet invisibility within, the conventional pantheon of deindustrialization's most recognizable performers is to consider him alongside another virtuosic dancing man, another of popular culture's "quintessential icons" of the "last days of the American working class": Tony Manero, the Brooklyn disco prince of *Saturday Night Fever*.[28] For historian Jefferson Cowie, Tony Manero, played by John Travolta, exemplified the unraveling and subsequent disappearance of the US working class as a highly visible social force at the end of the 1970s. Italian American Tony, nineteen, is a stunning success on the disco dance floor, which simultaneously offers both respite from his benumbing, dead-end job and the recognition denied him by a pileup of interpersonal failures and a collective class shame that permeates his neighborhood as well as almost every one of his interactions. This shame is exacerbated by a palpable sense of class obsolescence. Disco as personal expression, and as a tool of mastery in competition, remasculinizes Tony, setting him apart from his circle of loser friends whose quasi-tribal primitivity and lack of new economy skills seem to mark them for inevitable extinction. As Tony reaches the pinnacle of his community's weekend dance floor hierarchy, he discovers and exposes its big lie: that hierarchy, sustained by white racial privilege, is merely a cheap gilding barely concealing the crushing banality and casual violence of his and his circle's lives. Ultimately, he flees Brooklyn for Manhattan and the promise of a new start.

Cowie sees the film as such an exemplar of deindustrialization's blows to the working class that he uses the title of its breakout song, "Stayin' Alive" by the Bee Gees, for his analysis of the 1970s. He writes:

> As much as curmudgeonly Archie Bunker was the definitive character of the first half of the seventies, doomed to be on the losing side of history, Tony Manero served that role for the second half by battling his way toward the winning side of history. He showed that, for the able, "working class" may be something that could simply be rejected like any other style choice in the world of self-constructed identities, and that cost was merely severing all connections to the past. And not only *could* it be rejected but, if possible, it *should*.[29]

Surprisingly, for Cowie, as for many of the film's critics at the time of its release, the disco dancing so central to the plot is reduced to an aesthetically and contextually appropriate background against which the larger and more significant theme of coming of age in a time of seismic political economic shifts plays out. He makes this explicit when he notes:

> [The film's] classic cinematic theme of imprisonment or escape is pitch perfect, and the disco setting makes it emblematic of the seventies. The urgency and desperation of its themes *make it more than a dance flick*: *Saturday Night Fever* is both symptom and exploration of the most important breaking points in the nation's white, male, working-class identity.[30]

One reason for Jackson's comparative invisibility as a deindustrial working-class icon is nascent in this assessment of the role of dance in the film.

For Cowie, as for many historians and cultural critics, dance needs to partner with a "more than" to gain significance to issues of political economy, and even then only as a "setting." On its own, it is insufficient, practically a corporeal McGuffin compared with the film's "classic cinematic theme," which somehow operates independently of the moving bodies that produce it. To the extent that dance drives the plot at all in this reading, it is because it serves as an obvious stand-in for Tony's lack of "real" agency beyond the dance floor, while seemingly demonstrating its own inadequacies and contingency as a strategy for self-making. The characterization of dance as an ornamental feature of setting, and its attendant invisibility as a cultural force, arises from the persistent Romantic view relegating it to personal expression and/as a respite from work and therefore unintelligible within networks of production.[31] It overlooks both the role of production in the work of art generally and, as discussed later in this chapter, the specific intimate historical relationships between dance and/as industrial production.[32] The stubborn persistence of this view is especially ironic given that, in the service economy operating alongside and ultimately supplanting manufacturing, the "sensuous experience" and heightened affect of labor is itself a commodity, making the dancer the very model of what political philosopher Antonio Negri calls an "immaterial worker."[33] Finally, this view misses crucial opportunities for a deeper understanding of both the film and the figural economy of the deindustrial. To take dance seriously, without the need for a thematic "more than," is to recognize that Tony doesn't so much "battle" his way to the winning side of history as hustle (the disco dance) there. His mastery of multiple rhythms, from his elegant, liquid duet with Stephanie Mangano (Karen Lynn Gorney, "More Than a Woman") to his solo percussive, driving pelvic thrusts ("You Should Be Dancing") cinematically authorize his geographical and class "escape" by demonstrating that he possesses the requisite corporeal, affective, and aesthetic capital—if only as raw materials—and the talent for mobility that enables him to glide away from his old life. Simply put: Tony's affectively productive mobility on the dance floor is fungible, and therein lies his new economy potential.

When *Saturday Night Fever* was released in 1977, Michael Jackson was also nineteen, the same age as Tony Manero, and doing some of the same moves onstage. Also in that year, he and the Jackson 5 released their own anthem to literal and metaphoric mobility: the optimistically titled album *Going Places*, whose namesake track proclaims: "The world is bigger than this ole town / I wanna get my feet up / Off the ground."[34] Though the lyric refers to getting on a plane, getting one's feet up off the ground to "leave this ole town" also registers literal, dancerly movement and, for Michael in particular, moving produced spectacular social mobility. By 1977, the Jacksons had been escaping the contracting opportunities in the industrial Rust Belt for almost a decade, with Michael using his self-described pleasure at being onstage as further freedom from the hard physical labor of drilling and rehearsal needed for this initial escape. The character of Tony Manero worked in a hardware store; he was, in fact, a service worker, not the embodiment of the macho industrial prowess exemplified by the steel industry and, in turn, by Joseph Jackson, then transmitted via a lick from his belt and the demand for one more rehearsal to his sons. In one sense, Tony was always already at the end of the Fordist line; his dilemma was that nothing replaced the industry and its employment options that had left Brooklyn years before. Michael Jackson, by contrast, both explicitly referred to and simultaneously embodied the corporeal rigors of the industrial context from which he escaped, the fictive smoothness of that escape, and the ongoing physical service and affective labor—consumed by his audiences—that were required to sustain it: a much more complex repertoire of working bodies and regimes of labor layered one over another. Of course, all of these bodies were black, and therein lies another reason for Jackson's indiscernible deindustriality.

In addition to demonstrating dance's relegation to setting, Cowie's characterization of *Saturday Night Fever* as "both symptom and exploration of the most important breaking points in the nation's white, male, working-class identity" underscores the importance of race in the rapidly consolidating deindustrial imaginary of the middle to late 1970s.[35] Indeed, disco itself is a useful "index of popular white racial feeling in the United States."[36] Its inclusive impulse and its multiple genealogies of blackness and queerness were answered with what Cowie calls the "Beer Hall Putsch" of white heteronormative retrenchment: the "Disco Sucks" movement.[37] The disco wars were a proxy for larger battles over the "character and color of labor" at the end of the industrial moment, paralleling those that defined this moment's beginnings.[38] As social historian Eric Lott has observed of the United States in the mid-nineteenth century, "Class straits may energize interracial cooperation, but they are also often likely to close down the possibility of interracial embrace."[39] So it proved in the middle to late 1970s, when white racial animus, crystallizing around issues of court-ordered busing for school integration in the early part of the decade, fractured workers' solidarity even as the labor-management compact that sustained industrial era prosperity was itself fraying. Labor historian Judith Stein notes that, when George McGovern, who unsuccessfully challenged Richard Nixon for the presidency in 1972, stated that "bussing was 'one of the prices we are paying for a century of segregation in housing patterns,' he omitted the fact that the 'we' was defined by class."[40] For working-class whites, busing obviously and explicitly threatened both white racial privilege performatively reproduced through segregationist housing practices that often had the force of law when they were not the law outright and the patriarchal Fordist "provider" ethos at a moment when that ethos seemed increasingly imperiled.[41]

Interracial division, brought into high relief over busing, inhibited the formation of a robust cross-racial working-class coalition in the 1970s, consolidated the racial retrenchment of the Reagan era, and forged a "link in a chain of representations" that figured the normative working-class body in the public sphere as white, ethnic, and conservative.[42] As political theorist Adolph Reed argues, the hegemonic working-class deindustrial subject became an allegorical conflation of "ethnicity, attitudes, religion, place of residence, race, gender, and simplistic notions of 'blue collar' employment": figured as white male Rust Belt George Wallace voters at the beginning of the 1970s and Reagan Democrats at the end of them.[43] Michael Jackson—young, black, a Jehovah's Witness and, by this time, living in California—simply did not fit this figural bill. Four decades later, the normative working-class industrial and deindustrial body remains white and male: both a representational residue of racist employment practices in the US manufacturing sector from its inception and a reflection of a racial economy in which the black unemployed, disproportionally disadvantaged by the sector's contraction, are blamed for their own predicament. Deindustriality's presumptive whiteness, coupled with the relegation of dance to personal expression or entertainment, helps to explain why, despite a working-class background central to both his autobiography and the publicity apparatus promoting the Jackson 5, the only highly visible "Jackson" typically discussed in even the most progressive racial and cultural histories of US deindustrial decline in the late 1970s and 1980s is Jesse.

VIRTUOUS(O) WORK

Jackson's status as a transitional deindustrial subject arises directly from his virtuosity and from virtuosity as a figuration of self-evidently virtuous material and affective work. Concert dance is work: a job, the product of labor, enmeshed from beginning to end in networks of production and consumption. It is also both ideological and rhetorical: a "persuasive kinesthetic and visual means by which individual identities are called or hailed into larger group formations."[44] Both of these dimensions became increasingly obvious at the consolidation of the industrial age, when dance exemplified a kinesthetic modernity of "unstoppable motility."[45] With industriality waning in the West, dance now typifies the "hypermateriality" of so-called immaterial, affective service labor.[46] It is also figural: a "mix of making and reading" regimes of work "combined in one."[47] Dance's status as simultaneously hypermaterial, ideological, and figural makes dancers particularly significant rhetorical actors in public imaginings of bodies and work. Virtuoso dancers offer especially visible, potent representations of the ways work might be produced and consumed. Michael Jackson illuminates these dynamics with special clarity.

"Virtuosity" as conventionally understood migrated from Romantic classical concert music; the excessively self-evident individuality of the Romantic virtuoso was a bulwark against the encroaching alienations of the industrial age. Michael Jackson's virtuosity is both shaped by and contributes to the Romantic genealogy of virtuosity as spectacular individual excellence. This genealogy often begins with violinist and composer Niccolò Paganini (1782–1840), whose performances enraptured audiences and led peers to proclaim themselves "already dead," so great was the perceived gulf between his talent and their own.[48] David Palmer uses Paganini as the paradigm case for defining virtuosity as excellence: "the art of incredible skill which displays a heightened sense of self-expression, evokes a distinctive affecting presence and transforms ways of viewing human agency," to which dance scholar Gabriele Brandstetter, also using Paganini, adds the exceptional "charisma" projected by the performer.[49]

"Virtuosity" is also a keyword in contemporary discourses about the changing nature of work with performers serving as paradigm cases, albeit highly generalized ones, of post-Fordist immaterial labor. Performance studies scholar Shannon Jackson notes, "The finer points of how different virtuosos developed different kinds of affective skills or different ways of managing immateriality is less often recounted . . . when making these connections."[50] But managing immateriality is not the virtuoso's task alone, whether s/he takes the stage or the sales floor as a Wal-Mart greeter. The finer points of virtuosity *as a transaction*, both produced and consumed, are recounted even less often than the specific skills of the virtuoso herself, despite their centrality to the performer's figural potential.

Though its role is too often generalized as mere presence, the audience's consumption of the virtuoso's labor is central to virtuosity and involves more than simply "witnessing" a virtuosic event to authorize the labor of the performance in lieu of producing an actual product.[51] Virtuosity is an active spectatorial process in which both the virtuoso and the audience collaborate. Evaluative spectatorship is itself a form of work in this formulation, as in the case of managers whose job it is to observe and assess the affective comportment of service laborers. Consider social theorist Paolo Virno's "normal meaning" of virtuosity:

> By "virtuosity" I mean the special capabilities of a performing artist. A virtuoso, for example, is the pianist who offers us a memorable performance of Schubert; or it is a skilled dancer, or a persuasive orator, or a teacher who is never boring, or a priest who delivers a fascinating sermon.[52]

It is worth making explicit that Virno's dancer may be "skilled" in ways that seem self-evident, but assessments of memorability, persuasiveness, fascination, and, indeed, "skill," are relationally produced rather than simply witnessed.[53] Virtuosity is thus located betwixt and between performance, context, and reception: between the skills of the exceptional artist and the sets of expectations, narratives, and spectatorial relationships within which s/he operates.[54] It arises as much from the audience's assessment of the ethos and pathos evident in the performance as from their witnessing of the artist's execution of techne; this is the case both in the context of the artist as genius and in everyday scenarios of servile virtuosity wherein one's job depends on swift service with a smile. The audience verifies and evaluates those very "special capabilities"—technical facility, affective output, and their alignment with shared norms of "excellence"—and, in so doing, establishes the efficacy of the performance itself.[55] Virtuosity's cathectical potential resides in the fact that it is not the property of the performer alone, and its potential to figure virtuous work on the public stage resides in the relationship between the artist's execution and the spectator's interpretive, evaluative labor.

Virtuosity is thus both psychodynamic and sociohistorical: a transitional subjectivity in itself. Its cathectical potential lies in its ability to organize and package multiple elements, including the performer's skill and affective surplus, spectators' expectations and desires, and, in the case of Jackson, "theatrical [and deindustrial] constructs of blackness and whiteness in implicit and explicit relation to one another."[56] This theory of virtuosity, and Jackson's particular execution of it, readily accommodates what dance historian Susan Manning calls "cross-viewing": a process wherein audiences "catch glimpses of social locations that differ from their own," as well as recognition of aspects of these locations that are similar to their own.[57] Indeed, in Jackson's case, the potential for racial "cross-viewing" was an explicit element in the framing of his career beginning in his Motown years as part of Berry Gordy's racial cross-marketing.[58] In addition to this potential for racial cross-viewing, Jackson's repeated references to his childhood in Gary frame the potential for both class cross-viewing and class recognition as well, further contributing to his figural potential as deindustrialization's transitional subject.

Three additional aspects of virtuosic performance in Virno's "normal" sense illustrate the significance of consumption in assessments of virtuosity while contributing to the concept's critical slipperiness. First, the definitional precision of virtuosity is inversely proportional to its seeming self-evidence. Audiences "know it when they see it," and what they see challenges referentiality while inviting a veritable mash-up of metaphors. Virtuosos are "angels," "devils," "heroes," "monsters," "magicians," and "machines," sometimes all at once.[59] As these images suggest, the virtuoso is human, but not quite: there is something more than talent or execution, and definitions strain to capture both the performer's exemplary humanity and this peculiar excess that seems greater than the sum of its merely human parts. This "human/more than human" quality again marks the virtuoso as a transitional subjectivity and the spectator's experience as one combining vicarious identification with the artist's obvious humanity and aspirational consumption of those elements that seem to exceed it.

Second, definitions of popular virtuosity are most effectively operationalized in comparisons with nonvirtuosos, like Paganini's "dead" comparators. Michael Jackson's performance with his brothers as the reunited Jackson 5 at the televised celebration of Motown's twenty-fifth anniversary is illustrative. Jackson sang "Billy Jean" and introduced the moonwalk on *Motown 25: Yesterday, Today, and Forever*, but his solo effort was preceded by the group's rendition of Jackson 5 hits.[60] Michael is clearly the front man in this number, though the medley features shared choreography. Many of his moves seem almost throwaway—timekeeping or rhythmic punctuation—but are executed with a precision and vehemence rendered more compelling and eye-catching against the comparative docility and rootedness of his brothers. He inserts rapid-fire corkscrew kicks and effortless close-legged spins almost gratuitously. The casualness with which the spins are tossed off belies their tightness and smoothness: he looks as if he is on ice while his brothers are weighted down. In line formations, he is visibly more taut and, simultaneously, very loose-jointed. His hip thrusts are sharper, his dime stops (complete pauses, usually transitions between moves) more abrupt, and his crouches with turned in knees so extreme they are almost grotesque. Yet these moves resolve so quickly into other steps that the group choreography seems utterly staid by comparison, and this underscores Michael's virtuosity even further. His dancing is always so self-evidently better than that of his brothers, it is as if he is physically enacting the group's inability to contain him.[61]

Finally, the relational economy of virtuosity manages and organizes multiple dimensions of difference, paving the way for the simultaneous alienation and identification that funds the virtuoso's power as a figural actor. As I have argued elsewhere, an audience's "knowing virtuosity when they see it" is recognition of a preexisting—if barely articulated—consensual template for reading the performer's virtuous effort and for organizing the range of affective responses conjured by the performance. This template binds the audience to the performer, inviting attachment, identification, and desire across some dimensions of difference, for example, gender and race, while performatively reinforcing others, which are then coded as "talent" or "genius." In Jackson's case, his exceptional virtuosity as an artist also operated alongside his "Black American exceptionalism." As African American studies scholar Imani Perry argues in *More Beautiful and More Terrible: The Embrace and Transcendence of Racial Inequality in the United States*:

> The African American figure of note and achievement is evidence for, and in some instances a sign of, chipping away at the infrastructure of White supremacy. . . . And yet, the Americanness of the subject of Black American exceptionalism predicates idealized Blackness on claims to, or actual citizenship in, the American dream.[62]

Jackson's coupling of virtuosity and Black American exceptionalism was particularly potent at a time of structural economic change, sustaining "American mythologies of perfect democracy and unfettered possibility" when actual working-class possibilities were visibly diminishing, particularly for workers of color.

Simply put, virtuosity is a recognizable plot, activated in performance, into which audiences set an exceptionally skilled, charismatic performer. This plot organizes audiences' own attachments and longings by projecting these onto the artist, thereby enabling them to consume an "other" body onstage. "Virtuosity" enables audiences to attend to the noteworthy aspects of such bodies framed by the performance (the seemingly transcendent execution of virtuous, highly disciplined work) and to "appropriate" feelings about them (identification as well as alienation). Virtuosos incarnate plots of possibility for audiences—seeming mastery of one's own labor and the affective surplus it generates—even while demonstrating the audiences' inability to activate these plots themselves and thereby serve as objects of both attraction and anxiety simultaneously: reassuring and disturbing.[63] In the public sphere, their successful performances operate centripetally: pulling together affect and spectacularly efficient work, and their audiences' appreciative assessments and affective investments, so these coalesce apparently effortlessly and naturally into ideologically potent plots of virtuous, highly visible labor and its equally virtuous consumption.

Virtuosity as a relational economy is particularly complex in popular performance, where communal ideals of virtuous labor circulate within more elastic frames of reference than in classical concert music and dance disciplined by explicit canons. Consider the case of saxophonist Kenny G, who, musicologist Robert Walser asserts:

> is in fact a virtuoso of a particular kind. His intonation is flawless, even on the treacherous alto sax. He plays flurries of notes with tremendous technical precision. He controls his instruments perfectly, doing with them exactly what he wants to. He plays ornaments on his ornaments, with nuances on his nuances.[64]

Yet despite his popularity, Kenny G is also reviled, particularly by jazz aficionados, who, as Walser demonstrates, seem to delight in imagining his demise. For these detractors, Kenny G is not virtuous enough. He violates jazz norms of "finding music" through "struggle."[65] The jazz virtuoso should be more hero than magician, and more devil than angel. Walser argues that "violent reactions to [his] music . . . surely betray a widespread cultural discomfort with, even contempt for, sensitivity."[66] But, if Kenny G's perceived excessive emotionalism is too much, it is also the case that his seemingly effortless effort is not enough. He is too problematic an object for identification, at least for one potential fan base, to earn his virtuosity.

As a dancer, Michael Jackson demonstrates the exceptional skill, self-evident and almost fantastic agency, charisma, and transcendence of nonvirtuosic peers common to all Romantic virtuosos. In this his virtuosity is old school and resolutely middlebrow. His dancing is too often dismissed, in part because it falls between the conventions of exceptional concert dance and those of popular dance regarding the nature of virtuous work in performance. Virtuosity in classical or avant-garde concert dance is most obvious when it occurs on opposite ends of continua of labor visibility: battles with technique that are clearly battles and position the artist as hero, as in athletic butoh where dancers' muscles strain and whitened faces and bodies are streaked with sweat; those in which the technique is so overmatched by the performer that it looks easy, as in ballet or tap, which positions the artist to be read as angel, magician, or machine; or those that hold up "virtuosity" in the lay sense for interrogation as in the deceptively simple dances of Yvonne Rainer and Steve Paxton. In popular dance, virtuosity is most recognizable in obviously athletic, spectacular, clearly "difficult" moves that are, at the same time, strongly narrative and highly expressive. Michael Jackson's virtuosity is both subtler and more complex. He combines exceptional musicality and precise execution of a repertoire that draws from so many genres it is best described as polycorporeal with recurring invocations of hard work simultaneously belied by the apparent effortlessness of his performances. Conventional virtuoso popular dancers make visibly difficult moves look easy; Jackson takes deceptively easy steps and complicates them in performance. His virtuosity is a function of his execution of these moves, not any inherent difficulty of the moves themselves.

Critics of his dancing often miss both the virtuosity of his execution—the actual work he does in performance—and the multiple genealogies performatively reincarnated in the process. Instead, they default to seemingly unexamined presumptions about originality, range, and difficulty putatively intrinsic to particular steps, or aggressively re-site him in other histories of movement. For example, in an otherwise laudatory essay, dance critic Joan Acocella observes that Jackson "didn't have a lot of moves. You can almost count them on your fingers. . . . He created very little dancing that was different from his own prior numbers, or anyone else's."[67] She concludes that, in his short films, "dance is tertiary, even quaternary. . . Jackson didn't value his dancing enough."[68] Likewise, performance theorist Peggy Phelan describes Jackson as a "captivating (albeit relatively narrow) dancer" while noting his "two-step, the double gesture of appropriating and transforming" other artists' moves.[69] On the other hand, in a review that explicitly calls Jackson a "virtuoso dancer," critic Anna Kisselgoff recasts him as an "avant-garde" concert artist at the cost of his "street" (read "black") moves. She writes:

> Scrub away the the [sic] veneer of street dances in the performance he gave Thursday night at Madison Square Garden, look past the occasional suggestive gesture and rotating pelvis, marvel at the backward gliding moonwalk and the isolated body parts—seemingly set into motion on their own—[. . .] Yes, Michael Jackson is an avant-garde dancer, and his dances could be called abstract. Like Merce Cunningham, he shows us that movement has a value of its own and that what we read into it is provided by the theatrical context around it.[70]

These mixed assessments of Jackson's dancing also reveal a default hegemony of choreography, and presumptions about originality and range that derive from it, over techniques for executing it.

As dance studies scholar Marta Savigliano observes, "Choreography operates at a distant, privileged position as the creative, innovative, progressive dance-making force, the truly artistic undertaking that makes dance happen."[71] By this measure, one element of Acocella's critique is correct. Jackson was not given sole choreographer credit for many of his dances. He worked with Michael Peters to choreograph *Thriller* and with Vincent Paterson on *Smooth Criminal*. Though the moonwalk was his signature move, he did not create it so much as appropriate it and repurpose it in the two-step Phelan describes.[72] Judged against a very restrictive standard of choreography as putatively original authorship, Jackson is neither a creator nor an innovator.

Choreographer credit, however, is a particularly suspect way to assess choreographic agency for two reasons. First, as dance scholar Sally Gardner has argued, the separation of choreographer and dancer arises from modern dance's simultaneous resistance to, yet enmeshment within, a model of industrial era production that frames the relationship as a division of labor: one that fails to account for ensemble creation and an artist's ability to operate in both roles.[73] Second, choreography, particularly in the making of popular works with a superstar like Jackson, is an interactive process, not one of passive inscription wherein the dancer's movements are wholly shaped by a choreographer/author. As his choreographers have attested, working with him was highly collaborative.[74]

While Phelan avoids defaulting to such a simplistic view of choreography, her charge that Jackson is a "narrow" dancer conflates a negative assessment of the breadth of his repertoire with a negative assessment of his expressive and physical range. Even when these abilities are singled out for praise, as in Kisselgoff's review, they require recoding in a recognizable choreographic genealogy of "abstract movement" and a figural connection to a major choreographer. A view of Jackson as the terpsichorean child of Merce Cunningham is certainly more interesting than one that reduces his work to four removes from some fictively original choreographic ideal of pure value: Acocella's assessment that his dancing was "tertiary—even quaternary." But to fully grasp his complex virtuosity, its figural relationship to the changing nature of America work, and his racial critique-in-motion, it is important to reckon with the specific dynamics of his execution, as well as to probe the precise point where his supposed "narrowness" and his polycorporeal appropriations meet in performance.

Jackson's movement vocabulary was relatively small, though his repertoire became richer and more complex over the period under consideration here. *Thriller* (1983) and his performance of "Billy Jean" at the *Motown 25* anniversary concert (1983) are comparatively simpler than *Smooth Criminal* (1988): one reason why the first two are much more frequently reproduced by fans. Taken together, these three performances are representative of the range of Jackson's dancing at the height of his career. He makes extensive use of his knees, especially in Charleston-informed moves from turned in to turned out, as well as isolations, quick corkscrew kicks, closed-leg spins, pelvic thrusts, toe stands, variants on the electric slide and jazz struts (figure 2). He pops and locks his joints, juxtaposing these against seemingly weightless glides. He also makes extensive use of "the robot" and variants, and of the dime stop. It is not that these elements are difficult in and of themselves. Indeed, in *Smooth Criminal*, they are reproduced, albeit not nearly as well, by one of the children "spying" on Jackson in the film's nightclub setting. His specific virtuosity comes from the interrelationship of his musicality and the sharpness of his attack. Jackson seemed particularly proud of this dimension of his performance style, underscoring the point by invoking Fred Astaire, who reportedly called him "a *hell* of a mover."[75]

As critic Margo Jefferson has aptly observed, Jackson's moves, particularly his quick changes of weight, are both "liquid and percussive."[76] He is able to forcefully insert half and quarter steps while visibly working within, not against, the music, thus exemplifying the African American aesthetic structure of complicating and manipulating rhythmic flow.[77] He is also extraordinarily clean, even while extremely fast. His lean line emphasizes that every strut and kick is sharp and fully stretched: completed to the tips of his toes. In rapid-fire combinations, his precision, particularly his highly articulate management of his joints and his feet, makes him readily discernible from others in the ensembles he leads or in crowd scenes when you can't see his face or make out his costume. He also displays an impressive ability to clearly articulate contrasting moves in the same choreographic phrase. *Thriller* is an interesting case in point. In an early scene in which he and Ola Ray

Figure 2: Michael Jackson with *Smooth Criminal* ensemble. Note the precise geometry of his joints. Screenshot, *Smooth Criminal. Moonwalker.* Standard version. Warner Bros. Entertainment, 2010.

skip from the theater toward their eventual zombie encounter, Jackson's liquid, almost weightless skips are the counterpoint that makes his stiff-armed parodic zombie walks seconds later so extreme and, therefore, so playful. His dance with his zombie chorines begins with isolations on beat, then switches to quick pelvic gyrations: a simple physical passage that is rhythmically challenging to execute with the requisite sharpness, as demonstrated by hundreds of Jackson's flash mob imitators. A few of his moves were enabled by special effects: his "antigravity" forward lean (figure 3) and hyperspin in *Smooth Criminal* are two examples.[78] But these effects-assisted moves are interesting because they differ from the rest only in degree, not in quality: a bit more extreme, but the same intricate coupling of grace and vehement precision that characterizes Jackson's dancing in this period.

Romantic constructions of virtuosity obscure the mechanics of creative production, hence the mystifications of the performing "angel" or "magician." In contrast, Jackson routinely exposed the very labors virtuosic dance—and his particular percussive liquidity—generally conceal: disrupting conventional visual equations of economy of input yielding spectacular output. Here, efficiency and precision in performance are always described as *work*. Jackson insisted on narrating the labor involved, even in rare moments when he "let[s] the dance create itself," as was the case with the moonwalk in the "Billie Jean" performance on *Motown 25*.[79] Yet even here, as if to emphasize that no dance really creates itself, he also highlighted his efforts as a choreographer for the same show in ensemble numbers with his

Figure 3: Jackson's "antigravity lean." Screenshot, *Smooth Criminal. Moonwalker.* Standard version. Warner Bros. Entertainment, 2010.

brothers that he "choreographed and rehearsed . . . for *days*."[80] Jackson never colluded in the rhetorical consignment of his virtuosity to the ephemerally of talent. He certainly found performance pleasurable, but it was always produced through repetitive hard work. Most important, he did not improvise in performance; he consistently deployed the vocabulary of choreography and rehearsal as a way of establishing both the labor and the artistic pedigrees of his dances. In so doing, Jackson both exposed the unseen work of virtuoso performance—those labors that defined him by, in his view, erasing his childhood—and aggressively intervened in the stereotype of African Americans as "natural" dancers. He writes, "Black people are truly innovative dancers; they create many of the new dances pure and simple."[81] The agency articulated in "innovative" and "create" challenges racist dismissal of African American dancers as mere imitators of European culture just as the agency implicit in his adult invocations of hard work forecloses a priori attribution of his abilities to either "genes" or "genius."[82] On the rare occasions he presents himself as a uniquely gifted dancer, it is not as a choreographer, not as an instinctual artist, but rather as a quick study.[83]

DANCING MACHINE

In addition to his own physical facility and discipline, Jackson's virtuosity is inextricably linked to place and race: the socioeconomic landscapes from which it emerged or, as the popular mythos has it, the places from and to which he escaped. He was a child of the American industrial heartland, born in the steel mill town of Gary, Indiana, and molded in the self-consciously Fordist studios of Detroit's Hitsville USA: Motown. His repeated references to his childhood as a nonstop regimen of rehearsals and performances lay the narrative groundwork authorizing his virtuosity as something other than talent, charisma, or luck. This was not simply the dancer's pleasure of practice, though Jackson did write about his love of performing. Even so, from a very young age, he argues, he was another working stiff who did not and could not control his own labor. In his autobiography, he writes:

> I was reminded of that old song by Clarence Carter called "Patches," where the oldest
> son is asked to take care of the farm after his father dies and his mother tells him she's
> depending on him. Well, we weren't sharecroppers and I wasn't the oldest, but those
> were slim shoulders on which to place such burdens.[84]

Jackson's repeated references to the burdens of his childhood and the image of the sharecropper, albeit disavowed, underscore the black body's very specific and intimate relationship to oppressive regimes of work. Performance scholar Jayna Brown notes that this relationship was embodied by a much earlier generation of black child performers crossing the country, and the ocean, more than a century before

Jackson took the stage with new versions of some of their moves.[85] For Jackson this was a matter very close to home.

Michael Jackson was the driven son of a driven father. Joseph Jackson was a crane operator for U.S. Steel and an R&B guitarist.[86] In *Moonwalk*, he seems much more of a shift boss. Both father's and son's escapes from alienating regimes of work required strict adherence to more of the same: slowly building capital through "overtime" rehearsals and performances, the equivalent of second and third shifts to refine routines with Tayloresque precision. Reference to the sharecropper aside, Jackson's family was itself a site of industrial (re)production: a factory turning out professional entertainers. In Michael's account, Joseph's demands for productivity in this arrangement unrelentingly trumped the unstructured pleasures of childhood. In this regard, the Jackson family dynamic resonates powerfully with historian Robin D. G. Kelley's observations about the effects of racist exploitative labor practices within black working-class families. He writes that these families

> were sites for internal conflicts as well as key institutions for sustaining a sense of community and solidarity. If patriarchal families are, at the very least, a system by which exploited male wage earners control and exploit the labor of women and children, then one would presumably find a material basis for a good deal of intrafamily conflict, and perhaps an array of resistance strategies, all framed within an ideology that justifies the subordinate status of women and children.[87]

The trope of the family as locus of production was repeated when Michael Jackson and his brothers signed with Motown, whose corporate dynamic operated through a rhetorical sleight of hand that shifted between both of these, most notably in company founder Berry Gordy's uncanny ability to operate as paterfamilias and factory boss. Gordy had in fact worked at the Ford Wayne Assembly Plant and spoke explicitly about the line as Motown's production model.[88] This same tropic intertwining of family and factory circulated through the vernacular of American industrial modernity itself, with union "brothers" and corporations like General Motors (GM) serving as "generous mother." It also recalls other sites where black bodies, the family, and (re)production and/as work were intimately linked, including the plantation "family" where white "fathers *could* and *did* sell their sons and daughters," and troupes of black performers who were literally family (e.g., the Whitman Sisters) or were readable through that trope.[89]

Jackson's virtuosity is thus inextricably tied to working-class credentials forged through both his own labors and those of his father. In *Moonwalk*, he observed: "A part of my earliest memories is my father's job working in the steel mill. It was tough, mind-numbing work and he played music for escape."[90] In underscoring his class background, Jackson made the industrial working class generally, and the black industrial working class in particular, visible as creative cultural actors in the hegemonic American public sphere as deindustrialization was accelerating. This was in itself a meaningful intervention because, as noted earlier, the normative working

body of American industrialization was presumptively white and heteronorma-
tively male, and deindustrialization's folk model was the same. Jackson's insistence
on recognition of his labor pedigree also challenged typical representations of black
life as bimodal (elites versus the multigenerational poor), even as it challenged virtuosity as magically produced.[91] He thus performatively refuted the "sneering references" to black workers as lazy that "typified the manner in which whites could still
use Blacks as a counterpoint to come to terms with their own acceptance of steady
and even regimented labor" that persisted from the dawn of industrialization.[92]

Punched Out

Michael Jackson's transitional subjectivity was produced through his virtuosic
dancing, but in the mid-1980s it was energized by collective anxiety around the
industrial age vision of the good life now seemingly on life support, with the steel
industry as Patient Zero. As the biological son of a steelworker and the corporate
son of an autoworker, Jackson exemplified, in the most spectacular terms, the inter-
generational compact that sustained industrialization's patriarchal promise of class
mobility produced through disciplined physical labor. As Mike LeFevre, the steelworker whose oral history begins Studs Terkel's classic volume *Working*, put it:

> If you can't improve yourself, you improve your posterity. Otherwise life isn't worth
> nothing. You might as well go back to the cave and stay there. I'm sure the first cave man
> who went over the hill to see what was on the other side—I don't think he went there
> wholly out of curiosity. He went there because he wanted to get his son out of the cave.
> Just the same way I want to send my kid to college.[93]

A brief summary of key events and policy decisions leading to the steel industry's
systemic decline through the mid-1980s, read against milestones in Jackson's career,
shows just how clearly imperiled the possibility of improving both self and posterity in the mills actually was in this period, and why Jackson's spectacular success as
a son of the late industrial age was so figurally potent even as his deindustriality is
so seldom recognized.

In 1973, one year after Jackson's first solo record "Got to Be There," the OPEC
oil embargo and subsequent dramatic increases in fuel prices touched off a pernicious global recession, coupled with high inflation, from which the developed
world was slow to emerge. The economic malaise persisted through the mid-1970s.
President Jimmy Carter, fearing "the fragility of the world, not the U.S. economy,"
and ardently committed to "reduce inflation, where steel always played a role,"
forcefully advanced policies favoring steel imports despite accusations of foreign—
particularly Japanese—dumping.[94] Meanwhile, as the domestic industry suffered,
the Export-Import Bank was providing a multi-million-dollar loan to a South
Korean company to finance a new steel mill in that country.

The results of these policies were devastating and appeared very quickly. In September 1977, the year the Jacksons released *Going Places*, more than 2,500 workers at U.S. Steel in their hometown of Gary were ruled eligible for "trade adjustment assistance": benefits for those "who believe they have been or will become unemployed due to increased imports."[95] By the end of October, industry earnings were plummeting, with U.S. Steel's dropping by almost 76 percent in the third quarter.[96] In December, AFL-CIO president George Meany blasted Carter administration trade policies, arguing: "Free trade is a joke and a myth. And a Government trade policy predicated on old ideas of free trade is worse than a joke—it is a prescription for disaster."[97] He singled out the steel industry as particularly imperiled. By the end of 1977, 20,000 domestic steel jobs were lost as mills closed across the country.[98] By 1979, U.S. Steel alone had closed thirteen steel-making facilities, even as it invested in nonsteel assets, including real estate and energy. According to the American Iron and Steel Institute annual reports, employment in the industry declined by more than 50,000 workers between 1977 and 1980.[99]

The election of Ronald Reagan in 1980 did not reverse the industry's fortunes. By 1984 and Jackson's meeting with him at the White House, domestic steel had lost more than 160,000 additional jobs.[100] As noted earlier, Reagan steadfastly refused to implement policies he viewed as protectionist to help the steel industry, opting instead for voluntary agreements with other steel-producing nations. He also championed a strong dollar policy that imposed an additional competitive disadvantage: "the equivalent of taxing U.S. imports by 63% and providing U.S. imports with an equivalent subsidy."[101] By 1985, when *Ebony* magazine employed a Chicago artist to imagine Michael Jackson in the year 2000, aging "gracefully" into an urbane, prosperous if conventional maturity, it was increasingly apparent that "time could be a villain" to northwest Indiana, including his hometown.[102] The future of the entire region was in doubt due to the steel industry's contraction. A state business publication noted that 60,000 jobs had been cut from local payrolls between 1980 and 1985, and unemployment in the Gary–Hammond–East Chicago area was 13.9 percent. This was actually an improvement from a high of 19 percent the previous year.[103]

Hanging on to a job in the industry was no guarantee of insulation from precarity during this time, as the case of U.S. Steel demonstrated. The already adversarial relationship between the company and the United Steelworkers of America became increasingly strained as each blamed the other for the company's decline.[104] These tensions culminated in a six-month-long strike/lockout in 1986–87, at the end of which U.S. Steel, now renamed as the vaguely sinister-sounding "USX," forced wage concessions and elimination of more than 1,300 union jobs. After the new contract with the union was ratified, USX announced the closing of four additional plants affecting 3,700 employees, withholding the decision during contract negotiations so it could, in the words of labor historian John Hoerr, deliver "the final blow in the steel labor war of 1986–87."[105] Michael Jackson released his *Bad* album in 1987 as US steelworkers faced very bad times indeed. In this atmosphere of rising inequality and job uncertainty, Fordist labor conditions began to look like the good old days and Michael Jackson offered a reassuring spectacle: both the triumph of and the triumph over the human motor through the hard physical work, precision, and efficiency emblematic of industrial glories now clearly vanishing.

Automatic, Systematic

In his precise attack, preternatural cleanness and speed, and explicitly mechanistic movement vocabulary, coupled with his recurring testaments to repetitive hard work and invocation of his industrial lineage—"as much crane operator" as artist— Jackson both incarnates and transcends the trope of the human motor, combining the virtuoso's seeming mechanical exactitude with superhuman charisma. Historian Anson Rabinbach argues that this trope is "a paradigm of social modernity" linking "expanded output, greater work performance, and more energetic workers" to social reform through metaphors drawn from thermodynamics and a larger "science of work," including Taylorism.[106] Popular performance was central to the domestication of the trope. The Fordist production model that supplanted Taylorism as the paradigmatic integration of worker and machine was praised in explicitly dancerly terms with the noise of the line as the score.[107] It was "an experiment in tempo" that provided the "swing and exuberance" which would increase production.[108]

Concert and popular dance simultaneously embraced and resisted the trope of the human motor, and with it the American industrial imaginary, in its most pivotal early decades: the late 1910s and early to mid-1920s. Jackson's invigoration of it at the deindustrial moment draws directly upon this history, including updated versions of some of the same moves. Whether "internalizing the machine into the body" through biomechanics exercises and "machine ballets" or resisting Taylorized economies of gesture through exotic displays of highly personal affect in the dances of Isadora Duncan, Ruth St. Denis, and others, amateur and professional dancers offered their audiences templates for imagining how industrial structures of physical productivity, anti-industrial "authenticity," or preindustrial racialized "primitivity" operated corporeally and affectively.[109] On the popular stage, the chorus girl was especially evocative of connections between dance and industrial work, and black dance vocabularies were central to their figural potential. As Jayna Brown observes, the chorine incarnated both "industrial capitalism's disciplinary claims on the (white) body's time and energies and the potential freedom and pleasures technological innovation was making possible" in urban centers.[110] Black dance elements were key components of the repertoire across the color line: "Dance techniques developed by African American women vitalized the white dance instructor's choreography" of chorus routines.[111] Further, Brown argues that nostalgia for vanished modes of production from the "primitive" preindustrial past was read onto or against black popular dancers by both black and white audiences, particularly in the Depression era, when "black nostalgia, the desired return to a simpler time, ran alongside white romanticized versions of the black folk."[112] Half a century later, Michael Jackson would also evoke nostalgia at a moment of economic crisis, this time for the "simpler" life of the industrial worker.

While the pleasures of precision in an industrial imaginary were incarnated by the chorus line, theater historian David Savran notes that "cultural critics consistently displaced their anxieties about an exhilarating, frightening Machine Age" onto another mode of popular performance: jazz.[113] In *Highbrow/Lowdown: Theater, Jazz, and the Making of the New Middle Class*, he documents the rising anxiety around the "Fordized human subject," both white and blue collar, who in the 1920s had been "transformed into an extension, simulacrum, or machine." Jazz was both a reflection and an agent of industrial dehumanization: a "maddeningly monotonous music" that "had passed through the stereotyping machine to emerge as standard jazz-finished one-steps, as tinny and characterless and undistinguished as a school of Fords." Certainly there was a strong undercurrent of racial(-ist) anxiety in this jazz aversion as exemplified by the pains so many took to excise blacks from the idiom. George Gershwin, for example, "aimed to dispel the 'superstition that jazz is essentially Negro.' "[114] This excision of blackness is another hallmark of the connection between jazz and the industrial imaginary: both depended on whitening prior means of production. When white jazz dancers put "jazz music in motion" during this period, they literally followed in the footsteps of black artists who originated the moves.[115] Sixty years later, Jackson's virtuosity both challenged the putative whiteness of that industrial imaginary and answered charges that he and his black jazz antecedents were either characterless and limited or undisciplined primitives. He used moves—the shimmy, the Charleston, and the strut to name only three—drawn from jazz dance and African American jazz dancers to conjure the promise of mobility in that now-vanishing industrial age, even as manufacturing jobs chased increasingly globalized cheap labor to be replaced by lower wage service jobs when they were replaced at all.

In both the Taylorist and Fordist scenarios, the exemplary human motor combined speed, efficiency, the minimum gestural range deemed necessary, the illusion of overcoming fatigue, and visibly high productivity. Jackson presented all five united in/as virtuoso performance. He made the human motor lyrical, beautiful, and personally expressive. But, in his testaments to the hard physical labor of performance, he also challenged Romantic visions of the virtuoso as perfect human motor by insisting that dance was actually work, not the transcendence of it. He also challenged its presumed whiteness, as discussed later. His human motor operates as both a gestural performative and a performance: repeatedly producing the exemplary deindustrial body as both Gary and Neverland simultaneously, making the mastery of this paradoxical doubleness vicariously available to his audiences.[116] Further, his laborious virtuosity was contagious. As his countless imitators amply demonstrate, audiences were, and remain, not content to simply watch him. They continue to consume and reproduce him at the level of their own musculature, making Jackson both a motor and a generator.

Viewing Jackson's dancing through the trope of the human motor also invites reconsideration of his pacing, which is intimately connected to his rejection of consistent full-body shots over quick edits that isolate parts of the dancing body. This pacing is a central element of his virtuosity. Across his repertoire, Jackson performs quick combinations, pauses, then executes others. The pauses are complete—he is perfectly still—but they are also tensive: not relaxed, but poised for reactivation. The effect recalls William Faulkner's observation that "the cost of electricity was not in the actual time the light burned but in the retroactive overcoming of primary inertia when the switch was snapped."[117] Though he never conveys inertia onstage, Jackson does demonstrate absolute command of the energy needed to repeatedly snap the switch. Further, unlike "the master" Fred Astaire, who favored full-body shots, Jackson used editing to underscore this very specific pacing despite its fragmentation of the dancing body: the choice at the root of Acocella's charge that he "didn't value his dancing enough."[118] But Acocella's assessment ignores the relationship between editing, his phrase/pause pacing, and the importance of isolations in Jackson's repertoire.

Smooth Criminal is an interesting example; it has been described as among the most dancerly of the artist's films.[119] Midway through, the tempo slows dramatically as Jackson begins to moan, the ensemble moves as if in a collective trance, and a black cat walks across piano keys, the discordance underscoring the surrealism of the scene. In succession, Jackson nods with only his head moving rhythmically up and down in the frame, then snaps his fingers in a close-up of the snap, then repeatedly stamps his right foot in a full-body shot, then repeatedly flexes his right arm upward in a shot of his upper body. The tight and long shots have the same effect: underlining each isolation within this highly erotic, yet highly stylized sequence. Even in combinations without such obvious isolations, as in the *Thriller* zombie dances where shots often focus on Jackson's upper body, the editing directs the viewer to the single gesture (shoulder raises, in this case), inviting recognition of larger relationships between a percussive part and the flow of the whole. Put another way, this editing strategy emphasizes that precise "narrow" gestures are the drivers making the entire dance go in ways that parallel the relationship between the Fordist worker's individual production moves and the overall flow of the assembly line.

Automatic, systematic: Jackson's dancing romanticized the seamless fusion of dancer and/as machine, one "tuned and gentle to your vibe," fluidity always working within, not against, his percussive phrasings. His moonwalk is a prime example. The move's grace and elegance arise from his precision in producing the illusion of forward momentum while being carried backward: more evocative of a conveyor belt than of weightlessness.[120] In so doing, he recast the trope of the human motor itself as a site of nostalgic longing. Fordist mechanization viewed retrospectively through the anxieties of deindustrialization was not standardized racist wage slavery but a race-neutral vehicle for self-expression and mobility, just as Motown, modeled on the Ford assembly line, conveyed the Jacksons out of the inferno of Gary's steel mills to a phantasmatic place of control over their labor: "neverland" indeed.[121]

Full of Color

The trope of the human motor has a far older and darker history: mechanization effectively replaced slave labor, America's "other" human motor. Indeed, industrialization's human motor whitened manual labor and, in turn, the American ethnics most likely to embrace factory work as a tool of social mobility. As Lucius Brockway notes in Ralph Ellison's *Invisible Man*: "we the machines inside the machines."[122] This human motor, together with the history of black popular dances and dancers "swinging the machine" in the early decades of industrialization and the whitening of representations of the working class, exposes the figural force of Jackson's polycorporeal dance vocabulary, refutes dismissals of his "narrowness," and positions him as a critical agent coloring the deindustrial.[123]

Jackson's dancing exemplifies the Africanist aesthetics outlined by pioneering dance studies scholar Brenda Dixon Gottschild, particularly the high affect juxtapositions in shifts from playful or elegant moves to vehement, percussive ones, and the "kinesthetic intensity" she labels "ephebism."[124] But he is also a corporeal encyclopedia of black popular dances and dancers, quoting the moves of Josephine Baker, Cab Calloway, James Brown, Jackie Wilson, *Soul Train* dancers, and street and club dancers who were his contemporaries, as well as Fred Astaire and Gene Kelly, to name only a few.[125] The number of steps in his repertoire may be small, but the histories, choreographic strategies, and performance styles he draws on are anything but.[126] In this sense, Jackson is not a narrow dancer but a synecdochal one: the visible parts of his performances invite recognition of a much larger and more diverse corpus.

Thus, Jackson did more than invoke and lyricize a nostalgically idealized human motor and, with it, an entire mode of production. He also signified on it, reminding his audiences that it was "full of color" all along: performatively tricking back on both the whitewashing of black popular dance and racist exclusions of black workers from the promises and rewards of industrialization by drawing on tropes of African American performance going back decades.[127]

Northern industries, including steel and auto which birthed Michael Jackson, drew willing black workers from the American South to Gary and Detroit throughout the mid-twentieth century. More than 15 percent of the region's black population migrated to work in steel during the 1950s.[128] These workers were met with systemic racism from both management and unions across industrial sites; seniority systems kept them out of top jobs and affirmed racial hierarchies. As labor historian Bruce Nelson observed, "There was no united working class in steel."[129] Indeed, when Nelson interviewed black steelworkers, "what struck [him] most forcefully . . . was that in describing the racial discrimination they encountered in the workplace, they rarely distinguished between steel management and white workers."[130]

Institutionalized discrimination in the manufacturing sector was challenged both from below, as with the formation of counterunions like the Dodge Revolutionary Union Movement of autoworkers in Detroit in 1968, and from above, as in a 1974 consent decree between the federal government, United Steelworkers of America, and the steel industry that provided plant seniority for all, as well as by a generation of African American politicians elected to public office during this period. Indeed, the Jacksons themselves were very publicly part of this political process, performing two concerts in support of the re-election of Richard Hatcher, the first African American mayor of Gary, in 1971.[131] But the results of black workers' and politicians' efforts were undermined by federal policies sacrificing domestic manufacturing for trade and finance. To add insult to economic injury, in a repudiation of these battles to secure equal access to well-paying industry jobs, historian Judith Stein points out that institutional racism led to actively blaming victims of these policies for their effects: "During the 1960s, the nation attributed black unemployment to racism; during the 1980s, black unemployment came to be seen as a preference for idleness. . . . In both eras, racial ideology mystified the sources of black unemployment," effectively concealing the systemic redirection of capital to nonmanufacturing sectors.[132]

Against this bleak backdrop, Jackson's zombie routine in *Thriller*, his most popular and iconic dance, operates as an agential amalgam of race and deindustriality through a mechanistic movement vocabulary and literal and thematic mobility that define this period of his career and thus his potential as a transitional subject. The dance's many afterlives have been read as performative expressions of collective post-9/11 belonging, as a spectacle of postcolonial disciplinarity, and as a mode of contemporary choreoprotest, but the "rave from the grave's" figural potential at the time of its release gets less attention.[133] The film premiered on MTV in December 1983, racially integrating the network's music video roster. In describing the multiple ironies of its complex race, genre, and media crossover, performance studies scholar Tavia Nyong'o observes, "As an allegory of racial capitalism, and of lateral agency within it, *Thriller* could not work better."[134] But in the third year of Ronald Reagan's first term, with the overall US unemployment rate at almost 10 percent and the African American unemployment rate double that, Jackson's class background and labor bona fides, the mise en scène of the film, and its choreography remind us that it operated both as an allegory of racial capitalism *within a very specific deindustrial moment* and as a figuration of class "crossing over" as well: a combination ripe for intersectional cross-viewing.[135]

The film's premiere was bracketed by two other works that demonstrated deindustrialization's increasing visibility and urgency in the US cultural field during this period. Billy Joel's "Allentown" ("they're closing all the factories down") was released a year before in 1982, and Bruce Springsteen's "Born in the U.S.A" ("Born down in a dead man's town") a year after in 1984.[136] Both songs voice the anxiety, rage, and despair of working-class men with "nowhere to run, nowhere to go."[137] This sense of profoundly, perhaps permanently, arrested socioeconomic mobility was exacerbated by the federal government's sclerotic response to the crisis in manufacturing, exemplified by the Congressional Budget Office's study titled "The Industrial Policy Debate" (1983), released the same month *Thriller* premiered on MTV. The study, initiated at the request of Senate minority leader Robert Byrd (D-WV), assessed competing claims about the role of government in addressing the "short-term and long-term difficulties" facing US heavy industry about which "everyone agrees."[138] After noting that one consequence of maintaining current policy was that "new job growth will tend to be in the low-wage, low-productivity service sectors, and blue-collar workers will continue to suffer high unemployment," the study concludes that there is no "clear solution to the question of what, if anything, should be done," and indeed no consensus on the central "problems and goals" informing the debate.[139] The subjects of Joel's and Springsteen's songs were left to withstand the ravages of structural economic change wholly on their own. In their discussion of "Born in the U.S.A." as a "unified duality" of working-class identity riven by Vietnam and deindustrialization, Jefferson Cowie and Lauren Boehm observe: "In the absence of any real material aid, one answer to questions of lost wars, shuttered factories, and embattled hometowns was to accept the New Right's retooled discourse of populist nationalism."[140] But on-screen in *Thriller*, Michael Jackson, as deindustriality's transitional subject, offered another answer. One could virtuosically outdance the escalating zombification.

Like the African Americans to whom they were linked by transatlantic chattel slavery, zombies were also racialized human motors. They were putatively created in Haitian folklore by masters seeking untiring slaves, then became whitened as part of the consolidation of industrial capitalism with its anxieties around the anomie of wage labor and mass consumption.[141] Zombies are "proletarian pariahs" with neither the dapperness of Dracula and his vampire descendants nor the resources to support constant access to tailors, which, as singer-songwriter Warren Zevon reminds us, is required by werewolves.[142] They emerge with particular vehemence in times "associated with rapidly changing work under capitalism."[143] The year 1983 was just such a time.

In "A Zombie Manifesto," Sarah Juliet Lauro and Karen Embry note "the resonance of the zombie with the factory worker's mechanistic performance, [and] the brain-dead, ideology-fed servant of industry."[144] If the industrial zombie was produced by the mind- and soul-stripping routinization and alienation of factory labor, deindustrialization doubled down and stripped away the labor, heightening alienation through the resulting unemployment and further zombifying the working class.[145] As anthropologist Kathryn Marie Dudley observed in *The End of the Line*: "In this new symbolic universe [of the deindustrial], dislocated factory workers in America have fallen to their 'natural' level in the capitalist world economy; and like other 'primitive' social forms, they are portrayed as a vanishing breed, the contemporary representative of a dying way of life."[146] It has gone unremarked that the narrative arc of *Thriller* replicates this same atavist trajectory, moving from a teen horror mise en scène of 1950s postwar prosperity to the vaguely deindustrial uncanny: a dead landscape of vacant lots, deserted streets, hulks of dark, empty factory buildings, no one living to hear you scream. The abandoned house to which Ola Ray's character flees after the zombie dance could have been on a blighted block of Detroit or Gary in this same period or, indeed, today.

The zombie's association with routinized industrial labor as both a corporeal identity and a dying way of life is reflected in the film's choreography as well as its mise en scène.[147] Jackson's dancing in *Thriller* is the most obviously mechanistic of any in this period of his career, in part because, like the chorus lines of the 1920s and 1930s, it presents a synchronized and highly rhythmic execution of a limited number of moves done in a tight ensemble formation that disperses and recongeals. Indeed, its popularity and reproducibility as a social dance arise directly from these qualities; transcriptions in the dozens of available online instructions reproduce the steps, slides, stomps, and claps as a kind of prosody, with line breaks representing relationships between the moves and the rhythm.[148] There is staccato quality to the steps, another element that lends itself to simplification in these myriad textual tutorials. In signature ensemble moves—the quick pelvic thrusts embedded in slower sidewise advances downstage, elongated slides brought crisply to a close with the punctuation of a stamp and a clap, the clockwise pivot turn on the rooted right foot powered by percussive falls of the left, and windmill arms—the upper torso is static and the knees and elbows typically either sharply angled or tensively straight and rigid. With their stiff-legged lurching and popping left-right head isolations, their jaws opening and closing like nutcrackers, and their symmetrical feints to left and right with bent knees, flexed feet, and frozen claw-hands, these zombies operate less like the decrepit but recognizably human actors of George Romero's horror classic *Dawn of the Dead* than funky E. T. A. Hoffmann automatons. So angular and percussive is the ensemble dance that a cutaway to a zombie quartet featuring one member executing an extravagantly liquid frug seems to be from another film.

Jackson's dancing in this sequence delivers the reliable pleasures of his signature speed, crispness of line, notable moves like the toe stand, and vehemence of execution. His quick cross-steps are always a bit quicker, his joints sharper, his poses held just a split second longer than those of the other dancers before resolving in a millisecond as he rejoins the group choreography. His lability in shifting from the most mechanistic to the comparatively more fluid elements of the dance finds its thematic parallel in his shifts between his zombie incarnation and his virtuoso rock star persona. He is spectacularly mutable and mobile in multiple senses of the term, and these qualities are a form of new economy capital earned from the routinized labors of rehearsal even as they performatively conjure an industrial gestural repertoire. In spectacularly deploying that capital, Jackson demonstrates both his unquestioned leadership of zombie solidarity within an increasingly frightening deindustrial imaginary and the group's inability to contain or restrict him.

The *Thriller* zombies, and Jackson's and the film's enormous crossover success, suggest that virtuosic mutability and mobility just might be fungible to other types of race and class crossovers at a moment of collective choreoeconomic arrest. As Nyong'o observes, dancing might be a "form of dezombification," making *Thriller*, at the time of its release, a cruelly optimistic figure of corporeal new economy retooling.[149] Jackson's virtuosic efforts, honed and executed with industrial precision, coupled with the willingness and ability to shape-shift, were the tools needed to trick back on the process of zombification—to literally outmaneuver it—to emerge in a deindustrial moment of personal agency, play, and prosperity. No wonder so many subsequent imitators are still eager to step into Jackson's shoes. Writing of the 1970s, Cowie notes that, as deindustrial precarity was becoming increasingly legible, "there was little hope of a progressive working-class identity without confronting its full racial complexity, and on those grounds the nation's music failed to assist."[150] In the early 1980s, however, with that precarity spreading in the absence of any federal remedy, *Thriller*, with its multiracial zombies, infectious rhythm, Jackson's spectacularly mutable mobility on-screen and off, and record-breaking sales, suggested that his audiences too could perhaps play with the apocalypse and not only survive but thrive. Jackson offered and demonstrated a "dream life" of deindustriality: percussive self-assertion and/as graceful social mobility "democratized" by a young black working-class man.[151] He was the Fred Astaire of industrial decline.

Jackson's activation and transcendence of the trope of the human motor in this phase of his career positioned him as both an agent within an industrial imaginary that never wanted to include him and one even the most inclusive industrial moment could not contain. He was on the move to "neverland." Moreover, by invoking movements drawn directly from the African American dance repertoire, he performatively integrated the presumed whiteness of these industrial mechanisms, vehemently, percussively inserting bodily comportments that racist infrastructure first tried to exclude and then to pathologize. During this period, he deftly played both sides of virtuosity's rhetoric of transcendence. Jackson could perform both readily readable racial identity as an African American working body—his cosmetic surgeries had not yet made him appear racially ambiguous—and a Black American exception, as well as invoke the extraordinary artist's putative demographic transcendence using a tactical double positioning reproduced in movement. His transitions from splaying knees to multiple spins emphasized mastery of vocabularies popularly regarded as both racially particular and universal, dancing both together in ways the putative worker solidarity of industrialization never did, all the while performatively refuting racist charges of idleness and reduction to "nature," versus discipline and "culture."[152]

In his own "escape" from Gary to Neverland, Jackson seemed to incarnate the promise of mobility forged through Fordist labor: one rendered retrospectively simpler, more desirable, and more egalitarian by the emerging economic dislocations of deindustrialization. He could parlay the discipline and sweat equity of the mill and the assembly line into virtuosic class mobility. Of course, there are multiple ironies here. First, as noted previously, he could embody a generic American industrial imaginary that in fact consolidated itself through the exclusion and exploitation of black workers. Second, his father's insistence on flawless execution and his own perfectionism positioned Jackson as operating simultaneously within both a regime of industrial discipline and its affective successor, the neoliberal imperative to be excellent all the time as the only bulwark against one's own dispensability. Finally, Jackson could only embody a longing for this vanishing industrial past because he so completely escaped it. From the 1970s through the period covered here, he was the Horatio Alger story of the moment at which industrialization's putative promises were morphing into something else: something seemingly more precarious, more Darwinian. Indeed, the entire arc of Jackson's career parallels the dismantling of this very industrial infrastructure; both accelerated in the 1980s.

Relocated to Neverland in California, later in his career and in the period discussed in the following chapter, Michael Jackson could no longer embody both the virtuous results of industrial discipline and a virtuous escape from it. Instead, he seemingly enacted the flighty irresponsibility of capital itself, increasingly deterritorializing his earlier, carefully wrought relationships between effort and visibility, uncoupling the excesses of celebrity from the work of performance. In this new iteration, the body of the performer came to stand in for the *absence* of his own labor and exposed the very corporeal and socioeconomic incommensurabilities of production, consumption, and visibility that virtuosity was supposed to repair. As the deindustrial wore on for decades, he himself became an object of nostalgic longing: Where was the Michael Jackson of *Thriller*?

Michael Jackson's virtuosic activation of the human motor offered a fantasy of unalienated labor in an industrial modernity that was and never was. It could be mastered through hard work, activated as an aesthetic of personal and racial agency, even become, potentially, emancipatory: a way to transform industrial discipline into spectacular deindustrial success. Ultimately, though, the increasingly global flow of capital was itself a hell of a mover, and Jackson, no longer publicly a dancing virtuoso, became too much an embodiment of its irresponsible caprices and the devastating aftereffects of its failures. By the time of his passing in 2009, his American audience was already consigned to neoliberal neverland, left to the tender mercies of some very smooth criminals in a postmanufacturing age.

CHAPTER 2

Consuming Passions, Wasted Efforts

Michael Jackson's Financial(-ized) Melodramas

To serve all those new needs, urges, compulsions, and addictions, as well as to service new mechanisms of motivation, guidance and the monitoring of human conduct, the consumerist economy has to rely on *excess* and *waste*.

Zygmunt Bauman, *Consuming Life*[1]

Your bad debt looks unconnected, autistic, in its own world. But you can be developed. You can get credit after all. The key is to have interests. . . . You will have an investment, even in debt.

Fred Moten and Stefano Harney, *"Debt and Study"*[2]

"Dance shalt thou," said he. "Dance in thy red shoes till thou art pale and cold! Till thy skin shrivels up and thou art a skeleton!"

Hans Christian Andersen, *"The Red Shoes"*[3]

The Michael Jackson of the new millennium was not the Michael Jackson of *Thriller*, who could leverage a shared podium with the president of the United States as he had with Ronald Reagan in 1984. Among many other things, he was poorer, if not by any reasonable standard actually poor. In the year of his headline-making visit to the Reagan White House, he earned $91 million ($205 million when adjusted for inflation).[4] Ten years later, in 1994, he earned a comparatively meager $19 million ($30 million when adjusted for inflation). This figure included both "work" income from his concerts, recordings, and endorsement deals and investment income, most notably from his ownership of ATV, the music publishing company with a catalog containing more than 4,000 songs, including more than 200 Beatles titles. ATV was the jewel in Jackson's portfolio that included MiJac Music, which held copyright to his own songs; merchandizing deals for clothes and shoes; real estate; and a film, video game, and memoir all entitled *Moonwalk*. He outbid other investors to purchase ATV in 1985 for $47.5 million in what was widely hailed as a brilliant business move; song catalogs generate significant royalty income, and the revenue from ATV would sustain Jackson through the last decades of his life. In 1995, he sold a 50 percent stake to Sony creating Sony/ATV Music Publishing; his own remaining shares generated eight-figure annual payouts.[5] Like other wealthy Americans and indeed like the US economy itself, Jackson's revenue streams were becoming increasingly financialized through the mid-1990s into the new millennium, shifting from the real sector production of goods and services to those arising from investment and speculation. His investments were becoming at least as important to his fiscal well-being as his creative labor and arguably even more so.

In 2004, Jackson earned $20 million ($25 million adjusted for inflation), but his annual expenses were almost as much.[6] Sales of his album *Invincible* (2001) met neither his expectations nor his need for increased cash flow. By 2005, he faced both a trial on child molestation charges and the prospect of Bank of America (BOA) calling in a $270 million loan he made against his shares of the Sony/ATV catalog, putting his ownership of this key asset, and its steady income, in jeopardy. His attempt to refinance this loan using a private equity firm investing in distressed debt led to a lawsuit against him, a foreclosure, and yet another attempt to refinance, this time with success. Michael Jackson the human motor was now a heritage product that had long ago been subsumed into "Michael Jackson, Inc.," and in the run-up to and during the US Great Recession of 2007–9, he faced the very real possibility of complete economic collapse. His corporate viability looked every bit as imperiled in this period as had U.S. Steel's more than two decades earlier, when he had so successfully danced away from deindustrial devastation. But Bear Stearns, the now defunct brokerage firm whose investments in collateralized debt obligations lead to its failure in 2008, may be a more appropriate comparison than a declining industrial era behemoth. At the dawn of the US Great Recession, both Jackson and Bear Stearns were weighted down by debt, facing acute cash crises, and dogged by lawsuits and rumors of instability. Jackson was overexposed as a spectacular oddity but no longer publicly visible as a working artist because he hadn't toured significantly in a decade. He was adamantly opposed to returning to the concert stage, and, according to the *Wall Street Journal*, his cash crisis was so extreme he worried about paying his electric bill.[7] Yet in 2010, he earned $262 million, adjusted for inflation.[8] It was his highest annual gross ever, and he had been dead for a year. He died in 2009 in the midst of rehearsals for a comeback attempt that, in theory, would have paid off his enormous debts, put him on a more secure financial footing, and rehabilitated his reputation with fans. The comeback would feature his greatest hits. He would once again be the Michael Jackson of *Thriller*: once again the highly disciplined, virtuosic transitional subject with the fungible mobility to outmaneuver capital itself. Estimates of his debts at the time of his death ranged from $400 to $500 million.[9]

Michael Jackson was not only a virtuoso performer. In the last two decades of his life, he was also a prodigious spender and a spectacular debtor, with his earning potential deeply compromised by dismissals as "Wacko Jacko" for a range of strange stunts, accusations of child molestation, albums that failed to meet critical and financial expectations, and a string of business deals gone bad, frequently resulting in lawsuits against him. The virtuosic dancing, charismatic surpluses of talent and precision, and invocations of hard work central to the cathectical invitation to consume him in performance at the height of his career were now largely a memory, supplanted by a succession of tabloid melodramas: sensational accounts of bizarre behavior, disturbing allegations, and financial crises.

Here too Jackson is deindustrial. In this phase of his career, he enacted on the public stage the very economies of consumption, debt, and austerity that supplanted those of the industrial age human motor, and he did so in recognizably melodramatic terms: in images of excess, reversals of fortune, and pathos. Consider this phase the metaphoric "Neverland" to his earlier "Gary." His reputation for precision and intense rehearsal, his testaments to hard work inextricably linked to his Rust Belt beginnings ("as much crane operator" as artist), and his image as the epitome of industrialization's promise of race and class mobility through physical labor were now replaced by charges of undisciplined childish or childlike (depending on whether one was a critic or a fan) hyperindulgence, including accusations of untoward indulgences in actual children. According to accounts of both his financial advisers and his adversaries, he sustained an extravagant lifestyle on borrowed money while refusing to accurately assess and manage his own increasingly dire financial situation because he was not, or could not be, told "no." And he flew from place to place—Las Vegas, Bahrain, Ireland, various homes in Los Angeles—chasing the possibility of quick financial gains or, more frequently, departing just ahead of bills coming due or creditors' expectations of payment. Between 2002 and 2008 in particular, he seemed to embody the flighty short-termism of capital itself, abandoning his earlier incarnation of industrial discipline even as the US financial sector seemed to be doing the same.

Jackson's deindustriality operates differently in this "Neverland" phase of his career. Despite postmortem reconsideration of the depth and quality of his post-*Thriller* oeuvre, in the early years of the new millennium he was no longer the virtuosic transitional subject whose mastery of corporeal and class mobility generated both nostalgia for, and hopes of smoothly escaping, the putatively race-neutral disciplinary regime that produced him.[10] Late in his career he instead exemplified, in truly spectacular fashion, both the ideal subject of financialization and the failed one. He invested, made deals, consumed, borrowed, and refinanced on a grand scale: all of the operations essential to this new mode of production. But he also defaulted on loans, some say defrauded investors, was sued by employees and collaborators for nonpayment of wages and royalties, and abjured the most basic of financialization's imperatives: to be an ever-savvy, ever-vigilant, fully fiscally literate steward of one's own economic well-being. In performance, Jackson had both mastered and signified on industrialization's human motor from the Gary beginnings to the height of his career. In the last years of his life, he was still an exceptional performer, but as the fiscal exigencies necessitating his *This Is It* tour indicate, his debt called the tune. If *Thriller* is the perfect allegory of successful racial capitalism, as performance studies scholar Tavia Nyong'o has persuasively argued, the final years of Jackson's career are equally replete with figural potential, though of a very different kind. Where his virtuosic dancing had once made him an aspirational icon, his financial travails remade him as a racialized cautionary tale of considerable figural and moralistic potency.

Michael Jackson's personal financial melodrama, while uniquely compelling in its particulars, is not unique. His experiences with credit, debt, and an austerity regimen are "simultaneously at an extreme and in a zone of ordinariness, where life building and the attrition of human life" under financialized capital "are indistinguishable."[11] Representations of his financial travails materialize the "secret codes" of post-industrial capitalism: its presumptions and racialization, contradictory moral imperatives, its irrationality, and its constitution in the practices of everyday life albeit here a spectacular life.[12] They expose the process of consumption enabled by credit as both unsustainable and uncanny: an ersatz form of production that replaced the artist's previous onstage labors. Indeed, Jackson's copiously documented, seemingly insatiable consumption underscored the absence of these labors, especially his absence from live performance. His trial on charges of child molestation made the moral economy of debt and/as aberrant consumption spectacularly visible. And, in his dance routines on the *This Is It* DVD, released after his death during the recovery from the US Great Recession, he activates an aesthetic of austerity and exhaustion that makes the reigning political economic dogma of redemptive contraction legible at the corporeal level even as he generated nostalgia for both his earlier virtuosity and the spectacular class mobility it produced. Perhaps most profoundly, representations of Jackson also demonstrate that black consuming and indebted bodies are as central to the figural and material operations of financialization as their laboring and dancing bodies were to industrialization. In the run-up to, during, and immediately following the Great Recession, Jackson's fiscal melodramas reveal the melodramatic elements of deindustrial financialization itself.

This chapter examines Michael Jackson's financial troubles as a figural economy of deindustrial financialization, focusing on the period from 2002 and his vehement assertion of himself as a black economic subject in a public dispute with Sony Music executive Tommy Mottola, to 2014, five years after his death. It analyzes performances that frame him as both an ideal and a deviant economic actor, particularly Martin Bashir's documentary *Living with Michael Jackson* (2003), which presents him as a moral hazard in multiple senses of the term. It offers a reading of *This Is It* as an example of the temporal, affective, and aesthetic operations of austerity—albeit a sequined one. It begins by exploring the figural repertoire of financialization, ultimately reading this successor to industrial capitalism through the lens of melodrama with Jackson at the center of particularly fraught and visible examples: simultaneously an intoxicated, out-of-control consumer run amok; a predatory villain; a self-sacrificing, laboring victim; and a posthumous angel.

Though he does not say so explicitly, philosopher and cultural critic Bernard-Henri Lévy surely had Jackson's figural potential in mind when he posted "The Three Stations of the Cross in Michael Jackson's Calvary" in response to the singer's death. Lévy's curious meditation presents the artist as a self-consuming, self-sacrificing product/victim of contemporary consumer culture. A unique "dandy"/ "saint–/"piece of living limestone," Michael Jackson died from and for our collective consumerist sins.[13] Unlike Lévy, my concern in this chapter is less with Jackson's personal "long and terrible Calvary" than with the way he makes deindustrial financialization's routine roads of trials—their incoherence, moralization, and racialization—visible and intelligible. Jackson traveled his road in spectacularly public fashion with equally spectacular sums to gain and lose, but, particularly in the Great Recession, many others covered the same fiscal ground unnoticed and unassisted with far more modest sums. So do they still. Jackson's financial melodramas were extreme, but the actions setting them in motion were utterly banal: shopping, borrowing, refinancing, working to pay it all off.

By reading Jackson's very public fiscal melodramas as a figural economy of financialization, I neither imply nor assume he lacked agency to operate within its structures, nor that the agency he had was simply irrelevant. Rather, reading his travails figurally reveals that even his very considerable agency and privilege—his global stature, significant asset portfolio, powerful friends and advisers, capacity for exacting self-discipline, and astute business sense—*did not alter* the trajectory from consuming passions through near fiscal collapse to labors of redemption that characterized his own plight. Indeed, Jackson's case exposes the attachment to fantasies of a fully autonomous artistic agency as cruelly optimistic yearnings for spaces of creative production outside of capital: fantasies as perniciously color-blind and ahistorical as industrial nostalgia.

In examining Jackson's consumption, indebtedness, and postmortem redemption, I do not claim that his financial dilemmas are simply equivalent to those of the millions of everyday debtors who became new opportunities for capital and old scapegoats for racialized socioeconomic Darwinism. Nor do I diagnose his financial condition as the result of personal pathology or victimization. I do not offer a comprehensive analysis of every aspect of Jackson's fiscal life in the period discussed here. Instead, I analyze Jackson both as an exceptionally interesting case and as the protagonist in representative albeit extreme versions of American financial(-ized) melodramas playing out from the early years of the new millennium through the Great Recession. These melodramas emplot consumer financialization for maximum legibility on the public stage. Michael Jackson's very extremity powers his figural potential.

Certainly there are other individuals whose fiscal travails have played out publicly, including during this same period: Mike Tyson, Donald Trump, and Lindsay

Lohan, to name only three.[14] Yet they lack Jackson's unique capacity to figure key operations of deindustrial financialization for four reasons. First, their biographies and career trajectories do not trace the United States' move from industrialization through the deindustrial to financialization as explicitly and successfully as Jackson's. Second, they do not come close to Jackson's iconic status as one of the faces of global capitalism itself. He was a brand, a pitchman, a product, an investor, an investment, and corporeal collateral. This iconic status is directly proportional to his potential as a cautionary tale. He literally embodied global capital's ambitions, reach, and commodification of its subjects, then its subsequent collapse and attempted recovery, in the same period it was actually bubbling over, then collapsing and recovering: between 2002 and 2014. Third, Jackson's seemingly mutable identity—man/woman, black/white, Gary/Neverland—parallels the mutability of millennial finance capitalism, where consumption becomes a form of production, debt becomes profit, and financial risk becomes prudent wisdom. Finally, Jackson is sui generis in his cultural and commercial impact: selling 750 million records worldwide, with eight platinum or multiplatinum albums and forty-seven tracks in the Billboard Hot 100 among many other singular achievements during his lifetime, according to MTV.[15] His stature as an artist alone makes him an exemplary public actor of maximum figural significance. Simply and admittedly tautologically put: other celebrity fiscal melodramas do not figure financialization as clearly as Jackson's because they are not, and never were, Michael Jackson.

FIGURING FINANCIALIZATION

"Financialization" resembles "globalization" in its inverse relationship between explanatory force and definitional imprecision. Economic sociologist Ronald Dore observed that both are "convenient word[s] for a bundle of more or less discrete structural changes in the economies of the industrialized world."[16] In brief, the term "refers to the increasing importance of financial markets, financial motives, financial institutions, and financial elites in the operation of the economy and its governing institutions, both at the national and at the international level."[17] Financialized capitalism and neoliberal governmentality are partners in US deindustriality, the result of the strategic favoring of finance over factories that escalated during and continued long after the Reagan years. For the purposes of this chapter, "neoliberalism" is defined as a political movement that champions the authority of the free market while extracting public resources to sustain private profit.[18] At war with the commons, neoliberalism frames the individual and the family as the only legitimate social actors, as exemplified by Margaret Thatcher's famous assertion that there is no society.

Financialization is neoliberalism's optimal mode of production. This partnership operates at both wholesale ("en masse") and retail ("individual") levels in the Foucauldian sense.[19] Wholesale effects include the heightened significance accorded the financial sector over the real sector production of goods and services, the shift of income from the real sector to the financial sector, an accompanying increase in income inequality, and wage stagnation.[20] At the retail level, neoliberal financialization shapes work in its own image; "relations between capital and wage-labor have been . . . increasingly embedded in interest-paying transactions."[21] Everyday life too becomes financialized, with individuals' consumption and debt packaged as profit opportunities for the financial sector, even as the individual is held "responsible for managing her own human capital to maximal effect."[22] The "entrepreneurial subject" produced by this partnership finds its agency in the moves between an abstemious personal responsibility and a seemingly oxymoronic prudent risk.[23] "Personal responsibility" operates as a raced, gendered, and classed code for self-sustenance without recourse to a contracted public safety net.[24] "Risk" operates as a goad to enter the market so as to maximize wealth and opportunity and counter the "paralysis" of the moribund or suboptimal entrepreneurial subject.[25]

As political scientist Rob Aitken has trenchantly observed, capital in general has a materiality seemingly prior to representation.[26] This is especially true of financialized capital. Unlike the regime it supplanted, contemporary financialization offers no monumental factory infrastructure, no human motors. Where are the equivalents of the chorus girls, the machine ballets, and the biomechanical exercises that aestheticize, domesticate, and signify on this new mode of production? Capital is now everywhere and nowhere; the nanosecond mobility of financial transactions may be highly choreographed, but they are executed in fractions of time too small to be cognitively experienced by human beings. This level of abstraction is felicitous for the financial industry, supporting a view that its operations are both too difficult to be fully comprehended by the average person and also intrinsically rational, in contrast to the messy vicissitudes of the real sector with its unions and conflicts, bodies and feelings. Yet even—perhaps especially—here, in this most abstract mode of production, performance as both a method and an object of analysis is useful. Financialization becomes visible in enactments, both spectacular and banal, including performances that stage capital's seductions with a manifest fakery that confirms every iteration of antitheatrical prejudice since Plato.

Consider as only one example of theorizing financialization through performance-as-fakery anthropologist Anna Lowenhaupt Tsing's use of performance—"simultaneously economic performance and dramatic performance"—to theorize the "economy of appearances" that stimulates the global flow of capital.[27] For Lowenhaupt Tsing, economies of appearances rely on the deployment of spectacle to "dramatize dreams" that will attract investment. In her analysis of the rise and fall of Bre-X, a mining venture in Indonesia that was a highly publicized darling of investors in the mid-1990s before being exposed as a scam, Lowenhaupt Tsing notes:

> The self-conscious making of a spectacle is a necessary aid to gathering investment funds. . . . Start-up companies must dramatize their dreams in order to attract the capital they need to operate and expand. . . . In speculative enterprises, profit must be imagined

before it can be extracted. The more spectacular the conjuring, the more possible an investment frenzy.[28]

Here the power of economic and/as dramatic performance, particularly spectacle, is especially, though not exclusively, associated with "scams." In this case, performance is both a routine hegemonic tool and itself a kind of scam, reduced to the "trompe l'oeils" and the "conjuring acts" of capital that distract from its embeddedness in state violence and environmental ruin.

But what of performance's, including spectacle's, potential to expose as well as conceal the actual mechanics of financialization's enticements for developing the self, particularly when both the performance and the mechanics hide in plain sight, embodied by the same highly visible entrepreneurial subject? What if performance is also a way to pin the wholesale and retail operations of financialization to the board of representation, then caption them to make them legible, and not simply the means by which they defer or escape legibility? This chapter presumes that performance as both a strategy for and an object of analysis enables the critical spectator to bracket capital's moves long enough to counter its abstractions and probe the affective, aesthetic, and racial dynamics that set its economic work in motion.

If, as performance and dance studies scholar Randy Martin suggests, there is a lot to learn about the strange customs of financialization, figures like Jackson are important pedagogical resources: materializing in performance what the fine print of capital so routinely and deliberately obfuscates by literally staging it in heightened moments of everyday life, in state spectacles like trials, in dance, and in media products.[29] At the least, figuring financialization through Jackson's very public fiscal predicaments exposes its deeply corporeal dimensions, challenging the view of the market as an "invisible hand." To both describe and examine these predicaments, I draw on a mode that has used performers to represent the aesthetics, subjectivities, and machinations of capital since 1800: melodrama. Jackson is the object of my analysis; melodrama enables me to explicate his figural potential.

Fiscal Melodrama

Melodrama may seem wildly unsuitable as a lens through which to view the operations and fallout of financialization, even when exemplified by Michael Jackson's sensational(-ized) fiscal situation. Indeed, its affective excesses appear diametrically opposed to the algorithms and putative rationality that power contemporary finance. But, as media scholar Ben Singer points out in *Melodrama and Modernity*, the genre was intimately linked to the operations of modern capitalism from its inception. Drawing on Peter Brooks's and others' influential treatments of the genre, which were largely responsible for its critical rehabilitation, Singer argues that, from its first appearance after the French Revolution, "melodrama allegorized the modern situation" as this situation was just beginning to emerge.[30] It responded to the profound social shifts accompanying crises of feudal and religious authority in a newly "'disenchanted' world of moral ambiguity and material vulnerability."[31] Melodrama contained, and fictively soothed, a wide range of social and economic anxieties around "poverty, class stratification and exploitation, job insecurity, workplace hazards, heartless contractual systems of housing and money-lending... and similar components of the new capitalist system."[32] Singer writes about early twentieth-century films; the "new capitalist system" to which he specifically refers is the European postfeudal order. Yet his analysis easily aligns with mid-nineteenth-century American plays in which predatory landlords threaten virtuous young women whose families can't pay rent, mothers are reduced to penury because of husbands ensnared by deviant consumption (e.g., *The Drunkard*), and enslaved African Americans collateralize their owners' debts (e.g., stage versions of *Uncle Tom's Cabin*). Further, it is difficult to read this list of the anxiety-inducing operations of postfeudal capitalism and not reflect on the current versions generated by deindustrial financialization: from worker precarity to increasing income inequality to the subprime mortgage market implosion and subsequent wave of foreclosures. Melodrama's potential to reflect and fictively resolve the "stark insecurities of modern life" is elastic: as applicable to financialization in the new millennium as it was to the everyday lives of capital at the beginning of the nineteenth century.

Melodrama's historical elasticity is matched by its elasticity as a genre; the term has been used to classify plays, films, and novels and to describe a mode of highly affective theatricality at work in a wide range of cultural moments and products. In this chapter, melodrama refers to both a persistent, recognizable mode that typifies American popular narrative and a specific repertoire of texts and performances to which this mode often alludes.[33] After Brooks, I use the term's classic pejorative connotations as a useful definition. Melodrama as both a mode and a repertoire includes "the indulgence of strong emotionalism; moral polarization and schematization; extreme states of being, situations, actions; overt villainy, persecution of the good, and final reward of virtue; inflated and extravagant expression; dark plottings, suspense, breathtaking peripety."[34] Even on brief reflection this list of characteristics resonates with accounts of the machinations and trajectory of American financialization between 2002 and 2014: from the irrational exuberance that abjured any talk of asset bubbles to the subsequent apocalyptic rhetoric of global financial collapse, rebounding charges of villainy directed at "predatory lenders" and "predatory borrowers," dark plots of robo-signers cranking out fake signatures on bad loan documents with ratings agencies colluding in inflated assessments of subprime securities, and benighted homeowners facing foreclosure.[35] Indeed the Great Recession itself played out as melodrama but without the satisfying moral closure of vanquishing the financial industry villains and salvation for the imperiled innocents.

These same characteristics describe late-career Michael Jackson as well: his peculiar and excessive indulgences coupled with the adulation of his fans and the opprobrium of his detractors, his simultaneous depictions as a pure and childlike humanitarian and a calculating predator at his molestation trial, his deep fear that powerful corporate interests were plotting to divest him of his stake in the Sony/ATV catalog, his repeated claims of persecution by both the tabloid press and Santa Barbara district attorney Tom Sneddon, and the ultimate peripeties of his sudden death and postmortem rehabilitation. To Brooks's list of melodrama's characteristics I would add spectacular visuality linked to both Jackson's public persona and the nineteenth-century theatrical productions most associated with the genre.[36]

Randy Martin describes financialization as "both a subjectivity and a moral code."[37] Understanding it, he writes, "entails more than tracking new disequalities and distributions: it entails probing the new logics by which strange customs are made to feel normal."[38] Certainly the tabloid circulation of Jackson's widely publicized fiscal problems as a cautionary tale of purely personal excess rather than an extreme version of routine operations is one way these "customs" become "normal." His economic travails, read as melodrama, demonstrate the ways these strange subjectivizing and moralizing operations converge, producing the star as the simultaneously exemplary and deviant economic subject reviled, then redeemed in death.

Yet Martin's use of the formulation "new logics" suggests a set of internally consistent principles at work when that may not, in fact, be the case. As political economist Susan Strange observed, the comparative rationality of the factory has been replaced by "a gambling hall" of new financial instruments unbeholden even to probability theory, often relying on the (il)logics of spectacle, heightened emotion, and pious admonishment.[39] Finance capitalism's status as a respectable and rational regime is challenged when its routine operations are examined through melodrama's repertoire of victims and villains, heightened emotions, strange coincidences, and reversals of fortune, even when these are embodied by the same figure. Further, melodrama's status as a non-elite, even dubious mode—an embarrassing amalgam of the improbable and the overwrought—aligns well with the trashy tabloid scopophilia that defined Jackson's late career, though it can flip this freak show script if deployed critically. Here, Jackson's personal idiosyncrasies are not the main attraction so much as dramatic flourishes in his enactment of the routine operations of finance that are the real agents driving the action. A close reading of Jackson's financial(-ized) melodrama exposes not the new "logics" of deindustrial finance but its affective and rhetorical sleights of hand, its fictive resolutions of real contradictions, and its embeddedness in prior, highly racialized, modes of representation and cultural production.

Film scholar Linda Williams argues in *Playing the Race Card: Melodramas of Black and White from Uncle Tom to O. J. Simpson*, "Melodrama is the fundamental mode by which American culture has 'talked to itself' about the enduring moral dilemma of race"; melodramatic expression is particularly important in establishing a connection between racial legibility and moral legibility.[40] Though representations of Jackson analyzed in this chapter recall multiple genres of melodrama, including temperance melodrama, they are always racialized; the connection is yet another reason melodrama is a useful tool for probing the racial and moral economies of both millennial capitalism and Jackson's incarnation of it.

Figuring financialization as melodrama through Michael Jackson exposes yet one more way deindustriality circulates through representations of blackness and African Americans. Both financialization and deindustrialization are racial projects: generating racial injury and powered by racial(-ist) fantasy. Just as caricatures of African Americans as primitive and undisciplined enabled white workers to reconcile themselves to industrial wage labor, the moral(-ized) rhetoric of the personally responsible entrepreneurial subject and its racialized spendthrift, or ignorant, or publicly dependent other eased anxieties about this successor mode of production while deflecting attention from structural inequities in its distribution of opportunities and blame.

Specific examples of financialization as a moralized racial project, in general and in Jackson's case, are discussed in the remainder of this chapter, but two brief examples demonstrate its broad contours. It has been well documented that African Americans were explicitly targeted by predatory mortgage lenders during the period covered here. Victims of these unscrupulous lenders bore not only the brunt of the losses during the resulting subprime crisis but also the brunt of the blame. They were characterized either as fiscal illiterates who failed financialization's imperative to be informed self-managers or as scammers who gamed the system: precisely the "Tom (passive victim)/anti-Tom" (threatening villain) polarity Linda Williams identifies as central to America's ongoing racial melodramas.[41] Likewise, as I discuss in chapter 4, Detroit and its majority black population, from its pensioners to its elected officials, were widely figured as the fiscal and moral miscreants causing the city's descent into bankruptcy proceedings between 2013 and 2014, despite the fact that a major precipitating factor was a widely praised pension restructuring undertaken by then mayor Kwame Kilpatrick in 2005. UBS, Citigroup, and other major investment and insurance firms were all part of the deal to fund city pensions using derivatives and credit default swaps. It was a "disastrous gamble" that ultimately imploded.[42] The finance industry parties to the deal denied responsibility even as city pensioners were demonized.

Thus, figures of black profligacy or haplessness could function rhetorically as racialized aberrations in the putatively color-blind free market, enabling its agents in the finance industry to cork up their machinations while blaming their victims. Representations of Jackson's extravagance and seeming heedlessness of the risks involved in both his public comportment and his numerous failed business ventures with suspect partners, coupled with characterizations of him as a generous humanitarian who was simultaneously benignly childlike and ruthlessly shrewd, condense this same process of moralized racialization in one spectacular individual. Examining his fraught late-career financial saga using elements of racial melodrama also links him to the two best-known examples in the American repertoire: *Uncle Tom's Cabin* and *The Octoroon*. All three cases begin with debts and end with dead black bodies that live on in morally cleansed, highly profitable postmortem incarnations.

Michael Jackson was a black entrepreneurial subject. That this has to be stated explicitly has less to do with Jackson himself than with the stubbornly persistent and dubiously reassuring "pleasure of knowing [racial identity] through seeing" that Bryant Alexander links to the "performative sustainability of race."[43] Though the artist has been discussed either as an embodiment of post-raciality or as desiring to be white, such readings ignore two interrelated facts. Throughout this career, he consistently referred to himself as a proud black man, and in July 2002 he vehemently asserted himself as a black artist in a highly publicized attack on the head of his record label: Sony Music Entertainment's Tommy Mottola. This episode is notable for its own melodramatic elements: its odd and highly theatrical visuals, heightened affect, explicit moral polarities, plot reversals, and heavily moralized fallout. The action and the response it generated exemplify Jackson's entangled racial, moral(-ized), and material economies during this period, as well as the potency of accusations of "playing the race card" in dismissing both histories and claims of economic injury.

Jackson's denunciation of Mottola as racist and "very, very devilish," accompanied by large photos of the executive with what appeared to be hand-drawn devil horns on his head, was ostensibly an expression of his anger at the studio's efforts to promote his album *Invincible* (2001): efforts he believed were both wholly inadequate and responsible for what he believed were its lower than expected sales.[44] But it was also an attempt to flip the conventional script of black artists' subordination to white corporate power in the music industry. This effort was shared by the Reverend Al Sharpton and attorney Johnnie Cochran, who had convened the "Racism in the Music Industry Summit" in New York City in July 2002 to address the issue. Jackson's protest erupted in the context of the summit; he was scheduled to speak to the general theme, though his personal attack on Mottola came as a surprise to the organizers. It could have been viewed as another example, albeit a problematic one, of the artist's consistent commitment to taking charge of his own legacy and intellectual property evident in his breaking with Motown, firing his father as his manager, and acquiring both copyright to his own titles and ATV. Indeed, in each of these prior actions, Jackson exemplified financialization's ideal: the savvy, agential entrepreneurial subject who deploys his own capital as a form of personal racial redress. The historical basis of Jackson's claim—that black artists were treated unfairly by racist, exploitative entertainment executives—went unchallenged in media coverage of the anti-Mottola demonstration; coverage of the summit, though, was thoroughly upstaged by that of the diatribe.

Jackson set his self-perceived poor treatment by Sony both within this specific genealogy of exploitation by the music industry and, ultimately, within a global history of white racial(-ist) accumulation by dispossession. In a public statement he delivered at the summit, Jackson asserted:

> The recording companies really, really do conspire against the artists. . . . They steal, they cheat, they do everything they can, especially [against] the black artists. . . . People from James Brown to Sammy Davis Jr., some of the real pioneers that inspired me to be an entertainer, these artists were always on tour, because if they stopped touring,

they would go hungry. If you fight for me, you're fighting for all black people, dead and alive.[45]

Jackson's action backfired quickly and badly. It was disavowed by Sharpton and other black artists who came to Mottola's defense. Press coverage relied on the same contradictory imagery that was later used to describe Jackson's management of his debts. His protest was dismissed as both "bizarre," even crazy, and a Barnumesque "ploy, not a plight": a negotiating tactic to get himself out of his Sony contract and acquire his master recordings with the label ahead of schedule.[46] Any discussion of structural inequities in the music industry was pushed aside in favor of a heavily moralized narrative of the individual artist as crazy or crafty.

In keeping with the peripety intrinsic to melodrama, Jackson became the villain of the piece. His attempt to frame his actions within a larger history of institutional racism was wholly unsuccessful and was read, instead, as highly idiosyncratic, purely personal, and without merit. Perhaps predictably, he was accused of "playing the race card," which, as American studies scholar Anne Cheng has noted, is a curious contradiction: asserting that a liability is an advantage when that liability has been "diagnosed" as "sickly and aberrant."[47] Jackson's "playing the race card" was presented as either delusional or an opportunistic deflection of both his declining popularity and his personal responsibility for his current financial predicament. Alongside these charges were others insisting he was actually not black enough to play this "card." Ironically, given his invocations of James Brown and Sammy Davis Jr., Jackson too would ultimately agree to tour to stave off financial exigency.

Whether his denunciation was a strange public meltdown or a misplayed negotiating move, the media coverage soon settled on a consensus narrative. The issue was not a function of, or fueled by, a well-documented history of music industry racism whatever the merits of Jackson's specific case. The issue was not black and white at all, but red and green. In this consensus narrative, he was not really fighting Sony or Mottola but a flood of red ink and "a very real, very relentless green monster: a gnawing mountain of debt," accumulated to sustain "his extravagant lifestyle."[48] Eight months after his unsuccessful attempt to claim the racial, economic, and moral high ground was recast as a histrionic race card evasion of personal fiscal responsibility, audiences would see a new Jackson morality play: one promising a glimpse of that extravagant lifestyle while strongly implying that it, and he, might be both fiscally and morally bankrupt.

ACT I: CONSUMING PASSIONS

There were plenty of unsettling moments in British journalist Martin Bashir's documentary *Living with Michael Jackson* (2003; hereafter *LwMJ*).[49] For Jackson's fans, the film was an undisguised hatchet job deliberately and deceptively presenting their unsuspecting idol as a creepy, delusional, child-molesting monster. The normally staid *New York Times* television critic Alessandra Stanley lent credence to this reading by noting Bashir's "callous self-interest masked as sympathy" for his interview subject/victim.[50] Jackson granted Bashir unprecedented access to his life and home over eight months of filming. After the disappointing sales of *Invincible* and negative fallout from the anti-Mottola debacle, he was reportedly hoping for a public relations turnaround similar to that of Diana, Princess of Wales, another of Bashir's interviewees.[51] Jackson complained to British media regulators, the Independent Television Commission and the Broadcasting Standards Commission about what he saw as his grossly unfair treatment by Bashir and produced his own rebuttal video, *The Michael Jackson Interview: The Footage You Were Never Meant to See*, in the same year. For those who had dismissed Jackson's spectacular strangeness long ago, surely the most disturbing turn in *LwMJ* was his observation that he sometimes let children sleep with him in his bedroom, which he articulated while cuddling a preadolescent boy later identified as Gavin Arvizo, subject of the subsequent Santa Barbara County criminal trial, *The People of the State of California v. Michael Joseph Jackson*. In the same review Stanley registered her unease with Jackson as well, noting that, while Bashir's oily interview style may have made Jackson seem "crazy," at least "insanity is a defense."

Aside from a few steps he reluctantly executes in response to Bashir's persistent prodding, Jackson does not dance in the film. But he does shop in a scene that invites heightened attention both to his own consuming passions and, more important, to the uncanny, disturbing elements of US "millennial" consumption itself.[52] Consumption as an economic driver is not new, but its role in deindustrial financialization is. In its "ideological guise as consumerism," it powers financialization at the retail level.[53] It feeds the market for credit and generates consumer debt as a source of financial industry profit. It commodifies self-identity, which is then transmuted into products that sustain the ongoing production of this identity.[54] The same imperatives govern the ideal consuming subject at the mall as govern the entrepreneurial subject in the financial markets: the consumer must keep spending while exercising the obligatory fiscal literacy and rational self-regulation. Watching Jackson shop in *LwMJ* offers viewers a chance to assess his retail performance against this standard. But it also provides an opportunity to assess the rationality of the operations and query the appeals of millennial financialized consumerism. During the early years of the 2000s, as the US housing bubble was beginning to form and consumer debt was increasing, it certainly merited scrutiny. In the very simplest of terms, the fiscal melodrama of the Great Recession began with the aggressive marketing and securitization of subprime loans, which, in turn, stimulated consumption enabled by credit. As viewers would see, at the retail level, Michael Jackson's fiscal melodramas began in a similar way.

What could we learn about the role of consumerism within financialization if we resist the neoliberal imperative to individualize—to seek purely personal motivations or assign solely individual blame—even in the case of a notorious subject like the Michael Jackson of the early millennium? What if, instead, we read Jackson's retail performance in *LwMJ* figurally: not simply as a reflection of "his" agency, "his" pathology, or "his" transgressiveness but as an especially legible, dramatic, and compelling case of how financialized consumerism routinely works in this period, including its rebranding of agency as the ability to shop, debt as moral failure, and its own customers/revenue streams as irrational losers and illiterates?

Jackson's shopping scene in *LwMJ* offers an especially vivid example of the artist's figural potential to illuminate the credit-fueled consumerism of the early 2000s. Its potency as an exemplar derives both from his own spectacularity and from its resemblance to a classic American cautionary tale of consuming passions run amok, even as it glosses the specific disturbing elements of millennial consumption. In its voyeuristic invitation to watch Jackson shop and pass judgment on his excesses, the scene recalls a genre of melodrama that specialized in depicting battles between "spectacular indiscipline" and the self-regulatory imperative: temperance melodrama and its best-known and most popular work, William H. Smith's *The Drunkard* (1850).[55] Temperance melodrama is another example of the form's intimate connection to the emergence of modern capitalism. The temperance movement that inspired it arose directly from concerns around consumption, alterity, changing modes of work, and the ideal of rational self-discipline. *The Drunkard* features images of intoxication, delusion, debt, interpersonal devastation, eventual redemption, and a surprising number of references to finances. Theater historian Bruce A. McConachie calls it "business class" melodrama: affirming the values of respectability and moderation amid a changing economy.[56] In the play, as in the *LwMJ* scene discussed in this section of the chapter, wanton consumption is facilitated by enablers who lend money. It produces little or no apparent pleasure, seems insatiable, is represented through distortions of the body, is unsettling to watch, and proceeds unabated to an inexorable physical, fiscal, and moral reckoning.

In the play, Edward Middleton, an earnest, wealthy, promising young man "given to excesses," is ensnared by a predatory lawyer, Squire Cribbs, who introduces him to alcohol. Cribbs was an adviser to Edward's late father, possibly responsible for the elder Middleton's "failed speculations."[57] Cribbs's desire to destroy Edward arises directly from his own avarice; he is bent on illicitly acquiring both money and Edward's wife, Mary, as well as on seeking revenge for Middleton's saving Mary and her mother from eviction. Once Edward takes a drink, his consumption becomes unstoppable, leading to a series of unsavory public spectacles. Soon he is broke and delusional, but he keeps on drinking; at a crucial moment, Cribbs provides him the funds to continue his binge as a way to ultimately "line [his] own pockets."[58] In his darkest moment, Edward is saved from suicide and redeemed by a kindly benefactor while Cribbs is caught forging this same benefactor's signature on a bank check and will suffer the consequences he so richly deserves.

In the final years of his career, representations of Michael Jackson offered this same narrative arc of intoxicating consumption, public ignominy, and the embrace of possible economic redemption, figuring it on the national stage as the nation was moving through this same arc between 2002 and 2010. The scene from *LwMJ*

I discuss later in the chapter demonstrates the intoxication phase of this recognizable arc. In this scene, Jackson's intoxicants are the objects he so insatiably acquires and the credit that makes his acquisitions possible. In this he was exemplary but not unique. His credit intoxication was not his alone, even if he consumed and borrowed on a colossal scale. At the time he was buying and borrowing to do it, millions of US consumers were doing it too. The financial industry was eager to keep the intoxication going; indeed, it was itself binging on consumer credit. In the run-up to the Great Recession, there were plenty of besotted Middletons and enabling Cribbses.

If it seems a stretch to link the putatively rational process of credit-enabled millennial consumption to an overwrought nineteenth-century melodrama of a drunk on a life-altering bender, consider that contemporary commentators have made this same general connection in reflections on the causes of the Great Recession. For some, consumers being "drunk on credit" was a metaphor.[59] For others, it was a simple fact of neuroscience: a function of the stimulation of pleasure centers of the brain.[60] Nor was this drunkenness solely a matter of individuals given to wanton personal excess due to pathology or biology. Speaking about the role of mortgage-backed securities and credit default swaps in the Great Recession, former president George W. Bush asserted in 2008 that "Wall Street got drunk. . . . It got drunk, and now it's got a hangover. The question is, how long will it sober up and not try to do all these fancy financial instruments?"[61] A journalist reflecting on his remarks framed her opening query in recognizably melodramatic terms with a headline that read: "Was Wall Street Drunk, Stupid, or Evil?"[62]

Theater historian Amy Hughes observes that "today's audiences are thoroughly involved in the reprise, recycling, and revision of sensational scenes" reminiscent of nineteenth-century melodramatic theatrical spectacles.[63] These dynamics emerge with particular urgency in moments of cultural anxiety like the Great Recession of 2007–9.[64] But financialization's role in sensational scenes of credit and consumption in the years preceding it remains resistant to figuration. Scenes of Jackson's shopping offer a cinematic primer on these retail operations in part because they make credit-fueled private consumption publicly visible. Jackson's fiscal melodrama does not, of course, reproduce The Drunkard point for point; there is no one invidious individual who plays the role of Squire Cribbs, for example. Yet reading his shopping in LwMJ as a sensational scene of deindustrial consumerism through the lens of The Drunkard, with its recognizable moral arc from intoxication to redemption, makes its excesses, unsustainability, uncanniness, and the figural and moral politics of credit and subsequent debt visible as affective and corporeal, as well as fiscal, operations. The play relies on a barroom brawl and dramatizations of the delirium tremens (DTs) to illustrate the perils of alcohol consumption. LwMJ, however, demonstrates the unsettling dimensions of material excess in a scene that is simultaneously spectacularly opulent and recognizably routine.

This crucial scene in LwMJ comes just before Bashir questions Jackson about his plastic surgery, the extent of which the artist firmly denies against overwhelming visual evidence, and well before the infamous "bed" episode. It begins with Jackson and Bashir on a trip to the Grand Canal shops at the Venetian Hotel in Las Vegas. Bashir has announced that Jackson plans on spending "serious money," and Jackson has attested to his love of shopping. The Regis Galerie is his favorite store in the mall; it appears to specialize in highly ornate, weighty, and thickly gilded rococo-style furnishings, particularly urns, paintings, and other accessories. The items are crowded together, making narrow warrens of gilding that seem almost impassible. Jackson wanders through the store's multiple levels, identifying his previous purchases and adding more still more: "I bought that, these, these, this one. . . . Put that on the list." He seems affectively detached from the process of buying: neither dazed nor manic, yet disconnected from both Bashir and the trailing store manager as he points to items, generally without pausing for even a moment to inspect or ask questions about them.

The sheer number of acquisitions is dizzying. Meanwhile, crowds have assembled outside the shop with cameras flashing, pressing to get a look at or photo of Jackson. He is performing consuming even as he is a consumer performance consumed. Bashir notes that "80% of the shop [seems to have been] bought by" Jackson and futilely attempts to track the amount of money spent; the gallery manager prudently refuses to help. Price tags reveal that the very large ornate chess set Jackson purchased cost $89,000. He already has a similar one at home, we learn, but this one is bigger. A pair of gilded blue glass urns, about four feet high, are listed at $275,000 each, though Jackson assures Bashir he gets a discount: "Celebrities like bargains too." As Jackson contemplates two huge oil paintings he has just purchased, including one of nymphs bathing Apollo, Bashir observes that the dominant style of his choices seems imperial, "like Louis XIV," to which Jackson, the King of Pop, responds, "That's my taste."

On the surface, the scene of Jackson shopping at the Venetian presents him as the paradigmatic ideal consumer: one who loves to buy things as a form of recreation presumably because he can afford to. His seeming insatiability stimulates the US service economy, thus providing gainful employment for others; Bashir notes sardonically that the gallery's manager is the luckiest of his profession in the world. Certainly Jackson's indulgence in shopping was not unique; in the early years of the new millennium, there were plenty of others doing the same, albeit most on much smaller scales. In 2000, three years before the release of *Living with Michael Jackson*, consumer spending's share of the US GDP was almost 68 percent and was projected to increase.[65] Personal consumer expenditures accounted for almost 60 percent of total employment in the US economy in the same year; this percentage was also projected to increase.[66] These figures were only two indicators of the growing importance of this sector. In the two preceding decades, as domestic manufacturing declined, consumer spending grew dramatically, enabled by falling rates of savings, the rise of consumer credit and debt, and wealth generated in the stock market.[67] Personal consumption not only made the US economy go during the early millennial period but also was an enactment of US citizenship. President George W. Bush famously urged "full participation in the American economy" as an appropriately patriotic response to the 9/11 terrorist attacks: a statement that was widely para-phrased as a prompt to go shopping.[68]

Jackson is also ideal in that, in this scene, he has clearly, even genially, submitted to being tracked and consumed by others, epitomizing Zygmunt Bauman's assertion that, in the millennial consumer economy, individuals have become both promoters of commodities and commodities themselves.[69] Jackson is simultaneously an adver-tisement for his own brand and a commercial for the process of consuming: osten-sibly demonstrating its pleasures and its utility as a vehicle for public self-staging. In so doing, he seemingly re-enacts the *Lifestyles of the Rich and Famous* reality televi-sion model of simultaneously regulating and stimulating aspirational consumption wherein the ostentatiousness onscreen inspires revulsion at the excesses or tacki-ness, thereby affirming the viewer's own prudence, while also generating the nagging feeling that one's own staging of the self might not be up to snuff.

Yet there is something unsettling about the scene beyond Jackson's personal idiosyncrasies that invites critical scrutiny of consumption. Indeed, his very pecu-liarities underscore the uncanniness of consumerism in this period, making it, like Jackson himself, seem both familiar and strange. The sheer number of purchases, coupled with the items' ostentatious aesthetics and exorbitant prices, makes the artist appear a glutton, not a discerning connoisseur: a material manifestation of his status as a millennial oddity, no longer a working virtuoso. A fungible inauthen-ticity permeates the entire episode, linking the ersatz Venice, the unknown prov-enance of Jackson's purchases, his own highly modified appearance, and Bashir's transparently insincere attempts at rapport to shopping itself. Jackson's muted affect seems out of sync given his professed appreciation for the objects he buys. And he seems either oblivious or indifferent to both the specifics of his purchases and his own increasingly perilous fiscal situation.

The issue is not that Jackson prompts an entirely new recognition or critique of the problems with millennial consumerism in this scene. It is that he seemingly enacts these problems and demonstrates the validity of these critiques in a way that makes them spectacularly visible. Specifically, he exposes six key points about the retail operations of financialization in the early 2000s: the almost unimagina-ble resources separating elites from ordinary consumers, and their caprices from conventional metrics of value; the consumer economy's reliance on unsustainable excesses; financialization's uncoupling of consumption and production, particularly its occulting of labor through globalization; the contradictory characterizations of African Americans' relationships to commodity culture; the apparent affective hol-lowness and irrationality of this putatively rational process; and its dependence on, even intoxication with, credit.

In *Financialization of Daily Life*, Randy Martin remarks on financialization's new turn on

the familiar tale of a society where the concentration of wealth passes as a spectacle
for all to enjoy, even as most suffer being dispossessed of it. Stars, for example, are eye

candy, publicly displayed private lives for the vicarious, visual, and collective consumption of wealth. Perhaps this observation helps explain reports of ambivalence rather than resentment toward inequality.[70]

In *LwMJ*, Jackson is problematic as eye candy because, within the framework of the film, watching him shop is more a matter of voyeuristic curiosity than vicarious enjoyment. Certainly the individual prices of pieces he purchases attest to the wealth required of the Regis Galerie customer. In shopping there, Jackson stages himself as one of the winners of financialization: reaping the rewards of both his artistry and his savvy business deals despite widespread reports of financial problems. But the fact that he seems to buy these things in bulk raises questions about his judgment and, by extension, about the frivolity enabled by extreme wealth. Paying $89,000 for a chess set? And he has a similar one already? How many such chess sets does anyone need?

Jackson had long argued that his lavish expenditures on Neverland Ranch, with its carnival rides, its menagerie, and the staff needed to maintain it, were a function of his generosity. The ranch was, in part, "for the children": a quasi-charitable venture to entertain sick or disadvantaged kids and thus morally palatable as a drain on Jackson's funds. But it was hard to make a similar case for gigantic oil paintings and gilded urns. Bashir's relentless but ultimately unsuccessful attempt to figure out the total cost of the trip highlights the fact that, though likely stratospherically large, the final bill is apparently of no concern to Jackson. This visit to the mall happened during the same period disgraced former Tyco CEO Dennis Kozlowski was buying a $6,000 shower curtain.[71] It preceded former Merrill Lynch CEO John Thain's $35,000 office toilet.[72] These retail performances of wealth made the privileged caprices of the super-rich abundantly clear and attracted widespread opprobrium and ridicule. But Kozlowski, Thain, and other uber-consumers employed layers of decorators and assistants to mediate their purchases, affording them some measure of distance and deniability. In *LwMJ*, Jackson made his purchases himself and, in so doing, directly established a visual connection between the wealthy individual and his pricey, questionable indulgences.

Jackson seems to have an unlimited appetite for these accessories. He is vague about where he will put them all: not Neverland but another unspecified house. Yet if this acquisitiveness makes him a seemingly ideal consumer, it also aligns him with the classic morally fallen drunkard from a temperance melodrama: intemperate, out of control, even grotesque. Viewers' suspicions that Jackson's consuming passions may have gotten out of hand are amplified by his appearance. As press coverage widely noted, at this point in his career Jackson's looks were unusual not only when compared with his earlier visages but also in and of themselves in ways that rendered suspect both his taste, one component of "good" consumption, and his capacity for prudent self-regulation. Shots of his broad shoulders make him clearly readable as male, yet the dark, perfect parentheses of his eyebrows, the angular planes of his pale face, his pointy shard of a nose, and shoulder-length layered and straightened jet-black hair make him appear whitened and feminized, though not female. The issue is not that he appears simply race and gender indeterminate: a marketer's demographic nightmare, crossing multiple categories of segmentation at once. It is that he seems as conspicuously artificial as the things he buys, though without the urns' and the chess set's aesthetic consistency. He looks like a collection of discrepant parts. Like *The Drunkard*'s spectacle of Edward Middleton in the throes of the DTs, Jackson's material excesses seemed legible at the level of the body. Moreover, the ever-present, disconcerting visual evidence of the face he so clearly paid for, alongside the pile of purchases, begged the question: Did he know when to stop?[73]

That question was not relevant only to Michael Jackson. Environmentalists and scholars have noted the unsustainability of millennial consumption in increasingly urgent terms.[74] "Mindless" economic growth fueled by increasing consumer spending raises issues of resource depletion, environmental degradation, global inequities, and waste disposal.[75] As Zygmunt Bauman observes in an epigraph to this chapter, a consumer economy relies on excess and waste, and by the early 2000s, it was abundantly clear that the results were overwhelming the planet.[76] Watching Jackson's acquisitiveness—the repeated addition of new objects that seem both extravagant and almost wholly interchangeable—invites the question: How much of this is enough? It also recalls the admonishment of another performing artist whose work responded directly to the United States' millennial retail binge: Bill Talen, aka the Reverend Billy of the Church of Stop Shopping:

> Like crack cocaine or membership in the National Rifle Association, shopping is an annihilating addiction that must be slowed down to be stopped. Or flooded with new and different light. But people, please—*do something!* Think of something quick. The research phase is over. How many times do we have to hear that seven percent of the world's population is taking a third of the world's resources? How many neighborhoods need to be malled?[77]

Randy Martin may be correct that stars serve as eye candy, further embellishing conspicuous consumption for audiences' vicarious if ambivalent pleasures. But part of this consumer(-ing) fantasy, and part of the audience's ambivalence as opposed to outright resentment, may be that stars visibly work, producing entertainment products that performatively sustain their "starness." This work inoculates their consumption, marking it as, if not purely rational, prudent, or entirely meritorious, then at least earned. Interestingly, when Jackson was at the peak of his stardom during the *Thriller* years, his own spending was relatively modest given the magnitude of his commercial success. He lived at Havenhurst, his family's Encino estate, until he bought the property that would become Neverland Ranch when he was twenty-nine. But, beginning in the late 1980s, he was increasingly depicted as an excessive, and excessively strange, consumer. His reported attempt to buy the bones of Jos. Merrick, the Elephant Man, is a case in point. Jackson publicly denied it, but his biographer J. Randy Taraborrelli states that he initiated it as a Barnumesque publicity stunt that backfired badly, branding him as bizarre and entitled in ways that foreshadowed the scene at the Grand Canal shops.[78] By 2003 and the airing of *LwMJ*, reports of Jackson's out-of-control spending were commonplace, and he was more of a curiosity than a star: no longer touring and without a major commercial success even close to that of his prime. He was no longer the King of Pop, producing hit after hit. He was just shopping like one. In this, he exemplified the popular view of the US deindustrial economy: it didn't make things anymore; it simply devoured things made elsewhere.

As anthropologists Jean Comaroff and John Comaroff remind us, post-industrial consumerism is both a symptom and a cause of increasingly "mysterious relationships between production and consumption": a condition that "is integrally connected to the changing status of work under contemporary conditions."[79] Consumption's role in ameliorating the effects of structural change in modes of work is not new. Indeed, its history in this capacity both illustrates and explains its uncanniness.[80] It operates as a surrogate, partially filling in the gaps and fictively repairing the losses and alienations caused by these changes.[81] Marx's commodity fetishism locates this uncanniness at the very heart of production itself: congealing the work of laboring bodies, some consumed in the process, into the object of exchange. As the commodity effigies congealed labor, consumption surrogates the autonomy of the workers who produced it. In Bauman's retelling of this now familiar narrative, it is a palliative form of compensation:

> [Workers'] gradual surrender of one aspect of the craftsman's tradition—self-management—had to be obtained through the boosting of another aspect: market orientation and self-interest. . . . The search for freedom is reinterpreted as an effort to satisfy consumer needs through appropriation of marketable goods.[82]

The mythos of Ford's "wage" of five dollars per day, supposedly an amount that would enable his workers to buy Ford automobiles, is the classic example and is discussed in chapter 3. Consumption is also odd because it successfully perpetuates itself as a surrogate for autonomy not *despite* the fact but *precisely because* it is inadequate in the role: "The unsatisfied need for autonomy puts constant pressure on the consumer urge, as successively higher levels of consumption become disqualified and discredited for not bringing the hoped for alleviation of stress."[83]

In the United States, a stream of cheap imported goods, enabled by relaxed barriers to international trade, cushioned workers from the full effects of deindustrialization's reduced wages and purchasing power. Ultimately, deindustrial consumption occults relationships to production itself; the global race to the low wage bottom in sourcing manufactured goods has "put such a distance between sites of production and sites of consumption that their relationship becomes all but unfathomable, save in fantasy."[84] As the Comaroffs observe, these conditions generate "an intensification of efforts to . . . restore some transparency to the relation between production and value, work and wealth."[85] Watching Jackson shop mystifies rather than clarifies that relation. How, precisely, did he afford all of these things without touring or a major new hit?

Further, in neoliberal regimes of financialization, production is not just occulted. Its "perceived salience for the wealth of nations" is actually superseded by the workings of financial markets.[86] According to the Comaroffs:

> Above all else, the explosion of new monetary instruments and markets, aided by ever-more sophisticated means of planetary coordination and space-time compression, have allowed the financial order to achieve a degree of autonomy from "real production" unmatched in the annals of modern political economy. Indeed, the increasingly virtual qualities of fiscal circulation enable the speculative side of capitalism to seem more independent of manufacture, less constrained by the exigencies or the moral values of virtuous labor.[87]

Jackson, deindustriality's transitional icon, materializes precisely these dynamics. His own financialized income stream and his shift from highly visible virtuosity to spectacular notoriety effectively decoupled connections between his own labor, his sources of revenue, and his consuming passions. In *LwMJ*, his performance as a shopper surrogated his own creative production. *This* Michael Jackson stood as a reminder of the *absence* of his former labors as surely as the Venetian in Las Vegas stood in for the distant original. Jackson seemed to have danced away from work as financialization did the same: rendering labor—"real production"—apparently dispensable.

Unlike those of Dennis Kozlowski, John Thain, or other conspicuous consumers from the ranks of the financial elite, Jackson's retail excesses were widely cast as compensation for childhood injury, including by the artist himself: the abuse and unrelenting pressures he suffered at the hands of his father. By this logic, the elaborate furnishings he buys in *LwMJ* are the functional equivalent of toys, and if having them made him happy, so what? Wasn't shopping simply another way the neoliberal entrepreneurial subject could effect his own psychic repair: participating in both the "mood economy" and the retail economy at the same time?[88] As Bauman observes, happiness is the value most associated with consumerism:

> The society of consumers stands and falls by the happiness of its members—to a degree unknown and hardly comprehensible to any other society on record. The answers given to the question "are you happy?" by members of a society of consumers may legitimately be viewed as the ultimate test of its success and failure.[89]

Whether Jackson was truly happy or not either in the Regis Galerie or with his new furnishings is ultimately unknowable. But his muted affect and seeming detachment from his interlocutors and most of his purchases in this scene do not signal happiness in any obvious way. Indeed, the extravagance of these purchases is inversely proportional to the intensity of his emotional display in acquiring them. He is far more animated when waving to fans. He pronounces some of the objects beautiful, but there is no discernible joy, no frisson that comes with securing a bargain or a long-sought-after unique prize, in either his verbal or his nonverbal expressions. Nor does his demeanor register as the restrained intensity of the seasoned collector. He could be grocery shopping. Jackson's absence of visible delight onscreen belies one key appeal of both partaking in discretionary consumption and vicariously enjoying it by watching someone else shop: the palpable thrill that comes with imagining the new self nascent in the commodity, as well as an appreciation of the savviness and discerning eye affirmed in the process of acquisition. Because he seems both vaguely aware of, yet utterly oblivious to, any metrics of value, it is also difficult to read his shopping as a performance of consumer shrewdness that might generate its own pleasures. "Celebrities like bargains," but the specific nature of these bargains is unclear as he appears unconcerned about prices, painters, periods, or provenance. He doesn't remember some previous purchases, needing to check in with the store manager—"I bought this, right?" Given the sheer number of acquisitions, this is understandable though the objects themselves are highly distinctive, but it furthers the impression that he has no affective investment in any one piece in particular.

There is one childlike moment in the scene. Jackson summons the manager, who can't quite keep up, by trilling, "Yoo hoo." Viewed against the amount, aesthetics, and prices of the objects, and Jackson's clear authority as an uber-consumer, the trill seems incongruous even as it highlights the incongruities suffusing the entire episode. His inscrutable affect, the apparent lack of mediating minions or decorators to wrangle the manager and do the dirty work of adding up the bargains, the breathy "yoo hoos," the meandering, seemingly random nature of his acquisitiveness: all make shopping at this most spectacular level look less like fun and more like "a hedonic treadmill" of perpetual accumulation.[90] If the ultimate test of consumerism is happiness, in this scene at least Jackson does not advance a convincing case that it succeeds, any more than *The Drunkard*'s scenes of Middleton's manic ingestion make drinking look like a good time. Further, read alongside the scorn and notoriety he attracted for other consumer(-ing) episodes, and *LwMJ*'s framing of him as psychologically damaged, the last two decades of Jackson's life read as a demonstration of the abject hollowness of consumer pleasures both as a way to successfully stage the self and as a tool for repairing psychic wounds.[91]

Though his affect seems "off" throughout the scene, Jackson demonstrates that he is not an ignorant consumer, at one moment accurately identifying the iconography of Apollo in a painting he has just purchased. In an aside to Bashir, the gallery manager notes, "Mr. Jackson knows his art." Bashir responds snidely, "Obviously." Throughout the entire episode, Bashir's snarky faux sincerity underscores his utter disdain for Jackson's taste. It marks Jackson's consumption as both spectacular and banal: the trappings of imperial wealth and taste purchased at the mall, a gaudy middlebrow tourist spot. But Bashir's sarcasm and condescension also clearly signal to viewers that Jackson's taste should be regarded as even worse than just spectacularly banal. It should be read as *bad*: tacky, even grotesque, the opposite of respectable. As the two initially enter the mall area, Jackson proclaims the elaborately painted ceilings, meant to conjure works by Michelangelo, "amazing" and "incredible." Bashir coyly responds, as if trying to elicit a confession: "Isn't it a bit tacky?"—the qualifier amplifying his barb while seeming to cushion it. Jackson calls him "silly." Later, when Jackson identifies a pair of urns he considers especially beautiful, Bashir audibly gasps—"Oh my goodness!"—a theatricalized expression of shock at this assessment, not shared sentiment. He then notes sarcastically, "Only a half a million [dollars] for both." When he archly observes, "It's like you surround yourself with stuff that's like an emperor's house," it is abundantly clear that this is not meant as a compliment. Most egregiously, when Jackson notes that he currently has no girl-friend for whom to buy jewelry, Bashir patronizingly observes, "Well, there's time. You're still a young boy." When *LwMJ* was shot, Jackson was forty-three years old.

Whatever his intentions, Bashir's dismissals, condescension, and use of a racially charged diminutive activate a familiar scornful script that "black Americans are, at base, ill-equipped to manage wealth and are deserving of racist ridicule for their attempts to buy their way into the privileges of participation in public life."[92] As media scholar Roopali Mukherjee argues in "Bling Fling: Commodity Consumption and the Politics of the 'Post-Racial'": "In the post-racial milieu, as cultures of conspicuous consumption shape standards of taste and habits of over-indulgence across racial lines, public dismay and derision focus pointedly on black consumerism as uniquely pathological." Bashir's stagy gasps of horror and his observation that Jackson surrounds himself with "*stuff that's like* an emperor's house" imply that the artist is taking material liberties and doing it badly: that is, with tacky, inferior "stuff that's like" the *real* objects a *real* (read: white, upper-class, European) monarch might enjoy. This racialized contempt both disciplines its tar-gets and quells the anxieties of those who dispense it. As Pierre Bourdieu observes:

> Tastes (i.e., manifest preferences) are the practical affirmation of an inevitable differ-ence. It is no accident that, when they have to be justified, they are asserted purely nega-tively, by the refusal of other tastes. . . . The most intolerable thing for those who regard themselves as possessors of legitimate culture is the sacrilegious reuniting of tastes which taste dictates shall be separated.[93]

In a regime that equates consumption with identity, Jackson's taste—"like Louis XIV"—and his ability to shop like an emperor upset "material logics of [white] racial supremacy."[94]

Yet, in a retail variation on the race-card-playing/not-black-enough character-izations of his anti-Mottola demonstration, Jackson's consumption is both racial-ized and "post-racialized": the latter not simply because he personally appears racially ambiguous. As Mukherjee writes of the hip-hop moguls who were Jackson's millennial contemporaries, "stylized accoutrements of vertiginous class transcend-ence" were "dossier[s] of visual evidence" for the fictive racial equality enabled by neoliberal markets and financialized consumerism.[95] As I discuss in the next section of this chapter, the very same combination of fictive equality-before-the-market and opprobrium directed at black consumption undergirded the subprime mortgage bubble forming even as Jackson shopped at the Venetian, as well as the subsequent crisis when that bubble burst.

As he wanders through the Regis Galerie, Jackson illustrates the intoxication phase of financialized millennial consumption—its excesses, unsustainability, occulting of labor, and affective hollowness—even as Bashir signals its contradictory racial dimensions. But within the context of both the film as a whole and the widespread publicity about the state of Jackson's finances, this scene also demonstrates another of Zygmunt Bauman's crucial points: "The rationality of a consumer society is built on the irrationality of its individualized actors."[96] Jackson was the paradigmatic ideal consumer whose insatiability powered the economy. He also exemplified aberration because he appeared to be a zombie shopper whose limited emotional responses belied the promised happiness of shopping even while incarnating the unstoppable drive to consume further and because, when viewed through Bashir's obvious disdain, he consumed like an arriviste imperial wannabe: an undiscerning glutton with bad taste for inappropriate objects. But above all Jackson was financialized consumerism's cautionary tale because, like *The Drunkard*'s Edward Middleton in the throes of intoxication, at the time the film was shot and released, Jackson had neither the ready cash to spend so extravagantly nor, apparently, the firm grip on his fiscal situation required of financialization's ideal subject.

In the limousine before arriving at the Venetian, Bashir asks Jackson if he's good with his money. Jackson replies that he is, though he avers when asked his net worth, stating only that it's "up there." When Bashir presses, asking if the number is $1 billion, Jackson replies, "It's over there." Bashir confirms: "Over a billion dollars?" Jackson says yes. In fact, in 2003, he was in debt for at least $200 million, with the most generous estimate of his net worth at $350 million—much of that in nonliquid assets—and what *Forbes Magazine* called "a franchise in decline."[97] Jackson was heavily dependent on credit, and in 2002–3, when *LwMJ* was shot and released, the situation was becoming increasingly perilous. Indeed, some reports attributed his widely reviled anti-Mottola demonstration to his desperation at the prospect of missing a payment on his $200 million loan from Bank of America collateralized by his stake in SONY/ATV.[98]

This BOA loan was not the only one in the same period; there was an additional loan for $70 million. Media reports even had him pawning a $2 million diamond watch to raise cash.[99] Given this dismal financial picture, Jackson's characterization of his net worth in the film was either a PR move, a willful misstatement, or an indicator of deep denial, ignorance, or indifference. None of these options demonstrate the rationality intrinsic to the neoliberal financialized subject or the business savvy attributed to the Michael Jackson of the mid-1980s. Mischaracterizations could be easily and publicly disproved, further tarnishing the artist's image, and neither denial, ignorance, nor indifference would preempt an eventual reckoning. That

Jackson could afford a retinue of financial advisers only underscored his seeming fiscal fecklessness: either they were doing a very poor job, in which case Jackson failed in his due diligence, or he ignored their counsel by spending too much. Whatever the reasons for both his misstatement and his predicament, he certainly did not appear to be a paragon of the logical "homo economicus."[100] Financialization "figures individuals as rational, calculating creatures whose moral autonomy is measured by their capacity for 'self-care,'" even as it both elides and depends upon consumer irrationality.[101] As both an ideal consumer and a fiscal cautionary tale of irrational consuming passions, this image of Jackson exemplified these dynamics.

In light of the widely available information on the shaky state of his finances, Jackson's shopping at the Regis Galerie looks less like a recreational, albeit excessive and strange, outing and more like an out-of-control binge on credit with the prospect of a public fiscal downfall lurking in the wings. He was not binging alone. In the early 2000s, both financial institutions and ordinary consumers were doing versions of the same thing, though impelled by very different exigencies. This state of affairs was not the result of a rational market calibration of credit supply and demand. Liquidity, assets that could easily be converted into cash so as to be bought and sold, is "the life blood of financialization," and consumer credit played a crucial role in ensuring it.[102] As legal scholar Tayyab Mahmud and political economists Anastasia Nesvetailova and Ronen Palan trenchantly observe, "Demand for credit had 'to be created and liquidity relied critically on demand being whipped up.'"[103] Subprime mortgage lending was both a symptom and a result of this "whipped up" demand, but it was not the only one. Stagnant wages also fueled the demand for credit as consumers increasingly used up their savings and turned to credit cards to provide self-sustenance. Average household credit card debt increased 167 percent between 1990 and 2004, according to the Government Accountability Office; in 2005, personal savings dipped below zero.[104]

Jackson's cash flow, his credit and debt problems, and his seeming mischaracterization of his net worth generate the powerful temptation to attribute his fiscal travails to his own irresponsibility or pathology, with the artist having only himself to blame for the consequences. In this, *LwMJ*'s invitation to indulge in scopophilic disdain for his excesses mirrors precisely the racialized moral economy of neoliberal financialization; I probe the specific operations of this economy in the next section of this chapter. Here ordinary consumer "irrationality"—like binging on credit, depleting personal savings, overconsumption, and the inability or unwillingness to fully master one's own fiscal subjectivity—is solely an individual failure rather than the structural precondition for the financial industry's profit. As a function of generating liquidity, the industry's expansion of consumer credit created consumer debt that could then be securitized: "The purpose of making loans, mortgages and offering credit cards is increasingly the generation of tradable financial assets on a cycle of monthly payments."[105] Moreover, as I discuss later, expanding this asset base meant extending more, and much riskier, loans, while "hunting out economically marginalized groups for mortgage and consumer credit." As cultural theorists Fred Moten and Stefano Harney observe, "Creditors forgive debt by offering credit," prolonging the cycle.[106]

Consumers may or may not have made "rational" decisions to enter that cycle. But the very premises required for rational decision-making are unequally distributed, and sometimes intentionally so. It has been copiously documented that, from payday loan transactions to subprime mortgages, many consumers were simply lied to: taking on credit and debt obligations based on industry deception pure and simple.[107] But succumbing to financialization's unrelenting enticements to consume on credit is not simply an economic decision even in a fully transparent and equitable fiscal environment, and even for elites like Michael Jackson. As Lauren Berlant has written about food consumption, it is also about "expressivity," self-sustenance, and care for others.[108] Shopping may not be a fully effective surrogate for autonomy but is one way to "lubricate the body's movement through capitalized time's shortened circuit—not only speed up at work but the contexts where making a life involves getting through the day, the week, and the month."[109] Here consuming on credit "is also directed toward making a less-bad experience. It's a relief, a reprieve, not a repair."[110] Perhaps in order to generate just such "less-bad experiences" for themselves and their families and friends, some consumers may have shrewdly gamed the system that was gaming them. In any case, when individuals got into fiscal trouble due to payday loans or credit card bills, or financial institutions got into trouble because of their investments in subprime mortgages, charges of irrationality were leveled initially against the borrowers who merely consumed the intoxicant, not those who knowingly offered it, often while betting against these same borrowers. Such borrowers were simply moral, cognitive, or fiscal failures. How could they have taken on those loans, run up those charges, not read the fine print? What were they thinking? It was only later that commentators asked, was the entire system of lending and securitization "drunk, stupid, or evil"?

In this context, reading Jackson's consuming passions figurally as both an extreme version of routine industry operations and a financial(-ized) version of *The Drunkard* is instructive because, within the framework of the play, irrational intoxication is neither an individual's "fault" nor an inevitable consequence of one's propensity for excess. It is generated by an inherent property of the intoxicant itself: a property ruthlessly exploited by a predator bent on personal profit. Further, in *The Drunkard*'s moral economy, unlike that of neoliberal financialization, the financial professional who introduced Middleton to drink for nefarious reasons, then lent him the money to keep on drinking, was the object of disdain, not Middleton himself.

Like Edward Middleton, and unlike ordinary US consumers, Jackson had wealthy benefactors who came to his assistance: offering financial advice, providing lavish accommodations and refuge, lending money, and assisting in negotiations around the refinancing of his BOA loans. Some of these relationships devolved into lawsuits against him; others simply faded away. But Jackson continued to spend "like it was 1988," and perhaps more important, he continued to borrow to do so.[111]

Twenty-seven million people watched ABC's airing of *Living with Michael Jackson*, helping it win the night in the Nielsen ratings.[112] But it was only the opening act in an unfolding, highly publicized melodrama linking Jackson's purported fiscal and moral bankruptcy. An even more spectacular act was yet to come. In December 2003, ten months after *LwMJ* aired in the United States, Jackson was formally charged in Santa Barbara County with seven counts of performing a lewd act upon a child, two counts of administering an intoxicating agent for the purpose of committing a felony, and one count of conspiracy. Gavin Arvizo, the boy Jackson cuddled in the film, was the accuser. The subsequent criminal trial promised another titillating glimpse into Jackson's consuming passions. But ultimately it revealed far less about Jackson's sex life than it did about his money, and far less about his money than about the intertwined moral and figural economies of financialization in the new millennium.

ACT II: FISCAL DEVIANCE, FISCAL INNOCENCE

The People of the State of California v. Michael Joseph Jackson was a melodrama of the most public kind. Linda Williams has argued that the American jury trial could "'leap' into the melodramatic mainstream of popular entertainment" because of its astonishing stories; evidentiary spectacle, including the defendants' and witnesses' demeanors; and narratives and images of wronged innocence demanding redress.[113] Jackson's trial offered all of this and more to those who followed its extensive coverage in the mainstream and tabloid media. It also featured spectacles of pathos, including Jackson's seemingly extreme physical frailty, bizarre moments like his appearing in court wearing pajama bottoms, salacious testimony, moral polarization, and breathtaking plot reversals, including the prosecution's own witnesses turning against them on the stand. While these developments drew the headlines, the trial was also a fiscal melodrama hiding in plain sight: one demonstrating the contradictory moral and figural economies through which financialization disciplines its subjects. Specifically, competing characterizations of Jackson offered by the prosecution and the defense illustrate the ways "finance becomes us": its racialization, its transmutation of economic transactions into individuals' characters, its function as a moral barometer, and its "inverted structure of responsibility."[114] These competing characterizations crystallize in two seemingly unrelated pieces of testimony that framed the artist as an insatiable fiscal miscreant in the prosecution's case and as an innocent child in the defense's.

These are not racially neutral positions. On the contrary, they are the very same anti-Tom (predatory villain)/Tom (kindhearted if hapless victim) tropes Williams, after Leslie Fiedler, sees as central to US racial melodrama, both in general and in other spectacular trials in the decade prior to Jackson's: *California v. Orenthal James Simpson* (1995), in which the football star turned actor was acquitted of murdering his wife, Nicole Brown Simpson, and Ronald Goldman, and *California v. Powell* [et al.] (1992), in which four white officers who were videotaped beating African American motorist Rodney King were acquitted of all charges. Like these predecessors, Jackson's trial also generated images of black savagery in the "anti-Tom tradition" as well as black innocence wrongly abused: the "Tom" trope of black simplicity and martyred innocence originating with Harriet Beecher Stowe's novel *Uncle Tom's Cabin* and its countless stage and screen descendants. Race was not invoked specifically in actual proceedings, but the trial unfolded within a "racially saturated field of visibility."[115] Elements of that field included these two earlier trials, Jackson's initial embrace, then subsequent rejection, of the Nation of Islam during the proceedings, the selection of an all-white jury to hear Jackson's case, Joseph Jackson's statement to the media that American racism was to blame for his son's prosecution, a racial divide in perceptions of Jackson's innocence, Michael Jackson's own racially ambiguous appearance, and his racial self-assertion in his anti-Mottola demonstration. A comprehensive examination of racialization in the trial exceeds the scope of this chapter.[116] My intent here is to demonstrate that the anti-Tom/Tom tropes implicit in the cases against or in support of Jackson rehearsed the very same dynamics used against other racialized subjects of financialization, particularly the subprime borrowers of the Great Recession. These contradictory characterizations figure both the racialization and the moral asymmetry at the heart of financialization's everyday lives.

Jackson's molestation trial began with jury selection in Santa Barbara County in January 2005 and lasted fourteen weeks.[117] Near the end of his case, on May 3, lead prosecutor Tom Sneddon called forensic accountant John Duross O'Bryan to the stand to testify about the state of Jackson's finances over the strenuous objections of the defense team; reporters noted that evidence concerning the artist's finances had "been a sore point" between the prosecution and the defense throughout the trial.[118] Duross O'Bryan had only partial access to Jackson's financial records: reports and memos from his advisers between 1999 and February 2003 and one balance sheet from June 2002. On the stand he painted a dismal picture of the artist's fiscal situation. He testified that the 2002 balance sheet showed a net worth of negative $285 million, and that Jackson was regularly spending between $20 and $30 million dollars more a year than he had earned. In February 2003, when *LwMJ* aired, Jackson had only $38,000 in cash and unpaid vendor invoices totaling $10.5 million.[119] The jury was told that interest payments on the loans collateralized with his music catalogs came to $11 million a year. Personal expenses and expenses related to Neverland Ranch totaled $7.5 million and $5 million a year, respectively. When cross-examined by defense attorney Thomas Mesereau, who suggested that Jackson could have easily addressed the shortfall by taking up one of many offers to tour or license products, Duross O'Bryan replied, "If [the liquidity crisis] could have been solved, why wasn't it?" When Mesereau asked why, given these supposedly dire circumstances, Jackson had not been forced into bankruptcy, Duross O'Bryan drew a direct connection between Jackson's consumption, credit, and debt, answering: "He was able to continue to borrow."[120]

Testimony about Jackson's finances seems like an odd digression in a child molestation trial, but the prosecution saw it as crucial to establishing Jackson's motive on the conspiracy charge. They alleged that the artist and his team were so mortified by the damage *LwMJ* had done to his brand and future earnings potential that they held the Arvizo family against their will and attempted to force them into making a rebuttal video. Ostensibly the accountant's testimony would reveal the full extent of Jackson's fiscal precarity and desperation and thus explain his purported confinement of the family. But, given its strategic placement in the prosecution's case—near the very end and thus especially likely to stick in the minds of the jury—it is certainly possible that this testimony was also intended to evoke a fungible profligacy linking Jackson's seeming heedless irresponsibility with money to heedless irresponsibility with children. By this reasoning, in addition to its evidentiary value on the conspiracy charge, his financial situation could serve as a window onto his character. In this part of the prosecution's narrative, he was not just an irrational consumer binging on credit. He was also an amoral one: consuming children and willing to take extreme measures to cover his tracks as the costs of both types of consumption were catching up to him. His fiscal and moral situations were thus inseparable. The implications of this equation may also explain the defense's vehement resistance to the judge allowing this evidence. By raising the possibility that Jackson's considerable expenses and debts were a fiscal problem as well as problems of character, the prosecution could plant a question in the minds of the jury. If the artist couldn't be trusted to manage his money, credit, and debts, if he were fiscally pathological to this considerable extent, how could he be trusted with children in his bedroom, and how pathological was he when he got them there?[121] Making Jackson a spectacle of fiscal deviance and indebtedness could make him a spectacle of depravity as well.

Moral Hazards

The implied equation of profligacy and criminality was certainly not unique to Michael Jackson's trial. Indeed, it played out explicitly in the trial of former Tyco CEO Dennis Kozlowski—he of the $6,000 shower curtain—that unfolded in the same year as Jackson's. Yet Kozlowski's crime was "white collar"; he may have been greedy and extravagant, but he was not depicted as also morally depraved.[122] In Jackson's case, though, the prosecution's suggestion of fiscal deviance—the inability or unwillingness to control his appetites, to regulate his consumption, to assess risk and rationally calibrate his desires to his means—could conjure moral and sexual deviance in the minds of the jury because financialization itself is a moralizing project enabling precisely these kinds of extrapolations. Its moral(-ized) dimensions are yet another reason both melodrama as a genre and the melodramatic trial, with their emphases on virtue and villainy, figure its operations so well.

Philosopher Jane Bennett defines the "moraline" as replete with a self-certainty impervious to irony or humor, an overidealization of purity in which the good is "too tightly" linked to the pure, and harshly punitive.[123] These broad contours of a moralizing project are readily apparent in neoliberal financialization's unshakable faith in its own machinations even, indeed especially, when they fail catastrophically as in the subprime crisis; its idealization of the putatively free market; and its consignment of its "losers" to personal abjection. But the slippage between money and character nascent in the prosecution's use of financial testimony in Jackson's trial also relies on three interrelated elements through which financialization's moral project actually transforms deviance from its ideal subject into unscrupulousness, turning credit and debt into character: its shaping and deployment of that ideal subject as a moral standard, an asymmetrical structure of culpability and visibility through which this standard is enforced, and the ease with which this "moral code" aligns with racist anti-Tom figural economies.

As I have noted throughout this chapter, the ideal neoliberal financialized subject is wholly autonomous; supremely rational; smart enough and brave enough to assess and embrace profitable, appropriate risk; and always optimally self-regulating. This ideal subject is made, not born: hailed into being by financial industry discourses that link one's relationship to the market to the most intimate components of the self. In advertisements, directives from the financial advice industry, and programs of consumer education, finance becomes a mode of self-expression, an investment in self-knowledge, and an extension of one's own body with the attendant obligation to care for it. For example, as Randy Martin notes, in refining the ideal subject's ideal portfolio, "Risk is a 'friend' whose intimacy with your own emotional pulse allows you to know yourself."[124] Further, in finance as in diet:

> control is the key to a fit life. Mismanagement introduces "financial stresses" that strict adherence to the program can eliminate one by one. [Fiscal] [f]itness carves out a great middle like a Darwinian niche, where a harmonious relation to work, to debt, to charity, and to taxes allows the masses to live free of fear.[125]

Retail financialization thus becomes a way to incarnate the classical ethical ideals of self-knowledge, self-care, moderation, and autonomy in everyday life. Inattention to, resistance to, or ignorance of this regime becomes an ethical failure and not simply a money problem. Jackson exemplified this ideal in the *Thriller* years of the mid-1980s: seizing financial opportunities, taking well-informed fiscal risks, and relying on his personal capital to "heal the world." It was his very status as an exemplar that made the evidence of his dire financial circumstances in 2005 so useful in painting a negative picture of his character by setting the formerly beloved and highly disciplined King of Pop into a recognizable plot of the superstar/hero gone to seed: self-indulgent, surrounded by sycophants and enablers, and morally suspect. If he jettisoned financialization's moral code after proving he could master and profit from it, what other codes might he have actively disregarded?

Bennett observes that one way to challenge moralizing projects is to "depurify one's ideals with a sensibility attuned to the messiness of actual life": for example, by recognizing consumption on credit as a kind of reprieve.[126] Interestingly, the prosecution's forensic accountant, Duross O'Bryan, seemed to head in this direction in "Neverland Accounting," published four years after the trial on the occasion of Jackson's death. His essay attests to Jackson's figural potential by noting correctly that, though the artist came up short against financialization's self-regulatory ideal in a uniquely spectacular way, he was not by any means unique. Yet the essay also exemplifies the asymmetry of financialization's moral economy:

> Ah, but as with much of America, he turned to easy-access debt—in this case, using his ever-appreciating music catalogs as collateral—to act as financial ballast. The problem is, like a lot of American homeowners and businesses in recent years, Mr. Jackson had basically mortgaged his bedrock assets (in particular the Beatles catalog) to the hilt.... Mr. Jackson's expenditures may have been extreme and unusual. Unfortunately, though, his financial habits were all too common.[127]

Duross O'Bryan never suggests that the very ubiquity of these "financial habits" might have a structural explanation: one indicting the credit-debt industry along with "much of America." Here, as the use of "habits" suggests, it is solely the obligation of individuals (including businesses) to regulate their own financial behaviors and replace any dysfunctional patterns with better ones. Lenders are unmarked and invisible in this discussion of credit and debt, and therefore disappear from the moral landscape. As Martin explains, the self-management expected of the ideal financialized subject "requires ongoing learning and constant vigil to eliminate the flab of ignorance" or laziness, greed or denial: bad habits betraying an underlying moral laxity that would lead to ruin. In the asymmetrical moral economy of financialization, however, this obligation accrues to consumers alone.[128]

Good fiscal habits are morally pure, but, in millennial financialization, bad ones can be profitable. During the trial, Duross O'Bryan testified that Jackson could continue to spend because he could continue to borrow. But, given the dismal fiscal picture outlined in trial testimony, how could he still get loans? How could "much of America" get them in this same period, and why might they need them? In Jackson's trial this question was never asked. While it was not, strictly speaking, germane to the case, the failure to ask it attests to the pervasive common-sense notion of financialized morality as an individual responsibility whereas financial institutions are above the moral fray: beholden only to the workings of the market, the legal parameters set by regulators, and the imperative to be profitable.[129]

While individuals' consumption attracts its share of moralizing judgments, these are amplified in debt scenarios: the second acts in financialization's melodrama following credit intoxication. The sheer magnitude of Jackson's debts, coupled with his apparent inability or unwillingness to adjust to his diminished fiscal status, made him appear morally suspect, but it also made him an investment: one reason he could continue to borrow. In this he also figures the moral asymmetry of financialization wherein the lender bears no responsibility for extending credit—even in cases when doing so seems irrationally imprudent—and is barely even visible as a party to the transaction. Yet flouting conventional views of prudence is a viable, even laudatory tactic used by such lenders because, in capital's relentless search for growth opportunities, the riskier the investment, the greater the potential reward. Lenders who take on risky loans as investments are thus morally indemnified by the market logic of risk.

Jackson's situation exemplifies the way financialization's asymmetrical moral economy shapes borrowers as creditworthy investments not in spite of but precisely because of their debts, even as they attract opprobrium for the irrationality and unsustainability of their indebtedness. Further, as his travails unfolded during and shortly after his trial, he also demonstrated how financial elites forestall reckonings of their obligations by leveraging both their indebtedness and their connections to other elites. The *New York Times* reported that, in 2005, the year of Jackson's trial, the annual interest rate on his loans worked out to about 20 percent: "a toll more familiar in the world of credit cards, subprime lending, and loan sharks."[130] In April 2005, in the midst of the prosecution's case and before Duross O'Bryan's testimony, Jackson was in default on his BOA loans collateralized in part with his shares of the Sony/ATV catalog.[131] The Reverend Jesse Jackson interceded with BOA on the artist's behalf, but Michael Jackson's continued ownership of the catalog was clearly imperiled. Both Goldman Sachs and the private equity firm Blackstone Group were interested in acquiring a stake in his share of the catalog; accepting their offers to buy out a portion might have solved his debt issues and stabilized his finances, but he refused to sell. Ultimately, BOA sold his loan to Fortress Investment Group.

Fortress was "placing a bet" on Jackson's debts; it specialized in distressed debt, typically associated with overleveraged entities or those at risk of impending bankruptcy.[132] The firm and others like it "are designed for wealthy investors looking for big returns on riskier bets." Distressed debt was a risky investment, but it had considerable profit potential, either in the event of the entity's turnaround or because, in a lend-to-own strategy, the investor would acquire the asset should the debtor fail. In Fortress's case that meant a chance at owning Jackson's share of the music catalog. Fortress's acquisition of Jackson's debt was a risk so replete with profit potential that, even after the artist's death, an analyst questioned BOA's wisdom—not for continually lending to him but for removing the loan from its books.[133] Jackson ultimately defaulted on Fortress's loan as well. In 2006, Sony helped broker a restructuring, bringing in Citigroup and acquiring the option to buy as much as half of Jackson's stake in the Sony/ATV catalog in the process. When he subsequently defaulted on another Fortress loan secured by Neverland, sending the ranch into foreclosure, private equity real estate investor Tom Barrack's Colony Capital firm bought the note.[134] During and after his trial, Jackson was simultaneously a morally dubious distressed debtor in court testimony and a heavily leveraged 1-percenter who could consistently secure large bailouts, even after repeated defaults.

The prosecution's trial testimony about Jackson's fiscal situation, and its potential as a vehicle of moral aspersion in the courtroom, rehearsed the same general tropes deployed during the emerging US subprime mortgage crisis: the investment potential of debt morally indemnifying the lenders who became invisible in the process, the implication that borrowers were predatory failures, the melodramatic unfolding of fiscal crisis shaped in moral extremes, and bailouts for financial elites. In that crisis and subsequent global economic downturn, consumers were also investments because of their debts, though via an even more financialized process than Jackson's, for less desirable collateral, and without the prospect of rescue by powerful firms and friends.[135]

Detailed accounts of the subprime crisis are now widely available. In brief, financial innovations, including hedge funds and structured investment vehicles, coupled with regulatory relaxations, generated a demand for credit-enabled debt that could then be securitized as risky, but potentially rewarding, investments. Mortgages fit the bill. They were aggregated, then transformed into mortgage-backed securities (MBSs) and collaterialized debt obligations (CDOs). Banks and other financial institutions then invested heavily in MBSs and CDOs, even while hedging their bets with credit default swaps (CDSs): both a type of insurance against nonpayment and speculation on the possibility that a default would occur. The asset pool available for securitization was expanded as lenders sought out economically marginalized consumers to generate new loans, in the process aligning rhetorically with President George W. Bush's "ownership society."[136]

While cloaked in the noble, egalitarian rhetoric of homeownership, the "ownership society" initiative made minority and working-class potential homeowners particularly visible as targets of finance industry opportunity, transforming their legitimate needs and desires into profitable resources because of their potential for accruing debt, which could then be repackaged and sold as MBSs and CDOs. As in Jackson's case, the riskier the loans, the potentially greater the returns. "Subprime" consumers—those whose incomes did not qualify them for more conventional products—were specifically targeted by lenders despite the risks they might pose. Subprime mortgages were profitable in two ways: through the commissions and fees generated on the initial loans and, in aggregate, as high-risk securities that could be packaged and sold to investors.

As is now well documented, a significant number of subprime loans made in this period were based on lender fraud: talking consumers into either purchasing homes or refinancing them through adjustable-rate mortgages they could not afford, forging borrowers' signatures on government-mandated disclosure forms, and baiting and switching loan terms, including embedding paperwork for adjustable rate loans in that for fixed-rate ones so, when borrowers signed the former, they would be tricked into signing the whole package; then the fixed-rate forms could simply be thrown away.[137] When consumers could no longer afford the ballooning payments on these adjustable-rate mortgages, financial industry losses began to mount as MBSs and CDOs began to implode, with effects felt around the globe. Consumer scapegoats were quickly assigned the blame, most famously in a well-publicized 2009 rant by financial reporter Rick Santelli, who labeled these borrowers "losers."[138] Everyone but the lenders and generators of the securities was to blame, including basic cable; the HGTV Network was singled out as "the real villain" of the ensuing global economic meltdown because it supposedly stimulated undeserving buyers' appetites for homes they could not afford.[139] As it unfolded, the subprime collapse was widely and publicly figured as the fault of "predatory borrowers" who exploited innocent lenders.[140] Even fraudulent lenders were morally indemnified by financialization's logic of the market, the moral sleight of hand whereby securitizing aggregated loans diffused responsibility across multiple institutions and ratings agencies, and the asymmetrical deployment of its ideal subject as an ethical cudgel against individual debtors who somehow should have known better. The same elements of Jackson's fiscal melodrama were now playing out on an international scale two years after they played out in a Santa Barbara County courtroom: charges of individual indiscipline, indiscriminate borrowing leading to moral hazards and lapses, the invisibility of lenders as equally culpable agents, and the financially desperate person as also morally depraved.

As Fred Moten reminds us, "In the United States, whoever says 'subprime debtor' says black as well," underscoring financialization as a racial as well as economic regime. African Americans and Latinos/as were specifically targeted by predatory lenders.[141] They were also "disproportionately [adversely] affected by the foreclosure crisis and [stood] to lose homes faster than white borrowers" both during and after the crisis, causing lasting damage to their credit scores and "wip[ing] out a generation of economic progress."[142] And they were also figured as solely or at least equally responsible for the subprime collapse. As American studies scholars Paula Chakravartty and Denise Ferreira da Silva observe, neoliberal financialization's effectiveness in disavowing the adverse effects it routinely generates "can be comprehended only if one acknowledges that the success [of its moralizing project] rests on what the tools of raciality offer it, the appropriate *persons* and *places* to attribute moral failures."[143] The anti-Tom tradition of figuring African American men as devious and insatiable is just such a tool, enabling the slippage between putative predatory sexuality and predatory fiscal subjectivity. Williams argues that the trope was inextricably interwoven into American popular culture with D. W. Griffith's film *The Birth of a Nation* (1915) and became a definitive component of American racial melodrama as it was replayed continually in entertainment and spectacular race(-ialized) trials.[144]

The anti-Tom tradition is a figural economy of racial antipathy that includes the "welfare queen," its more recent feminized counterpart. Whether as the depraved black man whose lust for white women was transmuted into lust for easy credit or the devious but lazy black woman living large while fraudulently on the dole invoked by Ronald Reagan, the anti-Tom tradition sustained the asymmetrical moral economy of financialization.[145] It enabled shifting the blame for economic turmoil onto the most vulnerable consumers, as if they were equally or more morally culpable, even as financial institutions received federal bailouts; such bailouts were also risky investments in debt but deemed economically essential and therefore morally justifiable, even imperative.

Jackson's molestation trial had demonstrated this same convergence of racialized and financialized moral reasoning years before it played out on the global stage. Though the prosecution did not explicitly refer to race, the racialized field in which the trial unfolded facilitated the connection between the artist, the anti-Tom predator sexually preying on the innocent, and the entitled, devious, profligate welfare queen. To refute the connection between Jackson's shaky finances and his alleged sexual depravity, his defense did not respond with its own forensic accountant. But it did deploy another figure from American racial melodrama's and neoliberal financialization's shared moral repertoire: the gentle, abused black innocent of the Tom tradition.

FISCAL INNOCENCE

Michael Jackson defense team's rebuttal to the prosecution's financial evidence was implicit in the testimony of one of their very first, and by Mesereau's account one of their strongest, witnesses: former child star Macaulay Culkin.[146] Culkin testified that he had slept in the same bed as Jackson many times and that the artist had never done anything improper. Culkin described Jackson as "very childlike. He liked doing the same things we did."[147] This testimony reinforced the defense's portrayal of the artist throughout the trial beginning with opening statements. Jackson, the defense asserted, was "a man who lost his childhood to hard work and entertaining and wanted to help children," a "very gentle soul" whose overly trusting nature was abused by a family of grifters who saw him as an easy mark.[148] Mesereau described Culkin's testimony as a "big factor" in Jackson's eventual acquittal, certainly because it established the artist's sexual propriety with young boys. But Culkin's description of the artist as childlike and his characterization of their friendship as essentially that of one child star to another also linked Jackson to the innocence of childhood itself. His childlike nature was as potentially fungible for the defense as his fiscal profligacy was for the prosecution. By this line of reasoning, because Jackson was basically a child himself, he was not just sexually innocent. He was fiscally innocent as well: culpable neither for his current financial circumstances nor for any plot to kidnap the Arvizos and use them to protect future earnings. Further, his trusting nature and humanitarian commitment to children, a logical extension of his own blunted childhood, made him easy prey to more fiscally savvy scammers. In a classic melodramatic peripety, Jackson became the child in the defense's scenario and Gavin Arvizo, his accuser, became the canny, entrepreneurial subject who, along with his family, saw Jackson not for the fellow child he was but as a financial opportunity ripe for exploitation.

Mesereau's and Culkin's characterizations of Jackson as pure, honest, childlike—a nurturer of children—besieged by a heinously callous family easily aligned with the American Tom archetype. Performance studies scholar Robin Bernstein has persuasively argued that white attachment to the figure of Uncle Tom was rooted in the fungible innocence of white childhood:

> The white child's innocence was transferable to surrounding people and things, and that property made it politically usable. This transmission occurred, for example, when Little Eva and Uncle Tom cuddled ecstatically in book illustrations, dramatic stagings of *Uncle Tom's Cabin*, games, advertisements, and household items. . . . In these images, the propinquity between the sentimental white child, foundationally defined by innocence, and the enslaved adult caused the white child's aura of innocence to extend to an African American character.[149]

In his guilelessness and gentleness, Tom was transformed by Eva into a child himself. His innocence was further reinforced by the blatant injustice of his suffering at the hands of the evil Simon Legree, whose amorality and warped family dynamics were underscored by his greed. Like its anti-Tom counterpart, this figural component of the American racial dialectic also persisted in popular culture and in the melodramatic trial.[150]

By painting Jackson both as the functional equivalent of an innocent child, underscored by the testimony of his former child friends, and as a gentle soul unjustly set upon by an amoral, greedy family of predators, the defense could benefit, however unintentionally, from the Tom tradition's figural repertoire. Significantly, this repertoire included images of adult-child intimacy that "to the modern nose . . . might seem to stink of pedophilia": Eva's "chaste physical engagement" with Tom.[151] Set within this repertoire, Jackson could play the role of the ruthlessly exploited, nurturing Tom whose physical relationships with boys were equally chaste. Further, because of his well-documented history of charity, his appeals to the post-racial in his music, and his own much reported childlike tendencies, he could both vigorously assert his own raciality and be cast in the role of Eva, the tragic, racially innocent phenotypically white child. Here, as Bernstein observes, "Innocence was not a literal state of being unraced but was, rather, the performance of not-noticing, a performed claim of slipping beyond social categories."[152] Through this chain of associations, in the seemingly damning *LwMJ* scene where Jackson cuddled Arvizo and spoke of the love of sharing a bed with a child, he was simply caught "in the act of not-thinking about race, gender, age, or sexual desire."[153]

Jackson's status as a Tom tradition innocent, functionally a child, established his fiscal guilelessness as well. "Fiscal innocence" is a riff on Bernstein's theorization of "racial innocence." In her compelling formulation, "Childhood in performance enabled divergent [racial arguments] to appear natural, inevitable, and therefore justified."[154] "Fiscal innocence" works similarly. In the defense's characterization, Jackson's repeated performances of childish(-likeness)—his trusting nature,

"not-noticing" of age and sexual desire, love of games and play, and professed identification with Peter Pan performatively produced him as fiscally prelapsarian: outside the gritty, vulgar adult world of bankers and their money, even as he was also a
generous humanitarian of considerable means. This dual nature of fiscal innocence
could help the jury reconcile his status as a wealthy mark for greedy schemers with
his seemingly utter obliviousness to his potential in this regard. It could also morally neutralize Jackson's spending and subsequent debts. This was not irresponsible
rapacity that signaled other deviant appetites. It was instead simply the logical, if
dysfunctional, result of a deprived child's inability to further delay gratification.

In neoliberal financialization's moral universe, of course, there is no childhood
outside of the fiscal and no space of fiscal innocence. Whether as the generational
investment in helicopter parents' future class capital, even in utero, or as proto-
commodity speculators in the exchanges of Pokémon cards, childhood has been
thoroughly financialized.[155] Yet, within this moral universe, allusions to racialized
childhood also operated as atavistic counterweights to the discourses of "predatory borrowers" through racial(-ist) paternalism. Here too the ideal entrepreneurial
subject served as the moral standard that the childlike Tom figure failed to meet not
because he was devious but because he was not sufficiently educated or, perhaps,
educable.

Like its anti-Tom polar opposite, this element of financialization's racialized
moral repertoire operated implicitly in Jackson's molestation trial before it was
invoked explicitly a few years later in the subprime crisis. Both Sarita See and Fred
Moten have noted that subprime borrowers were figured simultaneously as wily
cheats and as "hapless, naïve victims of smarter, educated folk . . . victims of their
own pathos and ignorance."[156] With the victim position the moral code remains
asymmetrical: faulting consumers for their haplessness or failures of fiscal literacy
rather than the still largely invisible financial institutions. As Moten states, subprime indebtedness is thus "a function of always already disabled self-possession,
a fundamental incapacity for personal responsibility, an inability to mature, an
endless developmental delay, a reckless childishness that demands instant gratification after hundreds of years."[157] Because there is no escape from financialization's
imperative to be an ever-savvy, ever-vigilant self-manager, however, hapless debtors
got no reprieve from either moral(-ized) judgment or, in large measure, from their
loan obligations. Again, they had only themselves to blame and needed to submit
to a rigorous program of moral-as-fiscal consumer education designed to root out
their deficits and remedy their ignorance.

In classic melodramatic fashion, the financialization of credit and debt in the first
decade of the 2000s offered a moral binary of feckless innocents needing schooling
in the ways of the world versus grifters bent on scamming their way to an unearned
good life while lenders and financial institutions largely escaped figuration as moral
agents. This binary mapped neatly onto the United States' Tom/anti-Tom racial
dialectic. Jackson's molestation trial offered a preview of these dynamics: rehears-
ing the same tropes in competing visions of the artist as either a savvy predator

or a benighted childlike victim. After fourteen weeks of testimony and roughly thirty hours of jury deliberations, he was found not guilty on all charges. Yet, as one headline trumpeting the verdict made explicit, his "freedom was not free."[158] His financial problems were becoming even more dire. He was *legally* innocent, but the *fiscal* innocence conjured as a byproduct of defense testimony did not spare him a reckoning any more than it spared the subprime borrowers who were figured in similar terms. In the third act of his fiscal melodrama, Jackson would deploy himself as corporeal collateral, using his labors in performance in an attempt to out-dance his debts. If he succeeded, he would restore himself to his mid-1980s prime: a beloved virtuoso and an exemplary entrepreneurial subject. And, by reminding his audiences of who he was as an artist at the height of his career—the hard-working King of Pop, deindustrialization's masterful transitional subject—he could perhaps vicariously transport them back to those seemingly better days as well.

ACT III: WASTED EFFORTS

On March 5, 2009, Michael Jackson announced that he was returning to the concert stage in July for a ten-show engagement in London featuring "the songs my fans want to hear."[159] The engagement was entitled "This Is It," and it would be, in Jackson's words, "the final curtain call." He agreed to undertake the rigors of rehearsal again ostensibly so his three children could see him perform, though financial exigencies were undoubtedly also a major factor. His antipathy to touring was well known. Yet Tom Barrack of Colony Capital, the firm that bought the note on Neverland saving it from foreclosure, was among those who presented the artist with a stark choice: return to live performance or face impending bankruptcy.[160] When the ten announced concerts sold out almost immediately, Jackson's promoters, the Anschutz Entertainment Group (AEG Live), added forty more shows. By AEG's estimate, Jackson would have earned at least $50 million for the run: not enough to fully settle his debts but a solid start toward financial stability with "the potential to earn tens of millions—if not hundreds of millions—through additional touring."[161] Jackson's characterization of "This Is It" as "the final curtain call" was both ominously prophetic and inaccurate. He died of acute propofol intoxication on June 25, 2009, three and half months after his announcement. Yet he continued to dance across screens and generate new revenue in rehearsal footage compiled by Sony in cooperation with his estate released under the show's title: *This Is It* (*TII*).

Like his shopping scene in *LwMJ* in 2003 and the prosecution's use of his finances in his child molestation trial in 2005, elements of *TII* are replete with the figural potential to illuminate the operations of millennial financialization. The film was shot in early 2009 and released in October of that year at the conjuncture of the halting beginnings of economic recovery from the US Great Recession and increasingly strident demands for fiscal austerity from the US political right. In this section, I examine two ways *TII* materializes key moral, rhetorical, and affective elements of the emerging US austerity project. First, scenes of Jackson's thinness and seeming frailty corporealize characterizations of austerity as a regimen of diet and hard work designed to produce a body politic that is "tough and lean."[162] Second, both *TII* and the emerging US austerity project operate through a temporal fantasy of the redemptive "comeback" that generates a vision of the future as a return to a reinvigorated version of the past produced through sacrifice and labor in the present. Jackson's is a sequined austerity to be sure. The fiscal problems that sent him back to the concert stage are certainly not comparable to those of a low-income, out-of-work single mother faced with cuts to food stamps and unemployment benefits in the same period. Yet, while he may not be a representative austerity subject, in *TII* Jackson does fully figure the dubious logic of, and incarnate the metaphors for, the austerity program advanced by the political right: embracing its prescription for hard work and sacrifice to redeem previous excesses and restore fiscal stability. He also materializes and corporealizes the shrinkage austerity advocates see as a mark of that prescription's success.

Austerity is neoliberal financialization's redemption fantasy when markets fail. As political economist Florian Schui argues, "The persuasive power of austerity arguments lies in part in the way in which they allude to familiar moral and cultural categories of moderation, sacrifice, selflessness and cathartic cleansing," as well as the dangers of excess, the necessity for atonement, and the promise of redemption through hard work.[163] According to Schui, "Even when we do not understand the economic logic associated with austerity arguments—or where they are presented without a compelling economic argument—their emotional appeal is strong."[164] Emotional appeal, sacrifice, selflessness, cathartic cleansing, familiar moral and cultural templates: this is the stuff of melodrama. I argue here that both *TII* and the US austerity regime emerging at the same time are melodramas of redemption. Jackson's personal melodrama—replete with pathos and a trajectory that begins with excess and ends in his shocking death—figures US austerity's melodramatic, moralized dimensions.

I begin by examining both austerity's melodramatic dimensions and Jackson's incarnation of them in *TII* using one of those "familiar moral and cultural" templates: Hans Christian Andersen's tale "The Red Shoes." In the story as in *TII*, dance, debility, and death converge in a plot about the fraught labors of penance for flashy consumption. Andersen's story centers on a poor child, new to an adopted life of wealth and privilege, who covets, then acquires, a shiny pair of red shoes. When she wears them, she becomes a public spectacle and an object of disdain. She thinks of nothing but the shoes. But they are cursed. Once on her feet, they dance unceasingly of their own volition, and she is powerless to stop them even as she is consumed by this frenzy of motion. "Dance shalt thou," intones a mysterious figure who may be the source of the curse. "Dance in thy red shoes till thou art pale and cold. Till thy skin shrivels up and thou art a skeleton!" The girl wastes away from her dancing. Even chopping off her feet gets her no reprieve; the shoes dance on in front of her, reminding all who see them of her untoward desires. Her soul is ultimately redeemed when she accepts the yoke of demanding physical labor but redemption comes at the expense of her life. After she dies, seemingly of exhaustion, her soul "flew on the sunshine to God, and there no one asked after the red shoes." Michael Jackson was reportedly interested in the story, particularly its translation into the famous 1948 British romantic melodrama of the same name featuring a ballerina fatally torn between her art and love. Former Sony executive Amy Pascal tried to convince him to do a remake to no avail. "Michael's life became The Red Shoes, I'm afraid," she observed.[165]

Andersen's story fits austerity's compulsive, punitive, and penitential dimensions, and its insistence on contraction of the public body politic. It also fits Jackson's personal journey from the privations of his Gary childhood through his consuming passions that attracted widespread opprobrium, followed by the well-documented stresses of rehearsal for *TII*, and ending with redemption in death. Moreover, austerity as a form of fiscal contraction and Jackson's appearance in the film resonate with the tale's image of unsettling physical contraction as the materialization of both punishment and penance: "Dance till . . . thou art a skeleton." In this context, Jackson's efforts in rehearsals for *TII* are "wasted" because he died before he could personally reap the rewards of his labors ("a waste"/in vain) and because he was by most accounts prodigiously self-medicating throughout the process ("wasted"/intoxicated). But most important, "wasted" here refers to his physical emaciation: appearing to shrink before our eyes as he dances across the screen. Jackson's shocking and much commented upon thinness in *TII*, coupled with his parsing of effort and marking of steps in rehearsal, are a visual and kinesthetic analog for the emerging US austerity project characterized as a "diet," a racialized "morality play," and a pervasive ethos of "tough love."[166] Because exhaustion, anxiety, and death were the denouement of Jackson's efforts to shrink his debt, he also figures the debility produced by austerity regimes, and the cruel optimism for a better future rooted in a return to a straitened yet somehow more robust past.

None of this is to assert or imply that the Michael Jackson of *TII* is a purely tragic figure or that he did not find real pleasures and comfort in the labors of rehearsal and the camaraderie of his fellow performers. *TII* blurs the distinction between the artist's apparent and reported vulnerability and his creative control, between no choice—fiscal exigency—and the array of choices he made in advancing the production.[167] I do not claim that the fraught, thin Jackson described in so many accounts of *TII*'s production is any more "real" than the smiling, joking, exuberant Jackson we sometimes see on-screen. Nor do I offer a comprehensive reading of the film or Jackson's dancing in it here. I argue that, because *TII* was undertaken as redress for previous consuming passions at least as much as for pleasure or posterity, because specific features fit austerity's and Andersen's story's imagery of contraction demanded by past excess, and because it shares austerity's temporal imaginary of the future-as-return-to-the-past, it illuminates the mechanics of a barely coherent austerity project emerging at the same time it was produced.

As scholars and commentators have increasingly noted, austerity is not simply a state economic program. It is also an ethos of public atonement for putatively unaffordable past excesses: one particularly amenable to melodramatic figuration through "The Red Shoes" and Michael Jackson because it is a conceptual "absence."[168] As political economist Mark Blyth argues in *Austerity: The History of a Dangerous Idea*:

> For an idea so central to the governance of states and markets, austerity's intellectual history is both short and shallow. There is no well worked out "theory of austerity" in economic thought that extends back in time to some foundational statements that become more systematized and rigorous over time as there is, for example, with trade theory. We have instead what David Colander has called "a sensibility" concerning the state, embedded in liberal economics from its inception, that produces "austerity" as the default answer to the question what should we do when markets fail?[169]

This sensibility is a diffuse public feeling as well as a reflexive response to financialization's failures. Indeed, government austerity regimes both rely on and contribute to this public feeling.

In 2010, the year after *TII* was released, Merriam Webster Inc. proclaimed "austerity" number one on its list of the "Top Ten Words" of the year. According to the publisher, such words offered a window into "America's mood and interests" as determined by the number of searches they received in its online dictionary.[170]

> "*Austerity*" clearly resonates with many people," said Peter Sokolowski, Editor at Large.... "We often hear it used in the context of government measures, but we also apply it to our own personal finances and what is sometimes called the new normal."

In 2009, US conservative elites began aggressively pressing this "new normal" as the putatively inevitable consequence of consuming passions run amok. Schui explains that "austerity policies have many facets but ultimately they are about abstinence from consumption."[171] In practice, austerity is less about abstaining and more about actively contracting by "cutting back on government expenditure that funds individual and collective forms of consumption: for example pensions, health care, and education," as well as "lowering the cost of labour, that is, reducing wages and hence individual consumption."[172] Debt is a catalyst for state austerity regimes, specifically the perception that national debt has become dangerously high and must be reduced, even if by draconian measures. Thus, according to Blyth, cutting state budgets, debts, and deficits, "its advocates believe, will 'inspire business confidence' since the government will neither be 'crowding-out' the market for investment by sucking up all the available capital through the issuance of debt, nor adding to the nation's already 'too big' debt."[173]

Austerity continues financialization's racialization and moralization of relationships between consumption, debt, and work, both at the level of the state and at the retail level of personal morality. As it played out in the US popular press and in the halls of government in 2009 and 2010, it was also racial and political melodrama: characterized by racialized binaries, powered by seething racial(-ist) resentments, and figured in highly moralized terms.

A brief summary of the rhetoric leading up to the US government's turn to austerity measures during the recovery from the Great Recession is illustrative. In 2007, after the collapse of securitized subprime mortgages, the George W. Bush administration bailed out financial institutions deemed too big to fail, and in 2008, the Obama administration initiated a stimulus package designed to blunt the worst of the recession's effects. Though many economists, most notably Nobel laureate Paul Krugman, repeatedly argued that the stimulus was too modest, the resulting uptick in US government debt provided political cover for conservative Republican legislative majorities and their constituencies to attack not only the administration's stimulus initiatives but also the tattered remains of the welfare state—for example, food stamps and assistance to the long-term unemployed—and public workers under the guise of a looming US "debt crisis." These attacks began in earnest in 2009 and escalated sharply in early 2010, pitting upright "workers" against undeserving "moochers" who were supposedly bankrupting the country.

For example, though they were not the only vocal advocates of the austerity ethos, right-wing populist Tea Party activists gave political fuel to austerity hawks by explicitly calling for an end to government social support programs in a March 15, 2010, statement proclaiming, "The locusts are eating, or should we say devouring, the productive output of the hardworking taxpayers."[174] The figural continuity of ravenous locusts with Ronald Reagan's welfare queen was hard to miss. The Tea Party contributed significantly to the racialized and moralized ethos of austerity, fusing anxiety about national debt to resentment of perceived "moochers" who did not work, or work hard enough, and who were coddled by a government spending itself into the red to do so. Its rhetoric made austerity's moral calibration of consumption, work, and debt explicit and personal, as exemplified by members' placards proclaiming "You are not ENTITLED to what I have EARNED" and "Redistribute My Work Ethic."[175] As political scientists Theda Skocpol and Vanessa Williamson note in their study of the group, the vision of hard work as both an intrinsic good and a moral obligation was the primary catalyst behind calls for cuts to social spending: "Only through hard work can one earn access to a good income and to honorable public benefits."

Fueled by populist outrage at "moochers" who consumed but did not work, austerity emerged as both a racialized moral politics of blame for the United States' economic problems and a way to redress those problems, but it was also a form of white populist retrenchment. As *New York Times* writer Thomas B. Edsall noted in "The Politics of Austerity," "The conservative agenda, in a climate of scarcity, racializes policy making, calling for deep cuts in programs for the poor. The beneficiaries of these programs are disproportionately black and Hispanic."[176] Likewise, the right's rhetorical reframing of public employees as a putatively undeserving, privileged class with pensions and benefits increasingly unavailable to much of the workforce was also deeply, if less obviously, racialized because, "for black Americans, government employment is a crucial means of upward mobility. The federal workforce is 18.6 percent African American, compared with 10.9 percent in the private sector."[177] Austerity advocates argued that shrinking government spending would ensure that these undeserving constituencies had to "earn their place"; a culture of "entitlement" would be replaced by a work ethic that would produce "deservingness."[178]

Pro-austerity forces gained momentum throughout 2009 and 2010. Republican legislative majorities ultimately implemented austerity measures in the Budget Control Act of 2011, which mandated a decade of spending cuts. Later budget sequestration—additional across-the-board spending cuts—were triggered in 2013 when a legislative "supercommittee" failed to recommend its own reductions. As a consequence, the US public sector lost 787,000 jobs between June 2009 and July 2013, according to the Economic Policy Institute; all told, austerity cost the nation 3 million jobs in this crucial recovery period.[179] It "prolonged the pain of the Great Recession into 2014" and was described as an even tougher regime than imposed on Europe in the same period.

Early in this fraught period of contraction, as the moralized and racialized rhetoric was reaching a crescendo and the pace of recovery from the Great Recession was uncertain, a new Michael Jackson concert was a reassuring prospect, in part because it followed the broad contours of austerity's redemption fantasy and because it recalled the artist's iconic success in outdancing bad economic times a quarter century before. Not only would his return to the stage improve his own cash flow, but his appearance in new versions of his classic hits would also remind the older members of his audiences of their spectacular journey together through the darkest days of the deindustrial 1980s. He would be an icon of austerity: reinforcing its logic of hard work and embodying its promise of better days to come. But success would depend on his labors dispelling and redeeming his Wacko Jacko excesses. Surely the work ethic that once helped him escape the deteriorating steel mills of Gary would now power his own resurgence as the King of Pop and exemplify the can-do discipline touted in pro-austerity rhetoric.

Exhausted Dance

On March 8, 2009, three days before Michael Jackson announced his return to the concert stage, then House Speaker John Boehner twice proclaimed that it was time for the federal government to "go on a diet."[180] Boehner's advocacy of stringent fiscal austerity in the shaky early days of the US economic recovery relied on an inaccurate yet highly persuasive analogy comparing individual and household economies to that of the federal government: "American families are tightening their belts. But they don't see government tightening its belt." Yet Boehner's misleading analogy can be redeployed for figural effect: to materialize the anxiety and debility produced by austerity regimes rather than to extol their putative "common-sense" wisdom. Boehner's austerity "diet"—a remedy for prior consumption—is figured by the skeletal dancing child atoning for wanton consumption in "The Red Shoes." Michael Jackson makes this same image viscerally legible in the same period austerity rhetoric was gaining momentum: demonstrating that "diet" and "belt-tightening" did not necessarily produce a lean, reinvigorated body politic.

The Michael Jackson of *This Is It* is very thin.[181] In both ensemble and duet scenes, he is visibly skinnier than the young men and women dancing alongside him.

In his prime, Jackson had been well aware of public perceptions of his weight. He addressed the issue in his autobiography *Moonwalk* in the course of refuting allegations that he had plastic surgery, claiming that his new angularity was the result of dietary changes that left him healthier.[182] Weight per se, and not just health, is of paramount concern to Western concert dancers in both elite and popular genres: a matter of aesthetics and audience expectation and not simply one of fitness. Jackson's leanness served his aesthetic beautifully, particularly at the height of his career. It accentuated the length and crispness of his line, which was important because, at five foot nine, he was not a tall man. His exceptionally clean line in stretched and extended moves makes him legible in ensemble routines and visually underscores his command of both space and attention. His thinness also accentuates the precise geometry of his joints in isolations, making his angular moves seem especially sharp and aggressive. But even by his previous standards, he appears visibly emaciated in the *This Is It* footage. The film is cut so that it is not possible to reconstruct a strict chronology of his weight loss, yet he is clearly bonier in some sequences, those presumably later in the rehearsal process, than in others. His clavicle protrudes, his jawline seems razor sharp, his shoulders—which had always been broad, seem to have shrunk, and his hands, which always appeared large against his frame, seem even larger by comparison. He has no discernible butt. His clothes hang on him as on a hanger (figure 4).

Just as Jackson's frequent references to the hard work of rehearsals and the labor that, in his view, erased his childhood, operate alongside and relativize any pleasures he may have taken in performance practice, his extreme thinness in *TII* signals the corporeal and affective costs of his dancing in rehearsals: his labors toward fiscal redemption. These costs were recognized by fans and members of the production team; testimony on this point was entered into evidence in *Katherine Jackson v. AEG Live*, his mother's civil suit alleging that the promoters callously kept Jackson working through a punishing regime of rehearsals when he was clearly in no shape to do so. This evidence serves as a widely publicized supplemental commentary track to the film. For example, in an email sent to Jackson's longtime makeup artist Karen Faye, a fan Jackson invited to the *Thriller* section of the rehearsal described him as a "skeleton," noting with alarm that he "was only bones":

Figure 4: Michael Jackson, screenshot, *This Is It*. Fans and members of the crew expressed increasing concern over Jackson's thinness during the production. These concerns were raised again in *Katherine Jackson v. AEG Live*. Sony Pictures Home Entertainment, 2010.

> We don't know if he is anorexic and stopped eating as he told us, or if it's something more complicated than that, a disease or something.
>
> . . . I also know that it is humanly impossible for a human being to be a skeleton and dance for 2 hours straight without any danger.[183]

Faye forwarded the message on to Frank "Tookie" Dileo, Jackson's manager at the time, with a preamble: "Frank, unfortunately she is right. I am fearful he will make himself so sick he will die." In another email to Faye, a different fan wrote:

> It is painfully obvious that Michael is TOO THIN. I know that Michael's weight fluctuates, and he is often mostly too thin anyways, but NOW he is REALLY TOO THIN.[184]

Director Kenny Ortega sent out his own alarm in an email message with the subject line "Trouble at the Front" to AEG Live's CEO Randy Phillips, noting reports of Jackson's weight loss during a costume fitting and indicating that he (Ortega) was now feeding Jackson.[185] Phillips responded by telling Ortega not to play amateur psychiatrist or physician. Jackson's doctor Conrad Murray, later convicted of manslaughter in the artist's death, had pronounced him fit. The show must go on.

As Franz Kafka, historian Rudolph Bell, and performance studies scholar Patrick Anderson have shown in very different projects, extreme thinness is both a spectacle in its own right and a specific kind of interpretive invitation to those who witness it.[186] This is certainly true of Jackson's physique during this period, as the emails to Faye and Phillips attest. Whether he was intentionally anorexic or not, his appearance, like that of the skeletal girl in the red shoes, invites reading his shrinking frame not just in terms of his health but also in relationship to his earlier history of consumption. Where he was once described as wantonly excessive, he is now visibly stretched too thin. His diminished physique is also a physical indicator of the rigors of his labors: for example, dancing two hours straight. He seems to be physically wearing himself away in inverse proportion to his earlier spectacular accumulation, just as Andersen's dancing child did in enforced penance for her red shoes. This wearing away, over against earlier images of his consumption like the shopping scene in *LwMJ*, corporealizes the austerity imperative to shrink: "shrink spending, shrink debt, shrink deficits."[187] Read through his own history as both a consumer and a debtor, Jackson's emaciation literalizes the attrition demanded of austerity's subjects and does so within the regime of putatively redemptive work that was supposed to "save" them.

Though Jackson sometimes briefly breaks out and dances playfully or vehemently full stop in *TII*—catching himself and noting that he should be saving his energy—most of his stage time is spent marking moves: providing corporeal traces to be fleshed out later in the performance to come. This is prudent and standard for rehearsal. But his thinness, over against the robust athleticism of his young cohort of backup dancers, renders his markings as something more complex. They are simultaneously kinesthetic sketches reminding us of the distance between these moves and his past virtuosity, promissory notes for the performance to come and never to come, and a suggestion of his present frailty as he labors toward fiscal redemption. In light of his extreme thinness, and our own memories of his vigor in past versions of the numbers he now rehearses, these small gestures become more ambiguous and more disturbing than routine rehearsal tactics. Do we see typical marking here, or is this all that a dancing skeleton can do?

Certainly there is beauty to be found in Jackson's kinesthetic tracing of moves: in the play of his knees, at once exuberant and wobbly; in the rhythmic timekeeping that is precise and sometimes looks palsied; in the spins, complete though not tight. His performances in *TII* recall those of butoh dancer Kazuo Ohno, who continued to perform into his nineties. Ohno became a spectacle of both fragility and endurance. Watching him in his later years, like watching *TII* knowing Jackson's fate—inevitable given the film's posthumous release—reminds us of performance theorist Herbert Blau's observation that when we see a performer at work, we are witnessing mortality at work as well. As Blau put it, "The body in performance is dying in front of your eyes. Unceasing process is out there in the flesh."[188] Ohno probed codes of Romanticism, gender, pathos, and the uncanny in ways that resonate strongly with characterizations of Jackson as gender ambiguous, innocent, and otherworldly. But the spareness of Jackson's gestures also suggests that he has been worn out by the rigors of redemption even as they signal his faith that these labors could eventually redeem him in the concert for which they are a corporeal down payment. In watching Jackson dance, we see both his mortality and austerity's imperative to keep working in service of his comeback as "unceasing processes out there in the flesh."

Taken together, his thinness and spare tracing of steps, even with the occasional playful flourish, make his performances look like exhausted dance: a reminder that moralized fictions of redemptive work elide that work's actual physical and psychic demands. As courtroom testimony would later reveal, Jackson was breaking down during these same rehearsals. Ultimately he lost both the muscle memory and the physical facility to execute his signature moves; *TII*'s production manager testified that both he and Ortega were worried he would get hurt onstage.[189] Ortega reported that Jackson was shivering: "He was lost, cold, and afraid," literally incarnating the pale, cold, and skeletal child of "The Red Shoes." He was also desperate, begging Ortega not to leave him, afraid his shot at redemption, "this dream, this desire, was going to fall away."[190]

In "Don't Stop Till You Get Enough: Presence, Spectacle, and Good Feeling in *Michael Jackson's This Is It*," music scholar Jason King describes compelling "moments of shared surplus feeling between Jackson and his cast and crew": moments that "inundate the entire film with radiant good feeling."[191] He also notes Jackson's extraordinary ability to master multiple elements of the production. These elements undeniably appear alongside both the artist's perilous thinness and postmortem reports of his increasing debility, but they do not relativize or negate them. Indeed, they contribute powerfully to Jackson's compelling figural potential in this moment of tentative economic recovery when the US unemployment rate was almost 10 percent: the highest it had been since the height of Jackson's career in the mid-1980s. The very combination of on-screen good feeling and off-screen private anxiety also characterizes both the routine affective operations of creative production and the nature of work in millennial financialization. The performer, to say nothing of the contingent university faculty member or the service laborer, may be extraordinarily adept, suffused with the pleasures of fellow feeling in the course of doing her job, profoundly exhausted and worn away by its demands, and terrified that job "was going to fall away" at the same time. Under millennial financialization work is central to subjectivity to the extent that, as David Harvey has noted, "Sickness (or any kind of pathology) gets defined . . . as the inability to work."[192] All but the most privileged are compelled to don the red shoes of millennial capitalism and dance till we drop, and, as Jackson's case attests, even some of the privileged are not immune. That we may find moments of solace or joy in the process does not lessen the compulsion. The US austerity regime's intensification of the rhetoric of hard work as an absolute good when joblessness was at record levels and unemployment benefits were framed as "disincentives" heightened both workers' investment in and anxiety around labor in a time of precarity. Indeed, Jackson's hit that supplies King's chapter with its title could also summarize austerity advocates' disposition toward workers in this period: don't stop till you get enough because you are on your own.

Dance scholar André Lepecki coined the phrase "exhausting dance" to characterize choreography that breaks with dance's modernist ontology of unstoppable movement. In the crawling and stumbling of William Pope.L and the stillness of Jérôme Bel, Lepecki sees "potential for a critique of choreography's participation in this political ontology of modernity."[193] But Jackson's dancing in *TII* tells us a more complicated story: one of a dancer who is exhausted but neither stumbles nor stands still. In this exhausted dance we see both the attrition produced by financialized austerity's redemption fantasy of unstoppable momentum, even in subjects as unquestionably privileged as Jackson, and the cruel optimism that the work of performance might make that fantasy come true. Jackson's investment in and anxiety around his upcoming concerts remind us that dance's relationship to unstoppable mobility is not simply a choreographic disposition of modernity. It is also financialization's and austerity's moralized demand of those subjected to its operations, and a tactic for economic advancement virtuosically exemplified by Jackson himself years before. A quarter century later, worn down and wearing away, he was still at it.

Back to the Future

Why, given the harrowing accounts of his health, did Jackson keep at it? He had canceled concerts before. One reason is the powerful attachment artists and audiences have to the redemption fantasy of the comeback: an attachment they share with austerity advocates. *TII* demonstrates the very specific temporal imaginary that drives this fantasy.

First, the project was not conceived as a simple nostalgia act. It was to have been a dazzling, complete reimagining of fan favorites with effects to surpass all of the artist's previous productions, not simply a re-enactment of greatest hits: both retrospective and radically new. Second, because the actual performance was never to be, *TII* depends on rehearsal footage, which, by its very nature, gestures forward toward a future realization in performance. Watching these rehearsals is both retrospective and anticipatory. When we see versions of *I Want You Back, Smooth Criminal, The Way You Make Me Feel*, and other milestones, we recall the Michael Jacksons of the originals even as we mentally extrapolate from the marked moves on the screen, imagining the possibilities of the performance to come. *TII* documents the artist's dancing toward this future-past that would never arrive: he is suspended in the act of delivering on the show's promise of anticipatory retrospection. Fans' comments after the concert announcement attest to their recognition of *TII* as an image of a future-past defined by both Jackson's creative work and his figural potential over forty years.

> "We grew up listening to him," says Iram Tariq, 20, of Greenwich. "We have to go see him. He's the only legend of our time who has attained that level of success."
> Says Chloe Brown, 17, of London, "He is an icon and an inspiration."[194]

These responses demonstrate the affective investment not only in Jackson himself as a virtuoso artist but also in his inspirational ability to incarnate social mobility across modes of economic production. That the last decade of Jackson's life played out in sordid tabloid headlines made the appeal of his comeback even greater. The concert would affirm his potential as an artist and icon in a way that was also both retrospective, harkening back to his glorious *Thriller* years, and anticipatory at the same time: What could he do next?

Austerity too depends on this attachment to a temporal fantasy of a future as a reinvigorated version of the past. Cultural studies scholar Rebecca Bramall defines it as a "site of discursive struggle between different visions of the future"; nostalgia for an imagined past is mobilized in this struggle.[195] She is writing specifically about twenty-first-century austerity Britain where the revival of a wartime and postwar ethos—"Keep Calm and Carry On"—makes this connection between visions of the future and the nostalgic past explicit. The US austerity sensibility, however, relies not on conjuring a collective memory of shared sacrifice but on the fantasy of a return to generic former glory made all the more desirable by a degraded present requiring a redemptive combination of fiscal contraction and renewed hard work. This fantasy was made explicit in the Republican Budget Resolution of 2012, entitled "Path to Prosperity: Restoring America's Promise," the distillate of the populist austerity rhetoric of the previous three years.[196] It depicts the federal government in the moralized terms used to describe Jackson: as a profligate consumer that "squandered . . . savings" with the result that "overspending" led to "the brink of bankruptcy." Only a tough love regime of fiscal contraction would remind us of our "greatest strength: the exceptional character of . . . entrepreneurial, self-reliant, hard-working citizens." Only this morally and fiscally redemptive contraction could "restore the dynamism that has defined America over the generations."[197]

That Michael Jackson did indeed make a comeback in *TII* both exemplifies and belies the cruel optimism that sustains attachment to austerity's temporal fantasy. In 2010, the year after his death, his work earned more than in the six previous years combined.[198] Like the dancing, laboring child of "The Red Shoes," he was at last fully redeemed: once again financialization's exemplary entrepreneurial subject. Unlike her, he did not escape financialization's reach, even after he was dead.

PART II
Detroit's Deindustrial Homeplaces

CHAPTER 3

Combustible Hopes on the National Stage

Figuring Race, Work, and Home in

("not necessarily") Detroit

This is a city where the dream came true for more people than anywhere else on Planet Earth and the principal fulfillment of that dream was a private home and a secure front door behind which to enjoy the life that is every American's god-given due. And when those homes come tumbling down, the release of energy is something terrible to witness, a Dresden of dreams incinerated in an existential fire-bombing of hope.

Jerry Herron, *"Motor City Breakdown"*[1]

I want my hair to smell like the smoke from yesterday's fire.

"Mary," Detroit[2]

Speramus Meliora; Resurget Cineribus

We hope for better things. It will arise from the ashes.

Motto of the City of Detroit

Lisa D'Amour tells us that the "Detroit" of her eponymous play is "not necessar-ily" the actual city.[3] In fact, her specifications for "Place" explicitly exclude it. The play's actions unfold in "a first ring suburb outside of a midsize American city." If reviewers comment on the title at all, it is to echo or rationalize D'Amour's equiv-ocal disavowal. In their view, "Detroit" is "metaphoric"; we are not told of what.[4] Perhaps it should be obvious: the name seems the perfect empty signifier to conjure a contemporary knot of racial(-ist) and economic anxieties, industrial era nostalgia, and incendiary self-destruction set in the neighborhood, at the intersection of work and home. Still—she didn't call it "Dubuque."

Key aspects of Detroit's function within the figural economy of American deindustrialization are captured both in D'Amour's "not necessarily" and in the unexplained and surely unexamined consensus around the city's putatively obvious metaphoric potential. In the second decade of the new millennium, a lot of municipalities were characterizing themselves as either "not necessarily" or emphatically "not" Detroit, and this was more than a function of the city's fiscally straitened circumstances in its immediate prebankruptcy period: 2012–13.[5] In this chapter, I argue that Detroit spatializes and racializes the hopes, the nostalgic melancholy, the willful amnesia—the affective mess—spawned by three decades of the deindustrial: packaging it for circulation within our shared emotional and representational vernacular whether it operates as figure ("not necessarily Detroit") or as an actual place with a very specific history. This affective mess was particularly palpable during the long, uneven recovery from the US Great Recession: a period of deindustrial doldrums that stretched into the 2010s, characterized by labor precarity, wage stagnation, and omnipresent reminders that the shift from industrial to deindustrial production was not the smooth evolutionary progression of capitalism that elite economic and political actors had suggested.

Three plays (not necessarily) sited in Detroit expose the mechanics and limits of its representational fungibility on the national stage during this recovery/prebankruptcy period: the details of this figural packaging. Each play uses Detroit to explore the interpersonal fallout from the opportunities and crises of racialized capitalism. Each also offers audiences intimate and collective visions of capitalism's US industrial heyday: particularly compelling as the economic recovery dragged on and the actual city of Detroit was sliding closer to a fiscal abyss.

In examining D'Amour's *Detroit*, Berry Gordy's *Motown the Musical*, and Dominique Morisseau's *Detroit '67*, I ask: How does Detroit function as the synecdoche not only for deindustrialization but also for the multisystem failures of late capitalism that include but exceed a contracting domestic manufacturing sector? How are these failures themselves figured as both profoundly intimate and interpersonal and, at the same time, spectacularly, publicly combustible? Who are the agents and who the victims in such figurations? How does Detroit-as-figure reconcile the vernacular binaries we use to think about economic issues like work versus home, the precarity of the deindustrial versus the seeming solidity of what came before, or even the amorphous squishy vitality of affect versus the supposedly detached, bounded rationality of economics itself?[6] At the same time, how does Detroit-as-figure both enforce and ignore America's racial binaries, sometimes under the guise of putatively post-racial "good manners"?[7] When D'Amour says her play is "not necessarily" set in the Detroit of its title, what specifically does she acquire, avoid, evade, or evoke in doing so?

I begin by describing these three plays whose New York productions coincided with a series of crises facing Detroit, including the imposition of an emergency manager and the beginnings of its highly publicized descent into bankruptcy. Next I argue that, in their broad contours as well as their specific visions of the city, the plays expose the crucial and contradictory elements of the deindustrial that are reconciled by "Detroit-as-figure." These elements emerge with special clarity in the thematic connections between race, place, home, and work driving each plot: connections that depend upon specific elements of the city's history whether these are explicitly acknowledged, reworked, seemingly forgotten, or sidestepped. The thematic importance of performance in all three plays, coupled with Detroit's unique history of techno-managerial and incendiary racialized spectacles, lead me to posit "re-siting/re-citing" as a heuristic tool to expose specific moments of the city's history operating in each play and in the city-as-figure. Rooted in performance theory and performativity, "re-siting/re-citing" informs my subsequent analysis of each play's "Detroitness" and, in so doing, brings the city's racial and political economic history to bear on its work as a "metaphor" for the deindustrial.

DETROIT ON THE NATIONAL STAGE: AN OVERVIEW

Detroit was first produced in Chicago, itself often figured as "not Detroit," by Steppenwolf Theatre and opened off-Broadway at Playwrights Horizons on September 18, 2012, for a six-week run.[8] Though D'Amour's casting note calls for a flexible approach to characters' ages, their heteronormativity is as obvious as their raciality is unremarked. They are presumptively, though perhaps by the same logic informing the choice of title "not necessarily," white. Both Steppenwolf Theatre's and Playwrights Horizons' productions featured all-white casts.

The play is explicitly framed as a comedy, albeit a "scary-funny" or "tartly funny" one.[9] Ben and Mary, clinging by their fingertips to a middle-class life that is beginning to unravel due to his unemployment and her incipient alcoholism, extend neighborly hospitality to Kenny and Sharon, who recently moved in next door and are trying to make a new start (figure 5). Kenny and Sharon met in rehab, from which they have only just emerged, or earlier while clubbing in "Hotlanta," or somewhere—the particulars keep changing.[10] They have shaky work histories. Both couples have shaky relationships with the truth, making "Bright Homes," the name of the 1950s first-ring suburb in which now they reside, even more ironic as the setting neither delivers on its promise of self-illumination nor secures the sunny future ostensibly enjoyed by an earlier generation of residents. Things do light up in the end, however, to disastrous effect, leaving Ben and Mary staring at the ashes of their domestic lives as Kenny's uncle muses about the area's "magic times" now clearly past. The New York production presented the neighbors' front and back yards, their disintegrating social facades, and the climax of their literally combustible relationship sparely, intimately, and realistically. Perhaps no obvious theatrical flourishes are necessary in a play that turns on failed self-reinvention in the deindustrial doldrums.

Detroit was a finalist for the Pulitzer Prize, and the Playwrights Horizons production, the only one I consider here, was generally well reviewed. Charles Isherwood

Figure 5: Left to right: "Sharon" (Sarah Sokolovic), "Kenny" (Darren Pettie), "Mary" (Amy Ryan), and "Ben" (David Schwimmer). Lisa D'Amour's *Detroit*, Playwrights Horizons. Photo: Jeremy Daniel. Photo courtesy of The Publicity Office/Michael Borowski.

of the *New York Times* called it "a sharp X-ray of the embattled American psyche as well as a smart, tart critique of the country's fraying social fabric . . . as rich and addictively satisfying as a five-layer dip served up with a brimming bowl of tortilla chips."[11] Joe Dziemianowicz of the *New York Daily News* was somewhat less impressed, noting that "the play eventually implodes. It begins as an exploration of the corrosiveness of living with crunched economics and curdled desires, but takes a sharp, not altogether logical, detour."[12] I share Dziemianowicz's dimmer view, but, as I will argue in the pages that follow, it is the city of the title—boldly asserted then equivocally disavowed—that makes the play's fiery detour wholly, if disturbingly, logical.

Yet these reviewers' points of agreement are notable for what they reveal, both about the titular city as self-evidently metaphoric and, less obviously, about the definitional and affective elasticity of the deindustrial. Here Detroit, so inextricably linked to a specific downward trajectory from industrial might to deindustrial decrepitude is "not necessarily" the actual place because it also operates as a figure. It is synonymous with a larger national econo-affective crisis that is simultaneously personal and collective: one of "embattled psyches," "fraying" social relations, stagnant wages, and constricted hopes for economic mobility and self-reinvention now and in the foreseeable future. By this logic, in this period Detroit is to contemporary fiscal and social debility as Kleenex is to facial tissue: a generic descriptor. It is every place, no place, and a very specific place at the same time, even if—indeed *because*—that specificity is simultaneously invoked and disavowed.

This figural economy is true of both D'Amour's title and the ubiquitous formulations of "not Detroit"-ness used to characterize other American cities. Further, because Detroit's particular economic history remains nascent in its figural potential, its use as a metaphor for both a generic state of the economy and a state of mind expands the deindustrial itself beyond images of factory shutdowns and displacements into a much larger econo-affective formation that is local and national, working and middle class, both transracial and deeply racialized. Thus, in D'Amour's play, Detroit is synonymous with a ubiquitous sense of fiscal precarity and "curdled desires" regardless of which "-ation"—financialization, globalization, privatization, or literal deindustrialization—may be to blame. In addition, the city's prosperous past also fuels fantasies of a now-vanished moment seemingly free of these contemporary economic and affective, personal and civic devastations: one that included the comparatively greater social mobility and financial security purchased with the industrial era labor-management compact. "Detroit" stands in for both the precarious present and a fiscal-social solidity that seems irretrievably lost, providing a ready point of nostalgia against which contemporary diminishment and anxiety can be defined.

Detroit was the first play of the 2012–13 New York theater season to "not necessarily" figure the city, but it was not the last. *Motown the Musical*, Berry Gordy's autobiography-as-musical-review, which opened on April 14, 2013, ran until January 2015, and returned to Broadway in 2016, is also not necessarily set in Detroit. Here it is the show's glossy spectacle; the emphasis on Motown as a brand and a "family," not a place; an eventual relocation to Los Angeles; and a set rendering the original site of Hitsville USA as a generic outline of an urban street that repeatedly and, in my view, very deliberately distance the company and its founder from the city of their births. In *Motown the Musical*, raciality and heteronormativity are equally obvious. All the leading performers are African American, and white characters are almost always explicitly referred to as such within the production. In scenes depicting Gordy's relationship with Diana Ross, each calls the other "Black" both as an endearment and as a shared tactic to mark their battles with, and successes in prevailing over, a wide range of racist obstacles within and beyond the entertainment industry.

A rousing competition between the Temptations and the Four Tops opens the production, presaging the intracorporate, quasi-family rivalries to come. The scene depicts a rehearsal for the upcoming televised *Motown 25* anniversary celebration, the show that would feature Michael Jackson's famous performance of "Billy Jean"—which was not produced by Motown—that launched the moonwalk. As we join Berry Gordy in his plush Los Angeles sitting room, we learn that a crisis is brewing around the show. Gordy is demoralized; key members of the Motown "family" are refusing to participate in this commemoration of his legacy. In one of the show's recurring themes, an aide tells Gordy that he has only his own prodigiously capitalist work ethic to blame: "You told them to compete with you: the giant who controls their lives." We then flash back to critical moments in Motown's and Gordy's intertwined histories punctuated by the company's hits and two new Gordy songs. His relationship with Diana Ross is central to the action. It ultimately disintegrates, presented as yet another casualty of Gordy's work ethic and, perhaps, Ross's insufficient gratitude. Yet by the end, Gordy and his artists are one harmonious happy family again with Ross presiding. A rousing representation of *Motown 25*, without Michael Jackson's legendary performance of his non-Motown hit, concludes with the song "Ain't No Mountain High Enough": nothing will keep even Gordy's legal rivals from celebrating him.

If spectacle is the defining mode of contemporary capitalism, as Situationist theorist Guy Debord has asserted, this musical celebration of Gordy's business prowess is one of Broadway's most obvious examples.[13] The production's vibrant colors, virtuosic singing and dancing, and broad temporal and spatial sweeps underscore both its triumphalist narrative and the magnitude of the Motown legacy. Further, its lush score of recognizable favorites and sumptuously detailed 1960s and 1970s costumes, hair, and makeup (in contrast to the very spare sets, which avoid any recognizable references to actual places) offer an equally spectacular dual temporality. The show feels simultaneously "young"—energetic, hopeful, highly affective— and nostalgic: wistful and elegiac. But this nostalgia is not only a function of the Motown classics that propel the production. It also arises from the show's uncomplicated relationship to its post–World War II escapist musical predecessors: recalling the late industrial era's prosperity and potential for self-invention, even across racial lines, in the immediate post–Great Recession context.[14] Like these classic postwar Broadway musicals, there is also a "marriage plot," though I would argue that the real enduring love story *Motown the Musical* tells is not Gordy's romance with Diana Ross but his romance with capitalism.

Reviews for the show were decidedly mixed, with Isherwood of the *New York Times* noting that song placement is sometimes "forced if not ludicrous" and the dialogue "vinyl stiff."[15] Herb Boyd of the *New York Daily News* writes that, while the show has been dismissed as "slapdash, sketchy and lack[ing] coherence, . . . such negative notices have not dismayed or discouraged audiences at sold-out performances."[16]

The city of Motown's birth is fairly peripheral to the overall plot of *Motown the Musical*. Specifics like native son Joe Louis and the 1967 riots are included, but by act II and the company's move to Los Angeles, the few remaining references to the city are as generic and ambivalent as D'Amour's disavowal, for example: "You left Detroit but you still love it."[17] Here Detroit's figural potential is initially inseparable from the possibility of successful self-fashioning and social mobility synonymous with its industrial past, particularly for the African American residents who migrated from the South to work in the automobile industry. Gordy's parents did precisely this, moving from Georgia to the city a few years before his birth. Within the frame of the show, the city is, at first, both fertile and racially inhospitable ground for the individual expressive and entrepreneurial initiative and tireless canny capitalism embodied by Gordy and his Motown family: a continuation, and a racial rewriting, of the Fordist origin narrative of the hard-working inventive genius birthing a wildly successful mass phenomenon. As Detroit becomes "Motown" over the course of act I, it operates as both deeply racially specific (a uniquely African American cultural crucible) and race-transcendent—no longer a racialized place but the "Sound of Young America." In that process, the city itself as a racially specific crucible and shorthand for a mode of production—the literal Motor Town—recedes into the background, hollowed out like the outlines of an urban street and skyline that signal its location onstage in the production. Ultimately, it becomes an evolutionary relic, one that must be abandoned on the road to better things: here Los Angeles, a newer, wealthier "industry" town.

After the company's relocation to Los Angeles in 1972, Detroit is no longer the fertile ground where "every street corner" offered black talent and energy; it becomes, instead, a reminder of the small-time and the provincial. One of Gordy's aides challenges him by describing his spending as a mismatch between "LA." ambitions and a "Detroit budget." Within the logic of both race-specific and race-transcendent capitalism that defines the show and Gordy as a character, this relocation is not a betrayal of his hometown but the simultaneous acknowledgment of its inevitable limits and the fulfillment of its nascent promise. As the character Smokey Robinson observes as if to preempt the charge that Gordy abandoned the city—a charge tinged with racial abandonment as well—sometimes one has to leave home.[18]

Ultimately, *Motown the Musical* effortlessly—indeed spectacularly—aligns with evolutionary narratives of race-neutral global post-industriality as natural and inevitable: the next logical stage in capitalist development. Detroit, in this view, will either disappear, like vestigial gills, or be productively reshaped by these same evolutionary forces and a new relentlessly hard-working Gordy-esque visionary. *Motown the Musical* ends in 1983, affirming the interpersonal and transracial affective balm of the Motown sound: a nostalgic reminder of both the good old days—even when those days were sometimes awful—and the power of the exceptional individual's ability to fully transcend the city's (and nation's) racism, its narrow industrial focus, economic precarity, and family dysfunction and betrayal through capitalist genius and hard work. The show as a whole representationally severs Motown the brand from Motown the place at the precise moments—1972, 1983, and 2013—that this place was increasingly linked to obsolescence and urban decrepitude: to the obvious failures of its industrial era promise. Within the context of *Motown the Musical*, the city becomes "lovable" in its particulars precisely because, in 1972, 1983, and again in 2013, it could, indeed must, be left behind.

In Dominique Morisseau's drama *Detroit '67*, the first in her award-winning trilogy of plays set in and about Detroit, both the city and its infamous race riot are essential in their specificity, and are not metaphors.[19] The author describes the work as her "love song" to the actual place, though it is more accurately a love song to a vision of the city's potential nascent in its past, even in one of its most fraught moments.[20] The show, a joint production of the Public Theater and the Classical

Theatre of Harlem, opened at the Public on February 26, 2013, and, after moving uptown, closed at the National Black Theatre on April 14, 2013. It featured four African American actors, two men and two women, and one explicitly racially marked white woman; it too is strongly heteronormative.

Steady, reliable widow Chelle wants to set up an after-hours club in the basement of the home she and her brother Lank (short for "Langston") inherited from their parents. Lank and his best friend, Sly, have other ideas. Sly, an "honest hustler," has an ongoing and seemingly unrequited flirtation with Chelle.[21] Bunny, a playfully sexy, vivacious family friend, serves as Chelle's affective counterpoint; her breeziness conceals her keen powers of observation, neighborhood savvy, and self-awareness. As the 1967 riots come to a boil nearby, Lank and Sly return to the house with a battered white woman, Caroline, whom they found wandering dazed on the street. Caroline is on the run from an abusive relationship with a corrupt Detroit police officer: the very embodiment of the racist "pigs" who routinely brutalize the neighborhood and are now shooting black residents first and asking questions later, if they ask any at all. Chelle, deeply unhappy that this mystery woman and her racial baggage are now ensconced in her home, agrees to let her stay and work in the basement club till she's back on her feet. Caroline and Lank have a romantic connection, much to Chelle's vocal displeasure, but Caroline ultimately flees the house, afraid for the trouble she may bring to both Lank and herself. The trouble comes anyway. As the city burns and police surge into the area, Lank and Sly are caught in the crossfire, and Sly, who is unarmed and trying to protect his and Lank's new business, is chased down as a presumptive looter by the police, shot, and killed. Ultimately, Chelle concludes that she and Lank must move ahead and open "Sly and Lank's Feel Good Shack" and realize Sly's dream, but the final image—her solitary and melancholy dance to the Four Tops' "Reach Out, I'll Be There"—marks this decision as no simple, hopeful triumphalism.

Detroit '67 was realistically and intimately staged, the primary focus being Chelle and Lank's unfinished basement-club. The warmth of the space marks it as a site of black joy and self-sustenance. The violent spectacle of the riot—fetishized in local and national news of the period—is kept offstage here. The audience fully registers the devastation of Sly's murder by the police, but Morisseau privileges this intimate space of hope and solace over scenes of black subjection. Indeed, Chelle and Lank imagine the future "Feel Good Shack" as an extension of this very room: as communal infrastructure, "some way for people to dance and feel good."[22]

The play was awarded the Kennedy Prize for Drama Inspired by American History in February 2014. Yet, at the time of its New York production, *Detroit '67* received surprisingly negative reviews. Isherwood of the *New York Times* called it "tidy...formulaic,...and disappointingly bland."[23] *Village Voice* critic Alexis Soloski mystifyingly described it as a "comedy-drama," noting that it appeared to "vacillate uneasily between the naturalistic and the sitcomic" with an "anemic" structure and the riot plot "contrived."[24] Soloski's review ends curiously and glibly, focusing on the final scene in which Chelle dances alone to the song "Reach Out, I'll Be

There"; Soloski concludes lamely: "Whatever the Motor City may suffer, Motown will endure." This conclusion not only reiterates the same quasi-evolutionary logic severing the brand in its soothing, seemingly race-neutral nostalgia from the very specific troubling particulars of the city of its birth but also dismissively and utterly misreads the arc of the play, which is about the inseparability of this sound and the city as a site of black innovation. In so doing, this review reproduces yet another aspect of Detroit's figural work: the city is a sonic madeleine of the good old days with Motown's music as generically American, easily severable from a very specific racial history and politics that were very bad indeed.

Like *Motown the Musical, Detroit '67* turns on the promise of social mobility through a risky-wise use of capital and the affective balm of the Motown sound. But it explicitly repudiates both the facile slippage between that sound, the city as (no)place, and the salvific potential of a capitalist work ethic. In so doing, *Detroit '67* starkly underscores the racial particularity intrinsic to Detroit's current figural work. This racial specificity and an accompanying history of racial(-ist) violence operate alongside—indeed aggressively haunt—figurations of the city as a relic of white loss and a placeless sound that heals the nation's racial wounds. Though *Detroit '67* focuses on the immediate period of the riot, it also conjures the city's long history of African Americans' struggles for decent housing and equal opportunity, as well as its racist policing.

In Morisseau's Detroit, as in the city itself both before and after 1967, neither capital, hard work, nor that "Sound of Young America" is race transcendent, and economic precarity is a function of racism, not deindustrialization. Lank is invested in the industrial era promise of successful self-fashioning both despite and because of his clear-eyed assessment that this promise never fully applied to him and is itself already on the wane. In articulating his claim on that promise, he deploys perhaps the most persistent and genuinely transracial figural element of the city: its potential for both personal and civic rebirth. Hope literally defines Detroit. It is enshrined in the city's motto: "We hope for better things. It will arise from the ashes." Lank imagines the city as Malcolm X's Mecca, an African American utopia: "Colored folks moving this city forward."[25] Morisseau is clearly more concerned with this utopic potential of the actual city, and the personal costs of investing in it, than with whether the commercial beat goes on, though her hope too is rooted in an image of the city's prosperous past. Indeed, her "Playwright's Note" is strikingly similar in tone to the nostalgic monologue in the final scene of *Detroit.*[26]

Taken together, these three plays expose the basics of Detroit's figural function on the national stage. Detroit-as-figure contains and reconciles five interrelated yet contradictory elements in discourses of American deindustrialization by serving simultaneously as the following:

- generic for a quasi-evolutionary cycle of economic prosperity and decline independent of place, mode of production, or demographic particulars (Detroit as dinosaur);

- a stand-in for the irretrievable loss of a solid and unproblematically good middle-class life—a loss that is both inevitable and, if one is sufficiently visionary and hard-working, wholly avoidable (Detroit as ruin for most, while a springboard for capitalism's truly meritorious);
- a diffuse structure of feeling that appropriates blackness as race-neutral nostalgia (Motown as transracial balm);[27];
- *both* a very specific history of race, class, and labor whose violent particulars are too often forgotten *and* a contemporary raced dystopia whose current African American population is directly and solely responsible for the city's economic decline (Detroit as cautionary tale); and
- the undying personal and civic hope for better things, as well as the ashes that both inspire and befall it (Detroit as phoenix).

Each play's "Detroitness" locates these five dimensions at the dramatic intersection of race, place, home, and work; each is haunted by specific moments in the city's history of this intersection. Each plot takes up the interrelationships between domesticity, work (or lack thereof), and dreams of the good life. In both *Detroit* and *Detroit '67*, these interrelationships are exposed and undone by neighboring strangers. In *Motown the Musical*, they are undone by the market and by intimates, though both processes are represented as the inevitable consequences of a successful business. *Detroit* and *Detroit '67* end in fire. All three plays also take up performance in various forms: Kenny's, Sharon's, and Ben's dissembling in *Detroit* (performance as "faking"); boxing, self-fashioning, and, of course, Motown's theatricality and actual productions in *Motown the Musical* (performance as "making"); dancing, dissembling, self-display, and, again, the Motown sound in *Detroit '67* (performance as both "making" and "faking").[28]

In addition to the themes of domesticity, work, hope for a good (or at least better) life, and performance, acting in all three plays relies on conventions of theatrical naturalism to varying degrees. While the history and particulars of naturalist acting and mise en scène exceed the scope of my argument here, the spectatorial invitation extended by this mode of onstage representation is crucial to the figural economy of American deindustrialization generally and Detroit as figure in particular. Audiences of naturalistic productions are invited to engage the works psychologically, focusing on individual characters' personalities and motivations rather than larger structural forces as drivers of the behaviors which, in turn, drive the plot and outcome. Further, audiences are also invited to operate as quasi-ethnographers, albeit not, typically, critical ones: observing the patterns of expressivity, behavioral norms, visual and aural structures, and social rituals defining the worlds of the plays and against which individual characters are assessed.[29] This focus on the individual and "culture" is, to use anthropologist Micaela di Leonardo's apt phrase, one of the ways Americans historically "launder politics from the public sphere": simplifying or eliminating the effects of collective and structural forces and, frequently, eliding history altogether.[30] Indeed, in D'Amour's play in particular, Detroit's very specific racial history is laundered.

My analysis identifies the figural elements of "Detroitness" and follows the ghosts of the city's history conjured by all three plays using two interrelated operations: "re-siting" and "re-citing." These operations, rooted in performance theory, are central to the circulation and materialization of the city's representational potency onstage and off. They make Detroit-as-figure go by selectively invoking and sometimes whitewashing aspects of the city's history, burnishing or tarnishing its metaphoric potential in the process. Performance-based heuristics are particularly appropriate given one other element of the city's figural work: its intimate connections to performance in multiple modes.

DETROIT AND REGIMES OF PERFORMANCE

Detroit and performance have an uncanny—if largely unexamined—relationship, making theater a paradigm case for demonstrating the city's figural work and performance theory an ideal tool for investigating it. For example, D'Amour's slippery "not necessarily" reminds us of both Detroit's figural mutability—meaningful because it is and is "not necessarily" the actual place—and the "not/not-not" condition performance theorist Richard Schechner sees as constitutive of performance itself.[31] The actor is not the character, but she is not-not the character either. Schechner states that, though this betwixt and between condition is highly generative, it is also "precarious because it is subjunctive, liminal, transitional: it rests not on how things are but on how things are not; its existence depends on agreements kept among all participants, including the audience."[32]

Schechner's precarious subjunctive both closely glosses the themes of *Detroit* and *Detroit '67*, where liminality and the hypothetical are plot points, and describes the city "not necessarily" specified by D'Amour's title. The latter dimension was particularly apparent in March 2013, three months after *Detroit* closed its off-Broadway run, and two months before it won an Obie Award, when Michigan's Republican governor Rick Snyder appointed Kevyn Orr, a Washington, DC, bankruptcy attorney who worked on the Chrysler Corporation's 2009 restructuring, to serve as emergency manager: a position whose profile ultimately included planning for and presiding over the largest municipal bankruptcy in US history. With its elected officials still in office but stripped by the emergency manager of all meaningful authority, creditors demanding payment, the specter of major assets including city parks and Detroit Institute of Arts collections being sold off to satisfy them, and city services and salary and pension agreements with city workers increasingly uncertain, Detroit itself now occupied the precarious subjunctive at the most basic level of governance. One resident summarized the situation by observing, "The city is past being a city now; it's gone," though, one might add, not gone completely as more than 700,000 people still lived there.[33] Detroit was "not necessarily" a functional city during this period, but it was not-not one either and it has been figured this way in national media for more than thirty years.

Its status as precariously subjunctive before and during bankruptcy proceedings is not the city's only connection to performance. Detroit's centrality to the figural economy of the deindustrial also arises from its unique industrial era techno-managerial spectacles of productivity and efficiency.[34] Before Detroit was inextricably linked to the "ruin," these spectacles were central to its brand in the popular imaginary. *Motown the Musical* makes the connection explicit in the young Berry Gordy's telling slip of the tongue. After vividly describing his vision of a vertically integrated production process to his family-investors, he concludes excitedly: "At the end of the line [are] cars . . . uh . . . STARS!." Motown's indebtedness to the Ford assembly line is an obvious, though not unique, example. In the city as both place and figure, these spectacles of techno-managerial efficiency haunt its deindustrial iconography, like the abandoned thirty-five-acre Packard Plant designed by Albert Kahn, conjuring *both* past triumphs *and* current devastation. At the most basic figural level, the city functions as the deindustrial's longest-running drama: another way it secures its utility in D'Amour's title and as a "metaphor." Detroit's value as deindustrialization's tragedy, or dark comedy, arises from its spectacular ruination and resulting melancholic nostalgia, more than a century of American racial and underclass voyeurism, and the fiscal cliffhanger of its bankruptcy proceedings, coupled with the fact this ruination is cast as the mirror opposite of its former extraordinary industrial productivity. That productivity was also represented in spectacular terms. Indeed, the figural potency of Detroit as exemplar of both industrial might and deindustrial decrepitude often centers on images of the very same infrastructure, decades apart.

Industrial(-ous) Performances

The Ford Motor Company (FMC) River Rouge Plant, at one time the largest industrial facility in the world, exemplifies the city's palimpsest of cultural and techno-managerial performances, though without the affective charge of there/ then versus here/now that powers so much industrial nostalgia and racialized scopophilia. The plant was a tourist attraction. A Ford promotional film from 1939 noted that it hosted more than 1 million visitors from all over the world; it was a spectacular production of production as spectacle.[35] Indeed, visitors can still tour the Rouge. Currently billed as a "living lab," with efficiency restaged for the green era, the plant is "Detroit's #1 Automobile Attraction": "More than a walk along an assembly line, the Ford Rouge Factory Tour is an excursion where environmental innovation and industrial production combine."[36] The tour includes a "multisensory theater experience" in the "Art of Manufacturing Theater" where viewers can engage in virtual multisensory ethnography as they feel "the heat from blast furnaces, the rumble of stamping presses and the spray mist from paint robots," set to an original score performed by the Detroit Symphony Orchestra.[37] This realistic evocation of the plant experience is key to the Art of Manufacturing Theater's function as a quasi-ethnographic site: one echoed in the naturalistic stagings of *Detroit* and *Detroit '67* in particular. It reinforces the view that, even today, industrial production is to Detroit what *kecak* dance is to Bali: a genre of indigenous cultural performance. Further, factory tours and evocations of factory labor remind us of Schechner's insistence that performances depend on the agreements we keep when we audience such spectacles whether these feature capitalist efficiency in the plant or intimate domestic scenes—especially agreements about presumptive spectatorial positions: the spectacles' implied normative audiences. Thus, we can agree that simulated heat from blast furnaces and rumbles of stamping presses make for great theater, especially if/because we don't actually work with the real thing.[38]

Detroit's techno-managerial regimes of performance are particularly fraught around race in ways that reverberate across all three plays. Two examples of "spectacular efficiency" from the city's history underscore the presumptive racialization of normative spectatorship for the city's political economic dramas as white from very early in its industrial past. This presumption of a hegemonically white audience is crucial to understanding both the city as a figuration of deindustrial decrepitude and affective responses to deindustrialization itself; it is woven into nostalgia for the industrial age. Both of these exemplary historic techno-managerial displays turn on racial "rehabilitation" projects designed to produce model cities as spectacles of benevolent white efficiency on the local and national stage.

The first came from the man who built the River Rouge plant. In November 1931, in an attempt to "cast himself as the benevolent caretaker of black Detroit," Henry Ford "rescued" the village of Inkster.[39] Using rhetoric that would be recycled in later urban renewal initiatives, the area to be rehabilitated was characterized as a squalid black slum.[40] Staging himself as the "patriarch of Inkster," Ford provided much-needed services through a structure reminiscent of the sharecropping and debt peonage many African American residents left the South to escape. Historian Beth Tompkins Bates writes:

> Though often portrayed as an example of philanthropy, the Inkster project was actually a loan from Ford to black FMC workers and their families in Inkster. Rather than being made available in cash, the loan arrived in the form of commodities—food at the Ford commissary, coal delivered from the Ford factory, shoes from Ford-owned stores. Black Inkster residents repaid the loan with their labor.[41]

Ford's "web of obligation, requirements, and control" was not optional and was continuous with the work of the company's Sociological Department discussed later in this chapter.[42] The Inkster initiative arose from both Ford's personal racist paternalism and a PR plan designed as much to rehabilitate his image at the height of the Great Depression as it was to rehabilitate the village.[43] Like the Rouge plant, the Inkster project was praised as a spectacle of efficiency, though again spectato-rial perspective was key. Bates notes that the dire economic circumstances of 1931–32 meant it "was hardly a time for biting the hand that fed African Americans in Inkster," while noting: "The greater the distance from the project, the more posi-tive the evaluation."[44] Ford's Inkster initiative reminds us that techno-managerial performance as constitutive "making" may also include plenty of both PR "faking" and dispossessive "taking," and that urban "efficiencies" are themselves functions of racialized agreements about normative spectatorship.

The second example comes from the period touted as the city's industrial hey-day. In the early to mid-1960s, Detroit was praised as a "Model City" for attacking racialized poverty through wise stewardship of federal War on Poverty resources. "Model" was not simply a metaphor. The federal Demonstration Cities Act of 1966, a name remarkably replete with performance implications, enabled the designation of a section of Detroit's inner core as a "city within a city" where antipoverty efforts could be concentrated, then assessed.[45] Though federal funding particulars were never what city leaders had hoped for, Detroit was judged a top performer by a wide range of national assessors, including then vice president Hubert Humphrey. It was considered "one of the best programs in the nation" and was a tourist stop for administrators seeking model urban antipoverty operations.[46] These external asses-sors and other national actors were stunned when the city that so efficiently and publicly demonstrated progress on racialized poverty on the national stage erupted in violence in July 1967.[47] The city's African American residents, who did not share these glowing assessments, and who continued to navigate flagrantly segregationist housing policies and racist policing, were perhaps less surprised.[48] The 1967 riot was both a direct repudiation of the economic efficiency of the "Model City" and a national counterspectacle. Images of burned-out buildings, carcasses of the riot's aftermath, circulated nationally, including on the cover of *Life* magazine.[49] These images of internal combustion, so central to the current city's figural work, haunt each play discussed in this chapter.

RE-SITING AND RE-CITING DETROIT

Detroit, Detroit '67, and *Motown the Musical* all draw upon Detroit's history of highly efficient techno-managerial performance, now subsumed in "ruins," and its equally specific history of race, home, and work. Each play re-sites and re-cites elements of these histories. Detroit is the figure organizing the affective chaos of the deindus-trial. Re-siting and re-citing are two operations powering its figural potential on the national stage. For example, each city asserting itself as "not Detroit" affirms the figural potency of re-siting and re-citing by negation. Re-siting and re-citing are also heuristic tools for tracking the ways the city's history enters its various figura-tions. Elin Diamond and Richard Schechner, among many others, remind us that "re" is a core feature of performance.[50] Theater in particular is defined by operations of re-siting (changing plays' settings, changing staging) and re-citing (memorizing and delivering lines, the intertextuality of dramatic texts, actors quoting others' behavioral bits). Yet "re-siting/re-citing" brings a critical precision to discussions of Detroit's figural work in these three productions that compensates for both the formulation's expansiveness and its unwieldy proliferation of homophonic, hyphenated variants. It exposes the complex interconnections between race, (home-) place, and history and the subsequent repetition and circulation of these curious amalgams within figural Detroitness. In so doing, it presses us to regard D'Amour's "not necessarily" with suspicion.

Re-siting/re-citing is neither simple re-enactment nor an argument for the persistence of transhistorical patterns. It builds on "surrogation," Joseph Roach's term for the driver of the "three-sided relationship" between performance, history, and substitution, by insisting on the explicit inclusion of a fourth term: "place."[51] By insisting on the *geographic specificity* of historical patterns and tropes, "re-siting" calls D'Amour's slippery "not necessarily" to account. In that play, though not only there, "Detroit" is, and is more than, a substitute for nameless contemporary white middle-class precarity because the work's claims to affective authenticity, reinforced by its naturalistic acting and staging, arise directly from the sited specificity of the title, even if that specificity is disavowed. For example, "re-siting" conjures decades of urban renewal initiatives that literally re-sited, and in so doing disrupted, Detroit's established African American communities: part of the historical backstory to *Detroit '67*. Re-siting also describes white flight to the very first-ring suburbs in which *Detroit* is actually set.[52] The middle-class white couple at the center of this play's action is thus inextricably linked to an earlier generation of the city's white families not only by another character's wistful, nostalgic monologue about industrial era prosperity and neighborliness but by the larger historical reality that *these* people are here because *those* others, especially African Americans, were not.[53] When a whitewashed version of some of *those* others moves in next door, well, there goes the neighborhood. Re-siting likewise reminds us of Motown's move from the city of its birth to Los Angeles, and of runaway auto plants and suppliers leaving the so-called Rust Belt to set up shop in both the southern United States and the global south to avoid unionization and chase cheap labor. And it recalls those who cannot re-site so easily: residents like Chelle and Lank in *Detroit '67*, who are tethered to the city by family ties, personal property, or the stubborn hope for better things.

"Re-citing," as expressive retelling, underscores the interplay between historical fidelity and creative refashioning of specific historical events that powers *Detroit '67* and *Motown the Musical*, as well as *Detroit*. But it also illuminates a key element of the city's figural work perhaps best explained by contrasting it with performance theorist Joseph Roach's formulation, "surrogation." Trauma and loss are central to surrogation, which is, in its essence, a strategy of forging cultural continuity through imperfect representational repair; communally sanctioned substitutes are attempts to fill in "the cavities created by loss through death or other forms of departure."[54] These substitutes may exceed the gaps they fill, or they may fall short, but they always mark a temporal and narrative progression. Surrogation moves forward. Loss is a matter of the past, repaired more or less successfully by representational substitutes in the ongoing present.

Detroit's status as a seemingly self-evident metaphor for contemporary precarity and decrepitude depends on precisely the opposite type of temporality: the present is the wound/rupture that can only be further irritated, never healed, by representations of the city's prosperous past, however burnished and/or fictive such representations may be and however frequently they are offered. Detroit's manifold losses and this construction of a mythic golden age are inseparable: inextricably bound together by its unfinished racial economic business. To re-cite/re-site the city in these plays is to simultaneously conjure images of its mystified, putatively race-neutral golden age of industrial productivity (even when exposed as fictive) *and* those of its degraded, highly racialized, precarious present. As a figure characterizing and organizing the deindustrial's affective and racial fields, the city is meaningful because it conjures this here-now/there-then doubleness. Re-citing/re-siting the city always transplants both peril and promise, wound and balm: a tale of white industrial utopia and a racialized fall from economic grace.

This doubleness intrinsic to re-citing/re-siting deindustrial Detroit is central to the elegiac tone of all three plays, and to the countless encomia to the city itself. Further, hope—the city's affective currency for purchasing better things in the future—cannot fully fill present cavities caused by trauma and loss in any simple way. Hope is the most amorphous of strategies for representational and personal repair. As these three plays demonstrate, hope in the context of Detroit is either naively misplaced, a function of delusion; profoundly existentially costly with unrepaired and unrepairable wounds persisting alongside it; or not worth the trouble when the exceptional individual can simply leave and profit elsewhere.

"Re-citing," as both a representational and a critical methodological practice, reminds us of the work of textual citation: those rhetorical tactics establishing lines of evidence, provenance, and affiliation.[55] Yet, as the scholarly enterprise sometimes demonstrates, citation can also introduce errors: sloppy paraphrases, misquotes and inaccuracies, naive or well-meaning failures to discern or account for larger contexts, unintended or unwanted associations. Both types of re-citation operate in these three plays. The city's history is invoked as provenance authorizing *Detroit '67* and some moments in *Motown the Musical*; that same history is problematically paraphrased even as it is disclaimed in *Detroit*. As a critical operation, *re*-citing calls attention to such tactical deployments of citations, thus exposing how specific images and historical elements produce figural "Detroitness" through plot points or allusions.

All three plays re-cite tropes of their theatrical predecessors. *Motown the Musical* does this generically; it is the classic jukebox musical built on re-citing oldies. *Detroit* plays on and inverts the domestic disintegration of Edward Albee's *Who's Afraid of Virginia Woolf?*, with the younger couple as the agents of destruction and a seemingly imaginary dog replacing an imaginary son.[56] *Detroit '67* is in direct conversation with Lorraine Hansberry's *A Raisin in the Sun*. The name of one of the main characters, "Lank," is short for "Langston," recalling the line from Langston Hughes's poem "Harlem" ("What happens to a dream deferred?") that gave the earlier play its title. Plot particulars around investments of family funds are very similar. Both examine the fulfillment of family dreams, and both center on strong female characters, Chelle and Mama, whose "dynamic complexity" draws audiences into their personal pain.[57] Bunny's insouciance replaces Beneatha's emerging politicization, and the consequences of racist violence in Detroit '67 are lethal, though both plays end on hopes that better things will rise from the ashes of racist destruction.

"Re-citing" is directly linked to the normative workings of performativity, which Judith Butler defines as "citationality": a process that is not only discursive but also embodied and material.[58] Performativity acquires its social force through repetition, which produces stability as an effect. This perspective is particularly useful for illuminating the ways Detroit-as-figure subsumes and reconciles the various discourses and affects of the deindustrial. For example, the relentless circulation of Detroit's ruins imagery works in this way: performatively stabilizing the city as a figure of racialized atavism in the popular imaginary. In Butler's analysis, citation with a difference, as in drag's recoding of conventions of femininity, has the potential to expose and interrupt hegemonic constructions of privilege and identity. But, as my discussion of Detroit in particular will demonstrate, citation with a difference is not always replete with critical potential. On the contrary, sometimes re-citing reminds us that naive or reflexive reiterations of figural Detroitness merely reshuffle and rearticulate hegemonic terms and tropes, providing opportunities for regressive iterations of power and amnesia to insert, disguise, and perpetuate themselves. "Re-" further calls to uncritical reiterations of "common sense" understandings like Detroit as self-evidently and amorphously "metaphoric."

As critical tools, re-siting/re-citing insists on simultaneous attention to history, place, and racialized representations within figural economies. Further, re-siting/re-citing underscores the sited and citational nature of affect itself: the emotional forces and residues that course through or cling to history-in-place and are then repeated. Anthropologist Kathleen Stewart implicitly acknowledges this spatialization when she notes that "ordinary affects" are "a kind of *contact zone* where the overdeterminations of circulations, events, conditions, technologies, and flows of power *literally take place.*"[59] Re-siting/re-citing thus allows us to tease out relationships between bodies on- and offstage, history, and the peculiar amalgam of wishful thinking, willful amnesia, desires for racial containment, and for transracial mobility represented by Detroit-as-figure, both in the specific works examined here and in the figural economy of the deindustrial.

Re-siting/re-citing complicates theater theorist Soyica Diggs Colbert's "repetition/reproduction" dyad: a performative structure she sees as "the DNA of black expressive culture broadly, and drama specifically."[60] In her view, this dyad is linked to other "re-s"—reparations and "rituals of repair": "the symbolic reordering of the social and political hierarchy" articulated in the canon of black drama she examines.[61]

Motown the Musical works in just the way Diggs Colbert describes. Berry Gordy both repeats Fordist tactics and repeatedly disrupts racist hierarchies of cultural production even as the Motown sound repairs the nation's racial wounds, at least within the context of the play. In addition, the dulcet tones of the company's classic hits affectively suture together business rivals, intimates, races, and the show itself: nostalgic, acoustical repair of personal and collective traumas. On the other hand, *Detroit '67*, the play most specifically sited in the city, re-cites the visceral, irreparable trauma of the riot: personalizing it in Sly's murder and ending with Chelle's solitary grief and commitment. Yet, the most optimistic reading of this final scene does not demonstrate repair of Chelle's, or the neighborhood's, losses. Here, re-siting/re-citing Detroit's history onstage reminds us that repetition/reproduction does not always guarantee productive rethinking of the city's, or the United States', racial past, nor does it provide a template for a just and equitable future.

Rather than simple repair, the figural Detroitness reproduced in all three plays presses another question: What happens to reparations deferred? Certainly, as Langston Hughes's poem reminds us, there are explosions: the "Dresdens of dreams" Herron describes in the first epigraph to this chapter. These explosions are explicitly cited in *Detroit '67* and *Motown the Musical* and are troublingly re-sited/re-cited in *Detroit*. Further, in all three plays, these explosions are inseparable from their aftermaths: the ashes from which better things, we hope, will arise. All three plays, like the city itself, are haunted by this cycle of racial violence, the ashes of its dissipation, and subsequent stubborn hope that repeats, so far without repair.

Haunting is an effect produced by re-siting/re-citing: the ghost a recurring reminder of the now inaccessible dis- or replaced original. As sociologist Avery Gordon notes, haunting is "a constitutive condition of modern life."[62] It is also a constitutive condition of the theater, one theater historian Marvin Carlson memorably describes as the "ghostly sense [of] something coming back" onstage.[63] Detroit itself is often figured as a "ghost town."[64] *Detroit, Detroit "67*, and *Motown the Musical* are haunted by Detroit's history of racialized(-ist) political economy, including dreams of a good life in times of structural economic change. In all three plays the haunting begins at home. Homes in these plays are not simply the results of dreams come true and, as such, respite from the hard labors that produced them. They are also capital essential to attaining and staging the successful, decent, entrepreneurial self. Both Detroit's racial(-ist) history of industrial era prosperity and its present deindustrial precarity operate as ghost characters: "seething presence[s], acting on and often meddling with taken-for-granted realities" of homes in each play.[65]

HAUNTED HOUSES AND FORDIST GHOSTS

All homes are capital, of course: our biggest investment, we are often reminded. Characters in these three plays are intent on monetizing their assets to acquire a good life. *Detroit*'s Ben, a currently unemployed former loan officer, once helped others do precisely this. Now he works at home creating an online financial planning business: "helping people with their credit scores, that sort of thing," while referring to himself ("Ha-ha") as a "deadbeat." [66] Ben and his wife, Mary, own their home—or, more accurately, the bank owns it. Kenny and Sharon, living closer to the economic edge, appropriated the empty house of a deceased aunt. They "will probably buy it, though."[67] As prospective financial planner Ben coaches, "That's the way to do it—from a friend or family. You can avoid a lot of closing costs." Later we learn from Kenny's uncle that he and Sharon were squatters; they broke into the home through a back window. Is it this precarity, toxic envy, or both that impel Kenny to advise the would-be financial planner: "You've gotta hang on to that house, Ben."[68] Kenny is certainly the agent who renders this impossible as anything other than a hope to rise from the ashes.

Detroit '67 also stages the family home as capital and the tactical (mis-)appropriation of family assets. Chelle and Lank inherited money and their parents' home, which Chelle turns into an after-hours club: a "blind pig" in Detroit parlance of the time. The basement club is an investment, with profits to be reinvested in the house and in college tuition for Chelle's son Julius. In a direct parallel with *A Raisin in the Sun*, Lank has other ideas: to invest their inherited funds in Shepley's Bar and liquor license in a joint venture with his friend Sly. Racial re-siting enables the prospective purchase: the bar's white owner is decamping to the suburbs. This investment would pay both financial and social dividends: a chance to be "legit" and free from the increasingly brutal, racially motivated police crackdowns on unlicensed after-hours clubs.[69] Initially, the family home is enough for Chelle, and a bar is "a hustle-on-the-books."[70] Ultimately, in a turnabout that literally rises from the ashes of a burning city and the loss of their friend, the bar becomes a "stake in Detroit we ain't had before," one that could make the city itself a hospitable home.[71]

Motown the Musical also emphasizes the intersection of the family home, family capital, and visions of a good life. Berry Gordy must convince his extended biological family to provide start-up funds for the company, and, initially at least, they need convincing. The scene is set in the Gordy family home. Further, both in its opening and later, the play repeatedly stresses Motown as a corporate family, one that includes and subsumes other families (Gordy's, "Little" Stevie Wonder and his mother, and, most notably, the Jacksons) and is riven with internal rivalries set in motion by Gordy as the patriarch. Initially, Motown rents the company's "family home" on West Grand Boulevard from a reluctant white woman who testily announces she "has been burned by you people before." As the ashes from the 1967 riot begin to fall, Gordy advises his white office staff to leave for their own safety, telling them they would be safer at home. "This *is* our home," they emphatically reply. "Family capital" in the form of Motown artists' intellectual property also defines this home-business.

In the industrial era Detroit of *Motown the Musical* and *Detroit '67*, and whose aftermath is presented in *Detroit*, "family business" had multiple connotations.

More than retail "mom-and-pop shops," it signified the vision of an abstemious, Americanized, patriarchal nuclear family-as-self-sufficient-unit that was central to the city's industrial-affective bargain from its inception: rewarding takers with the "private home" and "secure front door" *behind which* is a good life. This bargain—whose legacy of the model middle-class family and community is remembered as fondly as its particulars are overlooked—involved trading the unruly potential of embracing difference for the possibility of personal prosperity. This bargain haunts all three plays even as it continues to power Detroit's figural work.

Self-Invention and the Wages of Living Decently

Initially Detroit could produce model families and communities like it produced Model Ts: according to Henry Ford's design. Ford's efforts began with his attempts to "build a better worker" through his five-dollar-per-day wage, the contours of which set the stage for both the private home as the city's dream delivered and the thematic foundation of the three plays discussed here.[72] As the *Detroit Free Press* explained in its coverage of Ford's announcement on January 6, 1914, five dollars per day was not a guarantee but a profit-sharing plan whereby all "workmen" over twenty-two years of age, estimated to be 90 percent of the workforce, could benefit. Women were initially excluded. Male employees under twenty-two who were "supporting families, widowed mothers, younger brothers or sisters, will be treated like those over 22 and young men from 18 to 22 years who show themselves sober, saving, industrious, and efficient will also share in the system."

Just as his Inkster project was cast as philanthropy, Ford's plan was described as a matter of "social justice" in the *Free Press* announcement. It was in fact an attempt to reduce costs caused by the astonishingly high turnover and absenteeism in his plant: literally compensation for the benumbing work. Protestant theologian Reinhold Niebuhr, who served as a pastor of a Detroit congregation, described the plan as one of the "ambiguous Mr. Ford's" "monstrous pretensions."[73] According to Niebuhr, Detroit's establishment, including its press, merely accepted "Ford's estimate of his own virtues."

If workers thought the new wage would mitigate the deadening routinization of the Ford assembly line, they were mistaken; instead, it meant that their home lives too would be Fordized. As historian Stephen Meyer III noted, "In the eyes of Ford, his officials, and his factory managers, a workman's efficiency in the factory and his home and family environment were thoroughly intertwined."[74] Therefore, the *Free Press* observed, "Ford employees are to be further benefited by the establishment of a sociological department [whose] work will be to guard against an employee's prosperity injuring his efficiency" on and off the job.[75] While not all Ford employees were to "benefit" from the Sociological Department, every employee who earned less than $200 per month was rigorously investigated in what was clearly a policy of class and ethnic profiling and policing central to "profit-sharing" from the very beginning.[76] Aggressive Americanization of recent immigrants was one of the explicit goals, though it was subsumed under the moralistic assertion that FMC "workers must live decently."[77]

The FMC Sociological Department was the decency police. Its operations relied on the city's characteristic amalgam of cultural and techno-managerial performances, extending the spectacle of productive efficiency to workers' homes and presentations of self. Department personnel were given "wide latitude in making their investigations. No red tape binds them."[78] Workers were subject to detailed interviews, and every aspect of their lives—from their personal habits to the quality of their furniture to the amount they held in savings to the look of their neighborhoods—was laid bare, recorded, and assessed as worthy or unworthy of participation in profit-sharing. Though women were initially unable to participate in the enhanced wage, they were still bound by the "decency" dictum. Wives of Ford workers were not allowed to have jobs outside the home; it was indecent by definition.[79] Personnel from the FMC Sociological Department operated as paternalistic corporate anthropologists: demanding tactical, nuanced presentations of self from working-class targets while yielding underclass spectacle for both researchers and their audiences in the mainstream press. Violations of WASP upper-middle-class decorum were circulated widely as a kind of vernacular "How the Other Half Lives." The *Free Press* story announcing that FMC "workers must live decently" is an interesting example, titillating and amusing with accounts of "scores sleep[ing] in shifts, seldom taking baths," and five "ducks waddl[ing] in the [bath]tub—Live ducks too!"[80] For workers, of course, this was no laughing matter; if they failed to meet the department's standards for living decently, they could be fired.

Set at the intersection of work and home, the Fordist decency bargain was affective as well as economic from the start: a way to dissolve boundaries separating production in the workplace from consumption-as-respite by regulating personal habits and decorum. The department's successes in instilling middle-class norms were used as stories of salvation, providing both moral uplift and good PR. Department accounts of investigations read like conversion narratives wherein the department investigator identifies and points out the vice, attachment to ethnic custom, evidence of obvious poverty, or other deviation from Fordist definitions of decency to the worker; provides assistance in remedying the fault; and produces a diligent, efficient, and prudent worker at the end of the process.[81] These conversion narratives, in turn, served as templates for future workers: reassuring them that any losses of control, privacy, and social and ethnic identity could be easily transmuted into a personally winning risk/reward calculation through inclusion in Ford's American dream.

Certainly there was resistance. Much of it also took the form of performance: dissembling, carefully staging evidence of "living decently," and trickster play with language to fudge answers to intrusive questions. Because marriage and obvious heteronormativity were essential components of decent living, single workers borrowed "wives"; historian Richard Snow recounts eleven boarding house residents presenting their landlady in this capacity as investigators never called on all of them at once.[82] In other cases, as in Snow's most compelling example of Sociological Department "conversion," workers betrayed no obvious resistance at all. A worthy Russian immigrant FMC worker, "Joe," saw his hardscrabble life and meager possessions redeemed for Fordist efficiency by a zealous investigator's ritual—and literal—fire. After renting new accommodations for Joe's family, the investigator proudly proclaimed that he

> "had their dirty, old, junk furniture loaded on a dray and under cover of night moved them to their new home. This load of rubbish was heaped on a pile in the backyard, and a torch was applied and it went up in smoke. There upon the ashes of what had been their earthly possessions, this Russian peasant and his wife, with tears streaming down their faces, expressed their gratitude to Henry Ford, the Ford Motor Company, and all those who had been instrumental in bringing about this marvelous change in their lives."

Snow wonders if these were only tears of gratitude. Perhaps, as in the aftermaths of so many of the city's fiery confrontations with difference, Joe and his family hoped for better things to arise from these ashes.

Perhaps its not surprising that the nonsmoking teetotaler Henry Ford insisted on the same behaviors from his workers. But one element of the bargain does seem curious: boarding houses were especially antithetical to the FMC definition of "living decently." Meyer notes, "Ford officials believed that the boarders, especially single men, violated the sanctity of the family unit."[83] The *Free Press* proclaimed that Ford "has declared war on tenements and squalid roominghouses and no employee of the Ford Motor Company will be permitted to exist in them."[84] On the surface, this appears to be a war on squalor, but, reading further, it becomes clear that the chaotic propinquity of the boarding house itself is the issue. "Married men who keep boarders in their homes" were to be "eliminated from the Ford organization." Ford himself is quoted:

> Married men should keep their households to themselves and their immediate families. They should not sacrifice family rights, pleasure, and comfort by filling their rooms with roomers and boarders. . . . [Moreover] men who earn from $5 to $9 a day do not need to have their wives take in boarders.

There were some pragmatic reasons for Ford's antipathy. Such queer, nonfamilial homosocial environments might enable other forms of fraternalism—like union organizing. Moreover, discouraging families from supplementing their incomes by taking in lodgers, like prohibiting wives from working, was a way the company could ensure that the FMC wage was the sole source of household support: one a worker might be reluctant to risk by participating in strikes or other forms of union activism. This would be particularly true if that worker had a mortgage, as

FMC strongly encouraged.[85] Finally, Ford's prohibition against boarding houses of necessity moved workers from Detroit's dense urban core out to neighborhoods of single-family homes and, in so doing, spatially reproduced the company's emphasis on the patriarchal nuclear family. Given the prevalence of Detroit's racial covenants in housing, racial segregation was a natural byproduct.

At the most basic level, Ford's bargain—possible personal prosperity at the price of potentially unruly diversity—was a way to control the strange and, from the company perspective, unproductive alliances likely to arise in highly concentrated urban areas, including cross-racial ones. Thus FMC regulated potential solidarity by regulating residential proximity. For example, as African American studies scholar Jeremy Williams notes in *Images of America: Detroit—The Black Bottom Community*, Polish immigrants and poor and working-class African Americans shared the same lower east side neighborhood during this period.[86] Living in such close proximity within structures of economic marginality necessitated the development of multiple, overlapping networks of cooperation. In his ethnographic study of contemporary Chicago tenement life, performance studies scholar Dwight Conquergood observed that "the chronic state of disrepair, breakdowns, and emergencies requires . . . a neighborly interdependence unheard of in efficiently managed middle-class properties."[87] The cross-familial, cross-ethnic, and cross-racial affiliations required for survival in such conditions had the potential to disrupt the model of the self-contained patriarchal family essential to the Ford organization, the ethnic/racial hierarchies on the shop floor, and the investment in white privilege as a form of worker capital that kept these hierarchies in place. They also had the potential to spawn antagonisms that might spill over into the workplace, disrupting production. Instead of complex solidarities borne of shared miseries, Fordism produced a "pit of individualism."[88]

Ford's bargain also imposed a highly racialized order on the city's industrial era population boom. US Census Bureau figures show Detroit's population more than doubled between 1910 and 1920, including large influxes of immigrants.[89] The African American population almost tripled during this same period, with the majority confined in or near downtown and the city's east side. The city was bursting at the seams, and there was an acute housing shortage. Pushing workers out of the dense urban core not only left that area open for more profitable commercial development but also reduced any perceived need for Progressive Era intervention in that core's increasingly fraught conditions.

Like the factory, the tenement was a site of affective, cultural, and economic production, but the interdependent improvisations required of its residents made it seem, at the time, to be the plant's ad hoc unruly, wholly inefficient mirror opposite, literally begging to be managed in service of industry. Through the efforts of the Sociological Department and later the FMC English School, Ford sought to reconfigure relationships between the two: to construct a new habitus so workers' home lives would both mirror and depend upon plant hierarchy.[90] In so doing, the Fordist "decency" bargain routinized and restricted paths of urban affect and affiliation. The patriarchal, putatively autonomous nuclear family was only the most obvious effect. Though versions of this same bargain were enforced in company towns across the United States, Ford's explicitness and the enforcement mechanism of his decency police, coupled with the city's industrial era prosperity, created figural "Detroit" as an object of the white industrial era nostalgia so prominent in the American deindustrial. This nostalgia includes fantasies of the abstemious, stable, patriarchal white nuclear family ensconced in its private home secured through vanishing modes of industrial work without the disciplinary, spatial, and, as I will discuss later, racial(-ist) mechanics through which these homeplaces were actually produced.

Pivotal moments in both *Detroit* and *Motown the Musical* make the successful internalization of this Fordist bargain very clear. Berry Gordy's corporate "family" never stops competing: the capitalist bargain is sanctioned company affect. And Gordy never stops working, even while on a quasi-honeymoon. His position at the top of a patriarchal production hierarchy is balm for even the most intimate of failures. After a substandard bedroom performance, Diana Ross reassures Gordy not with the usual "it happens to everyone" but by reminding him that he "is the boss of everything else." Even when legal challenges to the patriarch's distribution of family capital, and the flight of intimates, threaten to expose rifts in public, the smooth product itself—the Motown sound—repairs both the wounded father-boss and the credibility of the Fordist bargain itself in/as public performance.

That Fordist bargain is long gone in D'Amour's *Detroit*, but it lives on in wistful nostalgia. At the end of the play Frank, Kenny's uncle, surveys the ashes of Ben and Mary's burned-out home and recalls a past that seems as predictable and programmatic as the assembly line itself (figure 6). Bright Homes featured five models; while some customization was available, "mostly they just built it from the model."[91] Uniformity was not a concern; indeed, it was soothing. "It was no big deal that your house looked like a lot of the other houses." Fathers came home at "5:30 sharp, pulling into driveways in their Belvederes, their Furies." Their arrival times suggest that these were middle-class office workers, not factory workers, whose shifts did not align with the "nine-to-five" job and 5:30 dinnertime, though industrial nostalgia, like the spectacle of the Auto Manufacturing Theater, is heavily dependent on conjuring desire for these putatively "better days" in those who never actually worked in its trenches. Whatever mothers did, it goes unnoted. Community dances were held "two Saturdays a month," and the greatest deviation from this routine was the opportunity to stay at those dances past midnight. Above all, Frank wistfully observes, living in Bright Homes meant "you were safe." "Most of us were just living like this," he continues. "It was 1968. But the whole country wasn't hippies." Or civil rights workers. A closer look at the city's specific intersection of race, place, home, and work during the formative years of Detroit's Fordist industrial bargain reveals a pernicious racial(-ist) politics re-sited and re-cited in all three plays; all three feature houses haunted by it. The nature of this politics can best be summarized by paraphrasing Henry Ford's famous dictum on color choice

Figure 6: "Frank" (John Cullum) musing on the good old days in Bright Homes. Lisa D'Amour's *Detroit*, Playwrights Horizons. Photo: Jeremy Daniel. Photo courtesy of The Publicity Office/ Michael Borowski.

for the Model T: workers could have any decent style of living they wanted in the city or the suburbs as long as they were white.[92]

Racial(-ist) (In)Decencies

Despite Ford's active hiring of large numbers of black workers during the period of the five-dollar day, the Fordist bargain of exchanging the unpredictable potential of heterogeneity for possible personal prosperity utterly failed to remedy the abject housing situation of the city's African American residents.[93] As Bates observes, "During the height of his Five Dollar Day, Profit-Sharing Plan, Ford's proclamations warning about the evils of crowded houses did not lead him to challenge the rising walls of the ghetto."[94] The situation was not a secret. On the contrary, it was so dire and so public that it became the subject of numerous investigations by national black and white activists; these were widely covered by the local press. For example, a *Detroit Free Press* article from 1917 detailed one report by Dr. Charles F. Taylor of the Hampton Industrial School in Virginia, who came to the city with his own team of investigators under the auspices of the local Urban League chapter; the headline proclaimed, "City Faces Negro Housing Problem: Southern Clergyman Declares 25,000 Live in One Restricted Area."[95] After noting that the city's working-class African American residents, many of them new arrivals, lived "in three or four room houses for which they pay rents that would provide respectable whites' quarters in New York city," Taylor outlined the lethality of these conditions:

> They [black workers] were lured here by expectation of large wages, and when they got here, they were driven down into the disorderly house district.
>
> The lack of sanitation in their houses accounts for the high death rate among Negroes of Detroit, which is almost double that of any other section of the city.

The causes were no more a mystery than the conditions themselves; both an editorial and a letter to the editor during this period specifically identified racial discrimination as the source of the problem.[96] The remedy, however, remained unspecified undoubtedly because, as historian Thomas Sugrue notes, "race and class became more important than ethnicity as a guide to the city's residential geography" during this period; "residents of Detroit's white neighborhoods abandoned their ethnic affiliations and found a new identity in their whiteness."[97] For the white political and corporate elite, publicly calling for integrating the city's housing stock appeared simply unthinkable.

The FMC's absolute prohibitions against taking in boarders and "indecent" living conditions were not strictly enforced for its black workers; Bates suggests this comparative laxity arose from the calculus that it was better to let African American workers live in substandard conditions than be thrown into the street, as if these two were the only available options.[98] In fact, given the city's segregated housing, this was largely true. Well before *Corrigan v. Buckley*, the 1926 US Supreme Court case that affirmed the legality of racial covenants, city and suburban realtors aggressively wrote racial restrictions into property deeds outlawing occupation by African Americans, Asians, and Jews in perpetuity. Despite their FMC employment, African American workers in Detroit were the figural equivalent of "boarders" not owners, strangers not "family" in the city by force of law until 1948, when a case arising from the city, *McGhee v. Sipes*, argued by Thurgood Marshall, contributed to the Supreme Court overturning racial covenants as violations of the Fourteenth Amendment.[99] The ruling changed little on the ground; intractable de facto segregation was openly acknowledged. Orville Hubbard, the thirty-six-year white mayor of suburban Dearborn, Henry Ford's hometown and site of both his namesake museum and company headquarters, bluntly proclaimed an unwritten law against African Americans living there in the 1960s.[100] Thus, FMC's early cynical recalibration of "living decently" to exclude black workers not only reflected Ford's personal antipathy to racial equality but also aligned perfectly with the city's fraught racial history both before and long after the five-dollar-per-day period. It reinforced official and de facto segregation; established affective and material connections linking personal profit through self-reinvention, "decency," and racial homogeneity; and centered these operations on the family home.

The Fordist bargain of personal prosperity and/as self-reinvention in exchange for "decency" was white from its inception. The price of aggressively policing the same standards of "decent living" for black workers would have been massive restructuring of both specific residential geographies and the transethnic solidarity of whiteness consolidating in the city's middle- and working-class white neighborhoods and suburbs. Again, the issue is not that Detroit and FMC are historical exceptions, utterly unique in their racialization of industrial modernity. It is that the city's current status as deindustrialization's cautionary tale—crucial to its metaphoric utility—depends on recalling the promises of its industrial heyday while forgetting the racial and other costs, even as their legacy continues to operate both openly and spectrally within its figural work. All three plays re-site and re-cite elements of this racialized bargain using two themes drawn from Detroit's unique mix of performances: home-as-stage-for-self-production and home-as-site-of-interracial-conflict, even conflagration.

Detroit's African American workers, exceptions to FMC's decency bargain from its inception, embraced the possibility of industrial era self-fashioning without its structural opportunities; both *Motown the Musical* and *Detroit '67* re-cite crucial elements of this history. *Motown the Musical* makes the connection between self-invention and cross-racial encounter explicit. Early in the play, we flash back to the Gordy family home in 1938. Young Berry is listening to African American hometown hero, boxer Joe Louis, defeat German Max Schmeling in a knockout. The eight-year-old resolves to model himself on Louis. He recalls this moment at the end of the show, within the mis en scène of *Motown 25*, observing that he wanted "to make people happy like [Louis] did." The observation exemplifies the racial complexity managed throughout both the entire show and the history of Motown itself. Gordy's wish is both profoundly racially specific—to be a black man of unquestionable public achievement inspiring the pride of black audiences—and transracial. Louis's victory over the white Schmeling, coming at the nexus of both the end of the Great Depression and the dawning of World War II, was cause for national celebration: a moment with transracial potential not unlike that of the Motown sound within the frame of the show.[101]

Of course, an autobiographical musical is itself, almost by definition, an exercise in self-reinvention. In the script, Gordy's personal and ethical lapses are either sidestepped completely or actively neutralized; when he announces that his first wife, Thelma, is divorcing him because she "thinks [he's] a bum," his sister replies, "You may not be the best husband but you are the best brother." Yet sleight of hand with the facts of personal history aside, the ultimate vehicle of Gordy's spectacular reinvention is his prodigious work ethic and attunement to the market, even when the market's gatekeepers are explicitly racist. He is "never gonna give up on [his] dreams" and, within the context of the production, never has to. The company family may fail him—deserting him to pursue their own market dreams—and he has his "Edsel" moments, here incarnated in cringe-worthy performances by "Rick James" and "Teena Marie." Yet onstage in the fictional *Motown 25* within *Motown the Musical*, Gordy is celebrated as the paragon of both black and transracial capitalism that he unquestionably is.

Yet, as Suzanne Smith observes, while the Motown story hews closely to the general contours of the race- and place-neutral American dream, "Motown's economic success illustrates how capitalism operates by rules that cannot be held to a racial or local community agenda and how easily the enduring appeal of the company's music obscures this fact."[102] What was good for Motown was wounding to the city, a critique leveled by company insiders throughout the late 1960s. Significantly, *Motown the Musical* ends in 1983, the year US manufacturing reached a historic low, deindustrialization became a topic of political and social concern, and Michael Jackson was incarnating the very industrial rigors and choreographies now vanishing.[103] *Motown the Musical* offers audiences an "old life that feels real" due in equal measure to the persistence of the American dream narrative as the affective solace for deindustrialization's current predations and to the enduring popularity of the Motown sound.[104] Indeed, the public reframing of Detroit's postindustrial precarity as an invitation to personal entrepreneurship—discussed in chapter 4—finds a historical precedent in Gordy's own successful entrepreneurial challenge to industrial era racism, adding a measure of nostalgic transracial self-fashioning to that conjured by the "Sound of Young America."

In *Detroit '67*, Chelle is more interested in "survivin" than self-reinvention.[105] While her friend Bunny speculates on spending an imagined inheritance on trips to "Rome and Paris and all them high n' mighty places with my mink coat and my painted nails," Chelle accepts another version of the classic industrial era bargain: she'll get by so that her college-educated son can do better.[106] Lank's prospective bar is "too shaky," just something to lose.[107] For Lank, self-reinvention means literally rejecting the Fordist bargain altogether: "Pops was an auto man. Ford Motor Company. Served 'em til' his death half a year ago. He tried to get me in there . . . but that auto stuff ain't for me."[108] His romantic connection with Caroline, the white woman he rescues, is framed as part of this same rejection of the industrial bargain; Lank both rejects the benumbing nature of the work and the Fordist prohibition of unruly, even dangerous heterogeneity that goes along with it. Chelle is antagonized by both rejections. On learning of Lank's purchase of the bar, she explodes: "You always tryin' to have somethin' better! Can't never leave nothin' the way it is."[109] Tending his wounds after a police beating at the start of the riot, she confronts him, somewhat more gently this time, about his attachment to Caroline, linking it to her very clear sense of the classed and raced limits on self-reinvention Lank seems determined to escape:

> You get around her and you get further and further away from reality. Forgettin' who you are and what this world can do to you. You come in here with your new 8-track player and your new bar and this White woman, and you think you somebody you ain't.[110]

Those limits, she reminds Caroline later, are etched onto the city burning all around them: "Lank got his eye on the sky but Detroit ain't in the sky. It's right here on the ground. A ground with a lot of dividing lines. We on one side and you on the other."[111]

Chelle was speaking from history. Detroit's racial "dividing lines" circumscribing African American domesticity and/as self-invention, re-cited in *Detroit '67*, emerged with special clarity more than forty years earlier in the Ossian

Figure 7: Left to right: "Bunny" (De'Adre Aziza), "Chelle" (Michelle Wilson), "Lank" (Francois Battiste), and "Sly" (Brandon J. Dirden) in Chelle's basement club. Dominique Morisseau's *Detroit '67*. The Public Theater, the Classical Theatre of Harlem, and the National Black Theatre. Photo: Joan Marcus. Used with permission of the Classical Theatre of Harlem.

Sweet case of 1925. This case reinforced both the whiteness of industrial era opportunity and white resistance to integration. As in Morisseau's play, these industrial era dividing lines also came together at the nexus of home and inter-racial conflict and were rigorously policed. The city's police force was as central to the city's enforcement of industrialization's separate and unequal bargain for African Americans as the FMC Sociological Department was for white eth-nics: reminding newly arrived black workers that their prosperity depended on knowing their place.

In *Detroit '67*, Chelle's home and basement blind pig are sites of resistance to the most pernicious aspects of Detroit's racial(-ist) politics (figure 7). Her home is, in bell hooks's classic formulation, a "safe place where black people could affirm one another and by so doing heal many of the wounds inflicted by racist domination."[112] In the summer of 1925, however, the homeplace, site of self-reinvention and resis-tance, was armed.

That summer, Dr. Ossian Sweet, a highly regarded African American physician whose record of extraordinary self-invention included postgraduate work in Vienna and Paris, and who had come to Detroit from his birthplace in Jim Crow Florida, purchased a home on the city's near east side. As historian Kevin Boyle recounts in his comprehensive history of the case, *Arc of Justice*:

> The people who lived up and down the street didn't have the education, the credentials, or the polish of the lawyers, accountants, and college professors who lived in the city's

outer reaches. But they had all the attributes necessary to keep themselves out of the reach of the inner city, and that's what mattered most. Of course, they were white, each and every one. The vast majority of them were American born, and the few foreigners living on the street came from respectable stock; they were Germans, Englishmen, Irishmen, and Scotsmen, not the Poles or Russians or Greeks who filled so much of the east side.[113]

Sweet, his wife and young daughter, brother, and friends moved the family into the house over the Labor Day weekend. They brought guns with them. Sweet was profoundly aware of the potential for racist violence, including white attacks on African Americans who had previously purchased homes in white neighborhoods, as happened to a fellow Detroit doctor just three months before. That colleague had abandoned his home. Sweet, however, was determined to protect his investment. One Detroit police officer was dispatched for security at the request of one of Sweet's friends; the number was increased as night fell without incident. On the second night, however, a white crowd outside swelled to hundreds and let loose a volley of rocks and bottles, shattering windows as they rushed the house. A shot was fired from the house's second story, killing one member of the mob and wounding another. The police then entered the Sweets' home, arresting everyone inside. The Sweets and their friends were denied access to counsel, denied bail, and charged with murder, conspiracy to commit murder, and assault. In Boyle's account, officers on the scene initially denied there was any inciting white attack on the house at all: a lie they repeated at Sweet's subsequent trial.[114]

The (in)actions of law enforcement in the Sweet case were not unique. Racist policing is also part of Detroit's historic amalgam of race, homeplace, and work. Though African American workers were spared the intensive intrusions and denied outright the residential opportunities associated with FMC's decency police, they were at the mercy of city law enforcement, some of whom were neither decent nor particularly interested in the law. Police brutality is central to Morisseau's plot, which re-cites not only the force's history of harassment and charges of murder during the period of the riot itself but also a long record of racist practices that was openly acknowledged during the Sweet case.[115] The Ku Klux Klan allegedly had adherents on the force in both periods. Indeed, two months after the attack on the Sweets' home and during the period of Ossian Sweet's trial, it was actively seeking a public role in city government, with five Klan-backed candidates running for city council seats, and one for mayor.[116]

Through the efforts of James Weldon Johnson, executive secretary of the National Association for the Advancement of Colored People (NAACP), Clarence Darrow was persuaded to take the Sweet case, which first went to trial before an all-white jury on October 30, 1925. In his opening statement, Darrow began by explicitly linking African American industrial migration to the city, the promise of successful self-fashioning, complicity between racist residents and city police in enforcing segregation, the alignment of decency and respectability with homogeneous whiteness, and white class unease. In so doing, Sweet's defense laid bare the potency and precarity of whiteness as a consolidating class fiction in these formative years after the Fordist decency bargain.

Darrow stressed the relative modesty of the Sweets' new neighborhood; it was not an elite bastion of old money like the Grosse Pointes. Indeed, Sweet, with his medical degree and old-world bona fides, clearly possessed more educational and cultural capital than his neighbors, a point Darrow underscored by asking a white witness to pronounce the name of nearby Goethe Street, which she did as "Go-THEE."[117] In holding her up to ridicule, Darrow, likely unwittingly, demonstrated and reproduced the very anxiety that, in part, brought the mob to the Sweets' door. In a moment when auto plant hierarchy was etched onto the landscape in racially and ethnically segregated neighborhoods bulging with willing workers, whites at the edges of middle-class prosperity might find that racial privilege was only a fictive balm for their own dispensability.

Sweet himself explicitly invoked re-siting in his testimony, presenting the demonstrators as the incarnation of racism across time and place:

> When I opened the door and saw that mob, I realized in a way that it was that same mob that had hounded my people through its entire history. I realized my back was against the wall and I was filled with a peculiar type of fear—the fear of one who knows the history of my race.[118]

Holding legal title to his home was no more effective for him than ownership papers for Shepley's Bar proved for Lank and Sly in the world of *Detroit '67*, set forty years later.

The initial Sweet trial ended in a hung jury. Darrow returned for the retrial of Ossian's brother, Henry Sweet, which resulted in an acquittal and dropping of all charges against the remaining defendants. The victory was pyrrhic. Ossian's wife, Gladys, baby daughter, and Henry would later die of tuberculosis, likely as a result of time spent in jail before bonding out. Ossian sold the house in 1958, more than thirty years after regaining access to it; he barely lived there. Alone, broke, and suffering from chronic ill health, he committed suicide in 1960. The Sweet case reinforced racist dividing lines circumscribing African American residential ambitions for self-reinvention while demonstrating exactly how resistant many white Detroiters were to reconsidering their bargain of segregation for secure front doors and a modicum of personal prosperity.

Detroit most vividly re-sites/re-cites a seemingly race-neutral Fordist domestic decency bargain, exposing both its persistence as a point of affective attachment and the anxiety accompanying its utter dissolution: crucial elements powering the figural economy of the deindustrial, and Detroit-as-figure specifically, especially during the recovery from the Great Recession. In so doing, the play recalls the promise of agential self-fashioning combined with the acquiescence, outright dissembling, and willful—indeed necessary—self deception that led early FMC workers to submit their lives to scrutiny and their belongings to incineration, to borrow "wives," and to accept the possibility of five dollars a day for enduring the heat of the blast furnace and the benumbing rhythms of the plant. The legacy of this bargain is incarnated in the character of Frank, Kenny's uncle, who so wistfully recalls the good old days in Bright Homes. Frank is decent, though "the style of his clothes," like the postwar prosperity and the labor-management compact that sustained his good life in the subdivision, is "a little out of date."[119] He reminisces, asks solicitous questions, offers money. He wants to help. It "hurts" him to come back to the place.[120] Its reassuring uniformity has given way to bewildering unevenness: "Half the houses falling apart, the others so fancified they seem untouchable." He wants to preserve the neighborhood as he remembers it, creating an archive so "folks . . . could see what life used to be like": legibly homogeneous.[121] In Frank, industrial era decency has aged into benign, nostalgic arrest.

Early in the play, Kenny and Sharon appear only barely, if aspirationally, decent. They are seemingly renters, not owners, making them the equivalent of boarders in the neighborhood. They have low-level service jobs: Kenny in a warehouse and Sharon in a call center. Like Russian immigrant Joe, whose belongings were set alight by the FMC investigator, these two are making a new start with no furniture. The combined fictive normalcy and actual rarity of a neighborly meal brings Sharon to tears. Yet, again like the FMC workers subject to the Sociological Department's critical gaze, Kenny and Sharon always risk revealing those aspects of their former lives incompatible with their current presentations of aspirational decency: "Baby, we were going to keep that to ourselves."[122] "That" includes their histories of drug use, the fact that they broke into and were squatting in their home, Kenny's loss of his warehouse job and real name ("Roger"), the fact that he has a son somewhere and that he is a whole "can of worms" his uncle has, for years, preferred not to open.[123] They don't keep much of this to themselves for very long and, in the process, demonstrate a level of self-awareness unique among the other characters. Sharon announces that the dinner she hosts to reciprocate Ben and Mary's hospitality is themed "white trash, because I'm trying to own up to what I am these days."[124] Kenny's owning up comes after an edgy bonhomie with Ben over the prospect of going to a strip club; he proclaims, "I'm an *asshole* and it's too late for me."[125] Yet, staring at the ashes of their burned-out home, as if to underscore again that decency and delusion are so often partners at this moment of neoliberal deindustrial capitalism, Ben and Mary tell Frank that Kenny and Sharon were not bad people; the couple "enjoyed them."[126] Frank pauses and replies evenly, "Ma'am, they burned your house down."

Even before the play's final conflagration, it's clear that Kenny and Sharon don't play well with others. Sharon erupts in an extended profane rant over a pink-clad jogger's accusation of a dog they don't have. She relapses, necessitating being tied to the wall. The couple paws each other, leading Mary to finally, if futilely, recognize that "weird things are happening."[127] Sharon confesses that none of their previous neighbors wanted anything to do with them, instead hiding from the druggy decrepitude behind their own secure front doors.

Ben and Mary certainly appear decent, with savings and insurance, patio furniture, and a grill. They express the cruel optimism that mischaracterizes individual expendability and vulnerability as an invitation to personal entrepreneurship—"if you follow your passions, you're halfway there"—and their passions don't include freebasing heroin or arson.[128] Yet it's clear that their decency too is all front stage. Ben is a fraud. He has not been working on his financial services website. He's got nothing but a domain name: a title to no place, hence always both utopic and empty. Following Sharon's inexplicable observation that he seems "British," he confesses to "Ian," his fantasy British alter ego, who lives a genteel, if modest, life without Mary. Ben spends more time in "Brit-land," an online haven for those who want to be British, than building his own web business: their equal fictitiousness makes them largely interchangeable. By the play's end, conversing with Frank, Ben *is* "Ian," and the couple briefly muses out loud about moving to Britain to "have a farm": an artisanal-pastoral fantasy that served as an antidote to industrialization decades before.[129]

Mary's decency unravels in direct proportion to the increasing visibility of her alcoholism, betrayed in sloppy late-night emoting at Sharon's back door. From the beginning of the play, she seems brittle, concerned with appearances, and, like Ben, easily influenced. Her hostess duties read as overacting: frantic, excessive attempts to pull off a vision of what upper-middle-class entertaining should be, as if compensating for reduced circumstances. Her fantasy is living in the woods: also fraudulent as she and Sharon cannot even reach their campground site for their spur-of-the-moment immersion in nature. Both Mary and Ben are literally hobbled at various points in the play, unable to move forward due to plantar wart surgery and a deck mishap, respectively. Ben lets slip that the couple doesn't have any friends. At the end of the play, they are alone, with no family on site, and only Frank—a veritable stranger—to offer condolences and help.

Even the characters' houses appear indecent: the mirror opposite of the promise of uniformity in Bright Homes. Doors stick, patio umbrellas collapse and draw blood, decks give way, impaling limbs on shards of broken lumber. And the dreams dreamt there are strange, replete with rubber-walled, unhomey homes; a butcher's counter; and a broken-down boardwalk. In another dream, a banker keeps deposits in an Adidas shoebox under an old card table: a not so subtle allusion to the toxic mortgage crisis that spawned the recession of 2007, as well as to Ben's former employment as a loan officer. Real life for these characters feels like dreams, and the "old life"—Sharon's and Kenny's illicit pasts, Ben and Mary's membership in the middle class, perhaps Frank's rosy vision of Bright Homes that marked the apogee of the Fordist bargain—feels "real."[130]

Detroit's and *Motown the Musical*'s evocations of a vanished "old life" that feels more "real" than the present is at the very affective heart of the American deindustrial, and of repeated attempts to assert underexamined Fordist rubrics of, and bargains for, decency as timeless, race-neutral ideals while redefining industrialization's union-secured labor-management prosperity, the mechanism through which they were realized, as a fleeting, even unnecessary aberration. Lawrence Grossberg observed that we recognize structural change when "something 'feels' different."[131] While *Motown the Musical* stops just short of it, D'Amour's *Detroit* captures this affective difference accompanying the transition from industrialization to deindustrialization: the precarity left in the wake of the dissolution of the Fordist bargain, not only for Kenny, who once upon a time might have leveraged a measure of security from a shift at the plant, but also for the college-educated, middle-class Ben, who, as Kenny points out, is one month away from being just like him. In the character of Frank, this is a genial, sepia-toned bargain that was and never was: free of the boredom, the sexism that renders mothers too invisible to even bear mention in his nostalgic fantasy, any hint of racial diversity, and, of course, the nature of industrial work itself with its heat and sweat and noise, its crushing uniformity, and the accompanying hope, necessarily in some measure self-deceptive, for better things to be forged in the process for the next generation if not for oneself. In D'Amour's "not necessarily" Detroit, only the racial homogeneity remains unchanged.

That homogeneity takes an interesting turn in the penultimate scene of the play. At this point it is important to distinguish between D'Amour's script and the Playwrights Horizons production. In both, scene 7 is a kind of late-night bacchanal with the couples in Ben and Mary's backyard. Stage directions note, "Some kind of party music. Maybe music from Sharon's and Kenny's Hotlanta days? . . . Kenny is fake humping the grill. . . . They are all beer wasted."[132] In the production, the music is explicitly gangsta rap, underscored in both the text and the performance by Kenny's improvisations, "wail[ed], high-pitched R&B style," and Mary's performance in blackvoice: "Im a sexy mothafuckah on yo roof. I'm a sexy mothafuckah on yo back porch." The evening dissolves into desperately ecstatic confessions, overt and sloppy sex play, and the purgative promise of a ritual fire, punctuated by the imperative to testify:

MARY: Tell it baby tell it!
MARY AND KENNY: Tell it baby tell it!. . .
BEN: I'm feeling it!
MARY: Say it![133]

Kenny sets broken patio chairs alight. This ritual "burning up" is some sort of cleansing—seemingly the goal of this Dionysian breakdown. In the script, the fire gets out of control and spreads to the kitchen. In the production, things happen differently. As Ben and Mary are swept away in the sensory excesses of the moment—their reprieve from maintaining even the facade of their fraying decency—Kenny enters the kitchen and deliberately sets it on fire to the gasps of the audience. The house burns down: a spectacle of destruction whose early stages are shown onstage.[134]

The play presumes a white middle-class and upper-middle-class spectatorial position: the hegemonic status quo for mainstream New York and Chicago theater. All reviewers' references to "comedy" aside, the losses here are Ben's and Mary's, and so, too, is the trajectory of audience empathy. Ben and Mary are the victims of the new economy, the Great Recession, their neighbors, and their own self-deception. By scene 8, Kenny and Sharon are gone. They've burned their bridges, after all. Their front door—not theirs at all, we learn—is left wide open. This leaves Ben and Mary as the cautionary tale of what happens when "we dare to open ourselves to something new," the subject of the play according to its back cover.[135] On one level, this can be read as opening oneself to the vagaries of the neoliberal, financialized new economy where contingency and entrepreneurial self-invention are the order of the day, as well as to the self-deception needed to sustain a belief in the capacity to manage wholly on one's own bereft of any social safety net. But this play is "not necessarily" set in Detroit, where both the Fordist bargain recalled by Frank and its particular amalgam of race, place, home, and work were borne. In this larger context, and in light of the abundant racial signifiers that characterize the pivotal scene 7, "opening ourselves up to something new" also conjures a darker reading, haunted by the specific incendiary moments in the city's history, including the case of Ossian Sweet, whose neighbors were not about to be so open.

Internal Combustions

Homes in Detroit burn down a lot, and not just existentially as Jerry Herron's epigraph to this chapter suggests. Detroit's historic amalgam of race, place, home, and work is literally combustible in ways that continue to inform its figural work, even—indeed especially—in this putatively postracial moment. Homes burned down in March 1863 when a white mob descended upon black residences and businesses as word spread that one Thomas Faulkner, characterized as black but almost certainly white because he was listed on voting rolls, had violated two girls, one black, one white. In the mayhem that followed, at least one African American was killed, thirty-five houses and uncounted businesses burned, and more than 200 mostly black families left homeless.[136] The poem "The Riot," by "B. Clark, Sen., A Colored Man" described the scene in seventeen stanzas:

> Then they [white rioters] took the city without more delay,
> And fired each building that stood in their way,
> Until the red glare had ascended on high,
> And lit up the great azure vault of the sky.
> . . .
> Humanity wept, she lamented the sight,
> The groans, blood and tears of that terrible night;
> Yet, oh, may the town of Detroit never see
> Such a day as the sixth of March, sixty-three.[137]

Such a day did come eighty years later, in June 1943, when homes burned again. A scuffle between black and white youths at Belle Isle, the city's largest park, turned into a full-scale race riot lasting two days. Thirty four people were killed, 25 of them African American; 17 of these were shot by police. More than 600 were injured. In a now-familiar turn on the city's fraught industrial era housing/decency bargain, African American defense workers' occupation of a new project, the Sojourner Truth Homes, two months before was cited as a contributing factor.[138] White rioters burned black businesses, cars, and at least one apartment building. The violence prompted President Franklin Roosevelt to send in federal troops.

Houses burned yet again in Detroit's best-known racial conflagration: the 1967 riot re-cited in Morisseau's play. It began with a raid on a blind pig in the city's African American Twelfth Street neighborhood in what was widely seen as yet another example of its racist policing, which remained little changed since the days of the Sweet trials. During the riot, Isaiah McKinnon, one of the city's few black officers, who would go on to become police chief in the late 1990s, had worked a twelve-hour shift on riot patrol and was himself stopped and fired upon by white officers for violating curfew because they refused to believe he was a colleague.[139] The violence lasted for five days and ended with 43 people dead and almost 1,200 injured. Whole blocks were burned. Again, federal troops were dispatched to the city. When, in *Detroit '67*, Chelle expresses surprise that the events unfolding off-stage are being characterized as a race riot, Sly replies:

> That's what they say so. Makin' like we just hate honkies. But I wish they'd come askin' me some questions. I tell 'em—if this is about niggers hatin' honkies, then you tell me why White folks down there gettin' they lootin' in too. Naw . . . this is about pigs hatin' niggers. That's what this fire is about.[140]

Here, too, systemic residential segregation, coupled with racist policing, fanned the flames. The Twelfth Street neighborhood where the riot caught fire included residents re-sited from Detroit's Black Bottom/Paradise Valley when that neighborhood was razed in a series of urban renewal efforts between 1946 and 1963. These moves continued the early industrial era pattern of segregating high concentrations of African American residents in specific areas of the city with demonstrably fewer services.

As noted earlier, the 1967 riot became a national spectacle, demonstrating the combustibility of US race relations at the seeming apogee of industrial progress. While both *Motown the Musical* and *Detroit '67* re-cite the 1967 riot specifically, later conflagrations are more central to *Detroit* and the city's current figural work. These more recent fires operated alongside Detroit's deindustrial deterioration to become racial spectacles of another kind.

For the past thirty years, houses in Detroit have burned down on "Devil's Night," the evening before Halloween. Devil's Night is so closely associated with the city that the Wikipedia entry for the term indicates they are practically synonymous.[141] In *Devil's Night and Other True Tales of Detroit*, author Ze'ev Chafets describes it as an "orgy of destruction." "Spend the evening before Halloween with me and I'll show you something you've never seen before," Chafets's friend offers. "People try to burn down their own neighborhoods."[142] As this exchange suggests, Devil's Night spawned its own tourist industry in the late 1980s and early 1990s: an early precursor to the city's later ruins imagery. National and international reporters continued to keep the story alive and circulating. Residents of other states came; Chafets describes "a man from Dallas," race unmarked, who "come[s] up here every year. There's nothing like it. Ah [sic] never miss one."[143] That the city has a long history of whites burning down African American neighborhoods goes unremarked in these accounts. As performance theorist Joseph Roach has observed, "Forgetting is an opportunistic tactic of whiteness."[144]

Race is central to the affective force and scopophilic pleasures and horrors of Devil's Night spectatorship, just as it is to Detroit's "ruins" imagery and its figural work in general. Chafets makes this clear by repeatedly linking the fires to the city's demographic shift from majority white to majority African American, then characterizing that shift as literally continental: a kind of statistical and literal journey to the heart of darkness: "Within six years of the riot, it had a black majority and a black administration. . . . In most parts of town, most of the time, Detroit is as black as Nairobi."[145] White spectators are cast as mute witness/owner/exiles helplessly beholding this "orgy" of self-destructive irrationality at the hands of savages who are both indigenous and wholly alien: "The message was tacit but unmistakable—Look at what *they're* doing to *our* city."[146] Among Morisseau's achievements in *Detroit '67* is her reminder that, at many points in the city's history, African American residents made the same observation about the police.

In this characterization of white former residents' retrospective claim ("ours") on industrial Detroit, Chafets exposes a core component of Detroit's figural work: a toxic nostalgia in which industrial prosperity and whiteness are intimately linked, with the former putatively destroyed by black irrationality. Devil's Night spectacles become a racialized mirror opposite of industrial era efficiency instead of the latest in a long history of racialized internal combustions. Conservative radio talk show host Rush Limbaugh made this explicit when he cited Detroit's racial demographics as the cause of the city's 2013 bankruptcy filing with Devil's Night as evidence, popularizing Chafets's 1990 book as a primary source in the process.[147] In this view, despite being exempted from the Fordist decency bargain since its inception, African American Detroiters and their white progressive appeasers are cast as wholly responsible for the city's deindustrial decrepitude, reducing complex causalities of civic and governmental neglect to preindustrial "tribal animosity" that "seethes with the resentments of postcolonial Africa" and post-apocalyptic anarchy simultaneously.[148] For Limbaugh and his ilk, Detroit's devastation becomes evidence of both rational market evolution—the seemingly impersonal inevitability of deindustrialization—and racial pathology. Further, this invidious and inaccurate view inoculates civic and corporate neglect against charges of overt racism by fictively "proving" that, in a black city, the neoliberal rationality of abandoning it was right all along: Detroit was too "savage" and was best left to its own devices.

Thus, deindustrialization, read through Detroit-as-figure, becomes a way to imagine white loss at the hands of black savagery in a pernicious sleight of hand wherein putative black irrationality becomes the key symptom, if not the outright cause, of deindustrialization itself. The city's changed racial demographics become the pivot on which its status as industrialization's exemplar of unproblematic white middle-class prosperity turned to its figuration as aberrant cautionary tale demonstrating what happens when *"those people"* take over. Deindustrial hope and potential solidarity go up in flames: incendiary consequences of opening oneself to something (racially) new, even as industrialization's old racial(-ist) business is erased altogether. This is, of course, an old and not uniquely Detroit story. That said, as this city's hundred-plus years of racial(-ist) internal combustions demonstrate, when houses in a play entitled "Detroit" burn down, we need to pay attention.

The Figural Work of "not necessarily"

D'Amour's play re-sites and re-cites precisely this incendiary dynamic, including the spectacle of flames, through both spatial and racial sleights of hand and, in so doing, demonstrates how the city continues to operate as a figure of racialized deindustriality. *Detroit* is not necessarily set in Detroit because the "inner ring suburb" containing Bright Homes is not necessarily black. We know Kenny is a black sheep from boyhood troubles with the law ("graffiti, cheap wine"), heavy drug use, a son somewhere by a girl who used to clean houses, sexual appetites acted out in public, and "spells in jail."[149] He is deceptive and impulsive, can't hold a job, is edgy, angry and, of course, an arsonist. "Kenny" is not his real name; his mother has children with multiple partners and is herself unmarried. For all of Frank's wistful reflections on the bygone family-friendly days in Bright Homes, he has deliberately distanced himself from both Kenny and his mother; not all family is created equal, apparently. Perhaps this is because, in the world of the play, Kenny certainly, and perhaps Sharon as well, are not necessarily white: a reading strongly underscored by the blackvoice neo-minstrel performances of the backyard bacchanal, including hoodies and gangsta rap, in scene 7. Kenny blackens Ben and Mary in a contagious performance of abandoned decency, then blackens their home by reducing it to ashes. That's what happens when *those people* move next door and we invite them in. Just look at Detroit. Or *Detroit.*

It is certainly possible that D'Amour agrees with my reading, up to a point. Perhaps she means her "not necessarily" strategically as a way to disrupt precisely this connection between Detroit, contemporary fiscal precarity, blackness, and wanton destruction. In this reading, "not necessarily" may remind us that, in troubled times, incendiary encounters can happen anywhere; Detroit is both a unique place and just another example. Yet the figural residues of the city's very specific combustible racial(-ist) economic history, now selectively remembered and recoded as irrational black-on-white violence, coupled with its persistence as "ruins" on the national stage, can't be so easily stripped from the play by a coy equivocation. Further, in my view, Kenny's alignment with blackness both explicitly gestures toward Detroit's racial demographics and appeals to our oft-touted postracial self-congratulation. As Brandi Wilkins Catanese has argued in another context, to explicitly underscore the real Detroit's current racial makeup, and to make Kenny explicitly black, would be precisely the "bad manners" the play's "not necessarily" attempts to avoid.[150]

Yet racialization alone insufficiently accounts for Kenny's difference and the figural utility of Detroit in D'Amour's play. His very astute observation that, after Ben's severance runs out, Ben will be "just like him" belies the larger point that they are in at least one respect alike already—wholly expendable as economic actors—despite the fact that Kenny works with his hands by lifting heavy things and Ben does so at a keyboard. D'Amour's *Detroit* flattens the contemporary landscape of economic difference while selectively registering the affective force of the consequences: the dawning recognition of the precarity and isolation, to say nothing of the naiveté, of its middle-class subjects for whom things were not supposed to go this way. In so doing, D'Amour demonstrates another aspect of Detroit-as-metaphor. Because it figurally contains the nostalgia for a selectively remembered Fordist decency bargain, that bargain's currency as an affective attachment, and the profound anxieties wrought by its institutional dissolution, the city can offer class as well as racial fungibility, particularly to those who never paid dues on the shop floor. Not necessarily siting the play in the city of its title becomes a way to represent the upheavals of deindustrialization synonymous with Detroit as, at least affectively, transclass. In so doing, deindustrialization itself becomes elastic, encompassing multiple waves of late capitalist system failures: a collective shorthand for contemporary precarity and atavist anxieties in the face of market rapaciousness. Thus, even those who don't necessarily live there share a Detroit state of mind. The city is both a site of racial exception and a collective, generalizable affect.

ASHES TO ASHES?

At the end of *Detroit*, Ben and Mary are curiously muted. Maybe this is shock. Maybe it is stolidity enabled by savings, insurance, and quantifiable net worth. The two are not necessarily poor and not necessarily hopeless, even without family. They are not necessarily grounded in reality either, but this is the cruel optimism of neoliberalism's postindustrial bargain: the hope for better things achieved solely by relying on one's own devices. Rising from the ashes likely means embracing one's position as a member of the new and highly individualized creative class; everyone can become an entrepreneur on their own on the web somewhere—or nowhere. *Motown the Musical* reminds us that, once upon a time, this entrepreneurial self-fashioning was possible, particularly for those exceptional few who became the "boss of everything else." In contrast, *Detroit '67* insists we understand the racial limits of this transracial tale: the police can shoot and kill black business owners for no reason.

D'Amour says she liked Detroit when she visited it. After reassuring us that it is not all "burned-out neighborhoods," she expressed admiration for its "radical energy . . . : artists, activists, urban planners, and gardeners trying to re-imagine what this city could be."[151] She exempts the city's elected officials from this radical energy "because they have no money"; Michigan's governor did the same when he imposed the emergency manager. And she links this civic "energy" to what she "possibly proposes" at the end of her play, "which is what new things can we imagine other than these structures which are not working." This too is part of Detroit's current figural work. It is, we are told from many quarters, intrinsically dysfunctional and thus a productively blank canvas: industrialization's—and maybe even urbanity's—"closure dream," like the one Mary describes in the play's final lines.[152] What "new things" can we imagine—as if there are not people living there—neither artists, activists, urban planners nor gardeners—who are of necessity creatively imagining the city at the level of everyday life every day? What about those who, for generations, tried to imagine other structures of the good life like Russian immigrant Joe, Ossian Sweet, Berry Gordy, and, fictively, Morisseau's Chelle, Sly, Bunny, and Lank? What could these imagined "new things" do for them? Who, precisely, is the "we" that imagines these "new things"?

In *Cruel Optimism*, Lauren Berlant observes that older state-liberal-capitalist fantasies, like the Fordist decency bargain, shape adjustments to current structural pressures of crisis and loss.[153] These pressures, she argues, are wearing out the power of the good life's traditional fantasy bribe—benumbing work for the private home and secure front door—without wearing out the need for the good life. D'Amour's play, Detroit's re-sited and re-cited history, and Detroit-as-figure present something more complex. They demonstrate that this fantasy bribe is as self-rejuvenating as it is racialized. The deindustrial's version of the fantasy bribe is haunted by histories of incendiary racial violence as well as present-day tacit assumptions and explicit pronouncements that, if it were not for *those people*, all might be well. Within that fantasy, figurations of Detroit shape deindustrialization as both collective precarity and *those people's* problem because it is, somehow, their own fault. This current version of the fantasy bribe masks the fact that the bribe's rewards were always as unevenly distributed as its costs. And it reassures by continually reinvigorating the affective potency of capitalist self-invention fantasies at the nexus of home and work. After all, as the character Ben observes, websites don't burn, unlike Sly and Lank's "Feel Good Shack." Personal prosperity—if not collective justice—might just arise from the ashes one more time . . .

CHAPTER 4

Up from the Ashes

Art in Detroit's Emerging

Phoenix Narrative

Detroit is suddenly sexy. How'd that happen?

> Michael H. Hodges, *"How Detroit Got Its Groove Back"*[1]

Where are the black people?

> Nolan Finley, *Detroit News*[2]

By 2015, the year after Detroit emerged from bankruptcy, the city seemed to be transitioning from its deindustrial doldrums to a promising post-industrial future. Images of the city-as-ruin seemed increasingly passé: still in wide circulation but countered by a new figural economy depicting it as capitalism's latest phoenix rising from the ashes of its earlier decrepitude. Articles in the *New York Times*, *Harper's Bazaar*, and *Vogue* began extolling the city as a hip foodie, design, and shopping destination.[3] Earlier ad campaigns paved the way for this emergent civic rebranding. Chrysler's widely viewed "Imported from Detroit" 2011 Super Bowl commercial featuring white rap artist Eminem and the African American Selected of God Choir figured the city's muscular resurgence from its travails, despite the dismissals of "folks who've never even been here": "It's the hottest fires that make the hardest steel."[4] In 2013, Shinola, a luxury division of the conglomerate that includes the Fossil brand, launched a glossy print ad campaign for its watches, assembled in Detroit, prominently displaying local African American workers successfully retooled as artisanal craftspeople in the city's manufacturing tradition.[5] Apple, which neither makes its products nor locates an Apple store in the city, featured African American Detroit activist Jason Hall and his Slow Roll weekly bike rides in its 2014 commercial for the iPad, positioning the device as a form of grass-roots infrastructure generating interracial solidarity while aiding the city's comeback.[6]

The city's art and artists featured prominently in this new figural economy of economic resurgence, including these articles and ads. Diego Rivera's iconic *Detroit Industry* murals; Robert Graham's bronze *Monument to Joe Louis*, known locally as "The Fist"; and Eastern Market area murals on the city's east side, as well as Eminem and the choir, conjured the city's historic strengths: its demographics, work ethic, enduring fortitude, resilience, and creativity ready for glorious re-emergence in a post-industrial and seemingly post-racial comeback.[7] Perhaps Detroit would be the civic equivalent of early 1980s Michael Jackson: a spectacularly successful transitional icon whose boundless creativity and hard work fuel optimism for a bright future in a new mode of production.

Art and artists were not only inspiring backdrops to this emerging phoenix narrative, nor merely concrete manifestations of the can-do creative spirit that would make it possible. They were posited as active agents in the redevelopment process. Between 2011 and 2016, Detroit was also increasingly figured in the national media as the new Brooklyn or the new Berlin: offering affordable real estate, a seemingly self-evident bohemian authenticity, and untapped potential to reap hefty returns on investments in the city.[8] In this version of the phoenix narrative, art, artists, and their creative class compatriots—emblematic post-Fordist workers who embraced individual entrepreneurship and contingent employment—would fuel civic renewal.[9] As historian Julia L. Foulkes noted sardonically in a parody of this discourse, "Cheap places to live! Soul-crushing stories! Dancing (and rioting and repression) in the streets! Humanity exposed! All the city needs is a little SoHo-like gentrification to boost the economy and draw residents back to Detroit."[10]

"Back" is the key word. In this period, national accounts of art and artists as agents within figurations of Detroit-as-phoenix generally relied not on images of the resilience, know-how, and solidarity of the city's current residents but on its appeal to newcomers: a "risk oblivious cohort" of "pioneers" who would take advantage of its status as blank slate or frontier wilderness, making it "cool" for the "risk aware" cohort to follow.[11] These accounts of Detroit's putatively artist-led revival are generally light on descriptions of any actual art and operate from widely divergent presumptions of what art is and what artists do. The performing arts are not mentioned specifically as agents of renewal: strange given Detroit's history of innovation in music in particular.[12]

In these figurations, the city's post-industrial revival is as racialized as its deindustriality though by different means. African Americans are as invisible within most figural economies of Detroit's arts-led renewal as they were within earlier "folk models" of deindustrialization. The presumption that civic revival will be powered by outsiders moving "back" to Detroit, the generic "art" cited in redevelopment discourses, and the absence of references to the performing arts in particular are symptoms of what performance theorist Brandi Wilkins Catanese calls "the problem of the color-blind": the active disavowal of, or passive disregard for, "the material manifestations of race in society," including, in this case, Detroit's status as a majority African American city with a long and fraught history of profoundly racialized redevelopment initiatives.[13] Figurations of color-blind renewal, coupled with emphasis on outsiders moving in or back to the city, avoid the racialized "bad manners" of directly and explicitly equating that renewal with white newcomers.[14] Further, the invisibility of the performing arts in such figurations reinforces this color-blindness. Dance, music, and theater are generally embodied labors: inseparable from the specific bodies that produce and consume them, and from the specific locations in which these processes happen. Performers may be read as racially particular and venues as spatially particular: something a generic "art" within an equally generic "redevelopment" forestalls. In national, and even some local, figurations of artists as agents of Detroit's civic renewal, "art" and "artists" are wholly racially unmarked categories, enabling the cohort of pioneering "risk oblivious" newcomers to operate in the same way. Meanwhile, the "risk" to which this cohort is oblivious is left to inference: a "racial etiquette" that avoids directly acknowledging Detroit as a majority black and poor city whose residents have been explicitly indicted as the cause of its economic problems, and disproportionately adversely affected by prior urban renewal schemes.[15] Indeed Chrysler's, Shinola's, and Apple's corporate ad campaigns demonstrated greater attention to the city's actual demographics and what this might mean for civic revival than the often overheated rhetoric about Detroit as a new artists' mecca.

If Detroit has been the deindustrial's most obvious racialized cautionary tale for almost forty years, what do figurations of its arts-led, phoenix-like renewal tell us about the roles of race and art, both in its particular post-industrial incarnation and in capitalism's transitional periods? Will Detroit re-enact Michael Jackson's financialized melodrama on a civic scale, contracting in response to austerity imperatives? Will it exemplify an as-yet-unimagined just, egalitarian post-industrial capitalism?

This chapter examines figurations of Detroit's arts- and artist-led renewal between 2012 and 2016—the immediate pre- through post-bankruptcy period—to address three interrelated questions: How do these figurations depend on framing art and capital as color-blind partners reclaiming the city from its putative state of atavist wilderness? How do they reveal or obscure the racio-economic trajectories and austerity regimes of current redevelopment efforts? Finally, how can art intervene in fictions of seamless transitions between modes of capitalism by underscoring the racial, political economic, and affective dimensions of the deindustrial itself?

The chapter begins by surveying the ways art and artists operate in four city revitalization discourses beginning with the role of the Detroit Institute of Arts in the city's exit from bankruptcy. Taken together, these examples reproduce a familiar binary in figurations of art's relationship to capital. Art is both a timeless civic treasure that must defy monetization and a desirable amenity to be instrumentalized for redevelopment: a seemingly antithetical pairing that does significant rhetorical work within Detroit's phoenix narrative, as I discuss later. Further, many of these examples operate through presumptions about two types of racially unmarked post-Fordist workers as agents of urban redevelopment: the artist, whose flexible, affective, and generally low-wage labor creates an environment that appeals to her better-compensated counterparts—members of the creative class—whose appetite for "cool" attracts them to the city. Many rely on racialized presumptions or figurations of current city residents either as irrelevant—the city as blank slate or frontier wilderness—or as raw materials requiring the redemptive sophistication and savvy of newcomers from elsewhere.

This opening section of the chapter examines figurations of art within Detroit's emerging phoenix narrative, not practices of artist-led gentrification or the work of actual artists in the city. But two Detroit artists and their immersive installations do offer critical alternatives to these figurations: Tyree Guyton's *Heidelberg Project* on the city's east side and the late Mike Kelley's *Mobile Homestead*, sited at the Museum of Contemporary Art Detroit (MOCAD). The remainder of this chapter argues that these two works exemplify another role for art within urban deindustrial redevelopment: that of marking the deindustrial itself as a highly racialized transitional phase within modern capitalism, as a structure of feeling, and as a material element of the cityscape that is simultaneously selectively disappearing and selectively persisting. I describe the *Heidelberg Project* and *Mobile Homestead* as *gestic* art using Bertolt Brecht's theorizing of the *gest* as a critical marker of political economy in performance, then conclude with readings of each work's *gestic* operations: the ways each counters the fantasies of frictionless, logical, color-blind, "creative" redevelopment that so often permeate Detroit's current phoenix narrative.

THE ART OF THE COMEBACK

Detroit has been a comeback story since June 11, 1805, when a fire almost completely obliterated it, inspiring missionary priest Gabriel Richard to pen the lines that became the city's motto: "We hope for better things. It will arise from the ashes." Art was almost wholly peripheral to these 200-plus years of comebacks, but race was not. The city has been coming back from incendiary interracial violence since the Blackburn riots of 1833. Its industrial heyday was marked by both race riots and slum clearance/urban renewal initiatives so transparently racialized they were dubbed "Negro removal" by African American critics.[16]

Yet art was central to the most pragmatic, most financialized dimension of the city's latest comeback. The status of the internationally renowned Detroit Institute of Arts (DIA) collections was a key issue in the "Grand Bargain" that ultimately led to the city's successful emergence from Chapter 9 protection in December, 2014.[17] The DIA's artworks were viewed by the city's emergency manager, Kevyn Orr, and its creditors as assets to be liquidated to settle the city's debts.[18] The art was positioned at one end of a binary with retired city workers' pensions—averaging $19,000 per year—at the other; in the draconian austerity logic of the bankruptcy proceedings, one or the other would have to go.[19] Which was more important: the city's cultural patrimony or its retirees' economic survival?[20] In the ensuing controversy, the imperiled collections were described in terms reminiscent of those used to characterize the role of art in the industrial city a century before: as a civic "jewel" that "nourishes the imagination and ingenuity" of future entrepreneurs, as an intrinsic public good, and a "piece of American history."[21] The perilous state of the collections was indicted as yet another indicator of the United States' dismissal of art as "frivolous."[22] While pensioners ultimately agreed to reductions in benefits, the artworks were saved through a combination of foundation donations and state funds that offset the size of the pension cuts: a "Grand Bargain" that also transferred the museum from city ownership to a private trust.[23]

The outrage generated by casting DIA collections, purchased with city funds for the city's people, as potentially liquid assets was understandable and also reinforced a view of "art" as intrinsically "above"—both independent of and more important than—immediate political economic and long-standing racial justice concerns. Indeed, as a number of media outlets noted, while Michigan's Republican governor Rick Snyder, a former venture capitalist, refused to offer any "bailout" money for the predominantly African American city or its pensioners directly, thus avoiding any intervention in these concerns, he did contribute $200 million to the Grand Bargain to preserve DIA art as state cultural patrimony.[24] Details and figurations of the Grand Bargain also reinforced this view of the city's art as literally, even necessarily, removed from Detroit's social, political, and economic problems just as the city was being touted as an artists' haven. For example, according to one account, to "save" the museum's art from becoming a casualty of these very problems, the ad hoc partnership of private foundations and the state had to "ransom [it] from city ownership."[25] There was no talk of directly compensating the city for its historic support of the institution, as there would have been if the works had actually been sold. Instead, as the rhetoric of "saving" and "ransom" suggests, Detroit—not its creditors—was figured as a menacing captor whose hold on its art needed to be irrevocably severed.

These foundation and state actors were "saving" Detroit's art by effectively privatizing it even as art and artists were posited in the national media as "saving" the city for all. This set of figurations was not as contradictory as it might first appear. The rhetoric and logistics surrounding the Grand Bargain both reinforced art as a sphere apart from the city's material circumstances and dovetailed nicely with emerging discourses of a Detroit redeemed and repopulated by racially unmarked newcomers who would operate independent of actual city politics or substantive new public initiatives. In this version of the phoenix narrative, these artist-newcomers' purely private, individual efforts would generate new entrepreneurial infrastructure for the city without the need for direct state investment, while serving as an attractive amenity for an equally racially unmarked cohort of desirable, better-capitalized "creatives" to follow.

Figurations of art within the Grand Bargain were nationally compelling, though not unique, examples of the *kunst*-washing of Detroit's phoenix/redevelopment narrative. *Kunst*-washing is my variant on "greenwashing": the state and corporate practice of touting pro-environmental "green" values as rhetorical camouflage for their actual operations. *Kunst*-washing touts art and a loosely defined, fungible "creativity" as both a cover for and an agent of austerity and free-market logics, and the racialized dimensions, of post-industrial redevelopment initiatives. It often includes figurations of the current city as savage wilderness on which versions of this emerging phoenix narrative generally depend, sometimes explicitly and sometimes implicitly.

In the case of the Grand Bargain, the precarious position of the DIA's artworks generated an opportunity to "save" highly visible assets by stripping them from city ownership without compensation while leveraging other austerity measures, including cuts to pensions. While this bargain did stave off demands by the most predatory of the city's creditors, press coverage generally avoided a direct indictment of both those creditors and the highly financialized arrangements, initially lauded by Wall Street, that helped drive Detroit into bankruptcy. Instead, this coverage painted the city itself as the—at best—hapless landlord from which its art had to be "ransomed."[26] It reinforced a vision of public art and cultural patrimony as one end of an inherent binary with public pensions at the other, then offered a fictive sense of partnership between foundations, the state, the city, and vulnerable pensioners who would have had to absorb even larger cuts to their benefits without the art and the Grand Bargian to "ransom" them. This kunst-washed bargain operated as cover for both the privatization of the museum and the state's refusal to take any direct responsibility for providing the benefits negotiated and earned by city workers.

The *kunst*-washing of redevelopment has been central to relationships between artists and post-industrial cities since the early 1980s. Two examples from opposite ends of the deindustrial era are illustrative. Sociologist Sharon Zukin's *Loft Living* (1982) was an early pivotal analysis positing artists as vectors for an emerging financialization. Zukin's focus was SoHo, the deindustrialized New York neighborhood whose abandoned factories were repurposed by artists as living and studio space beginning in the mid-1960s. She writes:

> Looking at loft living in terms of *terrain* and *markets* rather than "lifestyle" links changes in the built environment with the collective appropriation of public goods. . . . [I]t directs attention to investors rather than consumers as the source of change. In the case of the loft market, analysis is mystified by explaining change in terms of "urban pioneers" instead of the opening up of a new real estate market to middle-class investors.[27]

As deindustrialization and capital flight from urban manufacturing centers became increasingly visible as national problems, "art suggested a new platform to politicians who were tired of dealing with urban poverty," particularly as the federal government suspended commitments to large-scale urban renewal and revitalization efforts in favor of private development subsidized with tax breaks in the late 1970s and 1980s.[28] While the artist-residents of SoHo did succeed in creating both generative artworks and self-sustaining models of urban collaboration, the loft "life-style" also operated as the *kunst*-washing of an emerging and increasingly aggressive real estate market such that, as of this writing, only one loft-as-performance-venue remains fully artist-owned.[29]

Early in the 2000s, when deindustrialized cities were no longer visibly new problems but seemingly intractable facts, the image of the artist as urban pioneer re-emerged in the work of management professor and consultant Richard Florida. In his book *The Rise of the Creative Class* (2002), Florida posits the eponymous class—those "paid to create new forms"—as central to civic revitalization.[30] For a strategy built on "creativity," the place of the arts and artists within Florida's creative class schema is both vague and ancillary at best. As he noted in an interview for his 2008 book, *Who's Your City?*:

> Public art plays two roles in a community: It *helps to create* an authentic sense of place and serves as a tool for revitalization. Quality of place is one of the defining issues of the creative economy. Places that are aesthetically pleasing *help to attract* innovative, creative talent. The arts *can also help play* a role in revitalization efforts. Investment in the arts (*galleries, public arts, common spaces, etc.*) provides public leaders with *a viable alternative to large capital investments* such as stadiums, convention centers, and so on.[31]

Aesthetics, to the extent that Florida addresses them, are unproblematically equated with "beauty":

> A community's aesthetics are extremely important; public art can play an important role in a community's overall appeal. Our research indicates that the higher people rate the beauty of their community, the higher their overall level of community satisfaction. Human beings crave physical beauty.

Florida aggressively marketed his "creative class" formulation to midtier cities as a *kunst*-cure for their deindustrial fiscal ills. In his view, art and artists offer capital low-risk routes to redevelopment because artists themselves shoulder much of the financial risk. They offer "authenticity"—presumably art can advance a free-market agenda because it is fictively apart from its homogenization and branding of urban space—and "beauty" to aestheticize and soothe capital's operations. These amenities are so fungible they can also be provided by "common spaces" in general. That galleries, public art, and members of the creative class might also stimulate public discourse on behalf of social justice and the public good is of less interest to Florida. "Creativity" for him is an agent of and for the free market, not an agent of critique or social change.[32] Indeed, when Florida was asked if his creative class of urban pioneers would "lead society in a better, fairer direction," he was reportedly "completely at a loss for a reply."[33]

With several very notable exceptions—Theaster Gates's work on Chicago's South Side and Rick Lowe's Project Row Houses in Houston's Third Ward—race does not feature prominently in studies of the role of art and artists in the redevelopment of deindustrial cities: as if it were incidental to either the cities' current populations or the hoped-for creative class newcomers.[34] While figurations of art as an agent of redevelopment within Detroit's emerging phoenix narrative often hew closely to Florida's creative class rhetoric, they too are generally "color-blind" in Catanese's sense of the term. Yet, on closer scrutiny, they are also profoundly racialized, particularly because most depend on implicit or explicit characterizations of the city's current majority African American population as either entirely absent (city as blank slate); as so atavist, benighted, or irrelevant that they do not factor in any redevelopment equation; or as a vague menace that provides gritty-yet-cool authenticity. These presumptions embedded in the latest version of Detroit's comeback suggest that *kunst*-washing and whitewashing of post-industrial redevelopment fantasies are intimately linked. Close analyses of figurations of Detroit's artist-led redevelopment offer opportunities to expose and challenge this "problem of the color-blind." In the sections that follow, I analyze three additional examples with three different relationships to the city: the redevelopment fantasy of a nationally renowned architect and urban planner, the real estate–based strategy of a transplanted New Yorker who literalizes the Detroit-as-new-Brooklyn version of the phoenix narrative, and a highly publicized foundation-driven plan that incorporated consultation with a wide range of Detroiters and local arts organizations.

Before proceeding further, it is important to note that, as of this writing, the City of Detroit has no arts-related or cultural affairs department or agency of its own despite the prominence of art in national and international figurations of its re-emergence. That department was eliminated in 2005. Indeed, a recent "Ideas City" conference located in and devoted to Detroit included the head of Chicago's Department of Cultural Affairs because Detroit had none.[35] It does have a Film Office, which incentivizes and supports production in the city. Moreover, its Arts Commission, which governed the Detroit Institute of Arts, was disbanded in 2014 as a consequence of the Grand Bargain that transferred the museum to a private trust and enabled the city's move out of bankruptcy. The State of Michigan has a Council for Arts and Cultural Affairs unit within its Economic Development Corporation, but as of this writing, neither Detroit nor Wayne County, in which the city is located, is represented in its roster of local arts councils. "CultureSource Detroit" is listed, but it is a membership-based professional organization, not a government entity.[36] Moreover, Wayne County government has no arts or cultural affairs departments that might represent the city.[37]

With no cultural affairs or arts-focused department, agency, or infrastructure in city government, it is difficult to know how the arts per se figure in current or future city government planning initiatives other than as existing anchor institutions that stabilize the area.[38] The administration of current Mayor Mike Duggan, who took office in January 2014, has continued earlier efforts to develop the city's rapidly gentrifying Midtown neighborhood. Midtown includes the Detroit Institute of Arts, now no longer city-owned; Wayne State University; and the College of Creative Studies, among other cultural and educational institutions. The most visible ongoing projects are a new hockey arena for the Detroit Red Wings—a public-private partnership subsidized by $250 million in taxpayer money with the team's owners to keep all the revenue—and the M-1 Trolley, another public-private partnership connecting the city's downtown to Midtown along Woodward Avenue.[39] Duggan accelerated city efforts to demolish vacant and blighted homes, with an additional focus on improving key neighborhood commercial corridors.[40] The absence of local government arts infrastructure in these efforts reinforces the view of art as separate from, if not wholly irrelevant to, actual on-the-ground redevelopment efforts except as ad hoc actions by individual urban pioneers operating outside state support, even as national and international media figure Detroit as a new arts hub.

"The Pink Zone"

For some, this absence of local government arts infrastructure is just fine—even ideal.[41] In "Why Detroit Is the New Berlin" (2014), Andres Duany, architect, urban planner, and author of The New Civic Art, presents "art" as synonymous with the libertarian ethos that will "save" the city. Duany's vision of the artist is a racially unmarked, intrepid millennial sojourner from elsewhere who will find Detroit desirable because it is a putative civic failure. He proclaims the city an anarchic wilderness where plucky newcomers can restore an "organic sequence" of urban redevelopment through a "Nike mentality: Just do it!"[42] He writes: "That Detroit is now attracting that first generation [of artist-pioneers] is an unintended consequence of its impoverishment. Detroit is now the city where the risk oblivious millennials can get things done." This risk oblivious cohort is "flummoxed and repelled" by regulation: "As evidence, observe the extraordinary numbers of millennials who are currently in the arts. Could it be that art and video are among the few things that can be made and sold without regulation—without the stranglehold of bureaucracy?" As noted earlier in this chapter, the "risk" to which this cohort of outsiders is oblivious is left to racial(-ist) inference.

Freed from the constraints of regulation, or even, in Duany's view, a functional city government, these "artists with a good eye, the penniless young people with a sense of adventure, and the fearless entrepreneurs" would follow in the footsteps of "the pioneers of the Left Bank of Paris in the 1870s, Greenwich Village of the 1920s, SoHo in the '60s, Miami Beach in the '80s, and Brooklyn today" and revitalize the city. Of course, this cohort of artist pioneers won't revitalize *all* of it, but "certainly a portion has the potential to become as rich and thriving as New York's trendiest borough." That these new pioneers might share locals' interest in high-quality local public schools and public transportation, or that they might be invested in critiquing the very structures of civic abandonment that produced this putative wilderness, is not considered.

Most damningly, Duany also fails to imagine that there are plenty of "artists with a good eye," as well as "penniless young people with a sense of adventure and fearless entrepreneurs," who now live in the city and have lived there for decades: suffering from, not benefiting from, its current conditions. His "Nike mentality" newcomers would be the city's "first generation" of artist-entrepreneurs; Berry Gordy, among so many others, apparently doesn't count. Duany dispenses with even the perfunctory nod to Motown, much less any other aspect of the city's rich arts history, that typically accompanies creative revitalization discourses.

This version of Detroit's artist-led phoenix narrative implicitly indicts its majority African American residents for being insufficiently creative, insufficiently risk oblivious, and insufficiently entrepreneurial to count as agents of civic renewal, or even register as agents within capital's newest frontier. There is no place for them amid the "cool" cohort of potential newcomers who would "make their own security arrangements" (private armed guards? a rifle in every studio?) and "make a cookie for sale without a certified kitchen, an accessible bathroom, and constant inspections." Duany's racialized presumptions of the city as atavist wilderness and his characterization of art as synonymous with libertarian politics *kunst*-wash his larger neoliberal, free-market prescription: to redevelop, Detroit should be designated a "Free Economic Zone which should be institutionalized as the first Pink Zone where [government] red tape is light."

One might ask why a risk-averse cohort of pioneers moving to a putative wilderness would need such a relaxation of regulation when government failure is supposedly the precondition for their arrival, but this would miss Duany's larger point. The "Pink Zone" is a way to free financialized capital from regulation, legitimate state abandonment of responsibility for those it has effectively already abandoned, and turn redevelopment over to the vicissitudes of the free market, not to empower creative artisanal cookie bakers. He makes this point directly when he notes that "developers like Dan Gilbert [founder and chairman of Quicken Loans and Rock Ventures LLC] are already renovating the big buildings" in the city because of "young people in-migrating": not as artists or independent entrepreneurs but as potential workers in the finance industry. He does not mention the $50 million in tax breaks from the State of Michigan Gilbert received to relocate the Quicken Loans corporate headquarters to Detroit.[43] In Duany's vision of Detroit's arts-phoenix narrative, artists are little more than stalking horses for state-subsidized private capital. His "risk oblivious" millennials who "just do it!" are merely color-blind cover for both the failure to address, and the license to ignore, the structural, systemic poverty of its current residents.

"Invest with Us"

The figuration of Detroit as the new Brooklyn was literalized in the December 2014 announcement that arts venue Galapagos was closing and relocating there.[44] Galapagos featured prominently in the redevelopment of Brooklyn's Williamsburg neighborhood. Executive director Robert Elmes made the connection between Detroit as the "new" Brooklyn/Berlin, its potential as a creative class hub with art as a catalyst, and its status as an emerging market ripe for infusions of new capital explicit on a section of the venue's website touting the move:

> For almost fifteen years, post-wall Berlin, Germany, lost population as people voted with their feet and moved west. Only after art and culture *made the city interesting* to curators and collectors did the city begin gaining population. This outcome was aided by efforts of the German government to attract business and industry to the city, and in turn art and culture helped attract these industrial and business interests.[45]

According to Elmes and others who view the city as a new arts colony, by setting up shop in Detroit, artist newcomers could do civic good while doing well creatively and financially.

While on the surface a color-blind "art" seems to occupy a more explicit and prominent place in this version of the phoenix narrative, it is art's ability to make a city interesting to equally color-blind curators and collectors who can insert it into structures of valuation, and then to business and industry, that will attract in-migration: essentially Florida's creative class trajectory of urban development. The city and its current residents are apparently not sufficiently interesting in and of themselves.

Unlike Duany, Elmes states his *kunst*-washed relationship to financialization outright in a section of the website entitled "Invest with Us": in Detroit, Galapagos is in the real estate business, and the city has abundant, cheap properties available. He has purchased more than 600,000 square feet in Detroit, including its highly desirable Corktown neighborhood, and in Highland Park: the impoverished, overwhelmingly African American municipality surrounded by Detroit that was the site of Henry Ford's first Model T plant. Further, in contrast to Duany's use of art to *kunst*-wash or ignore state subsidies to private corporations, Elmes is explicit about the need for state support; coverage of the move indicated that both the Michigan and Detroit economic development corporations were "supportive" of Galapagos's relocation, though it did not specify a monetary value.[46]

In the section of his announcement labeled "A New Funding Model," Elmes outlines his vision for Detroit's artist-led revitalization in terms that practically paraphrase Zukin's analysis of the SoHo loft as real estate market opportunity: "The arts are already in the real estate business—they just aren't being rewarded for it. . . . Moving the arts and culture away from the tin-cup mentality that has defined them for so long is an important focus for us as we begin our work in Detroit and Highland Park."[47] The Galapagos website does not specify how this new real estate–based funding model will move the city's artists away from a "tin-cup" mentality, but, as, Elmes notes in *Crain's Detroit Business*:

> "In New York City we created a no cost to low cost model for nonprofits, cultural groups and community groups to use the venue for fundraising and activism and presented over

600 fundraising events," [Elmes] said. "We're going to expand that here in Detroit and you'll see everyone big and small raising money through our infrastructure."[48]

Thus the "new funding model" does not so much move away from a "tin-cup" mentality as relocate it inside Galapagos's real estate holdings. But it is clear that Elmes expects to raise big money from his Detroit infrastructure. A year after he initially announced Galapagos's move to the city, he put one of his buildings, near the rapidly gentrifying Corktown neighborhood, on the market for $6.25 million. Elmes purchased the building for $3.92 per square foot; the sale price asks $45.29 per square foot.[49] In response to a firestorm of criticism over the sale, he responded by stating it was necessitated by his son's illness.[50]

Unlike Duany's vision of art as a synonym for generic, regulation-free entrepreneurship that must be imported into Detroit to pave the way for larger financial players, Elmes's real estate–based strategy does not wholly ignore local artists. The Galapagos website promotes a "Detroit Biennial": a "survey of new and important work being produced in Detroit" undertaken "in collaboration with local curators and galleries."[51] The Biennial will be presented by "Kunsthalle Galapagos"; an embedded hyperlink in the name takes the reader to a gallery space located not in Detroit but in Brooklyn.[52] Detroit may provide the artistic and curatorial talent (though as of this writing no specific Detroit artists, curators, or galleries are actually listed), but the real cultural capital—those "curators and collectors" who will actually make the city interesting—are apparently neither to be found nor to be enticed there.

While Elmes avoids the most risible and obvious figurations of the city as racialized atavist wilderness, it is clear that, for the Galapagos venture, Detroit's most valuable amenity is its potentially profitable, flippable raw square footage: one reason some Detroit-based critics paint its move as a New York City/manifest destiny land grab with profits siphoned back to the metropole. As one local critic noted at length:

> Don't let the cover of an artistic background fool you, this is just as troubling to me as Chinese real estate investment snatching up neighborhoods at the county tax auction. If land is the basis of freedom as Malcolm X suggests, it's disconcerting to know that residents around Detroit are loosing [sic] more and more of their freedom to landlords. When the Detroit art scene is having a hard enough time trying to be acknowledged on a national scale, having a big player airlift in, and control the narrative with property and big pockets, it is sure to push existing Detroit artists further to the sidelines of the converation [sic]. . . . [P]lenty of great Detroit creatives have built a very appealing brand that Galapagos is moving in to capitalize on. The rest of the great venues and art organizations around the city will just have to live in its big, New York–designed shadow. (I mean seriously? At least other out of town businesses would have hired local architects).[53]

Elmes's explicit *kunst*-washing of post-industrial redevelopment weds a fundamentally free-market, real estate–based approach to a quasi-colonial ethos. Detroit's vast stretches of cheap vacant land and its local artists offer resources that can only be properly processed—"made interesting"—elsewhere. The city itself remains the periphery: essentially spatial and aesthetic raw materials.

"Landscape"

The most famous, or notorious, of the nonprofit sector's plans to revitalize Detroit is *Detroit Future City* (*DFC*; 2012), supported by the Kresge, John S. and James L. Knight, and W. K. Kellogg foundations and by the nonprofit Detroit Economic Development Corporation. DFC began its transition to an independent nonprofit organization in 2015. (In this section of the chapter, *DFC* refers to the organization's published *2012 Detroit Strategic Framework Plan*—the document—and DFC to the organization.) The *DFC* document acknowledges input from a wide range of government and local stakeholders, as well as arts institutions including the *Heidelberg Project* and MOCAD, the permanent site of the *Mobile Homestead* installation, both works discussed later in this chapter. *DFC* focuses on Midtown as a model of successful civic redevelopment that must be sustained and supported. Most controversially, it calls for restructuring and reducing city services across its 143 square miles and ultimately designating "low vacancy" residential neighborhoods, particularly on the predominantly low-income, African American east side, as "Landscape" for agricultural and green uses.[54] Mayor Duggan's group executive for jobs and the economy called *Detroit Future City* his "bible."[55] Maurice Cox, Detroit's planning director, stated that he was "fortunate to inherit" *DFC*.[56]

It is difficult to overstate the level of scrutiny, often coupled with anxiety, suspicion, and outright hostility, with which local artists and activists regarded the *DFC* document upon its release. To take only one admittedly anecdotal example, in an October–November 2015 visit to the city as part of a Princeton Mellon Initiative course, "The Arts of Urban Transition," only three of the twelve artists and activists we met did not voice specific concerns about it. Most had heavily annotated copies of the document prominently displayed in their studios. This suspicion was explicitly acknowledged by a Kresge Foundation representative with whom we also met. In November 2016, on a return visit, artists' and activists' concerns were still palpable. Certainly some of the negative responses arise from the fact that the *DFC* document was produced by unelected agents. The plan was released shortly before the state's imposition of an unelected emergency manager in 2013; the city's school system is, as of this writing, still run by yet another state-imposed emergency manager.[57] In this context, it is understandable that *DFC* has been widely read, particularly by African American residents, as one more example of how they have been dismissed by white elites as incapable of self-governance.

Unlike other prescriptions for Detroit's redevelopment that figure current residents as raw materials to be made interesting or profitable by wealthy outsiders, New York cosmopolitans, and urban pioneers, or omit them entirely except as coextensive with civic failure, *DFC* explicitly acknowledges on its opening page: "Detroit is ... [h]ome to 714,000 residents who are resilient and already working to change the course of the city's prospects."[58] Its proposals and iconography identify, address, and reflect the city's majority African American population. It is explicit about serving the needs of and creating opportunities for current Detroiters rather than relying solely on fantasies of racially unmarked newcomers.

Art features prominently in the *DFC* document: as a model of "innovative development," a neighborhood amenity, corporate branding opportunity, strategy for information sharing, and a form of ecological infrastructure.[59] It is unique among nationally circulated Detroit-as-arts-phoenix discourses in noting the potential for art to advance critical dialogue. Further, the plan acknowledges the significance of community arts initiatives—both in general and, like the "Red Bull House of Art," specifically branded—as well as major Midtown arts institutions.[60] In its neighborhood-based schemas, art, along with "business, production, ... and lifestyle," will anchor "Live+Make districts," which, in turn, will "reinvent entrepreneurship for the 21st century within the space of discarded 20th century industry."[61]

On close examination, however, the actual place of art within the *DFC* vision is more problematic than it at first appears. In some cases, issues arise from the arts "precedents"—or lack thereof—highlighted in the document: foreshadowing potential conflicts arising when local needs and those of state or corporate capital diverge. Consider, as an example, the Red Bull House of Art, one of the "precedents" for neighborhood arts infrastructure. According to *DFC*, the House of Art offers an "artist residency program [for] Detroit-area artists."[62] This corporate-branded "authentic platform for the local arts community" will provide "exposure and interaction in a professional gallery venue." Yet none of the three artists in the House of Art's 2016 "Residency 1" cohort appear to actually reside in the city. They "live and work in the Los Angeles area" or are "based in New York City"; the third "lives and works in Brooklyn."[63] The House's website makes it difficult to determine whether artists in its previous eleven "cycles" are from the city or not, even as it touts residencies from "80+ local artists." While there are local artists and arts-related issues represented on the site, "authentic" residencies for artists who actually reside in arts metropoles reproduce the optics, if not also the practice, of corporate *kunst*-washing wherein Detroit's "authenticity" and private sector resources for local development actually serve corporations and individuals not located there.

Further, existing local arts initiatives run by residents of the city's neighborhoods are not cited as "precedents" for successful arts developments, or even mentioned by name, in the relevant arts sections of *DFC*. The *Heidelberg Project* is mentioned only on the list of stakeholders consulted. The widely praised Alley Project on the city's southwest side—touted as an excellent example of creative placemaking by the head of the Kresge Foundation—is not mentioned at all. Omissions of neighborhood art and artists from arts "precedents" in favor of a corporate branded operation whose current beneficiaries don't live in the city raise a bracing question: Whose art—in whose neighborhoods—really exemplifies DFC's long-term vision?

Related, and more disturbing, is art's alignment with the DFC's "shrinking city"/"right-sizing" strategy: the proposed recalibration and reduction of city services in lightly populated, predominantly African American and low-income areas. These neighborhoods would then revert to, or be rezoned as, "Landscape" labeled "Innovation-Production" and "Innovation Ecological." While this alignment avoids an obvious use of art to *kunst*-wash free-market ideologies in already gentrifying areas, it does offer a curious pairing of the *kunst*-washing and greenwashing within "austerity urbanism."

As critical geographer Jamie Peck defines it, US "austerity urbanism" is a program of extreme fiscal contraction imposed "in the context of reduced revenue flows and the withdrawal of state and federal assistance," particularly to cities viewed as "'home' to many of the preferred political targets of austerity programs—the 'undeserving' poor, minorities and marginalized populations, public sector unions and 'bureaucratized' infrastructures."[64] "Publicly designating some neighborhoods for active disinvestment while greenlining others, delivering residual services on a triage basis" is a hallmark strategy of austerity urbanism; Peck cites a plan by Detroit mayor Mike Duggan's immediate predecessor, Dave Bing, to shrink the city and aggressively cut services to neighborhoods as a paradigm case.[65] Yet, as urban sociologist L. Owen Kirkpatrick points out, to generate any substantial cost savings from this "right-sizing" strategy, residents of neighborhoods designated for triage would have to be encouraged—or forced—to move: recalling the racialized predations of urban renewal initiatives demolishing African American neighborhoods near the city's downtown without providing viable housing alternatives.[66] Bing was explicit that his "right-sizing" would entail such removals.[67]

Bing's proposed plan, which included support from DFC's foundation patrons and its precursor organization (Detroit Works Project), was met with vehement community resistance and scathing academic critiques. Critics characterized the proposal as the "dismantling" of the city and "essentially an effort to unlock real estate value currently 'contaminated' by a population in need of containment."[68] Given this recent history of resistance to urban triage, it was perhaps unsurprising that community activists and residents were highly suspicious of DFC's designation of vast stretches of the city as "Landscape" despite assurances on the part of DFC personnel and city planning director Maurice Cox that no one would be forced to move.[69] As Elena Herrada, a member of the Detroit Public Schools Board of Education, described DFC: "The foundations, which are really corporations in drag, are making sure that certain neighborhoods are . . . getting infrastructure improvements, lighting improvements . . . [while] other neighborhoods are decommissioned."[70]

The connection between the "arts" and the problematic "Landscape" designation is most obvious on a page of *DFC* illustrated with one of the city's most notable public artworks: the *Heidelberg Project*, though it is not formally identified. The project is located in one of the east side African American neighborhoods projected to become "Landscape." On page 287 of *DFC*, an unidentified thumbnail image of the project's signature *Dotty Wotty/People's House* illustrates a larger thumbnail with the following text: "Transitional Landscapes: Temporary landscapes that clean the soil and enable new forms of social life and creative displays: event landscape, remediation fields for forest, Artscape [*sic*], [and] Urban Meadow." A dialogue bubble seemingly produced by a silhouetted figure in the frame proclaims: "Support urban agriculture (small scale, organic, community/locally driven) through city policies and zoning." That one of the city's most visible and popular public artworks—one represented in the roster of *DFC*'s community stakeholders—goes unidentified does not suggest a commitment to invest deeply in, or even recognize, existing assets already enabling "new forms of social life and creative displays" in the neighborhoods. Moreover, an image of this iconic house topped by a figure touting the future of agriculture suggests the former may—or even should—be replaced by or subsumed into the latter.

How could a field or forest sustain works of art like the block-long *Heidelberg Project*? Would such works operate as islands in these proposed fields, forests, or meadows as the project's image operates on the page: an unmarked cipher within a pitch to rezone its site for farming? Was the installation itself viewed by *DFC* as "temporary" or "transitional"? Is it "artscape" or "landscape": a destination in and of itself or a blank canvas? What about the people who now live next to and near it—those who have kept up their homes for decades against massive civic disinvestment? Are they transitional or temporary too? Was the decision *not* to identify such a high-profile work by name on this page a tactic to obscure the social life and "artscape" that already exists in this "landscape"? Finally, in its push to imagine a post-industrial Detroit, did DFC consider that designating primarily African American neighborhoods as potential agricultural sites conjures images of the sharecropping/tenant farmer pasts forebearers of current residents moved to the city to escape? In the *DFC* document, visions of a post-industrial comeback sometimes appear explicitly preindustrial in deeply racio-spatialized ways.

In this and other examples within the *DFC* document, art outside of the Midtown area or the "Live+Work" zones operates as a *kunst*-washed palliative. It functions as a perfunctory nod to neighborhood social life within a greened-up austerity drive to rezone those very neighborhoods for agricultural use or pollution remediation without posing viable alternatives for people now living there. Further, as geographers Daniel Clement and Miguel Kanai argue, "The DFC's imagery of 'green and blue infrastructure,' 'desirable landscapes,' and 'flowering fields that clean contaminated soils' may be another trope to portray Detroit as investment-ready, whitewashing [its] problematic history of extremely uneven development at the metropolitan scale, marked by widespread racialized spatial injustice and oppression."[71] While other arts-phoenix versions of Detroit's redevelopment rely on figurations of the current city-as-blank-slate to entice newcomers, *DFC* proposes the creation of whole swaths of actual blank/green slate.

In redevelopment prescriptions for a post-industrial Detroit between 2012 and 2016, art has been figured as simultaneously trivial within the structures of city government and as an intrinsic and unassailable public good utterly divorced from the city's economic problems, as a symptom of a libertarian entrepreneurial ethos, a real estate venture, an amenity for a racially unmarked yet racialized creative class, a new form of production, and, when located in its predominantly African American neighborhoods, fungible with greened-up civic contraction. The remainder of this chapter argues for a different role for art in this transitional period: that of critically and explicitly marking the deindustrial itself as a specific, highly racialized phase within modern capitalism, as a structure of feeling and friction, and as a politics of location designating zones of productivity and abandonment. It posits two Detroit installations, Tyree Guyton's *Heidelberg Project* and the late Mike Kelley's *Mobile Homestead*, as "*gestic* spaces" in which the affective, racial, and spatial histories and effects of the deindustrial, and racialized trajectories of urban redevelopment, are especially clear.

The *Heidelberg Project* is a block-long installation-collage by African American artist and Detroit native Tyree Guyton consisting of reclaimed homes and lots on Heidelberg Street between Ellery and Mt. Elliott. Houses forming the core of the project were adorned with brightly colored painted polka dots, or LPs or stuffed animals nailed to their exterior walls; lots are filled with meticulously and densely layered piles of discarded shoes, toys, vacuum cleaners, and other objects. Guyton began the project in 1986; it now includes only what has survived multiple city demolitions and a dozen arson attacks. Described as a "sleepy, crazy Eden" amid its "postapocalpytic" surroundings, the *Heidelberg Project* is the third most visited tourist site in the city.[72]

Mobile Homestead, created by white artist Mike Kelley, is a full-sized replica of his family's suburban ranch house. The work includes both the replica and an elaborate basement level not open to the public. A "mobile" portion was transported through Detroit on a truck chassis pulled by a semi in 2010. Kelley envisioned *Mobile Homestead* as itinerant, ideally heading up and down Michigan Avenue "perform[ing] its social duty of useful public service."[73] The full installation opened in May 2013, almost a year and a half after Kelley committed suicide. It is permanently sited at MOCAD in Midtown, where it serves as a community gallery gathering space.

Both works are examples of what performance studies scholar Shannon Jackson has called "the expanded visual arts."[74] Both combine the structural and aesthetic components of the installation with theatrical, even spectacular, presentational elements and temporal dynamics that shape encounters with them as events; details of these dynamics are discussed later in this chapter. Spectator interaction and immersion are crucial components of both works. Guyton describes the *Heidelberg*

Project as an "environment"; Kelley conceived of *Mobile Homestead* as "performing its social duty," and in its current configuration, it operates as "an open clubhouse, a free zone for activity and exchange."[75] Though both have active social practice and educational components, I do not discuss these at length in this chapter. Instead, I locate each work's critical potential to illuminate and commemorate the city's deindustriality in its aesthetics, history, and location.

Both the *Heidelberg Project* and *Mobile Homestead* figure Detroit from within, offering intimate, insider critiques even as they, *Heidelberg* in particular, are also major tourist attractions and embedded in figural economies of the city circulating in national media. Both musealize and interrogate aspects of the deindustrial city as redevelopment efforts sweep it away with selective infusions of new capital, or propose erasing it entirely in greenwashed plans for civic abandonment. Detroit has been the nation's figural exemplar of deindustrial arrest: seemingly stuck between factories and financialization without a critical mass of either for more than thirty years. As the city becomes capitalism's new figural phoenix, the *Heidelberg Project* and *Mobile Homestead* insist that we confront and remember this liminal period— especially its costs, casualties, racialization, and selective debilitating persistence— in a direct challenge to fantasies of capitalism's natural, color-blind, benevolent evolution. Both offer alternatives to industrial nostalgia, cynical resignation, or blind faith in capital's ability to raise a shiny new city for all Detroiters from the ashes of its deindustrial debility.

I begin the next section of the chapter by defining "*gestic* space," based on Bertolt Brecht's theory of the *gestus* in performance. Next, I link the rhetorical work of the *Heidelberg Project* and *Mobile Homestead* to that of their most famous local industrial era counterpart, Diego Rivera's *Detroit Industry* murals. The three works form a geographical and *gestic* triangle connecting an icon of the city's industrial past to both its deindustrial present and visions of its post-industrial future. The *Heidelberg Project*'s and *Mobile Homestead*'s *gestic* potential to illuminate and interrogate the deindustrial arises from their most basic formal condition: both are homes in a period when relationships between homes and capital in Detroit are uniquely fraught. The chapter concludes with readings of the *Heidelberg Project* and *Mobile Homestead* that probe their deindustriality in/and their aesthetic particulars.

GESTIC HOMES

The *Heidelberg Project* and *Mobile Homestead* are *gestic* spaces because they materialize key aspects of Detroit's racial and political economic history in the city's deindustrial period in ways that directly challenge its current color-blind arts-phoenix narrative. The formulation "*gestic* spaces" builds on "*gestus*," Bertolt Brecht's term for "the mimetic and gestural expression of social relationships in which people of a particular epoch stand in relation to each other."[76] Both the comparative ("stand in relation to") and the historical ("of a particular epoch") dimensions of *gestus* are crucial to my analyses of the *Heidelberg Project* and *Mobile Homestead*. Reading the aesthetics and location of one against the other underscores the spatio-racial trajectory of capital in Detroit from the beginnings of deindustrialization through its increasing visibility in the mid-1980s to current visions of the city's post-industrial future. Further, these works offer *gestic* representations of deindustriality arising from the specific periods in which they were produced, as well as from their explicit engagements with the city's history.

The *gest* is a tactic of cultural production—something artists do—and an interpretive strategy: something audiences do. It is also both physical and rhetorical: "To view things *gestically* is to catch the gist in terms of gesture, or rather to position oneself at the point where one German word hovers indeterminately between two English ones."[77] In this chapter, I argue that the *Heidelberg Project* and *Mobile Homestead* are explicitly *gestic spaces* of the deindustrial and *read them gestically*, noting the ways their aesthetic particulars operate to critique or reinforce aspects of the period, particularly its racial dynamics. Both works require just such a "hovering" between gesture and gist. To understand how and why they are rhetorically potent and affectively moving, viewers have to physically move through them while engaging the kinesthetic and proprioceptive elements that animate their critical work.

Finally, the *gestus* theatricalizes political economy—"laying bare society's causal · network/showing up the dominant viewpoint as the viewpoint of the dominators"—through a materialist aesthetic that "excludes the psychological, the subconscious, the metaphysical *unless they can be conveyed in concrete terms*."[78] Herein lies the *Heidelberg Project*'s and *Mobile Homestead*'s particular significance as emblematic *gestic* spaces of the deindustrial. Both materialize the ways the deindustrial operates as a political economic and an affective state in two neighborhoods whose trajectories have increasingly diverged. Encountering these works means reckoning with manifestations of the metaphysical yearnings and existential anxieties, the resilience, debility, and uncanniness of the deindustrial as they emerge in specific spatio-racial environments. Both works are highly ambivalent, another indicator of their importance as *gestic* depictions of the period. They refuse the giddy optimism that routinely accompanies infusions of capital and/as redevelopment: capitalism's "phoenix" narrative. Yet they also refuse melancholy resignation and industrial nostalgia. Both *gestically* underscore the importance and contingency of affective attachment: to one's work and home, to the city, and to hope and history in capital's latest liminal phase.

The *Heidelberg Project* and *Mobile Homestead* form two arms of a *gestic* and geographical triangle linking them to Detroit's most iconic work of art: the DIA's *Detroit Industry* murals by Diego Rivera, completed in March 1933.[79] Rivera's murals monumentalize workers' achievements while critiquing the predations of the industrial age. The murals cover the four walls of a beautifully lit interior courtyard. One scene depicts factory workers dwarfed by the swirling inferno of the·blast furnace. A particularly famous panel features a multiracial formation of men straining against levers on the assembly line and reaching up to grasp components, appearing to hang from the line as if from meat hooks.[80] In another section, uranium miners glow a sickly green, poisoned by their labors. Tucked off to the side, in the lower corners of the work, industrialists and managers glower over plans or offer wan smiles, either oblivious to the workers who dwarf them or pleased with their own power to command such efforts. Rivera believed the murals were his finest work.[81]

The artist spent eleven months in Detroit, visiting the Ford River Rouge Plant, then the largest industrial site in the world, to conduct research for the project. He arrived in the city to begin working on the murals in April 1932, one month after the Ford Hunger March Massacre and the subsequent funeral demonstration for four marchers shot dead by the police: an event that drew 60,000 people, the largest "communist" mass protest in the United States since the funerals of Sacco and Vanzetti, according to the *Detroit News*.[82] Conditions in the city in this period, the height of the Great Depression, mirrored the despair and debility of its later deindustrial depths; Rivera "found a severely depressed city, where half of the people were working but two-thirds of them were living at the poverty level."[83] As art historian Linda Downs observes, "Rivera did not invoke the grave realities of the Depression in the Detroit murals. Instead, he concentrated on the strength of its indigenous industrial culture." When the work opened, in the midst of what was quite possibly a manufactured controversy characterizing the murals as communist and blasphemous, audiences turned out by the thousands to, in Detroit historian Jerry Herron's words, "see themselves depicted and to surprise themselves with the memory of who they were, in spite of history, in opposition to it."[84]

More than eight decades later, as Detroit's redevelopment efforts erase, or propose to erase, the city's ruined industrial infrastructure and some of the most obvious evidence of earlier civic abandonment, the *Heidelberg Project* and *Mobile Homestead* insist on figuring deindustrializaiton not as a frictionless transition in modes of production as putatively rational as the assembly line, not as a colorblind "creative" turn in capitalism's evolution, but as a fraught, racialized process that doubled down on those most excluded from industrial prosperity. Both also rely on an "indigenous" form: Detroit's "visually unspectacular" and "unbeautiful" neighborhoods of wood detached houses.[85] Whereas Rivera's murals monumentalize the triumphs and atrocities of the industrial age on the walls of one of the city's most venerable institutions, the *Heidelberg Project* and *Mobile Homestead* figure the deindustrial at its most intimate: not as monument but as home.

Poor Houses

The *Heidelberg Project* and *Mobile Homestead* are literal and *gestic* homes. They are composed of actual houses that mark and comment upon the racialized political economy of the city that contains them, and on the status of the home within it.[86] Whereas the three plays discussed in chapter 3 use Detroit's history to advance larger points about relationships between race, the private home, work, legacies of the industrial age, and contemporary precarity, these two installations focus specifically on the sometimes uncanny home within the deindustrial: a site of personal investment that both succumbs to and resists civic abandonment and private despair. Their *gestic* potential arises from the conjuncture of their specific aesthetics, the political and figural economies of houses in deindustrial Detroit, and the "unsettling multiplicity" of the house itself.

American studies scholars Paula Chakravartty and Denise Ferreira da Silva observe:

> A house is, in all its figurings, always thing, domain, and meaning—home, dwelling, and property; shelter, lodging, and equity; roof, protection, and aspiration—oikos, that is, house, household, and home. . . . Houses, as such, refer to the three main axes of modern thought: the economic, the juridical, and the ethical, which are, as one would expect, the registers of the modern subject.[87]

Yet their otherwise comprehensive list leaves out one element, one crucial to the *Heidelberg Project*'s and *Mobile Homestead*'s *gestic* work: the affective register that, in turn, registers the house as both object of and container for desire. Anthropologist David Graeber argues that "objects of desire are always imaginary objects, and usually imaginary totalities of some sort," and the house is precisely this.[88] Thing, domain, and meaning—to say nothing of work, life, emotions, and stuff—converge on/in the house-as-desire: in the desire for security, belonging, and distinction; for respite; for the agential performative production of the self and/as world. The house contains and, to use a real estate term, "stages" our relational materiality and our distinctiveness.

Detroit's homes, including the *Heidelberg Project* and *Mobile Homestead*, expose the confluence of the affective, the economic, the juridical, and the ethical registers—the unsettling multiplicities of the home—with particular clarity: highlighting the ways these registers operate in times of structural economic change. Moreover, because Detroit is a majority African American city, and because this fact is so central to its figural work, its homes also remind us that these registers are thoroughly racialized; for an account of the city's notorious record of housing discrimination in its industrial heyday, see chapter 3. Throughout its deindustrial period, images of Detroit's homes were simultaneously vivid examples of its seemingly unstoppable decline; evidence that this decline was stubbornly resisted by activist residents; examples of imperiled personal assets at risk of both government seizure and civic abandonment, sometimes both at once; and untapped potential sites for capital investment from as far away as China. To fully grasp the *gestic* potency of these two works within Detroit's current phoenix moment, it is essential to review key examples of this very public confluence: Detroit's residential ruins iconography coupled with the actual state of many of its neighborhoods, its highly publicized tax foreclosures and residential water shutoffs, and the role of the home mortgage industry in the city's redevelopment.

Images of blighted homes feature prominently in figurations of Detroit as deindustrial wasteland. Some of these images suggest residences' past grandeur still barely discernible despite overgrown foliage and trash. Others show houses sliding toward their own oblivion one piece at a time: not "homes" so much as fossils, their vitality long ago replaced by the compacted sediments of personal debility and institutional indifference. Still others feature actual homes, shabby though inhabited, standing alone on blocks as open and unobstructed as prairies, their persistence seemingly testifying to the disappearance of the neighborhoods around them. Such figurations present neighborhoods, and the city itself, as blank slates: frontier wilderness seemingly crying out for a capital takeover or destined for abandonment because they appear already abandoned. Indeed, civic abandonment of Detroit's neighborhoods has been very real, if not fully strategic. Former mayor Dave Bing unsuccessfully proposed shrinking Detroit's footprint and rationing services, but de facto rationing unfolded in an ad hoc manner apart from any city policy.[89] In 2013, an estimated 40 percent of the city's streetlights were not functioning either due to disinvestment or because they had simply disappeared, stolen by scrappers.[90] Trash collection was erratic.[91] In 2014, EMS response time to 911 calls averaged eighteen minutes; it took an ambulance more than twenty-five minutes to respond to a call from city hall involving a *Detroit News* reporter who appeared to be having a stroke.[92]

Detroit's broken houses and empty residential neighborhoods figure the deindustrial at its most personal and terrifying. They remind us that an earlier iteration of the state liberal capitalist bargain sustaining the desire for a good life has been willfully abandoned like so many empty city blocks. They also offer the same dubious pleasures of underclass voyeurism as did nineteenth-century tours of New York's Five Points. Detroit's shattered houses have been used as figural evidence in raced cautionary tales wherein the city's demographic shift to majority African American, not structural changes in the US economy and systemic private and public sector disinvestment, caused its post-Fordist decline.[93] This view is frequently articulated in white former residents' proprietary claims on the city's residential infrastructure, especially former family homes: a kind of absentee victimization-by-proxy that conveniently overlooks a seventy-year history of white and capital flight. To quote conservative commentator Rush Limbaugh's favorite author on the subject, "Look what *they're* doing to *our* city."[94] Both the *Heidelberg Project* and *Mobile Homestead* *gestically* comment on this unraveling of the Fordist bargain.

The overlapping affective, economic, juridical, and ethical registers of the deindustrial home are also evident in two widely publicized and highly controversial economic "recovery" initiatives: one undertaken by Wayne County, which includes the city, and the other by the Duggan administration. Each targets Detroit's residences as sources for "accumulation by dispossession," imperiling this poor city's poorest residents.[95] These initiatives are also crucial background for understanding the *gestic* work of the *Heidelberg Project* and *Mobile Homestead* because they underscore the fraught relationship between the family home, the deindustrial city, and the political economy of capital extraction in redevelopment periods.

In 2015, Wayne County planned to auction off more than 28,000 properties in Detroit, including 10,000 homes that were still inhabited, for property tax delinquency, ending the practice of avoiding tax foreclosure on those owing less than $1,700 and despite charges that the actions would deeply destabilize already precarious neighborhoods.[96] Data indicated that the overwhelming majority of those at risk of losing their homes to tax foreclosure were senior citizens, households with young children, or those facing an unanticipated crisis. Tax delinquencies rose as a direct result of the Great Recession when residential property values in Detroit plummeted but property tax assessments did not; a *Detroit News* investigation concluded that the city overassessed homes by an average of 65 percent. Unpaid property taxes accrued 18 percent interest penalties each year, though a 2015 law enabled retroactive lowering of the rate to 6 percent. Unable to afford these liabilities on homes shrinking in value, in neighborhoods often virtually bereft of city services, residents either abandoned them or faced tax foreclosure.

Critics labeled the auctions "Ebay on a city scale" and compared them to the accumulation of land through the dispossession of Native Americans.[97] African American homeowners were most affected even as the city was trying to attract new residents, and incentivizing corporate elites to move to downtown and Midtown with tax breaks and taxpayer funds. The foreclosures recalled forced relocations of African Americans during earlier city redevelopment initiatives, including one directly affecting the McDougall-Hunt neighborhood discussed later in this chapter: "a tragic and extreme version of a familiar pattern [of] . . . racial dispossession."[98] Properties were put up for auction online, including those with residents still living in them. In one tragic case, two buyers of a foreclosed home were killed in a confrontation with a relative of the occupant.[99] The foreclosures sparked vehement grass-roots resistance and produced new activist coalitions, most notably Detroit Eviction Defense, which makes highly theatrical spatial interventions on and near imperiled properties to save residents from being forcibly removed, in addition to mounting legal action on behalf of besieged homeowners.[100]

The Detroit Land Bank ultimately became the repository for those properties unsold in the auctions, including an estimated 4,500 that were still occupied. These are marketed on a website whose beckoning title recalls appeals to settle the US West a century and a half earlier: "Building Detroit. Neighbors Wanted."[101] Presumably this means "new" neighbors, not those already living in their foreclosed homes. The city's widely publicized inventory of putatively available residential properties attracted the attention of investors, including those from China. CNN reported that Detroit was the fourth most popular city for Chinese real estate investors:

> In the case of Detroit, the buyers often don't even do the repairs right away, according to Rachel Saltmarshall, president of the Detroit Association of Realtors. They're buying

at tax sales and foreclosure auctions and holding the properties, keeping them vacant, hoping that the city's comeback is imminent.[102]

Ultimately the Detroit Land Bank, which was "poised to own a quarter of the city—at least 86,000 properties" by the end of 2015, finalized a pilot program to sell homes back to those occupying them for $1,000 each, provided they met a strict set of conditions.[103] The tax foreclosure auctions underscore the contradictory nature of the deindustrial home: imperiled asset, civic revenue stream, frontier home-steading opportunity, and indicator of global investor optimism at the same time, each dimension thoroughly racialized. The *Heidelberg Project* and *Mobile Homestead* comment directly on this dizzying and debilitating confluence.

Another highly controversial element of "economic recovery" centering on the deindustrial home and its fraught intersection of affective, economic, juridical, and ethical registers began in 2014 when the Duggan administration announced it was shutting off water to residences with delinquent water bills. In July 2014, the NAACP Legal Defense Fund filed suit against the city seeking a halt to the practice, charging that the shutoffs were discriminatory and noting, "The folks who are being cut off are almost one hundred percent African American."[104] This was only one of the legal actions unsuccessfully seeking a moratorium on the shutoffs; Judge Steven Rhodes, who was also presiding over the city's bankruptcy proceedings, ruled that there was "no constitutional right to water service."[105]

In October 2104, there were 2,300 homes in the city without water due to shut-offs.[106] Between December 2014 and December 2015, a total of 23,000 accounts were turned off; in December 2015, a third of the city's water customers were sixty days or more past due on their bills and at risk of shutoff.[107] In some cases, the amount owed was less than $200; shutoffs were mandated for any amount delin-quent above $150.[108] In other instances, new owners were informed, after buying their houses, that they were responsible for five-figure unpaid water bills from the previous owners.[109] Residential water bill delinquencies were rolled into property taxes, threatening to push even more homes into tax foreclosure. Residents were terrified that both their children and their properties would be seized; lack of water was a reason social services could remove children to foster care.[110] Yet commer-cial scofflaws were not pursued.[111] The water shutoffs generated widespread local, national, and international outrage; protests, water activism, and charitable cam-paigns to pay bills and restore water service; and the involvement of the United Nations, which demanded the city restore access to residents' water as a basic human right and chastised it for gross incompetence in its billing processes.[112]

Detroit's abandoned and imperiled homes demonstrate the ongoing debilitat-ing precarity of the deindustrial, as well as grass-roots resistance to the home as a site of accumulation by dispossession; as discussed in the next sections of this chapter, the *Heidelberg Project* and *Mobile Homestead gestically* comment on both. But houses also figure prominently in Detroit's shift from factories to finance. Most notably, Dan Gilbert, founder of Quicken Loans, an online home mortgage broker, headquartered the company in the city in 2010 and subsequently bought up large tracts of its downtown. Described variously as Detroit's "superhero" and "monopoly man," Gilbert and his Bedrock real estate services owned more than eighty properties, almost 14 million square feet, with a total of $2.2 billion invested as of January 2016.[113] He also facilitated the relocation of consumer finance company Ally Financial to downtown.

Quicken Loans has a prominent place at the intersection of the affective, economic, juridical, and ethical dimensions of the home: particularly the point where desire for home ownership meets both the economic realities and the ethics of home financing in the city. In July 2015, less than a year after Gilbert was appointed a leader of an antiblight task force, the *Detroit News* reported that Quicken Loans had "the fifth highest rate of mortgages ending in foreclosure in Detroit over the last decade—and half of those properties are now blighted."[114] In April 2015, the US Department of Justice (DOJ) filed suit against the company, alleging that it improperly originated and underwrote mortgages insured by the Federal Housing Administration: accusing it of mortgage malfeasance by making irresponsible loans with US taxpayers ultimately responsible for the losses when those loans went into default.[115] Gilbert filed a preemptive suit against the DOJ and disputed the charges; Quicken's suit was dismissed, but the company succeeded in moving the DOJ suit to a federal courthouse in Detroit near its corporate headquarters.[116]

The home mortgage industry in Detroit is a crucial component both of the city's shift from industrialization to financialization and of its blighted deindustrial decrepitude. Even after the subprime loan crisis left the city with tens of thousands of foreclosures, the industry continues to both define and reflect the spatio-racial trajectory of the city's current redevelopment. As journalist Anna Clark argued in her essay for the nonprofit Next City Foundation: "Two different stories are playing out in Detroit. . . . There is the 'Midtown story,' the tale of select neighborhoods where the narrative is about revival. Historic residences in Detroit's most gracious communities are asking for eye-popping prices."[117] In contrast, "Across vast swaths of the city, this is not a story of revival; it is a story of war." Outside highly desirable areas, which is to say in most of the city's neighborhoods, it is virtually impossible to get a mortgage to buy a home, thus excluding all but those with ready cash on hand and resources to do the likely extensive rehabbing required to make it livable. Impediments include low appraisals of value, leaving no possible equity to be tapped for repairs, indeed even finding an appraiser willing to go into certain neighborhoods, and tax and water liens on homes outside highly desirable areas. Clark characterizes the situation as a new version of "redlining":

> Redlining is typically understood as the practice of denying access to home mortgages in certain areas to whole classes of people based on their race or ethnicity, and segregating them into less desirable areas. In today's Detroit, the phenomenon plays out differently, but the social impacts are no less intractable. Instead of an overtly racist and classist policy rendered with a boundary slashed across a map, it manifests as a cascading

series of obstacles that become apparent to a prospective homeowner when he or she approaches a bank to take advantage of what seems at first to be a buyer's market, open to anyone willing to invest in a rebounding city.

By virtue of their locations and their aesthetics, the *Heidelberg Project* and *Mobile Homestead* very precisely mark these "two different stories" of spatio-racial residential development. In so doing, they underscore the role of financialization in a city characterized simultaneously by capital investment from the finance industry and almost wholesale capital abandonment. Moreover, each pointedly, *gestically* asks its audiences to reflect on the racialized histories and futures of Detroit's deindustrial homes in this period of post-industrial transition.

The *Heidelberg Project* and *Mobile Homestead* are enmeshed in larger iconographic and political economic contexts of Detroit's deindustrial homes even as they *gestically* comment upon them. And they are not alone. Because Detroit's houses so vividly fuse the city's Fordist promise to the atavist anxieties activated by its dissolution, and so beseechingly evoke the affective and financial opportunities of homesteading a putative new frontier ("Neighbors Wanted"), they have a uniquely concentrated figural potency. I suspect this accounts for the remarkable persistence of the city's "shattered house" photojournalism and the number of Detroit artists whose works self-consciously reflect on the house as a site of play and loss. But the *Heidelberg Project* and *Mobile Homestead* are unique in their persistence and institutionalization, in their references to the city's racial(-ist) history, and in their abilities to simultaneously comment upon and attempt to repair the unsettling uncanniness of the long deindustrial moment that has come to exemplify Detroit on the international stage. The remainder of this chapter examines each work—its history, location, and aesthetics—reading its particulars as *gestic* interventions in the figural economies of Detroit, the deindustrial, and the city's emerging phoenix narrative.

THE *HEIDELBERG PROJECT*: WHAT TIME IS IT?

The *Heidelberg Project* stages confrontations with time. Both sides of Heidelberg Street between Ellery and Mt. Elliott are festooned with images of clocks. Brightly painted boards affixed to trees and utility poles depict hands stopped at 4:45 and 1:50, 3:52 and 11:40. The spreads of the clocks' hands make it seem as if time itself is being crucified on these poles and trees. Images propped up in lots, or nailed to the charred remains of a residential foundation, proclaim 1:40 and 11:30. There were houses here once, and families whose lives were set to factory shift and school schedules. Painted and chalked clock faces on the sidewalks register only hours, or only minutes because their hands have been smeared and faded by the weather or worn away by visitors, recalling Salvador Dali's famous images of melting clocks if they too were subject to the literal, pedestrian passage of time and not safely fixed on canvas. The proliferation of clocks, and of times, presses the questions: What time is it here on Heidelberg Street on Detroit's near east side? What time is it *really*?[118]

African American artist Tyree Guyton began the *Heidelberg Project* in 1986. Its most iconic component is the *Dotty Wotty House* (renamed *The People's House* after Barack Obama's election as president): his grandparents' white frame residence, which Guyton painted with brightly colored polka dots. His mother still lives there. When Guyton began the project, Detroit was already characterized as deindustrialization's racialized cautionary tale. He was thirty, a painter and sculptor by training. He grew up on Heidelberg Street, had worked in the nearby Chrysler Jefferson Assembly Plant as well as for Ford and as a city firefighter. The project was, from its inception, *about* his neighborhood as much as *within* it. The dots adorning his family home simultaneously conjured the jelly beans his grandfather loved, a postracial vision of a multihued city, and a defiant, colorful intervention into the neighborhood's blighted state. The playful exuberance of the *Dotty Wotty/People's House* tends to overshadow the darker edge, subversiveness, and complexity of the work as a whole. But the aesthetics of its current configuration, particularly its deployments of destruction, persistence, and accretion, and its ongoing visual dialogue with its own history and production exemplify the critical potential of *gestic* deindustrial spaces.[119]

In her 2001 analysis of the *Heidelberg Project*, poet and critic Wendy S. Walters described it as "a performance of history."[120] More than a decade, and multiple permutations, later, the work does not so much perform in and of itself as *gestically* stage multiple confrontations: with the site's history and its status in Detroit's latest phoenix narrative, with market and racial illogics of accumulation and abandonment that define the deindustrial, with what it means to be home in this African American post-Fordist city on the cusp of yet another comeback, and, above all, with the long deindustrial moment itself. The *Heidelberg Project* keeps time. It arose as a direct response to, and survives, the debilities of Detroit's deindustrial decline; marks this very history by confronting visitors with the scars incurred in the process of that survival; and, in its proliferation of clock faces, explicitly presses the question of what comes next. Is Detroit's latest comeback a time for hope and renewal or for cynicism? Is it a time to *kunst*-wash and whitewash the city's deindustriality or to greenwash its African American neighborhoods?

Time is a crucial component of the *Heidelberg Project*'s *gestic* work; its inextricability from Detroit's racial and political economic history is both its most basic condition and its subject matter. For those who know the installation well, the proliferation of clock imagery is a reminder that there is not just one *Heidelberg Project* but many over an arc of thirty years. The project has unfolded and changed over the course of Detroit's deindustrial period like the neighborhood itself: representing in microcosm the promise of a middle-class life in the city's industrial heyday exemplified by the family home, the racial(-ist) realities constraining that promise for the city's black residents, the incendiary history of these homes recounted in chapter 3, and the "demolition means progress" trajectory of current neighborhood redevelopment.¹²¹ Two successive mayors, irritated by the attention it brought to the neglect of the neighborhood and spurred on by the complaints of neighbors, tore parts of it down in 1989, 1991, and 1999. Guyton responded by creating new sculptures on the vacant lots and by adorning the increasing number of newly vacated structures. In the 2010s, the work was hit by multiple waves of arsons, burning some of the most iconic houses to the ground, including the *Obstruction of Justice ("O.J.") House*, the *House of Soul*, and the *Party Animal House*. Guyton then created new works on and within the burned remains of some of these: *gestic* acts that creatively adapted to deindustrial destruction without erasing it.

These new works in particular capture the deep ambivalence of "resilience" and "redevelopment" in Detroit's neighborhoods in its immediate pre- to post-bankruptcy period. For example, stuffed animals adorn the scorched foundations of the *Party Animal House*, gesturing back to those that originally decorated its exterior walls; it burned down in March 2014 (figures 8 and 9). For those who encounter the new version without prior experience of its predecessor, the creatures appear to be plucky, adventurous survivors assembled on an urban ark run aground. But they also look like benighted shelter pets: unsure how they ended up here, confined to this ruin where they face an uncertain future, an incipient danger signaled by the blackened brick walls that hold them fast. Are they, like Detroit's long-term residents, survivors or prisoners or both? Inside the shell of the basement foundations, which visitors must squat down to see, a blue high-heeled shoe topped with a naked white Barbie doll sits on a table as if on a stage; rows of chairs face the "stage" with single blue men's shoes on some of the seats. Guyton has created a blue peep show—both melancholy and mildly prurient—that reverses the racialized scopophilia of Detroit's "ruined home" iconography, first by making the naked white doll and not the city's African American residents the object of the gaze, second by underscoring that those who "look" from "outside" are voyeurs, and finally by highlighting the apocalyptic ethos of the scene: as if the audience inside this charred basement left their chairs in a hurry, leaving only single shoes behind because, like Cinderella at the ball, their times had run out.

Inside another charred foundation in the middle of the block, Guyton has assembled a strange quasi-domestic tableau: a black baby doll lying on a table, a charred set of steps hosting an array of dolls and doll heads looking around as if waiting for a party to start, another naked white Barbie sitting in what looks like a high chair. Atop the foundation, a guitar lays between a wig head looking out at the neighborhood on one side and shattered trophies on the other. The construction recalls an *offrenda*, an altar commemorating loss: the now-burned house, the Fordist domestic good life and good times, the long-forgotten victories signaled by these trophies. A large painting of a clock affixed to the assemblage shows 11:30: perhaps a reminder to remember those consumed by the city's decades of deindustrial losses as well as those still waiting for good times to return here.

The work's location is another of its foundational *gestic* elements. The McDougall-Hunt neighborhood, where the *Heidelberg Project* is situated, is north

Figure 8: The *Heidelberg Project, Party Animal House* (n.d.), before it was destroyed by arsonists in March 2014. Tyree Guyton, artist; Heidelberg Project, owner. Photo from Heidelberg Project Archives. Used with the permission of the Heidelberg Project.

of the now-vanished Paradise Valley, Detroit's historic African American cultural and economic center. It partially absorbed residents displaced when that neighborhood was razed in a series of urban renewal initiatives between 1946 and 1963 that were so transparently racialized they remain a point of contention more than fifty years later.[122] McDougall-Hunt featured prominently in coverage of the city's notorious Devil's Night arsons of abandoned houses and waves of schoolgirl rapes between 1980 and 1999, when Guyton was actively working on the project. From 1994 through the 2000s to the present it has been part of a federally designated "Empowerment Zone": another comeback plan. Empowerment Zones advanced objectives for revitalizing city neighborhoods, primarily through tax incentives for businesses.[123] If the Empowerment Zone initiative has left any lasting legacy in McDougall-Hunt, it is not readily apparent.

Now the neighborhood is one of the areas designated "Landscape" in *DFC*: from Empowerment Zone to green zone. Currently, the Detroit Land Bank is listed as owner of almost a third of its properties—the neighborhood's largest landowner: a testament to pervasive abandonment, demolition, skewed tax assessments, and tax foreclosures.[124] Detroit's Planning and Development Department is the next-largest owner. Property tax assessments in the neighborhood range from tax-exempt to over $74,000, with the highest assessment in the block of the *Heidelberg Project* at more than $19,000, wildly high given the area's property values.[125] Prices for

Figure 9: The *Heidelberg Project*, installation on the charred remains of the *Party Animal House* site (2015). Tyree Guyton, artist; Heidelberg Project, owner. Photo by Judith Hamera. Used with the permission of the Heidelberg Project.

properties in the area range from assessed value unknown to $59,000; of the four homes for sale in McDougall-Hunt nearest the project, all are foreclosures or auction sites.[126] The neighborhood is a *gestic* palimpsest of racialized deindustriality. Here the results of racialized urban renewal initiatives in the name of industrial era progress, nightmare landscapes of the deindustrial city, prior comeback attempts, fantasies of greened-up civic contraction, and the ongoing debility of civic abandonment and tax foreclosures write over one another unreconciled and seemingly unreconcilable.

If you were to stand in the middle of the *Heidelberg Project* in the early morning, you would be struck by the silence. You would hear birds, and perhaps the wind, but very little else. The quiet is the acoustic analog of the neighborhood's large swaths of open land; while the playful constructions and whimsy of the project's installations are compelling, it is the quiet that cues viewers to the fact that these constructions are here because houses, and people, are not. The silence and the sheer amount of empty space are unsettling and uncanny. The *Heidelberg Project* is barely three miles, yet an entire world, away from the bustling Midtown area, with its "meds and eds" redevelopment, its busy artisanal coffee shops, construction noise, and rising property values. The city did receive federal funds to increase the pace of demolition in the neighborhood and plant foliage as part of a storm water abatement strategy in 2015, but there is no visible new commercial or residential redevelopment. Clearly

McDougall-Hunt's "greening" is the only future policymakers have so far imagined for the neighborhood. With the notable exception of the project itself, and its large contingent of visitors, the phoenix has yet to arise here.

Yet the *Heidelberg Project* site is neither a park, nor "green infrastructure," nor simply "landscape." Part of its potency as a *gestic* space is the fact that it is still here, for now stubbornly refusing to disappear. In addition to its own spectacular constructions, African American residents' homes, with people sitting on porches or going about their business, are visible to the south, southwest, and, most dramatically, next door to one of the project's installations: the quasi-*offrenda* mentioned earlier. This house is well kept, with a prominent sign in front emphatically informing visitors that it is *not* a part of the *Heidelberg Project* and is not to be photographed. It too is a *gestic* intervention, both in the racialized scopophilia so apparent in images of "ruined" Detroit neighborhoods and in the DFC figuration of the site as suitable only for future green space.[127] With its admonition *not* to intrude, *not* to photograph, this house and its sign make spectatorship of both the *Heidelberg Project* neighborhood and the city's ruins imagery vexed and complex. Looking is not neutral. People live here, resist the racialized atavist narratives imposed on them from the outside, and look back. Further, in its very refusal to be subsumed into the project, this house reminds us that neighborhoods are contested spaces where dissent is a prerogative of citizenship, not simply raw material to be reconfigured by unelected actors.[128] Finally, this house and others surrounding the *Heidelberg Project*, like the project itself, push back against figurations of the city as blank slate, suitable only for greened austerity urbanism, even as they highlight the challenges of making the city work for residents in lightly populated neighborhoods. By its very location and surroundings, the *Heidelberg Project* refuses figurations of deindustrial Detroit as either simply debilitated or simply resilient.

Guyton has consistently articulated a vision of the *Heidelberg Project* as a site of post-racial civic healing, but neither that vision nor the work itself is "color-blind" in Catanese's sense. On the contrary, the artist explicitly and persistently presents the intertwined racial history and political economy of Detroit, and the United States, in ways that materialize black performance theory. As performance studies scholar D. Soyini Madison defines it, black performance theory

> works to translate and inspire, to politically interrogate and sensually invoke, how realms of performance struggles and troubles illuminate black agency and subjectivity within reimagined spaces of being. . . . [It] attends to performance histories, aesthetics, and orders of belonging governed by multifarious modes of un-freedom as well as the radical performances that violent constraint has invoked. But, as much as [it] is about politics, entangled within history and power, it is also an enterprise and a labor of the senses.[129]

While the *Heidelberg Project* is not a performance per se, it is a carefully theorized *gestic* production that stages confrontations with the very issues of race routinely "invisibilized" in the current color-blind phoenix narrative of Detroit's redevelopment.[130]

The project exemplifies an African diaspora aesthetic; as Walters and others have noted, it draws on African American fine arts antecedents, including Romare Bearden's collages and diasporic vernacular forms like the Kongo bottle trees, as well as European precedents like the work of Marcel Duchamp. Further, in (re) constructing the disappeared parts of the project, Guyton actively (re)constructs the neighborhood as black social and cultural space, aligning himself with earlier generations of African American residents who rebuilt their lives after the razing of Paradise Valley. This *gestic* (re-)construction is most obvious in his rebuilding of the *House of Soul*. The original was lost to arson on November 12, 2013. It was a meditation on spiritual and sonic sustenance, as well as the city's deep, rich history of African American music before, during, and after Motown. The bare wood two-story frame house was meticulously covered with LPs and 45 rpm records: a form of vinyl siding affixing the durable pleasures of black artistry, visually reinforced by the blackness of the disks, to the obvious frailty of the structure. The original *House of Soul* (figure 10) was also surrounded by images of clocks, some with records at their centers. Temporality was an explicit element of its message: nostalgia for better days coupled with a testament to enduring black artistic infrastructure on the LPs and in Guyton's design and creative labors. One of the disks nailed to an exterior wall was Lou Rawls's album optimistically proclaiming: *All Things in Time*.

Guyton's rebuilding of the *House of Soul* is a very explicit *gestic* act: a rare example of a "house" going up in McDougall-Hunt instead of coming down. But the new *House of Soul*, since renamed *The Sacred Place*, also adds an explicit political economic critique to the original's spiritual-sonic theme. In the new incarnation

Figure 10: The *Heidelberg Project, House of Soul* (n.d.), before it was destroyed by arsonists in November 2013. Tyree Guyton, artist; Heidelberg Project, owner. Photo from Heidelberg Project Archives. Used with the permission of the Heidelberg Project.

both the interior frame of the structure and its exterior walls are adorned with LPs: reinforcing visions of restorative black interiority and of music by black artists as homeplace infrastructure and internal support. Michael Jackson's *Thriller* is one of the LPs adorning the exterior (figures 11a and 11b). The spiritual element is

Figure 11a: The *Heidelberg Project, The Sacred Place* (2015). Tyree Guyton, artist; Heidelberg Project, owner. Photo by Alex Quetell. Used with the permission of the Heidelberg Project.

Figure 11b: Close-up of *Thriller* LP on *The Sacred Place*. Tyree Guyton, artist; Heidelberg Project, owner. Photo by Alex Quetell. Used with the permission of the Heidelberg Project.

explicit in crosses and an "Order of Service" listing the weekly rhythms of religious life, from 9:45 a.m. Sunday school to Wednesday night Bible study, nailed to the frame. But the exterior siding of *The Sacred Place* is also covered by signs saying, simply, "War," and by images of money: large representations of pennies, including fragments of Abraham Lincoln's head ringed by "In God We Trust" as if by a halo, and a sign for "MoneyGram International Money Transfers." A twisted, purple car body is nailed to one side, bisected by a purple cross that runs the full height of the construction, ultimately becoming a steeple: a car crucified. There are toy cars both inside and out: a reminder of Mo(tor)town—the sound and the Fordist mode of production—that sustained life in this neighborhood, both now gone. These coverings signal that here, less than three miles from Midtown, sites of black spiritual, sonic sustenance—the neighborhood's family homes, disappeared neighborhood churches, even the *Heidelberg Project* itself—are under siege: depleted by global capital flows away from the city and by local accumulation through dispossession in tax foreclosures, leaving only pennies, or fragments of pennies, behind.

The *Heidelberg Project* as a whole continually and explicitly reminds viewers that the work, McDougall-Hunt, and Detroit itself have always been spaces of what performance studies scholar Bryant Keith Alexander calls "raced relationality": where US racial(-ist) narratives and interracial confrontation are represented in particularly potent form.[131] *Move to the Rear*, a 1955 bus covered in painted polka dots and crosses, surrounded by car hoods and boards painted with grinning faces propped against or affixed to it, commemorated Rosa Parks's refusal to give up her seat to a white passenger in that same year.[132] The front of the bus marked Detroit's Rosa Parks Boulevard as its destination. The *Obstruction of Justice ("O.J.") House*, which burned twice in 2013 and was ultimately a total loss, had been densely layered with upside-down paintings of the American flag (an official distress signal), the painted initials "OJ," painted crosses, political campaign signs and a stop sign, images of clocks, and faces. A white toy car was set on the roof, conjuring O. J. Simpson's white Ford Bronco and the infamous slow-speed chase through Los Angeles that culminated in his arrest. For those who know the city's history, the piece also recalls Detroit's specific and notorious police abuses, including the Detroit Police Department's Stop the Robberies, Enjoy Safe Streets (STRESS) Unit, formed in the wake of the 1967 conflict. The overwhelmingly white department's STRESS Unit and its partner unit, the Big Four, were early civic adopters of an aggressive "stop and frisk" practice that harassed African American city residents before being disbanded by the city's first African American mayor, Coleman Young, in 1974. The unit is so notorious that there is still an online forum devoted to "STRESS memories."[133]

A recent iteration of Guyton's famous *Faces in the Hood* series is among his most pointed critiques of current "color-blind" redevelopment initiatives. *Faces in the Hood* are vibrantly colored portraits that cover the *Heidelberg Project*, painted in a faux-naive style with open mouths, some seemingly grinning, some seemingly shouting. The paintings are typically done on board and, most famously, on car

hoods, riffing on the intertwined history of the neighborhood, the auto industry, and urban vernacular for "a place where plenty of shit goes down."[134] They are
propped up in lots, affixed to homes, nested within *Move to the Rear*, and painted
on the sidewalks. The latest iteration lines the north side of Heidelberg Street, separating the sidewalk from the small patches of grass nearest the road: a row of faces
painted on the sides of cinder blocks, each topped with a "land line" telephone
(figure 12). Some of the phones are large, relatively new models clearly discarded
by an office as part of an upgrade. Some are small home phones with rotary dials.
Some of the blocks have toppled over and broken; some of the phones lie thrown
off to the side. The line of painted cinder blocks looks like a row of grave markers
ornamented by both the decedents' faces and technology that is increasingly obsolete. This piece, modest by *Heidelberg Project* standards, whimsically but *gestically*
forces the question: Are both the "hood" and the "faces" here—the representations
and their living counterparts—obsolete relics of a bygone age replaced by capitalism's latest phoenix narrative? Are they, too, outmoded in greened fantasies of
neighborhood contraction or in the aggressive redevelopment of Midtown so heavily populated by new white residents that a local columnist pointedly asks, "Where
are the black people?"[135]

Obsolescence and decay are key themes of the *Heidelberg Project*; both are activated by a visual logic of accretion. The work is literally constructed from, and
requires visitors to navigate, layers and layers of detritus: "the death of objects as
a means of [civic] transformation," according to Wendy Walters.[136] But both the
objects themselves and the nature of this transformation merit consideration, particularly in the context of Detroit's current arts-phoenix narrative. Consider, as an
example, one of Guyton's constructions made of discarded toys situated near the
quasi-*offrenda* mentioned earlier: a riot of neon-colored plastic children's chairs,
scooters, baby buggies, and cars are intertwined with child-sized basketball hoops,
plastic goalposts, dolls waving and doll heads grimacing, shopping carts, hobby
horses, and an orange caution cone, among many, many other items. This is a consumer economy hybrid of kiddie park and garbage dump. Toys are one site where
a globalized economy meets everyday domestic life. These plastic toys are almost
certainly imports: cheap to buy and thus easy to discard because of the same global
relocation to low-wage manufacturing sectors that contributed to the auto industry's downfall and the crisis of the US deindustrial. It is not unusual for visitors to
recognize their old toys in this and other carefully constructed piles, and the effect
is uncanny: moving from a quick, pleasant frisson of recognition through a slowly
dawning melancholy at the toys' very disposability, to a vexed pleasure in their
Heidelberg Project afterlives. In Guyton's precise, *gestic* arrangements, these objects
are not "dead," nor is their transformation into this pile a simple allegory of civic
rebirth. Instead, they persist both in their particulars and as an aggregate: attesting to the disposable desires fueling an economy where consuming things has
replaced making them, and the perseverance of the people and places discarded in
the process.

Figure 12: The *Heidelberg Project, Faces in the Hood* (2015), sidewalk of Heidelberg Street. Tyree Guyton, artist; Heidelberg Project, owner. Photo by Judith Hamera. Used with the permission of the Heidelberg Project.

While the plastic toys in this installation will likely endure in some form for centuries, other constructions emphasize their own decomposition. One of the most compelling is the *Ark*: a listing, dot-covered shell of a boat swamped by a gigantic, overflowing pile of stuffed animals. The work is whimsical and deeply ambivalent, particularly because it is open to weathering and decay. One reason the city gave for demolishing parts of the project was that this decomposition was a health hazard, ironic given the sheer number of abandoned, falling-down houses left in place in the area during that period. Guyton now routinely refreshes the more obviously perishable components of the work. Yet the *Ark*'s clear vulnerability is both inescapable and *gestic*. As it weathers, this pile and these layers literalize the "slow violence" of deindustrial era civic abandonment in Detroit's neighborhoods: wearing away residents' livelihoods, residences, and ultimately the neighborhood itself.[137] But they also challenge the fantasy of a color-blind art as a creative class amenity fueling the city's current phoenix narrative. Art that explicitly stages its own dirty, smelly decomposition over an extended period of time is not easily monetized and not easily reappropriated for bohemian coffee shop atmosphere.

The *Heidelberg Project* spans three decades of Detroit's deindustriality: *gestically* underscoring the era's protracted civic abandonment and extractive economics; probing color-blind plans for redevelopment that never reach the neighborhood; insisting that the city's African American identity, history, and creativity cannot be simply white-, green-, or *kunst*-washed away. It materializes the optimism, nostalgia, melancholy, and ambivalence arising from Detroit's seemingly never-ending series of comebacks and challenges the racial(-ist) voyeurism that atavizes and invisibilizes its residents. It stages a confrontation with post-industrial capitalism's discards. But its most obvious, and perhaps most bracing *gestic* work is its insistence that time, in transitional moments of capitalism, is always multiple, racialized, and never linear. As performance theorist Rebecca Schneider observes, "That time can be *porous, malleable, tactile, given to recurrence, given to cross-affiliate assemblage, given to buckling, given to rupture, given to return* is denied by the tick-tock of the time clock," as well as by figurations of redevelopment as color-blind, evolutionary, and intrinsically rational.[138] Less than three miles away, Guyton's contemporary, the late Mike Kelley, created another *gestic* work that also probes the problematics of Detroit's de- into post-industriality: not through *gestic* confrontations with time but with space.

MOBILE HOMESTEAD: "A TOTAL FAILURE"?

For much of 2015, getting to MOCAD, site of the late Mike Kelley's installation/sculpture *Mobile Homestead*, required careful navigation around a bustling construction site. Down much of Woodward Avenue, the city's main artery, workers were busy building the infrastructure for the M-1 Trolley, which would connect the vibrant Midtown, and by extension MOCAD, to downtown. Looking out from the museum's Woodward-facing facade, it seemed in this moment that figurations of Detroit as capital's latest arts-led phoenix barely kept up with the breakneck pace of actual redevelopment. MOCAD is adjacent to Wayne State University, the College of Creative Studies, and the Detroit Medical Center, each with robust Midtown expansions including new buildings. The Kresge Foundation, one of the forces behind *Detroit Future City*, has an office across the street from the museum. A new Whole Foods Market, attracted with $4.7 million in tax breaks, opened nearby in 2013.[139] The Detroit Artists Market and other gallery and studio spaces, and a Blick Art Materials store, are blocks away, as are an artisanal coffee house and a chic vegetarian restaurant. MOCAD has its own high-end cafe, and *Mobile Homestead*, which sits behind and slightly south of it, set back from the street, is directly across from one of the city's priciest restaurants.

Mobile Homestead was Mike Kelley's last project before he committed suicide in January 2012 at age fifty-seven. Kelley grew up in Westland, one of the city's southwest suburbs populated by white workers for the "Big Three" automakers (Chrysler, Ford, and General Motors). After studying art at the University of Michigan, he moved to Los Angeles in the mid-1970s and ultimately became an art world star: represented by powerful dealer Larry Gagosian and described as "one of the most influential artists of the past 25 years."[140] Some of his pieces sold for millions of dollars.[141] He produced highly conceptual works that explicitly mocked art world hierarchies and was perhaps best known as "the stuffed animal artist" who built collages and constructions with, and even quasi-morgues for, the toys in the 1990s, around the same time Tyree Guyton was nailing them to houses and piling them up in vacant lots on Heidelberg Street. By most accounts, Kelley had a deeply ambivalent relationship to Detroit. In a chapter from the catalog for the artist's Whitney Museum midcareer retrospective in 1993, David Marsh writes: "Though it may be true that [his] work is 'based on his rejection of Detroit . . . ,' [i]t's also true that the particularities of Detroit's popular culture remain[ed] firmly imbedded in the consciousness with which he approaches that work."[142] Kelley engaged the city's landmarks and landscape as well as its popular culture, including in a work done specifically for Detroit's tricentennial.[143]

Kelley was especially interested in probing the figural potential of his family home: an unremarkable white wood frame ranch with a Cape Cod peak. He featured it in *Educational Complex* (1995), a sculpture composed of architectural models of this home plus all the schools he ever attended. Later, he attempted to buy the actual Westland house as part of a "secret project, designed for my own perverse amusement," but the owner did not want to sell.[144] Kelley's interest in relationships between space and the personal uncanny—repressed memories of trauma, socially unacceptable desires and fantasies—became a theme in his work and ultimately a feature of *Mobile Homestead* as well. In 2006, when MOCAD opened, he approached museum staff with the idea of constructing a public sculpture, including a mobile component: an exact replica of the Westland home to be used as a community gallery space, with a portion traveling through the city as a service provider. The public sculpture reproduces the exact layout of the house, though without the furnishings. MOCAD partnered with Artangel, a London-based arts funder that supports site-specific work, to construct the project.[145]

Kelley dedicated the mobile portion of *Mobile Homestead*, basically the front of the house, in 2010. Prior to this formal dedication, it was trucked down Michigan Avenue, a major street connecting the city to its southwest suburbs. Along the way it passed landmarks like the shattered Michigan Central Depot and Greenfield Village, Henry Ford's eighty-plus-acre outdoor museum featuring Thomas Edison's light bulb lab, the Wright Brothers' workshop, and the house where Ford himself grew up, among others, before arriving in Westland, where it parked in front of the original (figure 13).[146] Work began on the MOCAD component in fall 2012 and was completed in 2013 (figure 14).

The first floor of *Mobile Homestead* houses community-based programming, from displays of the Detroit-based anarchist newspaper the *Fifth Estate* to meetings of a local quilting circle to experimental recycling workshops by the design and manufacturing collaborative Thing Thing. In 2016, MOCAD's Department of Education and Public Engagement, which oversees these exhibitions and events, added a multiyear examination of social practice art, "Art as Social Force," to the venue's roster. But *Mobile Homestead* also includes two lower levels not accessible to the public. As Kelley described it:

Figure 13: Mike Kelley's *Mobile Homestead* parked in front of his Westland, Michigan, family home. Image courtesy of the Museum of Contemporary Art Detroit and the Mike Kelley Foundation for the Arts.

A complex basement area will be built beneath the house, mirroring the floor plan of the original Kelley family home. Though the floor plan of the underground zone is the same as the house, the rooms may not be entered directly one from the other. To accomplish this architectural effect, the subground section of the house will be constructed two levels deep so that visitors must travel labyrinthian [*sic*] hallways and climb up and down ladders to reach the next space. The basement is being structured like this, specifically so that its floor plan is unrecognizable as the mirror of the house above. In this way, each room will take on a distinct cell-like quality. In contrast to the public orientation of the mobile section of the house and the community gallery/upper section, the lower levels are de-signed for private rites of an aesthetic nature. This section of the structure will be made available, on occasion, to individual artists or groups of my choosing. The underground zone will not be open to the public and the works produced there would have to be presented elsewhere, or not at all.[147]

MOCAD describes *Mobile Homestead* as "both a public sculpture and a private, personal architecture."[148]

Mobile Homestead gestically represents the alpha and omega of Detroit's deindustriality. By erecting a typical white (in multiple senses of the term) suburban home in the heart of Midtown—not yet booming when work on it began—Kelley both referenced and figurally reversed white flight from the city: one of the early spatio-racial dynamics that contributed to its emergence as racialized cautionary tale.[149] But *Mobile Homestead* also signals the hollowness of current figurations of Detroit's arts-led revival even as it offers a venue for the highly individual, often ad hoc activist interventions that contribute to and pose crucial critical questions about this revival. Some of *Mobile Homestead*'s *gestic* work is explicit and intentional. Other aspects of that work arise from its location, its public/private rhetoric and

Figure 14: Mike Kelley's *Mobile Homestead* at its permanent MOCAD site. Image courtesy of the Museum of Contemporary Art Detroit and the Mike Kelley Foundation for the Arts.

construction, and its surely unintentional conjuring of post-industrial capitalism's contradictory affective lives in Detroit, the deindustrial's most notorious exemplar.

The structure and aesthetics of the piece itself do not offer much to its audience apart from the community work exhibited inside. As Marsha Miro, director of MOCAD during the planning of the project, observed, the interior "feels like a stage set."[150] Like Kelley's oeuvre generally, it operates more powerfully as an idea than as a discrete object. Kelley imagined the work in ongoing *gestic* conversation with Greenfield Village: mocking Henry Ford's "grandiose notions of history" exemplified by Great Men through his own "every man's [*sic*] house."[151] Indeed, the house in its current setting does underscore the earlier intimate relationship between the now-vanishing industrial city and the dream of "the private home with the secure front door" that fueled its, and later its suburbs', growth.[152] This *gestic* spatialization of the city's residential and manufacturing history is compounded by the widely publicized fact that the MOCAD building next door was once an auto dealership. Now *Mobile Homestead* effectively situates the white industrial working-class "every man's house" at the epicenter of the city's post-industrial "new economy" revival. In so doing, Kelley also materialized many other former Detroiters' private dreams: to return to their former family homes, find them exactly as they were, and preserve them as personal bulwarks against the shifting tides of capital and as reminders of, if not better, then at least seemingly simpler days.[153]

But the work's whiteness is increasingly redundant in Midtown. Property values there have soared. A snapshot view shows that properties for sale in the immediate vicinity of MOCAD range from $64,000 to $3.3 million; unlike McDougall-Hunt, there are no foreclosures here.[154] Given that a 2015 US Census report identified Detroit as the poorest big city in the United States, with a median income of $25,769, with almost 40 percent of its population living below the poverty line, it seems unlikely that many of the city's predominantly (82.7 percent) African American residents are moving from their current neighborhoods into Midtown.[155] Indeed, 2015 saw a significant increase in the city's white population, with Midtown and the historic Corktown neighborhood singled out as attractors.[156] In this context, *Mobile Homestead*'s very whiteness now reads less like a *gestic* intervention reversing white flight than a *gestic* acknowledgment of both Midtown's current demographics and a newly awakened appetite for the city in white former suburbanites.

Further, in the midst of bustling Midtown, *Mobile Homestead*'s subterranean rooms no longer suggest only the uncanny, hidden lives of Fordism, the industrial era's repressed memories and traumas, or a place to hide from Fordist surveillance, the history of which is recounted in chapter 3. Instead, the unseen "cell-like" rooms *gestically* underscore what else is unseen in, and cordoned off from, this frenzy of redevelopment: the city's African American neighborhoods where, as in McDougall-Hunt, there are no nearby coffee shops or grocery stores. At the same time, these private levels—seemingly inaccessible from the public floor—recapitulate in spatial form the binary relationship between art and the community in figurations of Detroit's arts-led revival beginning with the opposition of DIA collections to pensioners' benefits. In *Mobile Homestead* as in many of these figurations, "real" art, exemplified by Kelley and his invited guests, is utterly separated from the community concerns of the first floor. Indeed, work produced in these lower levels can't even be shown above but must be exhibited "elsewhere or not at all," not unlike Galapagos's Detroit Biennial hyperlinked to the elsewhere of Brooklyn. Surprisingly, for an artist who spent the bulk of his career saying "fuck you" to art world elitism, these lower floors and "labyrinthian" trajectories reinforce a view of art in the city as a private space for initiates only.[157] Others have to keep out.[158] A detail of the site's exterior reinforces this perception at the scale of the entire piece. *Mobile Homestead*'s front lawn is fenced off from the street, signaling that even its "community space" is apart from the city's public space.[159]

In addition, the "private" nature of these lower levels spatializes and concretizes white former Detroiters' affective attachment to the city in terms of their own pasts, including former family homes typically, though not always, viewed through a racialized nostalgia for an imagined heyday that was and never was.[160] As Miro noted, Kelley himself thought of the lower levels in this way: "As a sculpture it would allow him to unearth things and explore ideas from his past in the two lower levels, which were to function sort of as his studio, where he would work when he was in Detroit."[161] In this private dimension of *Mobile Homestead*, the city is a site for a purely personal archaeology that would fuel equally personal "rites of an aesthetic nature."

Yet this widely known yet inaccessible private component of *Mobile Homestead* also functions as a *gestic* strategy of framing "agency in negative terms," particularly appropriate given the highly neoliberal trajectory of the city's current redevelopment.[162] As anthropologist Carol J. Greenhouse has argued, within the "pervasive condition of neoliberalism," including Detroit's highly racialized, uneven recovery, people may enact agency through recusal rather than assertion, opting for "the power to withhold consent, for example, or perform their resistance, to withdraw some part of their productive energy from what they see as 'the system.'"[163] In this reading, Kelley spatialized an aesthetic of recusal, if not outright refusal—not just an aesthetic of the personal or historical uncanny—into *Mobile Homestead*. These lower levels are the rare sites in today's Midtown that refuse the phoenix narrative: a refusal aesthetically underscored by the need to descend, not rise, to reach them. They refuse monetization, refuse commodification by creative class hipsters, and recuse themselves from city government's attempts to erase obvious markers of deindustriality, at least in highly desirable—that is, predominantly white—locations.

Kelley's *gestic* refusal extended to his ultimate vision for the work itself. He refused to sentimentalize the community/social service dimensions of *Mobile Homestead*. Indeed, at the end of his 2011 statement on the piece, before work on the permanent installation even began, he called it "a total failure" as a work of public art:

> Turning my childhood home into an "art gallery/community center" was simply a sign for social concern, performed in bad faith. The project, in its initial conception, expressed my true feelings about the milieu in which I was raised, and my belief that one always has to hide one's true desires and beliefs behind a facade of socially acceptable lies. But, perhaps, the failure of the *Mobile Homestead* project now, after being filtered through the institutions of the art world and community services, is successful as a model of my own belief that public art is always doomed to failure because of its basic passive/aggressive nature. Public art is a pleasure that is forced upon a public that, in most cases, finds no pleasure in it.[164]

"Failure" is also crucial to *Mobile Homestead*'s *gestic* potential: both because Kelley's statement very precisely underscores the ways "art" often operates as a sign for social concern performed in bad faith in capital's post-industrial redevelopment schemes and because *Mobile Homestead* has, in fact, failed to fail.

Kelley's explicit dismissal of public art is a bracing, if acidic, antidote to the *kunst*-washing of libertarian free-market ideology, real estate speculation, or austerity urbanism lurking within figurations of Detroit as emerging arts mecca. At least Kelley constructed an actual work with actual racial politics, unlike those figurations referencing a color-blind art, or none at all, as covers for financialization or civic triage. Yet *Mobile Homestead* fails to fail because it does indeed make meaningful interventions in the increasingly commodified and rapidly gentrifying

Midtown. As Kelley himself once noted, "Something done in bad faith can be successful."[165]

First, the events programmed into *Mobile Homestead*'s public floor generate their own explicit, critical interventions in the city, including those focused on its neighborhoods: bringing together the two worlds of Detroit's redevelopment at a level ignored by advocates of *kunst*-washed financialization. Unlike Duany's libertarian millennials, these interventions provide specific, pragmatic points of artist-neighbor solidarity. Panels about Detroit's "Little Libraries"—an initiative to fund and build libraries, and address local neighborhood "book deserts," are recent examples.

Second, *Mobile Homestead* makes a spatial claim for this solidarity in the heart of Midtown. To be sure, this is not the aggressive visual or explicitly racially attuned claim of the *Heidelberg Project*; the white house itself now seems dwarfed by the development around it. But these visuals reinforce the point: Where is the place for the arts to address communities' concerns amid this increasing gentrification? *Mobile Homestead* is that place, one likely to become even rarer given the area's pricey new developments. Indeed, its *gestic* potential will likely increase as the land on which it sits increases in value.

Finally, *Mobile Homestead* refuses to resolve its own contradictions: a public space fenced off from public life and from its own interior depths, a bad faith promise to advance the public good that actually does some good, a marker of both white flight and whitened gentrification, a mobile homestead that is immobile located in the one part of the city emphatically not a frontier wilderness ripe for homesteading, a "sentimental" work framed by a dyspeptic dismissal of its very premise.[166] The unresolved persistence of these aesthetic and affective contradictions is the work's most conceptual *gest* because it so clearly parallels the vexed and contradictory place of art in Detroit's latest comeback narrative: simultaneously a color-blind new economy harbinger, utterly apart from or irrelevant to official structures of civic life, a stalking horse for the finance or real estate industries, an inaccessible private playground, a site of community dialogue, a whimsical wonderland, and an open-air neighborhood *offrenda*.

Figurations of Detroit's arts-led revival depend on suturing a fantasy of art as color-blind, unalienated, highly individualized labor to deeply racialized plans for neoliberal financialization and Darwinian austerity urbanism. In contrast, both the *Heidelberg Project* and *Mobile Homestead* are *gestic* spaces where the racial frictions, profound irrationalities, and shocking unevenness of this transitional moment in capitalism become particularly clear. Neither offers a triumph over or a respite from capital's relentless churn or its increasingly ruthless triage operations. Both simultaneously conjure and refuse the simple hominess of "home," opting instead to materialize its intimate imbrication in racialized political economy.

What happens when the visible residue of the deindustrial—the evidence of decades of civic abandonment, the racial(-ist) bifurcation of civic space, the spatialization and materialization of capital's collapse—selectively disappears from Detroit's landscapes, then disappears from memory? Do we then forget the seismic shocks of structural economic change here in this city that exemplified these very traumas? Would this disappearance reassure us that the process of moving to the post-industrial is actually soothingly linear and evolutionary? What happens when deindustrial decrepitude selectively persists, unresolved and unremediated, leaving those consigned to dwell within it in a state of perpetual, perilous liminality? The *gestic* value of the *Heidelberg Project* and *Mobile Homestead*, particularly in a moment the deindustrial seems to be selectively disappearing, is not that they answer these questions. Rather, in contrast to color-blind, *kunst*-washed figurations of Detroit's latest comeback, the value of these works lies in their insistence that we must not avoid asking them.

Coda

Still Unfinished . . .

> "I don't care if you're a racist!" he shouted. . . . . "If you'll just bring back one [expletive] steel mill!"
> —Supporter of Donald Trump quoted in Jeff Sharlet, *"Bully Pulpit:*
> *Donald Trump, American Preacher"*[1]

Deindustrialization's normative subject, the white working-class male, exploded onto the public stage with a vengeance during the US presidential election campaign of 2016. This group was widely credited with, or blamed for, propelling Republican real estate developer and reality television show host Donald Trump to the presidency. It was as if the Reagan Democrats of 1980—the white blue-collar constituency exemplified by those living in Detroit's northeast suburbs—had returned. This time Trump's overt racism, xenophobia, and misogyny replaced Ronald Reagan's dog whistle appeals to states' rights and caricatures of the welfare queen cloaked in an aw-shucks affability. Trump was a prominent "birther" who argued against all evidence that President Barack Obama was not born in the United States. African American activists were roughed up, sucker-punched, and shouted down by Trump's supporters at his campaign events. That the candidate presented himself explicitly as a financial wheeler-dealer—a representative, if not the epitome, of the very mode of production that actively dismantled US manufacturing infrastructure—did not appear to give his supporters pause, nor did accounts of his stiffing small businesses that worked for him. They were seemingly powered by affect, and especially by anger. As one Trump supporter put it: "We all want to punch somebody in the face, and he says it for us."[2]

The so-called new economy—financialization, globalization, shift to services, whatever you called it—had not been kind to the white working class. For one thing, its members seemed to be dying younger than their parents, reversing decades of gains in life expectancy. A widely publicized 2015 study conducted by economists Anne Case and Nobel laureate Angus Deaton detailed steeply increasing mortality and morbidity rates for middle-aged whites between 1999 and 2003 due to suicide, drug and alcohol poisoning, and chronic liver disease. Those with a high school diploma or less who, forty years ago, might have secured a union job at a Big Three auto plant, were most affected. In the discussion section of their paper, Case and Deaton noted the possible impact of economic insecurity on mortality rates for this demographic: "After the productivity slowdown in the early 1970s, and with widening income inequality, many of the baby-boom generation are the first to find, in midlife, that they will not be better off than were their parents. Growth in real median earnings has been slow for this group, especially those with only a high school education."[3] In addition:

> The United States has moved primarily to defined-contribution [retirement] plans with associated stock market risk, whereas, in Europe, defined-benefit pensions are still the norm. Future financial insecurity may weigh more heavily on U.S. workers, if they perceive the stock market risk harder to manage than earnings risk, or if they have contributed inadequately to defined-contribution plans.[4]

For this group, US deindustriality, including financialization, was seemingly lethal.

Economists were also beginning to acknowledge that free trade—which had been decried by US trade unions since before Michael Jackson's *Thriller* heyday—was not the rising tide to lift all boats as had been touted by both Republican and Democratic elites. In a 2013 study, economists David Autor, David Dorn, and Gordon Hanson concluded:

> Exposure to Chinese import competition affects local labor markets not just through manufacturing employment, which unsurprisingly is adversely affected, but also along numerous other margins. Import shocks trigger a decline in wages that is primarily observed outside of the manufacturing sector. Reductions in both employment and wage levels lead to a steep decline in the average earnings of households.[5]

Yet, despite candidate Trump's railing against free trade, his promises to wrangle a better deal from the Chinese, and pledges to bring manufacturing jobs back to the United States, a global decline in overall manufacturing sector employment due to automation makes a new US industrial resurgence unlikely. As Nobel Prize–winning economist Joseph Stiglitz explained, "Global employment in manufacturing is going down because productivity increases are exceeding increases in demands for manufactured products by a significant amount. . . . The likelihood that we will get a manufacturing recovery is close to nil."[6]

Conservative elites derided Trump's supporters during the presidential primary season, blaming them for their own plight and piling on the opprobrium in a manner recalling indictments of African American Detroiters as having a "culture problem."[7] Most notorious was Kevin D. Williamson's screed in the *National Review*:

Nothing happened to them. . . . The truth about these dysfunctional, downscale communities is that they deserve to die. Economically they are negative assets. Morally they are indefensible. Forget all your cheap theatrical Bruce Springsteen crap. Forget your sanctimony about struggling Rust Belt factory towns and your conspiracy theories about wily Orientals stealing our jobs. . . . The white American underclass is in thrall to a vicious, selfish culture whose main products are misery and used heroin needles. Donald Trump's speeches make them feel good. So does OxyContin.[8]

Williamson's message to the white working-class communities that refused to concede to their own obsolescence: "Stonehenge didn't work out either: Good luck."

What happens when the postwar industrial era's "wages of whiteness" fall but "possessive investment in whiteness" does not?[9] Commentators posited that Trumpism is part of an emerging fascism in the West rooted in a diffuse but aggressive sense of white rural and working-class grievance: a response to structural economic change, coupled with perceived loss of white racial and patriarchal gender privilege. As Robert Kagan, fellow at the Brookings Institution, noted:

Fascist movements, too, had no coherent ideology, no clear set of prescriptions for what ailed society. "National socialism" was a bundle of contradictions, united chiefly by what, and who, it opposed; fascism in Italy was anti-liberal, anti-democratic, anti-Marxist, anti-capitalist and anti-clerical. Successful fascism was not about policies but about the strongman, the leader (Il Duce, Der Fuhrer), in whom could be entrusted the fate of the nation. Whatever the problem, he could fix it. Whatever the threat, internal or external, he could vanquish it, and it was unnecessary for him to explain how.[10]

Trump's almost parodic stagings of himself as a strong*man* who could, among other things, prey on women with impunity, certainly added to his appeal to white working-class men nostalgic for industrial era patriarchy; his rallies were characterized by violent spews directed at his Democratic opponent, Hilary Clinton, who actually won the popular vote. Clinton was decried as an out-of-touch elite who lacked "stamina": misogyny barely covered over with a veneer of right-wing antiestablishment populism.

But certainly the Trump phenomenon also relies on recognizable racist figural economies circulating in the United States for more than two centuries: those depicting racial and ethnic others as "stupid," "losers," and "rapists" intrinsically unfit for social inclusion. These figural economies provided the infrastructure around which white anger, grievance, and entitlement could congeal. For example, Trump's revival of Richard Nixon's racist dog whistle, "law and order," signaled his recognition of white fears as African American activists took to the streets demanding that "Black Lives Matter": casting black bodies in public space as intrinsically threatening and disorderly. This rhetoric both relied upon and resonated with more than a century of racial(-ist) figurations from blackface minstrelsy to forty-plus years of depicting Detroit, both the actual city and the metonym for industrial might, as a "victim" of its

African American population to be redeemed by the imposition of outside experts and an influx of new (read "white") creatives. Trump's rhetoric provided a new sticking place for earlier characterizations of *those people* as deviant financial actors whose putatively inept or willfully malign machinations spurred the subprime collapse. The unfinished political economic business of deindustrialization undoubtedly fueled Trump's political rise; the unfinished business of misogyny was unquestionably wind at his back. But the United States' unfinished racial business was no less essential.

Liminal periods like those betwixt and between dominant modes of production are intrinsically perilous times. In such periods it is tempting to cast a nostalgic eye back to fictive good old days. Trump's campaign slogan, "Make America Great Again"—widely paraphrased by both anti-Trump activists and the white supremacists who endorsed his candidacy as "Make America White Again"—was precisely such a move. The slogan epitomizes what the late Slavic studies scholar Svetlana Boym termed "restorative nostalgia": one that imagines itself as unassailable truth-under-siege locked in an epic battle between good and evil in its quest to restore the pure, transhistorical "lost home" where unquestioned race and gender privilege was coupled with a bygone labor-management compact.[11] As Boym reminds us, such unreflective nostalgia "can breed monsters."[12]

To counter Trumpist fantasies of unreflective white industrial nostalgia, it is useful to look back on those "great" days, and specifically on crises of industriality: not only strikes and their violent suppression, not only the physical debility, danger, and threat of dismemberment from the work itself, but also the daily, banal crises of tedious, alienating, racialized labor. In 1972, well before deindustrialization became a highly visible national problem, a Special Task Force on Work, part of the US Department of Health, Education, and Welfare, issued a report, "Work in America," that opened with a warning: "Significant numbers of American workers are dissatisfied with the quality of their working lives. Dull, repetitive, seemingly meaningless tasks, offering little challenge or autonomy, are causing discontent among workers at all occupational levels."[13] It described the routine debilities of industrial labor using a figuration from African American performance, "Blue-Collar Blues":

> There is now convincing evidence that some blue-collar workers are carrying their work frustrations home and displacing them in extremist social and political movements or in hostility toward the government.... [They] are characterized as alienated from their society, aggressive against people unlike themselves, distrusting of others, and harboring an inadequate sense of personal or political efficacy.[14]

Here blue-collar workers with "the blues" were described in precisely the same terms as Trump's deindustrial supporters over forty years later, but industrial jobs, and not their absence, were the cause. Further:

> Adequate and equitable pay, reasonable security, safety, comfort and convenience on the job do not insure the worker against the blues. The potent factors that impinge on

> workers' values ... are those that concern his [*sic*] self-respect, a chance to perform well
> in his work, a chance for personal achievement and growth in competence, and a chance
> to contribute something personal and unique to his work.

Notably, "The survey also found that minority workers, like whites, are dissatisfied with meaningless, routine, and authoritarian work, tasks, and environments. But for many employed blacks, problems of discrimination take precedence over many of these issues. (And, often, blacks express concern with these issues in terms of discrimination.)"[15]

"Work in America" a product of the Nixon administration, was hardly a progressive document as a whole, even for its time. Yet its explicit concluding calls for work to be dignified, meaningful (even "self-actualizing"); to be free of discrimination, and to pay a living wage; for the collective recognition that "the effects of monotonous jobs" constitute a form of "social-psychological pollution"; and for a federal government investment in work redesign seem wildly radical in the context of current deindustrial precarity, a diminished social safety net, and the rise of the highly individualized neoliberal entrepreneurial subject.[16] It seems unimaginable that a Trump administration would initiate or advance such a document.

We have lived in and with deindustriality for decades without systemic, structural remedies for the period's racial, gender, and widening income inequalities, much less any federal investment in ensuring meaningful and dignified work for all. Some economists, scholars, and activists have offered ideas for a more just and sustainable post-industrial future. For example, the basic income guarantee, advocated by as diverse a group as civil rights leader Martin Luther King and free-market evangelist Milton Friedman, has attracted renewed attention.[17] A robust union infrastructure might effectively counter the shocks and social Darwinism of deindustrial financialization, but increasingly aggressive Republican antiunion activism at the state level, fueled by seemingly limitless cash from right-wing antiunion donors, will make this a challenge. Local victories in battles to increase the minimum wage are promising. Yet any attempt to redress and repair the damage done by deindustriality is doomed as long as the United States' still unfinished racial business—its pernicious intertwining of race(-ism), work, and capital—remains unaddressed and unremedied in post-industrial figural and material economies. Trump's election demonstrates that, without the systemic dismantling of myths of white supremacy, interventions in structural inequality will be resisted by those who hold their white privilege dear as unearned "giveaways" to *those people*. Entitlement to fulfilling and well-compensated work cannot be hostage to racist and misogynist fantasies that post-industrial economic justice is a zero-sum game.

Almost a decade after his death, Michael Jackson, the Fred Astaire of the deindustrial, seems like a figure from another time. His music is still popular and widely played, but both his virtuosic transitionality and the melodramatic arc of his final years seem largely forgotten in their particulars. His ceaseless self-fashioning, his extraordinary work ethic, and his aggressive racial self-assertion have been sub-sumed into vague appreciations of his talent or equally generalized memories of his spectacular demise. He has become yet another tragic, self-destructive casualty of stardom—like Princess Diana or Marilyn Monroe—not a complex, potent example of a black economic actor surfing, and sometimes flailing in, the shifting tides of US capitalism. Meanwhile, a younger generation of African American entertainers—Kanye West, Jay-Z, and Rihanna, to name only three—has embraced their status as racially assertive entrepreneurs and brands without Jackson's Barnumesque stunts and melodramatic personal excesses. This generation offers a figural economy in which creative and financial prowess are seamlessly intertwined and equally virtuo-sic: black fiscal muscularity, artistry, and activism fully in tune with neoliberal finan-cialization. As Jay-Z famously rapped, "I'm not a businessman, I'm a business, man."[18]

The years since Jackson's death have seen some small improvements to his old Gary, Indiana, neighborhood if not to the city itself. African American artist Theaster Gates recently opened ArtHouse: A Social Kitchen, a community incuba-tor for art and entrepreneurship in partnership with city government and commu-nity organizations, with the support of the Bloomberg Philanthropies Public Art Challenge. There is still no Michael Jackson Museum; the town can't afford it, and private funding has yet to materialize. There is a website for it; the most recent item on the site's "News" link as of this writing is dated 2014.[19] But the Jacksons have pur-chased and renovated the house next door to the old family home on 2300 Jackson Street and partnered with state and local organizations to support additional resi-dential rehab efforts nearby.[20] As Michael Jackson's chronically underappreciated deindustriality recedes in favor of new spectacles of financialization, 2300 Jackson Street, and the block on which it sits, may be all that remains to remind us of his virtuosic embodiment of the postwar promise for vertiginous class transcendence in transitional times, and of the fickleness of finance capital which can turn figura-tions of its routine—even exemplary—operations into melodramatic cautionary tales (figure 15).

In Detroit, deindustriality is selectively fading away, including some of the period's most notable figurations. On August 14, 2016, Tyree Guyton announced that he would begin methodically dismantling the *Heidelberg Project* over a two-year period, leaving only the four extant houses. A new and as yet loosely defined initiative, Heidelberg 3.0, will succeed it. The new name, with its simultaneous conjurings of the project's thirty-year history and software updates numerically marking predecessors' obsolescence in a rapidly changing information economy, signals the work's accommodation of a fully post-industrial moment. So too does a new partnership with Shinola, the watch and luxury goods company touting its role in Detroit's revival with a mash-up of artisanal and industrial imagery noted in chapter 4. Shinola will erect a grandfather clock on the project's site. With that installation, and the removal of Guyton's colorful clock faces, there will only be one time prominently displayed on Heidelberg Street, and visitors will always know what time it is.

Figure 15: Photo of the childhood home of Michael Jackson, 2300 Jackson Street, Gary, Indiana. Taken by Volkan Yüksel. Wikicommons.

In interviews and in person, Guyton has been somewhat opaque about the reasons for his decision. He acknowledged the need to imagine a future for the work beyond what he could do alone with his own hands. The *Heidelberg Project* has consumed the bulk of his adult life; he acknowledged that, as an artist, it was time to do something new. He is now over sixty; surely the physical labor of maintaining the project is increasingly exhausting. Surely a dozen arson fires in the 2000s have been equally wearying. The *Detroit Future City* plan that consigned his neighborhood to "Landscape" with no new economic development that serves Guyton's neighbors potentially added to concerns for the work's persistence on the site, especially because some of the lots it occupies are owned by the Detroit Land Bank and could be purchased by any interested party. Perhaps Guyton—always a profoundly savvy tactician—is preemptively dismantling those elements most imperiled by city or private interests in neighborhood clearance for future agricultural development or, more likely, for further abandonment. Interestingly, possible future permutations of Heidelberg 3.0 are a neighborhood café and a cultural village: examples of Guyton imagining a vibrant future for Heidelberg Street in the absence of current city plans to do so.

New streetlights have come to McDougall Street in the neighborhood; the city successfully installed 65,000 LED lamps, completing the work in January 2017. The *New York Times* announced the news, illustrating the story not with a photo of the *Heidelberg Project* but, perhaps predictably, with one of an abandoned house.[21] And, in one more *gestic* indicator of the "two cities" nature of Detroit redevelopment in which downtown and Midtown vibrate with new businesses while the project's east side neighborhood continues to wither, the *Detroit Free Press* reported that the project's business offices would likely have to relocate; rising prices in Midtown prompted the owner of the building housing current operations to sell.[22]

Yet both its gradual disappearance from the vacant lots in McDougall-Hunt and the persistence of the four remaining houses continue the *Heidelberg Project's gestic* work. It still reminds visitors that the racialized losses and hopes of the deindustrial parallel those of the industrial age: the loss of jobs in the plants and of Motown, relocated to LA; the loss of homes and businesses in Paradise Valley and now in McDougall-Hunt; the loss of lives and dreams to incendiary racial violence; and the stubborn hope for a home in transitional capitalism free of racism and structural indifference. As deindustriality passes away in some parts of Detroit, and passes increasingly unnoticed in others, the *Heidelberg Project* underscores the fact that Detroit is also the place that racialized postindustrial capitalism has so far refused to completely redeem.

Meanwhile, in bustling Midtown, it is clear that Detroit's figural potential as phoenix is not yet exhausted. The Pistons, the local NBA basketball team, announced plans to move back to the city from the suburbs. Can a new stadium, subsidized with public funds, be far behind? Planning director Maurice Cox recently mused that the city could use a few more billionaires like Dan Gilbert to continue its resurgence on the national stage.[23] Despite an increase in retail stores and restaurants, and the promise of the new Red Wings hockey arena nearing completion, the same election that brought Donald Trump to the White House saw the narrow defeat of a tax initiative for a regional transit system linking Detroit to its suburbs. The city is not yet sufficiently attractive to merit white suburbanites' tax dollars in support of logistical integration.

On the city's east side, the activist Allied Media Projects is sponsoring the Detroit Narrative Agency with the explicit goal of generating new figural economies. The Detroit Narrative Agency is "a group of Detroiters who understand that the DNA of this city is made up of many stories, and who seek to shift the stories that are currently being told in and of Detroit toward justice."[24] The group recognizes that new narratives, local agency, and local figural agency are essential to the city's future and is, as of this writing, offering seed grants to artists and community members to create these new stories.

As figures and as material entities, Michael Jackson and Detroit function as nodes on which the racialized(-ist) projections, moralizing, and anxieties intrinsic to periods of structural economic change can accumulate even as they generate counterfigurations that aggressively challenge these operations. They made, and continue to make, material, political, and libidinal economies go. And they harken back to earlier racialized(-ist) figural economies of earlier transitional times. In the final page of *Love and Theft*, his monumental study of blackface minstrelsy at the dawn of the US industrial age, social historian Eric Lott quotes Karl Marx, who in

1867 wrote, "'Labour cannot emancipate itself in the white skin where in the black it is branded.'"[25] Lott concludes:

> Marx's image of labor as a great Blakean body, with certain of its parts immobilized owing to the shackling of others, gestures to the immensity of the "emancipation" these words invoke: not mere trade union unity—even less bourgeois "tolerance"—but a visionary conception of human collectivity.

A century and a half after Marx wrote his words, and more than two deindustrial decades after Lott wrote his, the racial(-ist) animus powering the Trump campaign and the persistence—indeed acceleration—of deindustrial debility in black and white working-class neighborhoods, including those in Detroit and Gary, show us the extent to which the task of realizing this visionary conception remains profoundly unfinished.

NOTES

PREFACE

1. Carol J. Greenhouse, "Introduction," in *Ethnographies of Neoliberalism*, ed. Carol J. Greenhouse (Philadelphia: University of Pennsylvania Press, 2010), 2.
2. Dwight Conquergood, "Performing as a Moral Act: Ethical Dimensions of the Ethnography of Performance," *Literature in Performance* 5, no. 2 (1985): 5.

INTRODUCTION

1. Jefferson Cowie and Joseph Heathcott, *Beyond the Ruins: The Meanings of Deindustrialization* (Ithaca, NY: Cornell University Press, 2003), 5.
2. President Franklin Delano Roosevelt called Detroit "the great arsenal of democracy" in recognition of the city's contributions to World War II, and specifically the retooling of its auto plants to accommodate military manufacturing. For a discussion of the designation, see Detroit Historical Society, "Arsenal of Democracy," *Encyclopedia of Detroit*, accessed February 14, 2016, http://detroithistorical.org/learn/encyclopedia-of-detroit/arsenal-democracy.
3. Despite speculation about Jackson's racial identity, the artist consistently and proudly asserted himself as a black man, most notably in interviews with Oprah Winfrey in 1993 and in a public action against the head of his record label, Tommy Mottola in 2002, which is discussed in chapter 2.

    Detroit's population is 84 percent black or African American according to the US Census Bureau; see Sonya Ragosti et al., "The Black Population: 2010," *2010 Census Briefs*, September, 2011, p. 14, accessed June 4, 2013, http://www.census.gov/prod/cen2010/briefs/c2010br-06.pdf. For the city's status during the Great Migration, see Richard Thomas, *Life for Us Is What We Make It: Building Black Community in Detroit, 1915–1945* (Bloomington: Indiana University Press, 1992); Elaine Latzman Moon, *Untold Tales, Unsung Heroes: An Oral History of Detroit's African American Community, 1918–1967* (Detroit: Wayne State University Press, 1993); and Isabel Wilkerson, *The Warmth of Other Suns: The Epic Story of America's Great Migration* (New York: Random House, 2010).

    On June 17, 1833, African American and white antislavery protesters engaged in armed confrontation with Detroit's sheriff to protest the arrest of Thornton and Ruth Blackburn, who had escaped slavery two years earlier and who were to be returned to their Kentucky owners. Ruth Blackburn was smuggled out of jail by two African American women visitors, one of whom switched clothes with her and stayed behind; Ruth reached freedom across the Detroit River in Canada. Thornton was freed during the subsequent confrontation and also safely reached Canada. The uprising resulted in what is believed to be the first US riot commission. Harsh reprisals against the African

American protesters led many to also relocate to Canada. See Karolyn Smardz Frost, *I've Got a Home in Glory Land: A Lost Tale of the Underground Railroad* (New York: Farrar, Straus and Giroux, 2007), 163–90.

4. Scholarly and critical studies of Jackson's career include Michael Awkward's "'A Slave to the Rhythm': Essential(ist) Transmutations; or, The Curious Case of Michael Jackson," in *Negotiating Difference: Race, Gender, and the Politics of Positionality* (Chicago: University of Chicago Press, 1995); Margo Jefferson, *On Michael Jackson* (New York: Vintage, 2007); Susan Fast, *Dangerous (33 1/3)* (New York: Bloomsbury, 2014); Tamara Roberts and Brandi Wilkins Catanese, eds. Special issue, *Journal of Popular Music Studies* 23, no. 1 (March 2011): 1–143; Susan Fast and Stan Hawkins, eds., "Special Issue on Michael Jackson: Musical Subjectivities" special issue, *Popular Music and Society* 35, no. 2 (May 2012): 143–319; Christopher R. Smit, ed., *Michael Jackson: Grasping the Spectacle* (Surrey: Ashgate, 2012); Joseph Vogel, *Man in the Music: The Creative Life and Work of Michael Jackson* (Toronto: Sterling, 2011); and Harriet Manning, *Michael Jackson and the Blackface Mask* (Surrey: Ashgate, 2013).

5. Michael Jackson, *Moonwalk* (New York: Crown Archetype, 2009), 107.

6. Berry Gordy worked briefly on the Ford Mercury assembly line in 1955. See Suzanne Smith, *Dancing in the Street: Motown and the Cultural Politics of Detroit* (Cambridge, MA: Harvard University Press, 1999), 252.

7. Recent analyses of Detroit include Dora Apel, *Beautiful Terrible Ruins: Detroit and the Anxiety of Decline* (New Brunswick, NJ: Rutgers University Press, 2015); Mark Binelli, *Detroit City Is the Place to Be: The Afterlife of an American Metropolis* (New York: Metropolitan–Henry Holt, 2012); George C. Galster, *Driving Detroit: The Quest for Respect in the Motor City* (Philadelphia: University of Pennsylvania Press, 2012); Rebecca J. Kinney, *Beautiful Wasteland: The Rise of Detroit as America's Postindustrial Frontier* (Minneapolis: University of Minnesota Press, 2016); and Charlie LeDuff, *Detroit: An American Autopsy* (New York: Penguin, 2013). An early discussion of Detroit as an exemplar of deindustrialization is Jerry Herron's *AfterCulture: Detroit and the Humiliation of History* (Detroit: Wayne State University Press, 1993).

8. Books of photographs include Dan Austin and Sean Doerr, *Lost Detroit: Stories behind the Motor City's Majestic Ruins* (Charleston, SC: History Press, 2010); Andrew Moore, *Detroit Disassembled* (Akron, OH: Damiani/Akron Art Museum, 2010); Julia Reyes Taubman, *Detroit: 138 Square Miles* (Detroit: Museum of Contemporary Art Detroit, 2011); and Camilo Jose Vergara, *Detroit Is No Dry Bones: The Eternal City of the Industrial Age* (Ann Arbor: University of Michigan Press, 2016).

9. US Bureau of Labor Statistics, "Detroit Area Economic Summary," updated April 30, 2014, accessed June 4, 2014, www.bls.gov/regions/midwest/summary/blssummary_detroit.pdf.

10. "Michael Jackson—Six Years after Death Estate Generated $2 Billion," *TMZ.com*, June 25, 2015, accessed February 14, 2016, http://www.tmz.com/2015/06/25/michael-jackson-6-years-death-anniversary-estate-money-billion-kids-children/.

11. Raymond Williams defines "structure of feeling" as "firm and definite as 'structure' suggests, yet it operates in the most delicate and least tangible part of our activities," and "will not appear to come 'from' anywhere." Williams, *The Long Revolution* (Peterborough, ON: Broadview Encore Editions, 2001), 64–65. Structures of feeling are "social experiences in solution." Williams, *Marxism and Literature* (Oxford: Oxford University Press, 1997), 133–34.

12. Steven High, "Beyond Aesthetics: Visibility and Invisibility in the Aftermath of Deindustrialization," *International Labor and Working-Class History* 84 (Fall 2013): 140.

13. The phrase is the subtitle of Stein's *Pivotal Decade: How the United States Traded Factories for Finance in the Seventies* (New Haven, CT: Yale University Press, 2010).

14. Lauren Berlant, *Cruel Optimism* (Durham, NC: Duke University Press, 2011), 3.

15. Berlant defines "cruel optimism" as "a relation [in which] something you desire is actually an obstacle to your flourishing." Ibid., 1.

16. According to the US Bureau of Economic Analysis, the gross output of the manufacturing sector for 2014 was $6,178.1 billion, a six-year high. "Gross Output by Industry," release date: November 5, 2015.

17. Thomas Sugrue argues that the deindustrialization of Detroit's auto industry through automation began in the 1950s. See Sugrue, *The Origins of the Urban Crisis: Race and Inequality in Postwar Detroit* (Princeton, NJ: Princeton University Press, 2014), 125–52. For deindustrialization escalating through the 1970s, see Stein's *Pivotal Decade* and Jefferson Cowie's *Stayin' Alive: The 1970s and the Last Days of the Working Class* (New York: New Press, 2010).

18. For an analysis of Black Lives Matter as a revolutionary social movement, see Keeanga-Yamahtta Taylor, *From #BlackLivesMatter to Black Liberation* (Chicago: Haymarket Books, 2016).

19. G. Epstein quoted in Thomas I. Palley, "Financialization: What It Is and Why It Matters," *Working Paper No. 525*, Levy Economics Institute, Bard College (December 2007), 1.

20. Mark Franko, *The Work of Dance: Labor, Movement, and Identity in the 1930s* (Middleton, CT: Wesleyan University Press, 2002), 30–31, 124–25.

21. See, for example, Kirk Fuoss, *Striking Performances/Performing Strikes* (Jackson: University of Mississippi Press, 1997).

22. See Jon McKenzie, *Perform or Else: From Discipline to Performance* (New York: Routledge, 2001), and Shannon Jackson, "Just-in-Time: Performance and the Aesthetics of Precarity," *TDR: The Drama Review* 56, no. 4 (2012): 10–31.

23. Jill Dolan, *The Feminist Spectator in Action: Feminist Criticism for the Stage and Screen* (Basingstoke: Palgrave Macmillan, 2013), 2.

24. One of the most notorious examples is conservative columnist George Will's ascription of the city's financial challenges to "cultural problems," characterizing the city as facing a "cultural collapse." *This Week with George Stephanopoulos*, ABC News, aired July 28 2013.

25. Micaela di Leonardo, "Deindustrialization as a Folk Model," *Urban Anthropology and Studies of Cultural Systems and World Economic Development* 14, nos. 1–3 (1985): 240.

26. David Roediger, *The Wages of Whiteness: Race and the Making of the American Working Class* (London: Verso, 2007), 96.

27. Eric Lott, *Love and Theft: Blackface Minstrelsy and the American Working Class* (New York: Oxford University Press, 1993), 148.

28. Roediger, *Wages of Whiteness*, 115.

29. Stanley B. Greenberg, *Middle Class Dreams: The Politics and Power of the New American Majority*, rev. ed. (New Haven, CT: Yale University Press, 2006), 39.

30. E. Patrick Johnson, *Appropriating Blackness: Performance and the Politics of Authenticity* (Durham, NC: Duke University Press, 2003), 5.

31. Ze'ev Chafets, *Devil's Night and Other True Tales of Detroit* (New York: Vintage, 1990), 5 (emphasis in the original).

32. Tina Fey, *Bossypants* (New York: Little, Brown, 2011), 155.

33. Barry Bluestone and Bennett Harrison, *The Deindustrialization of America: Plant Closings, Community Abandonment, and the Dismantling of Basic Industry* (New York: Basic Books, 1982), 6.

34. Robert Rowthorn and Ramana Ramaswamy, "Deindustrialization—Its Causes and Implications," *Economic Issues* no. 10 (Washington, DC: International Monetary Fund, 1997), 5.

35. Ibid., 1–2.

36. Ibid., 10.

37. "De-," *Oxford English Dictionary Online*, accessed January 7, 2016, http://www.oed.com. ezproxy.princeton.edu/view/Entry/47600?rskey=jnBXAt&result=3&isAdvanced=false #eid.

38. Daniel Bell, *The Coming of Post-industrial Society: A Venture in Social Forecasting* (New York: Basic Books, 1999), xc–c.

39. For a summary of these definitions, see Ash Amin, "Post-Fordism: Models, Fantasies, and Phantoms of Transition," in *The Post-Fordist Reader*, ed. Ash Amin (Oxford: Blackwell, 1994), 1–40.

40. For a definition of post-Fordism that includes the dismantling of the Keynesian welfare state, see Bob Jessop, "Post-Fordism and the State," in *The Post-Fordist Reader*, ed. Ash Amin (Oxford: Blackwell, 1994), 251–79.

41. Paulo Virno, *A Grammar of the Multitude* (Los Angeles, Semiotexte, 2004), 102.

42. For an account of the bill and its signing, see Paul Egan, "Testimony, Emails Shed Light on Right-to-Work Turmoil," *Detroit Free Press*, October 30, 2014, accessed October 31, 2014, http://www.freep.com/story/news/politics/2014/10/30/lawsuit-sheds-light-michigan-capitol-turmoil-right-work/18157739/.

43. In addition to Bluestone and Harrison; Cowie; Stein, *Pivotal Decade*; and Sugrue, see, for example, Steven High, *Industrial Sunset: The Making of North America's Rust Belt, 1969–1984* (Toronto: University of Toronto Press, 2003); Steven High and David Lewis. *Corporate Wasteland: The Landscape and Memory of Deindustrialization* (Ithaca, NY: Cornell University Press, 2007); John Hoerr, *And the Wolf Finally Came: The Decline and Fall of the American Steel Industry* (Pittsburgh: University of Pittsburgh Press, 1988): Judith Stein, *Running Steel, Running America: Race, Economic Policy, and the Decline of Liberalism* (Chapel Hill: University of North Carolina Press, 1998); and Anne Wren, ed. *The Political Economy of Service Transition* (New York: Oxford University Press, 2013).

44. Examples include Kathryn Marie Dudley, *The End of the Line: Lost Jobs, New Lives in Postindustrial America* (Chicago: University of Chicago Press, 1994); Sherry Lee Linkon and John Russo, *Steeltown USA: Work and Memory in Youngstown* (Lawrence: University Press of Kansas, 2002); Paul Clemens, *Punching Out: One Year in a Closing Auto Plant* (New York: Doubleday, 2011); Lisa M. Fine, *The Story of Reo Joe: Work, Kin, and Community in Autotown, USA* (Philadelphia: Temple University Press, 2004); Jennifer Hamer, *Abandoned in the Heartland Work, Family, and Living in East St. Louis* (Berkeley: University of California Press, 2011); Tracy E. K'Meyer and Joy L. Hart, *I Saw It Coming: Worker Narratives of Plant Closing and Job Loss* (Basingstoke: Palgrave, 2011); and Jennifer M. Silva, *Coming Up Short: Working-Class Adulthood in an Age of Uncertainty* (New York: Oxford University Press, 2013).

45. In addition to Apel and Cowie and Heathcott, see, for example, Tim Edensor, *Industrial Ruins: Space, Aesthetics, and Materiality* (Oxford: Berg, 2005), and Brent D. Ryan, *Design after Decline: How America Rebuilds Shrinking Cities* (Philadelphia: University of Pennsylvania Press, 2012).

46. One excellent example is Cathy Stanton, *The Lowell Experiment: Public History in a Postindustrial City* (Amherst: University of Massachusetts Press, 2006).

47. High, *Corporate Wasteland*, 10.

48. Ibid., 11.

49. Cowie and Heathcott, *Beyond the Ruins*, 5. Exceptions to this neglect of race are Cowie and Heathcott's *Beyond the Ruins* and Apel, *Beautiful Terrible Ruins*.

50. Notable discussions of relationships between art and deindustrialization include Richard Lloyd, *Neo-Bohemia: Art and Commerce in the Postindustrial City* (New York: Routledge, 2006); "Dancing in the Streets: The Arts in Postwar U.S. Cities," ed. Julia L. Foulkes and Aaron Shkuda, special section, *Journal of Urban History* 41, no. 6 (November

2015): 955–1072; and Aaron Shkuda, *The Lofts of SoHo: Gentrification, Art, and Industry in New York, 1950–1980* (Chicago: University of Chicago Press, 2016).

51. Representative examples include Randy Martin, *Financialization of Daily Life* (Philadelphia: Temple University Press, 2002); Tony Porter, *Globalization and Finance* (Cambridge: Polity, 2005); Maurya Wickstrom, *Performing Consumers: Global Capital and Its Theatrical Seductions* (New York: Routledge, 2006); Rob Aitken, *Performing Capital: Toward a Cultural Economy of Popular and Global Finance* (Basingstoke: Palgrave Macmillan, 2007); Paul Langley, *The Everyday Life of Global Finance: Saving and Borrowing in Anglo-America* (New York: Oxford, 2008); Jonathan Levy, *Freaks of Fortune: The Emerging World of Capitalism and Risk in America* (Cambridge, MA: Harvard University Press, 2012); and Miranda Joseph, *Debt to Society: Accounting for Life under Capitalism* (Minneapolis: University of Minnesota Press, 2014).

52. In addition to Joseph, see especially Stefano Harney and Fred Moten, *The Undercommons: Fugitive Planning and Black Study* (Brooklyn: Minor Compositions, 2013).

53. Notable exceptions include Max Haiven, *Cultures of Financialization: Fictitious Capital in Popular Culture and Everyday Life* (Basingstoke: Palgrave MacMillan, 2014); Paul Crosthwaite, Peter Knight, and Nicky Marsh, eds., *Show Me the Money: The Image of Finance, 1700 to the Present* (Manchester: Manchester University Press, 2014); and Leigh Claire La Berge, *Scandals and Abstraction: Financial Fiction of the Long 1980s* (New York: Oxford University Press, 2015).

54. Randy Martin, "A Precarious Dance, a Derivative Sociality," *TDR: The Drama Review* 56, no. 4 (Winter 2012): 66.

55. "Figure," noun, *Oxford English Dictionary*, accessed July 15, 2014, http://www.oed.com. ezproxy.princeton.edu/view/Entry/70079?rskey=9UiSVH&result=1&isAdvanced=fals e#eid.

56. "Figure," verb, *Oxford English Dictionary*, accessed December 20, 2015, http://www.oed. com.ezproxy.princeton.edu/view/Entry/70080?rskey=zUNIYv&result=2&isAdvanced =false#eid.

57. My use of "figural" is also indebted to Donna Haraway, *Modest_Witness@Second_ Millennium.Femaleman©_Meets_OncoMouse™: Feminism and Technoscience* (New York: Routledge, 1997), 8–14.

58. Eric Auerbach, *Mimesis: The Representation of Reality in Western Literature*, 50th anniversary edition, trans. Willard R. Trask (Princeton, NJ: Princeton University Press, 2003), 195–96.

59. Hayden White, *Figural Realism: Studies in the Mimesis Effect* (Baltimore: Johns Hopkins University Press, 1999), 51.

60. See Jean-François Lyotard, *Discourse, Figure*, trans. Antony Hudek and Mary Lydon (Minneapolis: University of Minnesota Press, 2011), with an especially clear summation on p. 74.

61. D. N. Rodowick, *Reading the Figural, or, Philosophy after the New Media* (Durham, NC: Duke University Press, 2001), 10; 70 (emphasis in the original).

62. Ibid., 49.

63. Ibid., xi, xvi, 53.

64. Kiff Bamford, *Lyotard and the Figural in Performance, Art, and Writing* (London: Continuum International, 2012), 18.

65. See, for example, Mike Higton, *Christ, Providence and History: Hans Frei's Public Theology* (London: Continuum/T&T Clark, 2004), 167; Jacques Rancière, *The Flesh of Words: The Politics of Writing*, trans. Charlotte Mandell (Stanford, CA: Stanford University Press, 2004), 75; and Terry Cochran, *Twilight of the Literary: Figures of Thought in the Age of Print* (Cambridge, MA: Harvard University Press, 2001), 56.

66. Theodor W. Adorno and Max Horkheimer, *Dialectic of Enlightenment*, trans. John Cumming (London: Verso, 1997), 123.

67. Thanks to Jayson Beaster-Jones for this observation.

68. Thanks to Sally Ann Ness for this very apt description of Jackson.

69. Eve Kosofsky Sedgwick quoted in Emily Apter, "Acting Out Orientalism: Sapphic Theatricality in Turn-of-the-Century Paris," in *Performance and Cultural Politics*, ed. Elin Diamond (New York: Routledge, 1996), 16.

70. Apel, *Beautiful Terrible Ruins*, 79.

71. Herron, *AfterCulture*, 9.

CHAPTER 1

1. Michael Jackson, *Moonwalk* (New York: Crown Archetype, 2009), 111.

2. Quoted in Caryn Rousseau, "Gary Tours Pay Tribute to the Jackson Family," *USA Today*, August 19, 2009, accessed February 22, 2011, http://usatoday30.usatoday.com/travel/destinations/2009-08-19-gary-jackson-tours_N.htm.

3. Jackson 5, "Dancing Machine," *Dancing Machine* (Motown, 2010), CD.

4. CNN reports that Jackson said, "I'm very, very honored. Thank you very much, Mr. President and Mrs. Reagan." "Michael Jackson's Meeting with the Gipper," *CNN Political Ticker*, June 26, 2009, accessed October 31, 2014, http://politicalticker.blogs.cnn.com/2009/06/26/when-jackson-met-reagan/. J. Randy Taraborrelli reports fifteen words in *Michael Jackson: The Magic, the Madness, the Whole Story 1958–2009* (New York: Hachette, 2009), 306.

5. Taraborrelli, *Michael Jackson: The Magic, the Madness, the Whole Story*, 307.

6. Ibid., 308 (emphasis in the original).

7. "Michael Jackson's Meeting with the Gipper."

8. Jackson, *Moonwalk*, 289.

9. "The Nixon-Presley Meeting 21 December 1970," National Security Archive, George Washington University, accessed April 22, 2015, https://nsarchive.gwu.edu/nsa/elvis/elnix.html.

10. In Reagan's case, the caricature came in the form of cartoonist Gary Trudeau's 1987 creation "Ron Headrest," a conflation of Ronald Reagan and the popular digitally generated character "Max Headroom." Jackson's characterization by the British press as "Wacko Jacko" similarly took hold later in the decade.

11. For more on this period of Ronald Reagan's career, see Timothy Raphael, *The President Electric: Ronald Reagan and the Politics of Performance* (Ann Arbor: University of Michigan Press, 2009), 153–94.

12. American Iron and Steel Institute in Steven Greenhouse, "LTV Problems Stir Concerns on Survival of Steel Industry," *New York Times*, July 28, 1986, accessed April 22, 2015, http://www.nytimes.com/1986/07/28/business/ltv-problems-stir-concerns-on-survival-of-steel-industry.html?pagewanted=all.

13. The Congress of the United States Congressional Budget Office, "The Effects of Import Quotas on the Steel Industry: A CBO Study" (Washington, DC: Congressional Budget Office, July 1984), 29.

14. Quoted in Judith Stein, *Running Steel, Running America: Race, Economic Policy, and the Decline of Liberalism* (Durham, NC: University of North Carolina Press, 1998), 273.

15. The formulation "virtuosity as precarious excellence" was developed by Gabriele Brandstetter, Bettina Brandl-Risi, and Kai van Eikels in the context of the research project "Scenes of Virtuosity," Collaborative Research Centre, "Cultures of the Performative," Freie Universität Berlin. It captures both the constraints of economized, post-Fordist virtuosity and the seemingly structural instability in the concept itself: "Virtuoso performances do

not subject their value to generally binding social structures of productivity. . . . This very individuality and display of self-will has also made virtuoso performers suspicious in the eyes of their contemporaries." Gabriele Brandstetter, "The Virtuoso's Stage: A Theatrical Topos," *Theatre Research International* 32, no. 3 (July 2007): 2.

16. For representative examples, see Kobena Mercer, "Monster Metaphors: Notes on Michael Jackson's 'Thriller,'" *Screen* 26, no. 1 (1986): 26–49; Michael Awkward, "'A Slave to the Rhythm': Essential(ist) Transmutations; or, The Curious Case of Michael Jackson." in *Negotiating Difference: Race, Gender, and the Politics of Positionality* (Chicago: University of Chicago Press, 1995), 175–92; Cynthia J. Fuchs, "Michael Jackson's Penis," in *Cruising the Performative*, ed. Sue-Ellen Case, Phillip Brett, and Susan Leigh Foster (Bloomington: Indiana University Press, 1995) 13–33; Susan Fast, "Difference That Exceeded Understanding: Remembering Michael Jackson (1958–2009)," *Popular Music and Society* 33, no. 2 (May 2010): 259–66; and Tavia Nyong'o "Have You Seen His Childhood? Song, Screen, and the Queer Culture of Childhood in Michael Jackson's Music," *Journal of Popular Music Studies* 23, no. 1 (2011): 40–57.

17. Lauren Berlant, *Cruel Optimism* (Durham NC: Duke University Press, 2011), 1. In the case of the waning industrial moment, cruel optimism resided in "a fantasy of the good life" sustained by rhetorics of "retooling" industrial workers for undefined new opportunities.

18. Winnicott always maintained that "transitional objects" were not simply things in the material sense but were "intermediate area[s] of experience." D. W. Winnicott, *Playing and Reality* (London: Tavistock, 1971), 2.

19. Ibid., 12.

20. Richard Schechner, *Between Theater and Anthropology* (Philadelphia: University of Pennsylvania Press, 1985), 109–11.

21. Jeffrey C. Alexander, "The Celebrity Icon," *Cultural Sociology* 4, no. 323 (2010): 325.

22. As Karen Sternheimer notes in *Celebrity Culture and the American Dream*, "Rather than simply superficial distractions, celebrity and fame are unique manifestations of our sense of American social mobility. . . . [T]he fluctuating nature of celebrity culture reflects and reveals the so-called American Dream itself, a dream that continues to evolve and change along with our expectations about what it means to achieve success in America." Karen Sternheimer, *Celebrity Culture and the American Dream: Stardom and Social Mobility* (New York: Routledge, 2011), xii.

23. Jackson's specific movement vocabulary and the exigencies of the deindustrial moment exemplify the "conjunctural" circumstances in which Mark Franko sees dance as political. In such circumstances, "forms of movement and sociopolitical life take shape simultaneously." Dance may reflect such conjunctural moments, critique them, or both, as in Jackson's case within the emerging deindustrial imaginary. See Mark Franko, "Dance and the Political: States of Exception," *Dance Research Journal* 38, nos. 1/2 (2006): 4.

24. Section heading from the lyrics to "Stayin' Alive," written and performed by the Bee Gees, which played over the opening shots of the film *Saturday Night Fever*: "It's all right. It's okay. You may look the other way." The song offers what Brenda Dixon Gottschild would term an "aesthetic of cool" in the face of social marginalization and economic precarity. Barry Gibb, Maurice Gibb, and Robin Gibb, "Stayin' Alive" (1977). "Aesthetic of cool" from Brenda Dixon Gottschild, "First Premises of an Africanist Aesthetic," in *Digging the Africanist Presence in American Performance* (Westport, CT: Praeger, 1998), 16 (emphasis added).

25. Jefferson Cowie, *Stayin' Alive: The 1970s and the Last Days of the Working Class* (New York: New Press, 2010), 357. For additional discussion of Springsteen as working-class icon, see Jefferson Cowie and Lauren Boehm, "Dead Man's Town: 'Born in the U.S.A.,' Social History, and Working-Class Identity," *American Quarterly* 58, no. 2

(2006): 353–78, and Jim Cullen, *Born in the U.S.A.: Bruce Springsteen and the American Tradition* (New York: HarperCollins, 1997).

26. Tricia Rose, "A Style Nobody Can Deal With: Politics, Style, and the Postindustrial City in Hip Hop," in *Microphone Fiends: Youth Music and Youth Culture*, ed. Andrew Ross and Tricia Rose (New York: Routledge, 1994), 71.

27. Jackson may also fail to register as obviously deindustrial because he began his career as a child, albeit by his own account a child laborer. But this too is a misremembering as children and child labor were essential to the dawn of the United States' industrial age.

28. Cowie, *Stayin Alive*, 314.

29. Ibid., 318.

30. Ibid., 314 (emphasis added).

31. Two trajectories contribute to this view. Andrew Hewitt argues that the Schillerian view of dance as ludic was replaced by dance as a model of work, though the replacement never fully stuck in popular usage. In addition, pioneers of US modern dance framed it as unalienated personal expression, positioning it explicitly against the regimentation of the industrial age. Andrew Hewitt *Social Choreography: Ideology as Performance in Dance and Everyday Movement* (Durham, NC: Duke University Press, 2005), 37–77.

32. On the failure to recognize art as a mode of production, see Raymond Williams, *Problems in Materialism and Culture: Selected Essays* (New York: Verso, 1980), 46.

33. Antonio Negri, *Empire and Beyond*, trans. Ed Emery (Cambridge: Polity, 2006), 7.

34. "Goin' Places," written and composed by Kenneth Gamble and Leon Huff, sung by Jackson 5 (Epic Records and Philadelphia International Records, 1977).

35. Cowie, *Stayin' Alive*, 314. *Saturday Night Fever* has a very interesting "love and theft" relationship with blackness that consolidates the whiteness of working-class life it depicts. These dynamics are perhaps best captured when one of Tony's entourage notes that the goal of preparing for the evening is looking as "sharp as you can look without turnin' into a nigger." See *Saturday Night Fever* (Paramount Pictures, 1977).

36. Eric Lott, *Love and Theft: Blackface Minstrelsy and the American Working Class* (New York: Oxford University Press, 1993), 5.

37. Cowie, *Stayin' Alive*, 321.

38. Lott, *Love and Theft*, 237.

39. Ibid.

40. Judith Stein, *Pivotal Decade: How the United States Traded Factories for Finance in the Seventies* (New Haven, CT: Yale University Press, 2010), 63.

41. As Cowie's indigenous Virgil of deindustrial decline, autoworker Dewey Burton asserted, "I'm not going to pay big high school taxes and pay more for a home so that somebody can ship my son 30 miles away to get an inferior education." Cowie, *Stayin'' Alive*, 4.

42. Adolph Reed, "Reinventing the Working Class: A Study in Elite Manipulation," *New Labor Forum* 13 (Fall 2004) : 18.

43. Ibid., 21. For a detailed historical discussion of the early formation of the whiteness of labor, see David R. Roediger, *The Wages of Whiteness: Race and the Making of the American Working Class*, new ed. (New York: Verso, 2007).

44. Franko, "Dance and the Political," 6.

45. André Lepecki, *Exhausting Dance: Performance and the Politics of Movement* (New York: Routledge, 2006), 3. See also Mark Franko, *The Work of Dance: Labor, Movement, and Identity in the 1930s* (Middleton, CT: Wesleyan University Press, 2002), 2–3. Dance's status as work does not reside solely in movement. Indeed, it is equally, and perhaps particularly, visible as work when produced by the exhausted body, the failing body, or, as Lepecki indicates, the body demonstrating dance's own exhaustion. Here too Michael Jackson is a useful exemplar, spectacularly embodying the interrelationship of work and exhaustion with particular clarity, as I discuss in chapter 2.

46. Shannon Jackson, "Just-in-Time: Performance and the Aesthetics of Precarity," *TDR: The Drama Review* 56, no. 4 (Winter 2012): 19. Jackson's point is that so-called immaterial labor is in fact inseparable from the body that produces it, hence "hypermaterial."

47. Angus Fletcher, *Allegory: The Theory of a Symbolic Mode* (Ithaca, NY: Cornell University Press, 1964), 10.

48. Brandstetter, "Virtuoso's Stage," 178. For an additional discussion of virtuosity with Paganini as paradigm case, see Jim Samson, *Virtuosity and the Musical Work: The Transcendental Studies of Liszt* (Cambridge: Cambridge University Press, 2003).

49. David Palmer, "Virtuosity as Rhetoric: Agency and Transformation in Paganini's Mastery of the Violin," *Quarterly Journal of Speech* 84, no. 3 (August 1998): 345; Brandstetter, "Virtuoso's Stage," 178.

50. Jackson, "Just-in-Time," 15. Jackson points out that Paolo Virno in particular underemphasizes the specific skills of the performer to advance his larger argument. That Virno's use of dance to analogize post-Fordist labor neglects the very rich partnership between popular dance and Fordist labor, as discussed later in this chapter, reinforces Jackson's point and argues powerfully for historical precision in the use of dance as a figure for virtuous work.

51. Paolo Virno, *A Grammar of the Multitude* (Los Angeles: Semiotext(e), 2004), 52–53.

52. Ibid., 52. As Shannon Jackson notes in "Just-in-Time," Virno both deploys and undermines this view of virtuosity in the "normal" sense to advance his larger argument about immaterial labor, ultimately claiming that no special skill is needed to be a virtuosic immaterial laborer in the management of affect. Michael Jackson's exceptionality is virtuosity both in the "normal" sense of individual excellence and in the sense of an immaterial laborer.

53. In "Just-in-Time," Shannon Jackson notes that virtuosity is relationally produced, though she does not explicitly discuss the audience's role in that process. Virno's later work does, however, include acknowledgment of the role of the audience, albeit not in the production of the virtuoso. In his reworking of Freud's study of the joke, Virno asserts that, in addition to the author and the object of the joke, a "third person" is "absolutely necessary": a "spectator who evaluates the witty remark, understanding perfectly the meaning of the remark and takes pleasure in it." Paolo Virno, *Multitude: Between Innovation and Negation*, trans. Isabella Bertoletti, James Cascaito, and Andrea Casson (Los Angeles: Semiotext(e), 2008), 80–81. For a discussion of the audience reading virtuosity in concert dance as apart from skill or craft, see Matthew Reason and Dee Reynolds, "Kinesthesia, Empathy, and Related Pleasures: An Inquiry into Audience Experiences of Watching Dance," *Dance Research Journal* 42, no. 2 (Winter 2010): 58–62.

54. I introduce this view of virtuosity as inseparable from the economy of spectatorship in Judith Hamera, *Dancing Communities: Performance, Difference and Connection in the Global City* (Basingstoke: Palgrave Macmillan 2007), 40–43.

55. Virno's use of Glenn Gould is an interesting example of the way the affective and behavioral excesses of virtuosity operate as transactional, between performer and audience, even when the audience is not present to witness them firsthand. In Gould's case it is not, as Virno suggests, simply *where* he performs (in the recording studio, not the stage) or *what* he produces (records, not live performances) that demonstrates virtuosity's dependence on witnessing in lieu of product. Virtuosity is also established in accounts of *how* Gould produced his performances regardless of their ultimate status as self-contained products—his perfectionism, behavioral tics, craziness, or genius. Indeed, accounts of these excesses are themselves performances that make Gould's products desirable as virtuosic. Virtuosity, then, is as much a flow of narratives and images about the affective and behavioral dynamics of production, stabilized through prior performances, as a singular enactment. Virno, *Grammar of the Multitude*, 53.

56. Susan Manning, *Modern Dance, Negro Dance: Race in Motion* (Minneapolis: University of Minnesota Press, 2004), xv.

57. Ibid., xvi–xvii, xviii.

58. For a discussion of Gordy's explicitly cross-racial marketing, see Suzanne E. Smith, *Dancing in the Street: Motown and the Cultural Politics of Detroit* (Cambridge, MA: Harvard University Press, 1999). For a discussion of raciality and viewership in contemporary media productions of African American popular dance, see Thomas F. DeFrantz, "Hip-Hop in Hollywood: Encounter, Community, Resistance," in *The Oxford Handbook of Dance and the Popular Screen*, ed. Melissa Blanco Borelli (New York: Oxford University Press, 2014), 113–31.

59. See Brandstetter, "Virtuoso's Stage," 178; Palmer, "Virtuosity as Rhetoric," 341; Hamera, *Dancing Communities*, 40–41.

60. Michael Jackson and the Jackson 5 medley, *Motown 25: Yesterday, Today, Forever* (MGM/UA Home Video, 1983).

61. For a discussion of the significance of *Motown 25* in developing Jackson's fan base, see Joseph Vogel and Anthony DeCurtis, *Man in the Music: The Creative Life and Work of Michael Jackson* (New York: Sterling, 2011), 76–79.

62. Imani Perry, *More Beautiful and More Terrible: The Embrace and Transcendence of Racial Inequality in the United States* (New York: New York University Press, 2011), 128.

63. See Hamera, *Dancing Communities*, 42.

64. Robert Walser, "Popular Music Analysis: Ten Apothegms and Four Instances," in *Analyzing Popular Music*, ed. Allan F. Moore (Cambridge: Cambridge University Press, 2003), 34.

65. Ibid., 36.

66. Ibid., 37.

67. Joan Acocella, "Walking on the Moon: Michael Jackson in Motion," *New Yorker*, July 27, 2009, 77.

68. Acocella's assessment that Jackson "didn't value his dancing enough" is challenged by multiple indicators that he valued it a great deal. For example, in *Moonwalk*, he notes that, after receiving acclaim from both Fred Astaire and Gene Kelly for his *Motown 25* performance, "I felt I had been inducted into an informal fraternity of dancers, and I felt so honored because these were the people I most admired in the world." Jackson, *Moonwalk*, 215. Another indicator is the title of his book of poems, released in 1992: *Dancing the Dream* (New York: Doubleday, 1992).

69. Peggy Phelan, "'Just Want to Say': Performance and Literature, Jackson and Poirier," *PMLA* 125, no. 4 (2010): 944.

70. Anna Kisselgoff, "Stage: The Dancing Feet of Michael Jackson," *New York Times*, March 6, 1988, accessed October 19, 2014, http://www.nytimes.com/1988/03/06/arts/stage-the-dancing-feet-of-michael-jackson.html. In contrast to Kisselgoff's, Acocella's, and Phelan's assessments, see the description of Jackson's dancing in the Dance Heritage Coalition's description of him as one of the United States' "Dance Treasures." Dance Heritage Coalition, "America's Irreplaceable Dance Treasures: The First 100," accessed May 14, 2015, http://www.danceheritage.org/jackson.html.

71. Marta Savigliano advances this view to critique, not endorse, the relationship between choreography as a "processor of difference" and so-called world dance. Marta Savigliano, "Worlding Dance and Dancing Out There in the World," in *Worlding Dance*, ed. Susan Leigh Foster (Basingstoke: Palgrave Macmillan, 2011), 175.

72. For more on appropriation and ownership of African American popular dance, see Anthea Kraut, "'Stealing Steps' and Signature Moves: Embodied Theories of Dance as Intellectual Property," *Theatre Journal* 62, no. 2 (2010): 173–89.

73. Sally Gardner, "The Dancer, the Choreographer and Modern Dance Scholarship: A Critical Reading," *Dance Research: The Journal of the Society for Dance Research* 25, no. 1 (Summer 2007): 35–53.

74. See, for example, Kina Poon, "Remembering Michael Jackson," *Dance Magazine*, September 2009, accessed November 26, 2014, http://www.dancemagazine.com/issues/September-2009/Remembering-Michael-Jackson.

75. Jackson, *Moonwalk*, 213 (emphasis in the original). Jackson idolized Astaire and took great pride in repeating Astaire's assessment. That said, I wonder if I am alone in hearing a touch of opprobrium in Astaire's use of "mover" instead of "dancer" or "artist."

76. Margo Jefferson, *On Michael Jackson* (New York: Vintage, 2006), 87.

77. Here my description is indebted to Thomas F. DeFrantz's "Performing the Breaks: Notes on African American Aesthetic Structures," *Theater* 40, no. 1 (January 2010): 31–37.

78. Jackson co-invented, and filed a patent application for, special shoes to produce this lean in live performance (wires were used in the film). The patent expired in 2005 because the patent maintenance fee was not paid. See Richard Mescher, "Timely Filing of Patent Applications: Lessons learned from Michael Jackson and Smooth Criminal," *Technology Law Source*, December 31, 2013, accessed May 9, 2015, http://www.technologylaw-source.com/2013/12/articles/intellectual-property-1/timely-filing-patent-applications-lessons-learned-from-michael-jackson-and-smooth-criminal/; and David S. Ferriero, "How to Be a Smooth Criminal," *The National Archives AOTUS Blog* April 1, 2011, accessed December 14, 2014, http://blogs.archives.gov/aotus/?p=2574/#respond.

79. Jackson, *Moonwalk*, 210.

80. Ibid., 208 (emphasis in the original). One might argue that Jackson's frequent references to hard work in his autobiography are self-staging, but even if this is the case, his decision to stage himself explicitly as a hard-working artist rather than a genius is significant.

81. Ibid., 210.

82. Gottschild, *Digging the Africanist Presence*, 110.

83. See, for example, Jackson, *Moonwalk*, 136.

84. Ibid., 150.

85. For example, Jayna Brown notes that transatlantic touring "picaninny choruses" were linked to the working child of industrial England through an undifferentiated comparison of all exploitative labor to chattel slavery, suggesting that "the appeal of the scampering, resilient black children on stage was perhaps that it brought an imagined health to the bodies of the factory children." Jayna Brown, *Babylon Girls: Black Women Performers and the Shaping of the Modern* (Durham, NC: Duke University Press, 2008), 42. That appeal may also have been nostalgic. With the coupling of blackness and childhood coded as doubly "primitive," these laboring youngsters may have also conjured a longing for the putatively carefree days of the agrarian past or the sunny climes of English colonies in the global south where dark-skinned children and their parents also toiled.

86. Joseph Jackson's job as a crane operator is notable. In the "Preface to the Third Edition," of *The Wages of Whiteness*, David Roediger writes:

    Historically the skill of crane operating was one that could be learned with relative speed, and many of the hookers who assisted crane operators were African Americans. Thus it seemed unlikely that crane operation would long survive as a craft job preserved for white workers. That it did remain subject to color bars, across stretches of space and of time, testifies to the brutal effectiveness of racism by employers, white workers, and unions. Roediger, *Wages of Whiteness*, ix.

    That Joseph Jackson held this position may testify to the same unrelenting drive he brought to bear on shaping his sons' careers: a drive both deeply embedded in and a vehement response to industrial era racism.

87. Robin D. G. Kelley, *Race Rebels: Culture, Politics, and the Black Working Class* (New York: Free Press, 1996), 36. For a reading of Joseph Jackson's violent child-rearing and Michael Jackson's music in the context of expectations of heteronormative black

masculinity, see Andreana Clay, "Working Day and Night: Black Masculinity and the King of Pop," *Journal of Popular Music Studies* 23, no. 1 (2011): 4–5.

88. Smith, *Dancing in the Street*, 14.
89. Hortense Spillers in Brown, *Babylon*, 24 (emphasis in the original).
90. Jackson, *Moonwalk*, 8.
91. For discussion of representations of black life as bimodal and the limited representations of the black working class in the context of racist structures of employment, see Steven Pitts, "Organizing around Work in the Black Community: The Struggle against Bad Jobs Held by African Americans," in *Race and Labor Matters in the New U.S. Economy*, ed. Manning Marable, Immanuel Ness, and Joseph Wilson (Lanham, MD: Rowman and Littlefield, 2006), 99–124.
92. Roediger, *Wages of Whiteness*, 180.
93. In Studs Terkel, *Working* (New York: HarperCollins, 1975), 3.
94. Stein, *Running Steel*, 234.
95. "U.S. Certifies 2,500 Steel Workers for Special Unemployment Help," *New York Times (1923-Current file)* 21 Sep. 1977, ProQuest Historical Newspapers *The New York Times* (1851–2007), ProQuest, accessed February 14, 2011.
96. Agis Salpukas, "U.S. Steel Earnings in 3d Quarter Fell 75.9% to $27 Million," *New York Times (1923-Current file)* 26 Oct. 1977, ProQuest Historical Newspapers *The New York Times* (1851–2007), ProQuest, accessed February 14, 2011.
97. Jerry Flint, "Meany Asks More Protectionism to Stop Loss of Jobs to Imports," *New York Times (1923-Current file)* 9 Dec. 1977, ProQuest Historical Newspapers *The New York Times* (1851–2007), ProQuest, accessed February 14, 2011.
98. Stein, *Running Steel*, 235.
99. Figures for the United States from the International Iron and Steel Institute *Annual Statistical Report*, in David G. Tarr, "The Steel Crisis in the United States and the European Community: Causes and Adjustments," Table 7.1, in *Issues in US-EC Trade Relations*, ed. Robert E. Baldwin, Carl Hamilton, and André Sapir (Chicago: University of Chicago Press, 1988), 174.
100. Ibid.
101. Stein, *Running Steel*, 269.
102. The artist who reimagined the mature Jackson was Nathan Wright. See Wright, "Portraits of the Stars: What They May Look Like in the Year 2000," *Ebony*, August 1985, 163.
103. Will Turbow, Elizabeth A. Cloyd, and David C. Allen, "Northwest Indiana Pushes for Economic Development," *Indiana Business*, January 1986, ProQuest US Newsstream accessed November 29, 2015. For a summary of the racial and political economy of Gary in this period, see S. Paul O'Hara, "Envisioning the Steel City: The Legend and Legacy of Gary, Indiana," in Cowie and Heathcott, *Beyond the Ruins*, 219–36.
104. See, for example, Harland Prechel, "Steel and the State: Industry Politics and Business Policy Formation, 1940–1989," *American Sociological Review* 55 (1990): 648–68.
105. John Hoerr, *And the Wolf Finally Came: The Decline and Fall of the American Steel Industry* (Pittsburgh: University of Pittsburgh Press, 1988), 560.
106. Anson Rabinbach, *The Human Motor: Energy, Fatigue, and the Origins of Modernity* (New York: Basic Books, 1990), 293. "Taylorism" is the putatively scientific system for managing work devised by Frederick Taylor and first published in 1911. Its key features include time-motion studies, task allocation, and standardization of tools.
107. For differences between Taylorism and Fordism, see Bernard Doray, *From Taylorism to Fordism: A Rational Madness*, trans. D. Marcey (London: Free Association Books, 1988), and Rabinbach, *The Human Motor*, 280–84.

108. The description is poet Ezra Pound's. Pound quoted in Felicia M. McCarren, *Dancing Machines: Choreographies of the Age of Mechanical Reproduction* (Stanford, CA: Stanford University Press, 2003), 134.

109. Ibid., 130. Jayna Brown argues that racialized fantasies of the preindustrial under-pin modern dance from its inception and indeed made it "modern": "The mothers of modern dance shaped their sexual mysticism from Orientalist fantasies, spun from the hootchy-cootchy dancers on the midway fairgrounds." Brown, *Babylon Girls*, 157.

110. Brown, *Babylon Girls*, 5. Connections between the chorus girl and industrialization involve more than the repertoire. To take only one example, John Tiller, a bankrupt English industrialist, and his wife opened a school to train chorines as an alternative to factory work. See Brown, *Babylon Girls*, 165; Susan A. Glenn, *Female Spectacle: The Theatrical Roots of Modern Feminism* (Cambridge, MA: Harvard University Press, 2000), 176, 178. For more on the relationship between the chorus girl and industrial labor, see Franko, *The Work of Dance*, especially 30–31 and 124–25.

111. Brown, *Babylon Girls*, 169.

112. Ibid., 194. In addition to racialized preindustrial nostalgia, the 1930s brought a harden-ing of genre divisions separating white modern dancers, especially those active on the political left, from white culture industry professionals often characterized as apoliti-cal. This division obscured larger relationships between dance and specific ideologies of work, as well as all dancers' rhetorical and social authority as workers. One lasting legacy of this split is the paucity of critical attention paid to contemporary popular per-formers, and virtuosi in particular, as clarifying examples of "virtuous" work. For a fuller history of this division and its consequences, see Franko, *The Work of Dance*, and Ellen Graff, *Stepping Left: Dance and Politics in New York City, 1928–1942* (Durham, NC: Duke University Press, 1997).

113. David Savran, *Highbrow/Lowdown: Theater, Jazz, and the Making of the New Middle Class* (Ann Arbor: University of Michigan Press, 2009), 139.

114. Ibid., 71.

115. Jacqui Malone, *Steppin' on the Blues: The Visible Rhythms of African American Dance* (Urbana: University of Illinois Press, 1996), 91. See also Jayna Brown, "From the Point of View of the Pavement: A Geopolitics of Black Dance," in *Big Ears: Listening for Gender in Jazz Studies*, ed. Nichole T. Rustin and Sherrie Tucker (Durham, NC: Duke University Press, 2008), 157–79.

116. Carrie Noland develops the gestural performative in *Agency and Embodiment* (Cambridge, MA: Harvard University Press, 2009), 170–205.

117. William Faulkner, *Absalom, Absalom!* (New York: Vintage, 1972), 88.

118. Acocella, "Walking on the Moon," 77.

119. This editing to emphasize isolations over full-body shots in *Smooth Criminal* may be part of the film's, and Jackson's, complex dialogue with Fred Astaire's work in its mul-tiple references to director Vincente Minnelli's Astaire–Cyd Charisse vehicle *The Band Wagon* (1953), specifically the number "Girl Hunt: A Mystery in Jazz." See Elena Oliete, "Michael, Are You Okay? You've Been Hit by a Smooth Criminal: Racism, Controversy, and Parody in the Video Clips 'Smooth Criminal' and 'You Rock My World,'" *Studies in Popular Culture* 29, no. 1 (October 2006): 66. For discussion of *Smooth Criminal* as "all dancing, all the time," see Megan Pugh, *America Dancing: From the Cakewalk to the Moonwalk* (New Haven, CT: Yale University Press, 2015), 306. Performance analysis from Michael Jackson, Sean Lennon, Kellie Parker, Brandon Adams, Joe Pesci, Jerry Kramer, Colin Chilvers, David Newman, and Bruce Broughton, *Smooth Criminal, Moonwalker*, standard version (Warner Bros. Entertainment, 2010).

120. Jackson did not originate this move either. For one account of his learning the "back-slide," see Thomas Guzman-Sanchez, *Underground Dance Masters: Final History of a Forgotten Era* (Santa Barbara, CA: Praeger, 2012), 121–22.

121. Though a complete survey of Jackson's work between 1982 and 1988 exceeds the scope of this chapter, note that many of his films explicitly evoke the heyday of American urban industrialism.

122. Ralph Ellison, *Invisible Man* (New York: Knopf Doubleday, 2010), 217.

123. For a discussion of African American popular dancers swinging the machine in the 1920s and 1930s, see Joel Dinerstein, *Swinging the Machine: Modernity, Technology, and Africa American Culture between the Two World Wars* (Amherst: University of Massachusetts Press, 2003).

124. Gottschild, *Digging the Africanist Presence*, 15.

125. Of course, Astaire and Kelly were themselves quoting the movement styles of African American predecessors and contemporaries. See Ibid., 32–34.

126. Jackson's well-documented borrowing of steps from predecessors and street dancers can be productively explored using embodied theories of intellectual property. As Anthea Kraut demonstrates in "Stealing Steps," these theories, including the parameters for acceptable "stealing [of] steps," enabled African American dancers to negotiate author-ship in the context of segregation and prior to dance's copyright protection in 1976. Kraut, " 'Stealing Steps,' " 179.

127. For a discussion of black social dance as signifying and as corporeal orature, see Thomas F. DeFrantz, "The Black Beat Made Visible," in *Of the Presence of the Body: Essays on Dance and Performance Theory*, ed. André Lepecki (Middleton, CT: Wesleyan University Press, 2004), 64–81.

128. Stein, *Running Steel*, 39.

129. Bruce Nelson, *Divided We Stand: American Workers and the Struggle for Black Equality* (Princeton, NJ: Princeton University Press, 2001), 145.

130. Ibid., xix.

131. "Jackson 5 Returns Home in Mayor Hatcher Benefit," *Jet*, February 18, 1971, 57. The caption to one of the accompanying photos singles out "Showman Michael" for special attention. For an account of black politics and the steel industry in Gary, see Greer, *Big Steel: Black Politics and Corporate Power in Gary, Indiana* (New York: Monthly Review Press), 1978.

132. Stein, *Running Steel*, 321.

133. For *Thriller* as a form of post-9/11 collectivity, see Harmony Bench, "Monstrous Belonging: Performing 'Thriller' after 9/11," in *The Oxford Handbook of Dance and the Popular Screen*, ed. Melissa Blanco Borelli (New York: Oxford University Press, 2014), 393–411. J. Lorenzo Perillo analyzes the layers of postcolonial disciplinar-ity and mimicry in the inmates of the Cebu (Philippines) Provincial Detention and Rehabilitation Center's rendition of *Thriller* in " 'If I Were Not in Prison, I Would Not Be famous': Discipline, Choreography and Mimicry in the Philippines," *Theatre Journal* 63, no. 4 (December 2011): 607–21. Tavia Nyong'o discusses *Thriller* in the context of the Occupy London protests; "The Scene of Occupation," *TDR: The Drama Review* 56, no. 4 (Winter 2012): 136–62. Kobena Mercer reads the original as a self-reflexive celebration of Michael Jackson's movie star status, a parody of cinematic codes of horror, and a "supplementary commentary on the sexuality . . . of Michael Jackson." This and "rave from the grave" from Mercer, "Monster Metaphors," 39, 40. Performance analysis from Michael Jackson, "Thriller," *Number Ones* (New York: Epic Music Video, 2003).

134. Nyong'o, "Scene of Occupation," 146.

135. The 1983 unemployment rate is from US Department of Labor, Bureau of Labor Statistics, "Labor Force Statistics from Current Population Survey: Unemployment Rate," Series Id: LNU04000000, accessed May 16, 2015, http://data.bls.gov/timeseries/LNU04000000?years_option=all_years&periods_option=specific_periods&periods=Annual+Data. African American unemployment figures from US Census Bureau, "Figure 13.1: Unemployment Rate, by Race and Hispanic Origin: 1980–1998," Labor Force, Employment, and Earnings, US Census Bureau *Statistical Abstracts of the United States* (1999), 406, accessed May 1, 2015, https://www.census.gov/prod/99pubs/99statab/sec13.pdf.

136. Billy Joel, "Allentown" (CBS, Inc., 1982); Bruce Springsteen, "Born in the U.S.A." (ASCAP, 1984).

137. Springsteen, "Born in the U.S.A."

138. US Congressional Budget Office, "The Industrial Policy Debate" (December 1983), xiii, accessed May 1, 2015, https://www.cbo.gov/sites/default/files/98th-congress-1983-1984/reports/doc29a-entire.pdf.

139. Ibid., 60, 69.

140. Cowie and Boehm, "Dead Man's Town," 361, 369.

141. Zombie lore is extensive, but for a useful survey, including a Haitian genealogy, see Deborah Christie and Sarah Juliet Lauro, eds., *Better Off Dead: The Evolution of the Zombie as Post-Human* (New York: Fordham University Press, 2011).

142. Jean Comaroff and John Comaroff, "Alien-Nation: Zombies, Immigrants, and Millennial Capitalism," *South Atlantic Quarterly* 101, no. 4 (Fall 2010): 783. In the song "Werewolves of London," Zevon sardonically notes that he'd like to meet the tailor of one of the titular characters.

143. Comaroff and Comaroff, "Alien-Nation," 795–96.

144. Sarah Juliet Lauro and Karen Embry, "A Zombie Manifesto: The Nonhuman Condition in the Era of Advanced Capitalism," *boundary 2* 35, no. 1 (2008): 92.

145. As the Comaroffs note in "Alien-Nation," the industrial era "ate up the bodies of its producers." Comaroff and Comaroff, "Alien-Nation," 780.

146. Kathryn Marie Dudley, *The End of the Line: Lost Jobs, New Lives in Postindustrial America* (Chicago: University of Chicago Press, 1997), 177.

147. One additional parallel between the film and the figure of the zombie: *Thriller* was not performed "live" prior to the film shoot.

148. The most notable of these tutorials for its "prosodic" representation is Ines Markeljevic's Thrill the World "Thriller Dance Script" (2010), accessed May 1, 2015, www.thrill-theworld.com.

149. Nyong'o, "Scene of Occupation," 142.

150. Cowie, *Stayin' Alive*, 325.

151. Morris Dickstein, *Dancing in the Dark: A Cultural History of the Great Depression* (New York: Norton, 2009), 357, 408.

152. Jackson's virtuosic use of black vernacular dance and his insistence on explicitly marking his labor as a black dancer invite a racialized historical consideration of Paulo Virno's "servile" virtuosity. In addition to its association with immaterial affective labor, the formulation also conjures a century and a half of American racialized performance and spectatorship that turned on spectacles of black "servility," most notably minstrelsy, the corked-up parody of black vernacular dance that was, in turn, executed by black performers themselves to forge a living out of the genres of public performance available to them. Historian Edward E. Baptist makes a similar point about virtuosity as a survival strategy of the enslaved African Americans. See Baptist, *The Half Has Never Been Told* (New York: Basic Books, 2014), 163–64. Jackson's explicit incorporation of tropes of

African American vernacular dance also spoke back to this very different history of "servile virtuosity."

CHAPTER 2

1. Zygmunt Bauman, *Consuming Life* (Cambridge: Polity, 2007), 38 (emphasis in the original).

2. Fred Moten and Stefano Harney, "Debt and Study," *e-flux journal* 14 (March 2010), accessed October 5, 2013, http://www.e-flux.com/journal/debt-and-study/.

3. Hans Christian Andersen, "Text of 'The Red Shoes,'" in *Project Gutenberg's Andersen's Fairy Tales*, updated January 26, 2013, accessed July 25, 2015, http://www.gutenberg.org/files/1597/1597-h/1597-h.htm#link2H_4_0018.

4. Zack O'Malley Greenburg, *Michael Jackson, Inc.: The Rise, Fall, and Rebirth of a Billion-Dollar Empire* (New York: Atria/Simon and Schuster, 2014), appendix, 250.

5. In 2005, during Jackson's child molestation trial where his finances took center stage, CNN reported that the Sony/ATV catalog was worth $400 million; this was likely only the value of Jackson's share. It also reported the value of MiJac Music at $75 million. Krysten Crawford, "Michael Jackson to Lose Beatles Catalog?," *CNN Money*, May 5, 2005, accessed December 14, 2014, http://money.cnn.com/2005/05/05/news/newsmakers/jackson_loan/index.htm?cnn=yes. The *Wall Street Journal* reported a value of more than $1 billion during the same period. Ethan Smith and Kate Kelly, "Michael Jackson's Other Battle: Staving Off Financial Disaster," *Wall Street Journal*, June 8, 2005, accessed December 14, 2014, http://www.wsj.com/news/articles/SB111819644592353818?mg=reno64-wsj.

6. Greenburg, *Michael Jackson, Inc.*, 251.

7. Smith and Kelley, "Michael Jackson's Other Battle."

8. Dorothy Pomerantz, "Michael Jackson Tops Forbes' List of Top-Earning Dead Celebrities, with $140 Million Haul," *Forbes*, October 15, 2014, accessed May 31, 2015, http://www.forbes.com/sites/dorothypomerantz/2014/10/15/michael-jackson-tops-forbes-list-of-top-earning-dead-celebrities/. Greenburg, Michael Jackson, Inc., 251.

9. *Billboard* reported the $400 million figure; "Michael Jackson Died Deeply in Debt," *Billboard*, June 26, 2009, accessed November 4, 2013, http://www.billboard.com/articles/news/268276/michael-jackson-died-deeply-in-debt. The *Daily Mail* reported $500 million in its account of forensic accountant William Ackerman's testimony in Katherine Jackson's suit against AEG. Hayley Peterson, "Michael Jackson Owed $30 Million Annually in Interest Payments on the $500 Million in Debt He Accrued over Two Decades," *Daily Mail*, August 13, 2013, accessed December 30, 2014, http://www.dailymail.co.uk/news/article-2391485/Michael-Jackson-paying-30MILLION-annually-just-payments-debt.html.

10. See, for example, Susan Fast, *Dangerous (33 1/3)* (New York: Bloomsbury, 2014).

11. Berlant, *Cruel Optimism*, 96.

12. Rob Aitken, *Performing Capital: Toward a Cultural Economy of Popular and Global Finance* (New York: Palgrave Macmillan, 2007), 4.

13. Bernard-Henri Lévy, "The Three Stations of the Cross in Michael Jackson's Calvary," *Huffington Post*, August 1, 2009, accessed October 22, 2014, http://www.huffingtonpost.com/bernardhenri-levy/the-three-stations-of-the_b_224224.html.

14. Former heavyweight boxing champion Mike Tyson filed for bankruptcy in 2003. Companies bearing real estate developer Donald Trump's name filed for bankruptcy in 1991, 1992, 2004, and 2009. See Chris Pizzello, "Celebrity Bankruptcy: Mike Tyson, Donald Trump," *Los Angeles Times*, April 16, 2015, accessed July 30, 2015, http://touch.latimes.com/#section/-1/gallery/p2p-77298571/?related=true. Actress Lindsay Lohan's fiscal travails are recounted in "Lindsay Lohan Money: Actress' Earnings and Debts in 2012,"

Huffington Post, December 12, 2012, accessed May 19, 2016, http://www.huffingtonpost.com/2012/12/17/lindsay-lohan-money-actress-earnings-debts-2012_n_2317617.html.

15. Eric Ditzian, "Michael Jackson's Groundbreaking Career by the Numbers," *MTV.com News*, June 26, 2009, accessed February 2, 2015, http://www.mtv.com/news/1614815/michael-jacksons-groundbreaking-career-by-the-numbers/.

16. Ronald Dore, "Financialization of the Global Economy," *Industrial and Corporate Change* 17, no. 6 (2008): 1097.

17. G. Epstein quoted in Thomas I. Palley, "Financialization: What It Is and Why It Matters" (Working Paper No. 525, Levy Economics Institute, Bard College, December 2007), 1.

18. For a discussion of relationships between neoliberalism and financialization, see Natascha van der Zwan, "Making Sense of Financialization," *Socioeconomic Review* 21, no. 1 (2014): 99–129.

19. Michel Foucault, *Discipline and Punish: The Birth of the Prison* (New York: Vintage, 1991), 137.

20. Dore, "Financialization of the Global Economy."

21. Tayyab Mahmud, "Debt and Discipline," *American Quarterly* 64, no. 3 (September 2012) : 475.

22. Ibid., 483.

23. As Wendy Brown notes in *Edgework: Critical Essays on Knowledge and Politics* (Princeton, NJ: Princeton University Press, 2005), the "entrepreneurial subject" is one "who rationally deliberates about alternative courses of action, makes choices and bears responsibility for the consequences of these choices" (43–44).

24. See Miranda Joseph, *Debt to Society: Accounting for Life under Capitalism* (Minneapolis: University of Minnesota Press, 2014), 96–100.

25. Ibid., 98–108.

26. Aitken, *Performing Capital*, 3.

27. Anna Lowenhaupt Tsing, *Friction: An Ethnography of Global Connection* (Princeton, NJ: Princeton University Press, 2005), 118.

28. Ibid., 57.

29. Randy Martin, *Financialization of Daily Life* (Philadelphia: Temple University Press, 2002), 8.

30. Ben Singer, *Melodrama and Modernity: Early Sensational Cinema and Its Contexts* (New York: Columbia University Press, 2001), 134.

31. Ibid., 132.

32. Ibid., 133.

33. Here I draw on the work of Linda Williams, who writes: "Melodrama should be viewed … as the typical form of American narrative in literature, stage, film, and television." Linda Williams, "Melodrama Revised," in *Reconfiguring American Film Genres: History and Theory*, ed. Nick Browne (Berkeley: University of California Press, 1998), 50. See also Singer, *Melodrama and Modernity*, 7.

34. Peter Brooks, *The Melodramatic Imagination: Balzac, Henry James, Melodrama, and the Mode of Excess* (New Haven, CT: Yale University Press, 1976), 11–12.

35. Former senator Phil Gramm famously labeled victims of deceptive and subprime loans "predatory borrowers" during the Great Recession. See Gramm quoted in Eric Lipton and Stephen Labaton, "The Reckoning: Deregulator Looks Back, Unswayed," *New York Times*, November 16, 2008, accessed January 5, 2015, http://www.nytimes.com/2008/11/17/business/economy/17gramm.html?pagewanted=all&_r=0.

36. For a discussion of capital and/as spectacle, see Guy Debord, *The Society of Spectacle*, trans. Donald Nicholson-Smith (New York: Zone, 1995).

37. Martin, *Financialization of Daily Life*, 9.

38. Ibid., 8.

39. Susan Strange quoted in Jean Comaroff and John L. Comaroff, "Alien-Nation: Zombies, Immigrants, and Millennial Capitalism," *South Atlantic Quarterly* 101, no. 4 (Fall 2002): 781.

40. Linda Williams, *Playing the Race Card: Melodramas of Black and White from Uncle Tom to O. J. Simpson* (Princeton, NJ: Princeton University Press, 2001), xiv.

41. Williams's analysis in *Playing the Race Card* is indebted to Leslie Fiedler's characterization of the "Tom/anti-Tom" dialectic in the US racial imaginary. Williams, *Playing the Race Card*, xv.

42. For details of Detroit's debt deal, see Nathan Bomey, "Disastrous Kilpatrick Debt Deal May Have Been Illegal, but the City May Settle Anyway," *Detroit Free Press*, September 25, 2013, accessed August 10, 2015, http://archive.freep.com/article/20130925/NEWS01/309250023/Detroit-swaps-legality-pension-Kevyn-Orr-Chapter-9-bankruptcy-debt.

43. Bryant Keith Alexander, *The Performative Sustainability of Race* (New York: Peter Lang, 2012), 107.

44. Thomas J. Lueck, "Record Industry Is Attacked by Top Star," *New York Times*, July 7, 2002, accessed March 11, 2015, http://www.nytimes.com/2002/07/07/nyregion/record-industry-is-attacked-by-a-top-star.html.

45. Jennifer Vineyard, "Michael Jackson Shocks Al Sharpton by Calling Tommy Mottola Racist," *MTV.com News*, accessed January 10, 2015, http://www.mtv.com/news/1455976/michael-jackson-shocks-al-sharpton-by-calling-tommy-mottola-a-racist/.

46. "Michael Jackson May Face a Cash Crunch," *CNN/People*, July 29, 2009, accessed January 10, 2015, http://edition.cnn.com/2002/SHOWBIZ/Music/07/29/cel.jackson/.

47. For the "race card" allegation, see Jeane MacIntosh, "Jacko Got Off-Tracko, Rev. Al Says," *New York Post*, July 8, 2002, accessed January 10, 2015, http://nypost.com/2002/07/08/jacko-got-off-tracko-rev-al-says/; Anne Anlin Cheng, *The Melancholy of Race: Psychoanalysis, Assimilation, and Hidden Grief* (New York: Oxford University Press, 2001), 101–4.

48. MacIntosh, "Jacko Got Off-Tracko."

49. *Living with Michael Jackson*, dir. Julie Shaw, Granada Television, Released February 6, 2003 (USA).

50. Alessandra Stanley, "Television Review; A Neverland World of Michael Jackson," *New York Times*, February 6, 2003, accessed January 10, 2015, http://www.nytimes.com/2003/02/06/arts/television-review-a-neverland-world-of-michael-jackson.html.

51. Tania Branigan, "I Was Betrayed by Bashir, Rages Jackson," *Guardian*, February 6, 2003, accessed July 12, 2015, http://www.theguardian.com/news/2003/feb/07/uknews.

52. Anthropologists Jean Comaroff and John Comaroff use "millennial" as an adjective to describe both post-industrial consumer financialized capitalism at the start of the new millennium and its "messianic, salvific, even magical manifestations." See Jean Comaroff and John L. Comaroff, "Millennial Capitalism: First Thoughts on a Second Coming," in *Millennial Capitalism and the Culture of Neoliberalism*, ed. Jean Comaroff and John L. Comaroff (Durham, NC: Duke University Press, 2001), 2.

53. Ibid., 4.

54. Matthew McDonald and Stephen Wearing, *Social Psychology and Theories of Consumer Culture* (London: Routledge, 2013), 47.

55. Amy E. Hughes, *Spectacles of Reform: Theater and Activism in Nineteenth-Century America* (Ann Arbor: University of Michigan Press, 2012), 60.

56. Bruce A. McConachie, *Melodramatic Formations: American Theatre and Society, 1820–1870* (Iowa City: University of Iowa Press, 1992), 188.

57. William H. Smith, "The Drunkard; Or, The Fallen Saved; A Moral Domestic Drama in Five Acts: The Acting Edition, No. 136 (New York: WM Taylor and Co. 1850)," in *Uncle Tom's Cabin*, dir. Stephen Railton (Institute for Advanced Technology in the Humanities, Electronic Text Center, University of Virginia, 2002), act I, scene 1, http://utc.iath.virginia.edu/sentimnt/snplwhsa11t.html.

58. Ibid., act III, scene 1.

59. To take only one of numerous examples, see the consumer finance website "Motley Fool": Tim Beyers, "America's Drunk on Credit," *Motley Fool*, August 9, 2006, accessed July 23, 2015, http://www.fool.com/personal-finance/general/2006/08/09/americas-drunk-on-credit.aspx.

60. Melissa Leong, "Spending Problem? Blame It on Your Brain," *Financial Post*, January 23, 2013, accessed July 23, 2015, http://business.financialpost.com/personal-finance/retirement/rrsp/is-your-brain-high-on-spending-trick-it-into-saving.

61. Sheryl Gay Stolberg, "A Private, Blunter Bush Declares, 'Wall Street Got Drunk,'" *New York Times*, July 23, 2008, accessed July 23, 2015, http://www.nytimes.com/2008/07/23/washington/23bush.html?_r=0.

62. Heidi N. Moore, "Was Wall Street Drunk, Stupid, or Evil?," *Wall Street Journal*, July 23, 2008, accessed July 23, 2015. http://blogs.wsj.com/deals/2008/07/23/was-wall-street-drunk-stupid-or-evil/.

63. Hughes, *Spectacles of Reform*, 157–58.

64. Ibid., 160.

65. Mitra Toossi, "Consumer Spending: An Engine for U.S. Job Growth," *Monthly Labor Review*, November 2002, 13.

66. Ibid., 15.

67. Ibid., 13.

68. See "Text: President Bush Addresses the Nation," *Washington Post, eMediaMillWorks*, September 20, 2007, accessed December 19, 2014, http://www.washingtonpost.com/wpsrv/nation/specials/attacked/transcripts/bushaddress_092001.html. See also Andrew J. Bacevich, "Going for Broke: He Told Us to Go Shopping. Now the Bill is Due," *Washington Post*, October 5, 2008, accessed December 19, 2014, http://www.washingtonpost.com/wpdyn/content/article/2008/10/03/AR2008100301977.html.

69. Bauman, *Consuming Life*, 12.

70. Martin, *Financialization of Daily Life*, 16.

71. "Kozlowski, Tyco Face More Questions," *CNN Money*, August 7, 2002, accessed July 11, 2015, http://money.cnn.com/2002/08/07/news/companies/tyco_kozlowski/.

72. Heidi N. Moore, "John Thain's $35,000 'Commode on Legs' Outrage," *Wall Street Journal*, January 23, 2009, accessed July 11, 2015, http://blogs.wsj.com/deals/2009/01/23/deal-journal-explainer-the-35000-commode-outrage/.

73. For a connection between cosmetic surgery, the neoliberal entrepreneurial subject, and consumerism, see Bauman, *Consuming Life*, 101–2.

74. McDonald and Wearing, *Social Psychology*, 114–18.

75. Dirk Philipsen, *The Little Big Number: How GDP Came to Rule the World and What to Do about It* (Princeton, NJ: Princeton University Press, 2015), 4.

76. Bauman, *Consuming Life*, 38.

77. Bill Talen, *What Should I Do If Reverend Billy Is in My Store?* (New York: New Press, 2003), xiii.

78. J. Randy Taraborrelli, *Michael Jackson: The Magic and the Madness* (Basingstoke: Palgrave Macmillan, 2004), 369.

79. Comaroff and Comaroff, "Alien-Nation," 728, 783.

80. One very basic aspect of consumption's uncanniness is an ambivalence baked into it at the etymological level:

    The English-language word "consumption" entails both an act of *destruction* (which explains why it often seems to make more sense to speak of "consuming a hamburger" than "consuming a cathedral") and an act of creation (bringing to a climax, reaching a peak, achieving a promised fulfillment).

    David B. Clarke, Marcus A. Doel, and Kate M. L. Housiaux, "General Introduction," in *The Consumption Reader*, ed. David B. Clarke, Marcus A. Doel, and Kate M. L. Housiaux (London: Routledge, 2003), 1.

81. This definition of surrogation comes from Joseph Roach, *Cities of the Dead: Circum-Atlantic Performance* (New York: Columbia University Press, 1996), 2–3. Roach sees surrogation as intrinsically uncanny.

82. Zygmunt Bauman, "Industrialism, Consumerism, and Power," in *The Consumption Reader*, ed. David B. Clarke, Marcus A. Doel, and Kate M. L. Housiaux (London: Routledge, 2003), 58.

83. Ibid.

84. Comaroff and Comaroff, "Alien-Nation," 784.

85. Ibid., 786.

86. Comaroff and Comaroff, "Millennial Capitalism," 4.

87. Comaroff and Comaroff, "Alien-Nation," 784.

88. Jennifer M. Silva, *Coming Up Short: Working Class Adulthood in an Age of Uncertainty* (New York: Oxford University Press, 2013), 115.

89. Bauman, *Consuming Life*, 45.

90. Ibid.

91. Reviewers' comments almost invariably include references to Jackson's apparent mental state in *Living with Michael Jackson*; Stanley's characterization of him as seeming "crazy," cited in this chapter, is only one example.

92. Roopali Mukherjee, "Bling Fling: Commodity Consumption and the Politics of the 'Post-Racial,'" in *Critical Rhetorics of Race*, ed. Michael G. Lacy and Kent A. Ono (New York: New York University Press, 2011), 186.

93. Pierre Bourdieu, *Distinction: A Social Critique of the Judgement of Taste*, trans. Richard Nice (Cambridge, MA: Harvard University Press, 1984), 56–57.

94. Mukherjee, "Bling Fling," 186.

95. Ibid., 185.

96. Zygmunt Bauman, *Society under Siege* (London: Polity, 2002), 188.

97. Brett Pulley, "Michael Jackson's Ups and Downs," *Forbes*, November 21, 2003, accessed January 10, 2015, http://www.forbes.com/2003/11/21/cz_1121jackson.html.

98. Greenburg, *Michael Jackson, Inc.*, 188.

99. Roger Friedman, "Jacko Pawned $2 Million Watch to Raise Dough; Banker Claims: 'I've Kept Him Alive,'" *FoxNews.com*, April 19, 2002, accessed July 17, 2015, http://www.foxnews.com/story/2002/04/19/jacko-pawned-2-million-watch-to-raise-dough-banker-claims-ive-kept-him-alive.html. The report provides an interesting example of racialized borrowing. Though the piece uses "pawned," Jackson was actually using the watch as collateral to borrow from a bank. "Pawn," however, conjures a pejorative image of ghetto finance.

100. Peter A. Ubel, *Free Market Madness: Why Human Nature Is at Odds with Economics* (Cambridge, MA: Harvard Business Review Press, 2009), xi.

101. Brown, *Edgework*, 6–7.

102. Mahmud, "Debt and Discipline," 476.

103. Ibid., 478.

104. Ben Woolsey, "Credit Card Industry and Personal Debt Statistics (2005 and Prior)," *Credit Card News*, September 13, 2007, accessed July 17, 2015, http://www.creditcards.com/credit-card-news/credit-card-statistics-2005-prior-1276.php.

105. Mahmud, "Debt and Discipline," 447.

106. Moten and Harney, "Debt and Study."

107. See, for example, Nobel Prize–winning economist Joseph Stiglitz, "Moral Bankruptcy," *Mother Jones*, January/February 2010, accessed July 15, 2015, http://www.motherjones.com/politics/2010/01/joseph-stiglitz-wall-street-morals.

108. Berlant, *Cruel Optimism*, 115; see also Sarita See, "Gambling with Debt: Lessons from the Illiterate," *American Quarterly* 64, no. 3 (September 2012): 495–514.

109. Berlant, *Cruel Optimism*, 115–16.

110. Ibid., 117.

111. Greenburg, *Michael Jackson, Inc.*, 203.

112. Allan Johnson, "ABC on Top with King of Pop Special," *Chicago Tribune*, February 8, 2003, accessed November 20, 2013, http://articles.chicagotribune.com/2003-02-08/news/0302080284_1_nielsen-ratings-viewers-living-with-michael-jackson.

113. Williams, *Playing the Race Card*, 262.

114. Martin, *Financialization of Daily Life*, 55; Robert Kuttner, *Debtors' Prison: The Politics of Austerity versus Possibility* (New York: Vintage, 2015), 234.

115. Judith Butler quoted in Williams, *Playing the Race Card*, 266.

116. I will not, for example, examine the racialization of the Arvizo family, though this is a fascinating topic. They are also persons of color.

117. Jury selection began on January 31, 2005.

118. Associated Press, "Jackson's Finances Probed," *Topeka Capital Journal/CJ Online.com*, May 4, 2005, accessed December 18, 2014, http://cjonline.com/stories/050405/pag_jackson.shtml.

119. John M. Broder, "Witness Says Jackson Had 'Cash Flow Crisis,'" *New York Times*, May 4, 2005, accessed December 18, 2014, http://www.nytimes.com/2005/05/04/national/04jackson.html?pagewanted=print&position.

120. Associated Press, "Jackson's Finances Probed."

121. See Joseph, *Debt to Society*, 19–25, on credit and trust.

122. Kozlowski was not accused of flouting financialization's "moral code," merely of reappropriating its logics to his own ends.

123. Jane Bennett, "The Moraline Drift," in *The Politics of Moralizing*, ed. Jane Bennett and Michael J. Shapiro (New York: Routledge, 2002), 13. Specifically, Bennett is interested in "moraline theory," but the characteristics she enumerates are useful for outlining the contours of a moralizing project as well.

124. Martin, *Financialization of Daily Life*, 85.

125. Ibid., 92.

126. Bennett, "The Moraline Drift," 20.

127. J. Duross O'Bryan, "Neverland Accounting," *Forbes*, July 2, 2009, accessed August 5, 2015, http://www.forbes.com/2009/07/02/michael-jackson-bankruptcy-opinions-contributors-king-of-pop.html.

128. Martin, *Financialization of Daily Life*, 92.

129. Milton Friedman, the economist perhaps most responsible for the dominance of neoliberal financialization, explicitly rejected any moral or social responsibilities of finance capitalism in his book *Capitalism and Freedom* and in a famous *New York Times Magazine* essay, arguing: "There is one and only one social responsibility of business—to use its resources and engage in activities designed to increase its profits so long as it stays within the rules of the game, which is to say, engages in open and free competition without

deception or fraud." Milton Friedman, "The Social Responsibility of Business Is to Increase Its Profits," *New York Times Magazine*, September 13, 1970, 32–33, 122–24. As I discuss later in this chapter, the subprime loan collapse amply demonstrates that "increase[d] profits" fully negated any finance industry criminal and moral responsibility for "deception and fraud."

130. Timothy O'Brien, "What Happened to the Fortune Michael Jackson Made?," *New York Times*, May 14, 2006, accessed December 30, 2014, http://www.nytimes.com/2006/05/14/business/yourmoney/14michael.html?pagewanted=all&_r=1&.

131. Ethan Smith and Kate Kelly, "Michael Jackson's Other Battle: Staving Off Financial Disaster," *Wall Street Journal*, June 8, 2005, accessed December 14, 2014, http://www.wsj.com/news/articles/SB111819644592353818?mg=reno64-wsj. The article notes that Neverland and MiJac, which held copyright to Jackson's songs, were collateral for other loans.

132. Crawford, "Michael Jackson to Lose Beatles Catalog?"

133. Matt Phillips, "MarketBeat: Michael Jackson: Bank of America Got This Loan Off Its Books, but Should It Have?," *Wall Street Journal*, June 26, 2009, accessed July 29, 2015, http://blogs.wsj.com/marketbeat/2009/06/26/michael-jackson-bank-of-america-got-this-loan-off-its-books-but-should-it-have/.

134. Greenburg, *Michael Jackson, Inc.*, 214.

135. I can find no evidence that Jackson's loans were securitized, and he was never a "subprime" debtor in the strictest sense. There are figural connections to the subprime, however, including one analyst's characterization of music catalogs' investment potential as "real estate" and the foreclosure on Neverland.

136. This was a classically neoliberal financialized initiative combining tax cuts and credits, subsidies from public funds to nonprofits, and a challenge to lenders to increase mortgages to minority consumers. "Fact Sheet: America's Ownership Society: Expanding Opportunities," George W. Bush White House Archives, August 9, 2004, accessed September 9, 2013, http://georgewbush-whitehouse.archives.gov/news/releases/2004/08/20040809-9.html.

137. Every one of these scams is detailed in the opening pages of Michael W. Hudson, *The Monster: How a Gang of Predatory Lenders and Wall Street Bankers Fleeced America* (New York: St. Martin's/Griffin, 2011).

138. Eric Etheridge, "Rick Santelli: Tea Party Time," *New York Times "Opinionator" Blog*, February 20, 2009, accessed July 10, 2015, http://opinionator.blogs.nytimes.com/2009/02/20/rick-santelli-tea-party-time/?_r=0.

139. Shawn Shimpach, "Realty Reality: HGTV and the Subprime Crisis," *American Quarterly* 64, no. 3 (September 2012): 515.

140. Phil Gramm quoted in Lipton and Labaton, "The Reckoning."

141. Fred Moten, "The Subprime and the Beautiful," *African Identities*, 11, no. 2 (2013): 240.

142. Renae Merle, "Minorities Hit Harder by Foreclosure Crisis," *Washington Post*, June 19, 2010, accessed August 21, 2015, http://www.washingtonpost.com/wp-dyn/content/article/2010/06/18/AR2010061802885.html. Ylan Q. Mui, "For Black Americans, Financial Damage from Subprime Implosion Is Likely to Last," *Washington Post*, July 8, 2012, accessed August 21, 2015, https://www.washingtonpost.com/business/economy/for-black-americans-financial-damage-from-subprime-implosion-is-likely-to-last/2012/07/08/gJQAwNmzWW_story.html.

143. Paula Chakravartty and Denise Ferreira da Silva, "Accumulation, Dispossession, and Debt: The Racial Logic of Global Capitalism—An Introduction," *American Quarterly* 64, no. 3 (September 2012): 373 (emphasis in original).

144. Williams, *Playing the Race Card*, 7. Williams notes that Leslie Fiedler, whose Tom/anti-Tom schema she adapts, saw the anti-Tom novel as a precursor.

145. The welfare queen returned to the Republican rhetorical repertoire in 2012 during the recovery from the Great Recession as lawmakers labeled Barack Obama the "food stamp president." John Blake, "Return of the Welfare Queen," *CNNPolitics.com*, January 23, 2012, accessed August 11, 2015, http://www.cnn.com/2012/01/23/politics/weflare-queen/.

146. Thomas Mesereau, *Larry King Live*, aired June 14, 2006, *CNN.com Transcripts*, accessed August 6, 2015, http://www.cnn.com/TRANSCRIPTS/0506/14/lkl.01.html.

147. Tamara Jones, "Culkin Shared Jackson's Bed but Says He Wasn't Molested," *Washington Post*, May 12, 2005, accessed August 6, 2015, http://www.washingtonpost.com/wp-dyn/content/article/2005/05/11/AR2005051102197.html.

148. Mesereau, *Larry King Live*.

149. Robin Bernstein, *Racial Innocence: Performing American Childhood from Slavery to Civil Rights* (New York: New York University Press, 2011), 6.

150. Williams makes a particularly compelling case for the film *The Green Mile* as a "Tom" example. See Williams, *Playing the Race Card*, 301–7.

151. Bernstein, *Racial Innocence*, 92–93.

152. Ibid., 6.

153. Ibid., 7.

154. Ibid., 4.

155. See Max Haiven's "Play: Coming of Age in the Speculative Pokéconomy," in *Cultures of Financialization: Fictitious Capital in Popular Culture and Everyday Life* (Basingstoke: Palgrave Macmillan, 2014), 102–29.

156. See, "Gambling with Debt," 495.

157. Moten, "The Subprime and the Beautiful," 243.

158. Edna Gundersen, "Jackson's Freedom Isn't Free," *USA Today*, June 14, 2005, accessed July 16, 2015, http://usatoday30.usatoday.com/life/people/2005-06-13-jackson-finances_x.htm.

159. Cesar G. Soriano, "Michael Jackson Announces 10-Concert Comeback," *USA Today*, March 5, 2009, accessed February 23, 2015, http://usatoday30.usatoday.com/life/music/news/2009-03-05-jackson-comeback_N.htm.

160. Greenburg, *Michael Jackson, Inc.*, 213–14.

161. Ibid., 218.

162. Jennifer Szalai, "First Words: The Tough Love of 'Austerity,'" *New York Times Magazine*, August 4, 2015, 13.

163. Florian Schui, *Austerity: The Great Failure* (New Haven, CT: Yale University Press, 2014), 13.

164. Ibid., 9.

165. It is not fully clear which version of "The Red Shoes"—Andersen's or the film's—Pascal meant here, but certainly there was no evidence that Jackson committed suicide because he was torn between his art and a normal life. Indeed, his life with his three children was clearly sustaining to him. Josh Rottenberg, "Michael Jackson's Movie Ambitions Included 3-D Film of 'Thriller,' 'Red Shoes' remake," *Entertainment Weekly*, October 30, 2009, accessed February 1, 2015, http://www.ew.com/article/2009/10/30/michael-jackson-movie-ambitious.

166. "Diet" used by House Minority Leader Robert Boehner, "The Obama Plan to Rescue the Economy: Can We Afford It?," *Transcript: Face the Nation* (CBS Broadcasting, Inc., March 8, 2009), 5; "morality play" from Mark Blyth, *Austerity: The History of a Dangerous Idea* (New York: Oxford University Press, 2013), 12; "tough love" from Szalai, "First Words."

167. Thanks to Carol Greenhouse for her keen observation on this point.

168. Blyth, *Austerity*, 8.

169. Ibid., 98–99.

170. "Word of the Year," *Merriam-Webster, Inc.*, December 20, 2010, accessed September 3, 2015, http://www.merriam-webster.com/word-of-the-year/2010-word-of-the-year.htm.

171. Schui, *Austerity*, 2.

172. Ibid.

173. Blyth, *Austerity*, 2.

174. Quoted in Thomas B. Edsall, "The Politics of Austerity," *New York Times*, November 5, 2011, accessed September 3, 2015, http://campaignstops.blogs.nytimes.com/2011/11/05/the-politics-of-austerity/?_r=0.

175. Theda Skocpol and Vanessa Williamson, *The Tea Party and the Remaking of Republican Conservatism* (New York: Oxford University Press, 2012), 66.

176. Edsall, "The Politics of Austerity."

177. As Edsall indicates in "The Politics of Austerity," the percentages of African Americans are highest in just those agencies that are most actively targeted for cuts by Republicans: the Department of Housing and Urban Development, 38.3 percent; the Equal Employment Opportunity Commission, 42.4 percent; and the Department of Education, 36.6 percent.

178. Skocpol and Williamson, *Tea Party*, 64, 74.

179. Figures cited in Chad Stone, "Austerity Prolongs the Pain," *U.S. News & World Report*, September 5, 2014, accessed September 3, 2015, http://www.usnews.com/opinion/economic-intelligence/2014/09/05/recession-austerity-spending-cuts-have-had-lasting-impact-on-jobs.

180. Boehner in "The Obama Plan to Rescue the Economy."

181. Randy Phillips, Kenny Ortega, Paul Gongaware, and Michael Jackson, *Michael Jackson's This Is It* (Sony Pictures Home Entertainment, 2010).

182. Jackson, *Moonwalk*, 227.

183. Exhibit 311-1 [9, Faye, 1/3/13] "Jackson V AEG Live Trial Exhibits," *TeamMichaelJackson.com*, accessed July 11, 2015, http://www.teammichaeljackson.com/archives/8832. While the posting on the Jackson site is certainly an indicator of vested interest, the exhibits bear court markings, and material contained in them was repeated, often verbatim, in media coverage of the suit.

184. Exhibit 330-1 [10, Faye, 1/3/13] *TeamMichaelJackson.com*, accessed July 11, 2015, http://www.teammichaeljackson.com/archives/8832.

185. Exhibit 307–2 [AEGL 000137453], *TeamMichaelJackson.com*, accessed July 11, 2015, http://www.teammichaeljackson.com/archives/8832. See also Alan Duke, "Lawsuit Evidence: Michael Jackson Lost Dance Moves in Last Days," *CNN Entertainment*, June 16, 2013, accessed December 30, 2014, http://www.cnn.com/2013/06/14/showbiz/jackson-death-trial/index.html.

186. Franz Kafka, "A Hunger Artist," in *The Penal Colony: Stories and Short Pieces*, trans. Willa Muir and Edwin Muir (New York: Schocken, 1961), 231–77; Rudolph M. Bell, *Holy Anorexia* (Chicago: University of Chicago Press, 1985); Patrick Anderson, *So Much Wasted: Hunger, Performance, and the Morbidity of Resistance* (Durham, NC: Duke University Press, 2010).

187. Szalai, "First Words."

188. Herbert Blau, *The Audience* (Baltimore: Johns Hopkins University Press, 1990), 366.

189. Duke, "Lawsuit Evidence."

190. Alan Duke, "Kenny Ortega Brings Tearful Testimony to Michael Jackson Death Trial," *CNN Entertainment*, July 11, 2013, accessed October 30, 2015, http://www.cnn.com/2013/07/10/showbiz/jackson-death-trial/.

191. Jason King, "Don't Stop Till You Get Enough: Presence, Spectacle, and Good Feeling in *Michael Jackson's This Is It*," in *Black Performance Theory*, ed. Thomas F. DeFrantz and Anita Gonzalez (Durham, NC: Duke University Press, 2014), 200.

192. David Harvey, *Spaces of Hope* (Berkeley: University of California Press, 2000), 106.

193. André Lepecki, *Exhausting Dance: Performance and the Politics of Movement* (New York: Routledge, 2006), 45.

194. Soriano, "Michael Jackson Announces 10-Concert Comeback."

195. Rebecca Bramall, *The Cultural Politics of Austerity: Past and Present in Austere Times* (Basingstoke: Palgrave Macmillan, 2013), 1, 10–11.

196. US House of Representatives, Committee on the Budget, "The Path to Prosperity: Restoring America's Promise," *Fiscal Year 2012 Budget Resolution*, n.d., 10–11. Curiously, the document advocates government austerity to avoid the "harsh austerity credit markets would impose upon us" (59).

197. Ibid.

198. Greenburg, *Michael Jackson, Inc.*, 251.

CHAPTER 3

1. Jerry Herron, "Motor City Breakdown: Detroit in Literature and Film," *Places*, April 2013, accessed June 1, 2013, https://placesjournal.org/article/motor-city-breakdown/.

2. Lisa D'Amour, *Detroit* (New York: Faber and Faber, 2011), 27.

3. Ibid., 5.

4. Charles Isherwood, "Desperately Trying to Stay Stuck in the Middle," *New York Times*, September 18, 2012, accessed June 1, 2013, http://theater.nytimes.com/2012/09/19/theater/reviews/detroit-with-amy-ryan-and-david-schwimmer.html?_r=0.

5. San Jose, Baltimore, Cleveland, and New York are only a few of the cities designated "not Detroit." See Blair Lee, "At Least Baltimore Is Not Detroit," *Gazette.Net: Maryland Community News Online*, September 27, 2013, accessed October 28, 2013, http://www.gazette.net/article/20130927/OPINION/130929269/-1/why-baltimore-is-not-detroit&template=gazette; the Fresh Brewed Tees ad for a shirt extolling "Cleveland: At Least We're Not Detroit," accessed October 28, 2013, http://www.freshbrewedtees.com/tees/cleveland-at-least-we-re-not-detroit.html.; Josh Koehn, "San Jose Is Not Detroit," *San Jose Inside*, October 2, 2013, accessed October 28, 2013, http://www.sanjoseinside.com/news/entries/10_2_13_san_jose_detroit_xavier_campos_new_york_times/; and Bill Keller, "New York Is Not Detroit But . . . ," *New York Times*, July 21, 2013, accessed October 28, 2013, http://www.nytimes.com/2013/07/22/opinion/keller-new-york-is-not-detroit-but.html?_r=0.

6. In this chapter I use "affect" in the generic sense, not the Deleuzian sense.

7. Here I am riffing on Brandi Wilkins Catanese's observation that, in a putatively post-racial era, raising the issue of race is "bad manners." See Brandi Wilkins Catanese, *The Problem of the Color[blind]: Racial Transgressions and the Politics of Black Performance* (Ann Arbor: University of Michigan Press, 2011), 5.

8. For only one example of innumerable references to Chicago as "not Detroit," see Randall W. Forsyth, "Chicago Is Not Detroit," *Barron's*, November 21, 2013, accessed March 31, 2014, http://online.barrons.com/article/SB50001424053111904253404579205921128206510.html. In the analysis that follows, I refer to both the published text of *Detroit* and the Playwrights Horizons production, indicating discrepancies where they occur. *Detroit* viewed in the Theatre on Film and Tape Archive, New York Public Library for the Performing Arts, taped October 24, 2012, accessed July 12, 2013.

9. D'Amour, *Detroit*, back cover.

10. Ibid., 39.

11. Isherwood, "Desperately Trying to Stay Stuck in the Middle."

12. Joe Dziemianowicz, "Theatre Review: 'Detroit,'" *New York Daily News*, September 18, 2012, accessed June 1, 2013, http://www.nydailynews.com/entertainment/music-arts/theater-review-detroit-article-1.1162183.

13. Guy Debord, *The Society of the Spectacle*, trans. Donald Nicholson-Smith (New York: Zone, 1995), 12.

14. For an excellent summary of the post–World War II musical and its values, see the "Introduction" to Stacy Wolf's *A Problem Like Maria: Gender and Sexuality in the American Musical* (Ann Arbor: University of Michigan Press, 2002).

15. Charles Isherwood, "Hey, Diana, Smokey, Stevie: You're on Broadway!," *New York Times*, April 14, 2013, accessed August 3, 2013, http://theater.nytimes.com/2013/04/15/theater/reviews/motown-the-musical-berry-gordys-story.html?pagewanted=all&_r=0.

16. Herb Boyd, "Harlem Week: Lackluster Reviews Don't Dismay Director of 'Motown the Musical,'" *New York Daily News*, August 6, 2012, accessed August 3, 2013, http://www.nydailynews.com/new-york/uptown/harlem-week-lackluster-reviews-don-dismay-director-motown-musical-article-1.1417402.

17. Quotations are taken from *Motown the Musical*, Lunt-Fontanne Theatre, New York, New York, July 12, 2013.

18. Motown was heavily criticized for leaving Detroit, and such critics included company insiders. See, for example, Suzanne Smith, *Dancing in the Street: Motown and the Cultural Politics of Detroit* (Cambridge, MA: Harvard University Press, 1999), 239–43.

19. The other plays in Morisseau's Detroit trilogy are *Paradise Blue* (2012), set in the city's African American Paradise Valley neighborhood in 1949, and *Skeleton Crew* (2016), set in 2008 and depicting workers and managers at a small, beleaguered auto-stamping plant.

20. Dominique Morisseau, *Detroit '67* (London: Oberon Books, 2013), 5.

21. Ibid., 8.

22. Ibid., 95.

23. Charles Isherwood, "Down in the Basement, Family Tensions Stir," *New York Times*, March 12, 2013, accessed June 1, 2013, http://theater.nytimes.com/2013/03/13/theater/reviews/detroit-67-at-the-public-theater.html?pagewanted=all.

24. Alexis Soloski, "Detroit '67: Get Ready," *Village Voice*, March 13, 2013, accessed June 1, 2013, http://www.villagevoice.com/2013-03-13/theater/detroit-67-get-ready/full/.

25. Morisseau, *Detroit '67*, 23.

26. See ibid., 5.

27. Here I work from E. Patrick Johnson's discussion of "appropriating blackness," particularly in the context of imagining and performing black music as putatively transracial. Johnson writes of gospel music:

> Like other black cultural art forms when they are let loose into the world, gospel music has become enshrouded in identity politics. . . . Like all identity politics and notions of "authenticity," the [white] choir members' appropriation of blackness is both/and rather than either/or. Each time the choir performs gospel music they participate in what has become one of the most recognizable signifiers of black culture. In that regard, they perform blackness when they sing. On the other hand, their performance of blackness does not diminish the white-skin privilege they enjoy in their country or in the United States.

> I argue that the Motown sound and other elements of figural "Detroitness" can be appropriated by white audiences as simultaneously "black" and "transracial," while regarding the current city itself, and its majority African American status, as fixedly "black." See E. Patrick Johnson, *Appropriating Blackness* (Durham, NC: Duke University Press, 2003), 218.

28. "Making" and "faking" are allusions to Victor Turner's famous revisioning of performance in light of the Platonic antitheatrical bias as "making, not faking." Too often, "making" and "faking" are reduced to binary opposites, with "making" a simple response to the Platonic critique of mimesis. The three plays discussed here, and Henry Ford's intervention in Inkster discussed later in this chapter, remind us that, on the contrary, "making" and "faking" are very often partners across genres of performance. See Victor Turner, *From Ritual to Theatre: The Human Seriousness of Play* (New York: PAJ Publications, 1982), 93.

29. My characterization of naturalistic theater's ethnographic appeal to spectators draws from Kiri Miller's analysis of *Grand Theft Auto* as an ethnographic encounter. Naturalistic performance partakes of the same "family resemblances and distinctions" as game worlds and field sites, particularly when such sites are coded as racially or culturally "other": a coding, I believe, that is also an intrinsic element of "Detroitness." Spectatorship of naturalistic performances recalls Miller's observation of game play: "Suspend your disbelief and treat the gameworlds [or the developments onstage] like actual places with human inhabitants" (35). Miller is particularly astute in her reading of subjects of color in such "ethnographic" structures. See Kiri Miller, *Playing Along* (New York: Oxford University Press, 2012), 32–37.

30. Micaela di Leonardo, *Exotics at Home* (Chicago: University of Chicago Press, 1998), 9.

31. Richard Schechner, *Between Theater and Anthropology* (Philadelphia: University of Pennsylvania Press, 1985), 112.

32. Ibid., 113.

33. Monica Davey, "Financial Crisis Just a Symptom of Detroit's Woes," *New York Times*, July 8, 2013, A1+.

34. My argument here is both indebted to and a departure from that of Jon McKenzie in *Perform or Else*. McKenzie describes three paradigms of performance and performance research: cultural/aesthetic, organizational, and technological, arguing that this threefold division resists a simplistic reading of binary oppositions between modes. This may be a presentist construction, however. A close reading of early Fordist labor practices, from the company's assembly line to the Sociological Department, reveals that the organizational and technological regimes collapse into one highly disciplinary techno-managerial mode. See Jon McKenzie, *Perform or Else* (New York: Routledge, 2001), 5–19.

35. *Harvest of the Years* (Ford Motor Company, Dearborn, MI: 1939). A clip from the film may be viewed at http://www.youtube.com/watch?v=TcXfk0op6JA, accessed July 31, 2013.

36. "Ford River Rouge Factory Tour America's Greatest Manufacturing," *The Henry Ford*, accessed June 8, 2016, http://www.thehenryford.org/rouge/index.aspx.

37. "Ford River Rouge Factory Tour—Art of Manufacturing Theater," *The Henry Ford*, accessed July 31, 2013, http://www.thehenryford.org/rouge/theater.aspx. The name of the theater has since changed to the "Manufacturing Innovation Theater."

38. Here it is worth noting that the scenes conjured in the Art of Manufacturing Theater are not racially neutral. As Thomas Sugrue noted, by 1940,

> half of all blacks in the automobile industry nationwide were Ford employees; nearly all of these workers were concentrated in the Ford River Rouge Plant. Wherever they were employed, most blacks worked in service jobs, especially on plant janitorial and maintenance crews, or in hot, dangerous jobs in foundries or furnacerooms[.]

Thomas Sugrue, *The Origins of the Urban Crisis: Race and Inequality in Postwar Detroit* (Princeton, NJ: Princeton University Press, 2014), 24.

39. Beth Tompkins Bates, *The Making of Black Detroit in the Age of Henry Ford* (Chapel Hill: University of North Carolina Press, 2012), 145.

40. As Bates notes, the reality was far more complex. Inkster was 73 percent white, and the African American community was actively self-reliant and ably assisted by a highly

entrepreneurial African American city councilman. The Great Depression wiped out many of the village's earlier gains and brought real suffering to the area. See ibid., 146–49.

41. Ibid., 148.

42. Ibid., 154.

43. Ford came under heavy criticism for closing the Rouge at the height of the Depression, adding significantly to the rolls of Detroit's unemployed. The Ford Hunger March Massacre, the killing of four unemployed workers by Dearborn police and Ford security employees, took place several months after the initiation of the Inkster project.

44. Ibid., 156.

45. Sidney Fine, *Violence in the Model City* (Ann Arbor: University of Michigan Press, 1989), 88.

46. Ibid., 90.

47. Ibid., 1.

48. Ibid., 92.

49. That cover, titled simply "Detroit," shows firemen and a bystander fully surrounded by billowing smoke and flames: the city as apocalyptic inferno. *Life*, August 4, 1967.

50. Diamond notes the ubiquity of "the terminology of 're' in discussions of performance, as in *re*member, *re*inscribe, *re*configure, *re*iterate, *re*store." Elin Diamond, "Introduction," in *Performance and Cultural Politics* (London: Routledge, 1996), 2. Schechner defines performance as "restored behavior." Schechner, *Between Theater*, 35.

51. Joseph Roach, *Cities of the Dead: Circum-Atlantic Performance* (New York: Columbia University Press, 1996), 2. Roach's three-sided relationship includes "memory," not "history." I argue here that Detroit's role in the figural economy of the American deindustrial is a function of its history: specifically, in the case of these three plays, the history linking work to homeownership summarized in Herron's epigraph to this chapter. That said, memory is also crucial to my discussion of *Motown the Musical*.

52. D'Amour, *Detroit*, 5.

53. Thomas Sugrue notes that Detroit's systemic racial segregation of housing was not merely an artifact of the early twentieth century. On the contrary, it intensified in the 1970s and 1980s, the beginning of the city's highly visible industrial downturn. See Sugrue, *Origins of the Urban Crisis*, 269.

54. Roach, *Cities of the Dead*, 2.

55. See Judith Hamera, "Regions of Likeness: The Poetry of Jorie Graham, Dance, and Citational Solidarity," *Text and Performance Quarterly* 25, no. 1 (January 2005): 15–27; Della Pollock, "Performing Writing," in *The Ends of Performance*, ed. P. Phelan and J. Lane (New York: New York University Press, 1998), 73–103.

56. One reviewer notes D'Amour's script plays out like *Who's Afraid of Virginia Woolf?* as if retooled by Sam Shepard. See Donald Hutera, "Detroit: State of the Nation," *Theatre News Online*, n.d., accessed August 8, 2013, http://www.theaternewsonline.com/LondonTheatreReviews/STATEOFTHENATION.cfm.

57. Soyica Diggs Colbert, *The African American Theatrical Body: Reception, Performance, and the Stage* (Cambridge: Cambridge University Press, 2011), 27.

58. Judith Butler, *Bodies That Matter: On the Discursive Limits of Sex* (New York: Routledge, 1993), xxi.

59. Kathleen Stewart, *Ordinary Affects* (Durham, NC: Duke University Press, 2007), 3 (emphasis added).

60. For "localness of race," see John Hartigan, Jr., *Racial Situations: Class Predicaments of Whiteness in Detroit* (Princeton, NJ: Princeton University Press, 1999), 13–16. For the "repetition/reproduction" dyad, see Diggs Colbert, *African American Theatrical Body*, 13.

61. Harry Elam and Michele Elam in Diggs Colbert, *African American Theatrical Body*, 4.

62. Avery F. Gordon, *Ghostly Matters: Haunting and the Sociological Imagination* (Minneapolis: University of Minnesota Press, 1997), 8.

63. Marvin Carlson, *The Haunted Stage: Theatre as Memory Machine* (Ann Arbor: University of Michigan Press, 2002), 2.

64. While there are many examples of the city characterized as a "ghost town," see Peter Hitchens, "From Motown to Ghost Town: How the Once Mighty Detroit Is Headed Down the Road to Ruin," *Daily Mail Online*, July 9, 2011, April 14, 2014, http://www.dailymail.co.uk/news/article-2012971/From-Motown-Ghost-town-How-mighty-Detroit-heading-long-slow-road-ruin.html.

65. Gordon, *Ghostly Matters*, 8.

66. D'Amour, *Detroit*, 13.

67. Ibid., 9.

68. Ibid., 68.

69. Morisseau, *Detroit '67*, 21.

70. Ibid., 24.

71. Ibid.

72. "New Industrial Era Is Marked by Ford's Shares to Laborers," *Detroit Free Press*, January 6, 1914, sec. 1+, ProQuest Historical Newspapers.

73. Reinhold Niebuhr, "Lessons of the Detroit Experience," *Christian Century* 82 (1965): 487.

74. Stephen Meyer III, *The Five Dollar Day: Labor Management and Social Control in the Ford Motor Company* (Albany, NY: SUNY Press, 1981), 123.

75. "Workers Must Live Decently," *Detroit Free Press*, April 18, 1914, sec. 1+, ProQuest Historical Newspapers.

76. Meyer III, *Five Dollar Day*, 129.

77. "Workers Must Live Decently."

78. "New Industrial Era Is Marked by Ford's Shares to Laborers."

79. Meyer, *Five Dollar Day*, 141.

80. "Workers Must Live Decently."

81. For a detailed discussion of the structure of both investigations and their write-ups, see Meyer III, *Five Dollar Day*, 125–41.

82. Richard Snow, "Henry Ford's Experiment to Build a Better Worker," *Wall Street Journal*, May 9, 2013, accessed July 20, 2013, http://online.wsj.com/article/SB100014241278873 24059704578471112978065632.html.

83. Meyer III, *Five Dollar Day*, 145.

84. "New Industrial Era Is Marked by Ford's Shares to Laborers."

85. "Workers Must Live Decently."

86. Jeremy Williams, *Images of America: Detroit—The Black Bottom Community* (Charleston, SC: Arcadia, 2009), 14.

87. Dwight Conquergood, *Cultural Struggles: Performance, Ethnography, Praxis*, ed. E. Patrick Johnson (Ann Arbor: University of Michigan Press, 2013), 188.

88. Niebuhr, "Lessons of the Detroit Experience," 1.

89. US Census Bureau, "Table 23. Michigan—Race and Hispanic Origin for Selected Large Cities and Other Places: Earliest Census to 1990," July 15, 2005, accessed April 4, 2014, http://www.census.gov/population/www/documentation/twps0076/MItab.pdf.

90. Sociologist Pierre Bourdieu defined "habitus" as "a "structured and structuring structure" that, when internalized, operates as "a disposition that generates meaningful practices and meaning-giving perceptions." Pierre Bourdieu, *Distinction: A Social Critique of the Judgement of Taste*, trans. Richard Nice (Cambridge, MA: Harvard University Press, 1984), 171, 170.

91. D'Amour, *Detroit*, 92.

92. The dictum is most often known through paraphrase: "You can have any color you want as long as it's black." Henry Ford, *My Life and Work (1922)*, Project Gutenberg, 2005, accessed April 30, 2014, http://www.gutenberg.org/cache/epub/7213/pg7213-images.html, 71.

93. For an insightful discussion of Ford's reasons for recruiting black workers and the stakes for the workers themselves, see Bates, *Making of Black Detroit*, 54.

94. Ibid., 96.

95. "City Faces Negro Housing Problem: Southern Clergyman Declares 25,000 Live in One Restricted Area," *Detroit Free Press*, March 12, 1917, 13, ProQuest Historical Newspapers.

96. Len G. Shaw, "Detroit's New Housing Problem," *Detroit Free Press*, June 3, 1917, sec. E1, ProQuest Historical Newspapers; J. W. Rawlins, "Letter to the Editor: Detroit Has Problem in Housing Conditions," *Detroit Free Press*, June 23, 1917, ProQuest Historical Newspapers.

97. Sugrue, *Origins of the Urban Crisis*, 22. Sugrue sees this shift in identification as beginning in the 1920s, but the FMC emphasis on white settlement in homogeneous neighborhoods and suburbs from early in the five-dollar-per-day profit-sharing initiative suggests it actually began a few years earlier in the late 1910s.

98. Bates, *Making of Black Detroit*, 98.

99. The McGhee House, 4626 Seebaldt on Detroit's west side, is now a Michigan Historical Site.

100. See Shawn G. Kennedy, "Orville L. Hubbard of Dearborn; Ex-Mayor a Foe of Integration," *New York Times*, December 17, 1982, accessed July 31, 2013, http://www.nytimes.com/1982/12/17/obituaries/orville-l-hubbard-of-dearborn-ex-mayor-a-foe-of-integration.html.

101. In an interesting extratextual moment in the production, even in Berry Gordy's show Michael Jackson exceeds the structures of Motown; reviewer Isherwood notes that "something close to rapture spreads across the audience" when the character of young Michael takes the stage, attesting once again to the uncanny affective potency of his many afterlives. The production I attended demonstrated this same dynamic. In the performance I saw, the young Jackson character's songs were the most wildly applauded by far.

102. Smith, *Dancing in the Street*, 248.

103. Ronald E. Kutscher and Valerie A. Personick, "Deindustrialization and the Shift to Services," *Monthly Labor Review*, June 1986, 7.

104. In *Detroit*, Sharon reflects on being told in rehab that her "old life" as a drug addict would feel real and her new life like a dream. The construction parallels the industrial nostalgia that frames the Fordist bargain as an old life that feels real and its successor mode of production as a dream, even as such nostalgia dispenses with the political realities of racism, union confrontations, and violent resistance. See D'Amour, *Detroit*, 57.

105. Morisseau, *Detroit '67*, 24.

106. Ibid., 12.

107. Ibid., 25.

108. Ibid., 54–55.

109. Ibid., 68.

110. Ibid., 70.

111. Ibid., 86.

112. bell hooks, "Homeplace (a site of resistance)," in *The Woman That I Am*, ed. D. Soyini Madison (New York: St. Martin's, 1994), 449.

113. Kevin Boyle, *Arc of Justice: A Saga of Race, Civil Rights, and Murder in the Jazz Age* (New York: Henry Holt, 2004), 16.

114. Ibid., 39.

115. See Morisseau, *Detroit '67*, 22–23. "The Big Four" cited in the play were cruisers, which "had a gestapo-like image" in the black community. "The three plainclothesmen and the uniformed driver riding in these vehicles, none of them integrated before 1965, were armed with shotguns, machine guns, and tear gas." Fine, *Violence in the Model City*, 100–101.

116. Bates, *Making of Black Detroit*, 106; Boyle, *Arc of Justice*, 162.

117. Boyle, *Arc of Justice*, 322.

118. Ibid., 290.

119. D'Amour, *Detroit*, 91.

120. Ibid., 94.

121. Ibid., 95.

122. Ibid., 21.

123. Ibid., 93.

124. Ibid., 49.

125. Ibid., 68 (emphasis in the original).

126. Ibid., 94.

127. Ibid., 83.

128. Ibid., 13.

129. Ibid., 96.

130. Ibid., 57.

131. Lawrence Grossberg, "Postmodernity and Affect: All Dressed Up with No Place to Go," *Communication* 10 (1988): 275.

132. D'Amour, *Detroit*, 77.

133. Ibid., 85.

134. Thanks to Norm Hirschy for this distinction between burning up and burning down.

135. D'Amour, *Detroit*, back cover.

136. The 1863 riots were not the first racial conflagration in the city, though they were the first with documented accounts of homes set on fire. The first "race riot" in Detroit was the Blackburn Riot of June 1833, in which a group of African Americans stormed the city's jail to free Thomas Blackburn. Blackburn and his wife, Lucy, had escaped slavery in Kentucky and fled to Detroit but were apprehended with the intent of forcibly returning them to bondage. Both were freed and escaped to Canada. The jail was set alight by African American demonstrators. For more on the Blackburn Riot, see Karolyn Smardz Frost, *I've Got a Home in Glory Land: A Lost Tale of the Underground Railroad* (New York: Farrar, Straus and Giroux, 2007).

137. B. Clark, "The Riot," in *Anti-Negro Riots in the North, 1863* (New York: Arno Press and the New York Times, 1969), 24.

138. jruss, "The 1943 Detroit Riot," *jruss's blog*, Walter P. Reuther Library, Wayne State University, June 12, 2012, accessed July 31, 2013, http://reuther.wayne.edu/node/8738.

139. Robyn Meredith, "5 Days in 1967 Still Shake Detroit," *New York Times*, July 23, 1997, accessed August 1, 2013, http://www.nytimes.com/1997/07/23/us/5-days-in-1967-still-shake-detroit.html?pagewanted=all.

140. Morisseau, *Detroit '67*, 77.

141. "Devil's Night," *Wikipedia*, accessed September 16, 2013, http://en.wikipedia.org/wiki/Devil's_Night.

142. Ze'ev Chafets, *Devil's Night and Other True Tales of Detroit* (New York: Vintage, 1990), 3–4.

143. Ibid., 5.

144. Roach, *Cities of the Dead*, 6.

145. Chafets, *Devil's Night*, 22, 24.

146. Ibid., 5 (emphasis in the original).

147. Julie Hinds, "Rush Limbaugh Prompts Republishing of Detroit Book 'Devil's Night,'" *Detroit Free Press,* August 24, 2013, accessed October 1, 2013, http://www.freep.com/article/20130824/ENT03/308240026/Devil's%20Night%20Chafets%20Rush%20Limbaugh.

148. Chafets, *Devil's Night*, 25.

149. D'Amour, *Detroit*, 93.

150. Catanese, *The Problem of the Color[blind]*, 5.

151. Patrick Pacheco, "Playwright Lisa D'Amour on 'Detroit' and the Vultures of Mid-Size American Decline," *BLOUINARTINFO International*, September 12, 2012, accessed July 4, 2013, http://www.blouinartinfo.com/news/story/825086/playwright-lisa-damour-on-detroit-and-the-vultures-of-mid-size-american-decline.

152. D'Amour, *Detroit*, 97.

153. Berlant, *Cruel Optimism*, 7.

CHAPTER 4

1. Michael H. Hodges, "How Detroit Got Its Groove Back," in *Canvas Detroit*, ed. Julie Pincus and Nichole Christian (Detroit: Wayne State University Press, 2014), 9.

2. Nolan Finley, "Where Are the Black People?," *Detroit News*, December 15, 2014, accessed January 12, 2015, http://www.detroitnews.com/story/opinion/columnists/nolan-finley/2014/12/14/black-people/20322377/.

3. Jennifer Conlin, "Choice Tables: In Detroit Revitalizing Taste by Taste," *New York Times*, October 8, 2014, accessed October 8, 2014, http://www.nytimes.com/2014/10/12/travel/in-detroit-revitalizing-taste-by-taste.html?_r=0; "Carolyn Murphy's Detroit," *Harper's Bazaar*, October 2014, 236; Hamish Bowles, "The Hamish Files: Detroit by Design," *Vogue*, December 14, 2014, 196.

4. "Imported from Detroit," February 5, 2011, accessed October 9, 2014, https://www.youtube.com/watch?v=SKL254Y_jtc. For a superb local critique of the ad, see Dora Apel, *Beautiful Terrible Ruins* (New Brunswick, NJ: Rutgers University Press, 2015), 113–21. See also Sarah Banet-Weiser's discussion of the Chrysler ad as a kind of nationalist rebranding: "Branding the Crisis," in *Aftermath: The Cultures of Economic Crisis*, ed. Manuel Castells, Joao Caraça, and Gustavo Cardoso (Oxford: Oxford University Press, 2012), 107–31.

5. Thanks to my colleague Harris M. Berger for his critique of Shinola's artisanal-industrial mash-up. For a local critique of Shinola, see Jon Moy, "On Shinola, Detroit's Misguided White Night," *Four Pins* March 26, 2014, accessed February 8, 2016, http://fourpins.com/life/shinola-detroits-misguided-white-knight.

6. "Apple-Ipad-Jason Hall-Slow Roll," accessed February 12, 2016, https://vimeo.com/112254143. For a local critique of the ad and the absence of an Apple store in the city, see Aaron Foley, "Apple Shot a Commercial in Detroit; It's Great but Also Sucks," August 13, 2014, accessed October 10, 2014, http://detroit.jalopnik.com/apple-shot-a-commercial-in-detroit-its-great-but-also-1620773281.

7. The Chrysler ad features both *Monument to Joe Louis* and Rivera's *Detroit Industry* murals in the Detroit Institute of Arts (DIA). Apple's iPad ad features the Eastern Market area, including its murals. The *Heidelberg Project*, discussed in this chapter, and the DIA are noted in "Murphy's Detroit," p. 236.

8. National Public Radio's *Tell Me More* asked: "Is Detroit the Next Brooklyn?" Audio program, July 21, 2011. See also Stuart Braun, "Danielle de Picciotto: 'Detroit Is the New Berlin,'" *DW.com*, November 21, 2013, accessed February 19, 2016, http://www.dw.com/en/danielle-de-picciotto-detroit-is-the-new-berlin/a-17241866. But the list of

sites Detroit supposedly replaces in cool cities buzz is far longer. For example, the *New Republic* included Detroit in its review of "cool" cities, noting that it was one of many hyped as the "new Seattle." Thomas Rogers, "The Life and Death of a 'Cool' City," *New Republic*, September 12, 2014, accessed February 19, 2016, https://newrepublic.com/article/119394/new-berlin-rise-and-fall-cool-cities. Detroit's own *Metro Times* commented on the proliferating list; see Michael Jackman, "Is Detroit the New LA?," *Metro Times*, January 28, 2015, accessed February 19, 2016, http://www.metrotimes.com/Blogs/archives/2015/01/28/is-detroit-the-new-la. Even *National Geographic*, better known for its articles on wilderness, noted Detroit's re-emergence by relying on these same tropes in Susan Ager, "Tough, Cheap, and Real: Detroit Is Cool Again," *National Geographic*, accessed February 29, 2016, http://www.nationalgeographic.com/taking-back-detroit/see-detroit.html.

9. The artist's autonomy, contingent employment, "creative" output, and operation without the support of institutional health benefits and pensions, coupled with theorizations of post-Fordist labor as "affective," "immaterial," and embedded in expectations of "virtuosity," make her an exemplary post-Fordist subject. For theories of affective, immaterial labor and post-Fordist labor as virtuosity, see, respectively, Michael Hardt, "Affective Labor," *boundary 2* 26 (1999): 89–100; Maurizio Lazzarato, "Immaterial Labor," in *Radical Thought in Italy: A Potential Politics*, ed. Paolo Virno and Michael Hardy (Minneapolis: University of Minnesota Press, 1996), 133–47; and Paulo Virno, *A Grammar of the Multitude* (Cambridge, MA: Semiotexte, 2004). For a discussion of the "creative class" as the "new precariat," see Rosalind Gill and Andy Pratt, "In the Social Factory? Immaterial Labour, Precariousness and Cultural Work," *Theory, Culture & Society* 25, nos. 7-8 (2008): 1–30. Richard Florida's specific definition of the creative class is taken up later in this chapter.

10. Julia L. Foulkes, "Dancing in the Streets: The Arts in Postwar Cities—Introduction," *Journal of Urban History* 41, no. 6 (November 2015): 955.

11. Andres Duany, "The Pink Zone: Why Detroit Is the New Berlin," *Fortune*, January 30, 2014, accessed February 2, 2016, http://fortune.com/2014/01/30/the-pink-zone-why-detroit-is-the-new-brooklyn/.

12. In addition to its innovations in blues and techno music and, of course, Motown, the city currently has an active Afrofuturism performance scene, including the nationally renowned Complex Movements artist collective. See, for example, Aaron Robertson, "The Future Was Already Here: Detroit's Afrofuturist Enclaves," *Metro Times*, August 10, 2016, accessed August 12, 2016, http://www.metrotimes.com/detroit/the-future-was-already-here-detroits-afrofuturist-enclaves/Content?oid=2459448.

13. Brandi Wilkins Catanese, *The Problem of the Color[blind]: Racial Transgressions and the Politics of Black Performance* (Ann Arbor: University of Michigan Press, 2011), 6.

14. As Catanese notes, "Race is the unruly chin hair on the face of an otherwise unblemished America: only bad manners would compel anyone to bring it up." Ibid., 5.

15. "Good manners" plays on Catanese's critique of color-blind discourse in which reference to race is "bad manners." See ibid. "Art's" partner, "culture," was used in one of these indictments of city residents: George Will's notorious characterization of Detroit as having a "culture problem." *This Week with George Stephanopoulos*, ABC News, aired July 28, 2013.

16. For information on the Blackburn uprising, see Karolyn Smardz Frost, *I've Got a Home in Glory Land: A Lost Tale of the Underground Railroad* (New York: Farrar, Straus and Giroux, 2007). James Baldwin characterized urban renewal as "Negro removal" in 1963. See Kenneth B. Clark, "A Conversation with James Baldwin," in *Conversations with James Baldwin*, ed. Fred L. Standley and Louis H. Pratt (Jackson: University of Mississippi Press, 1989), 42. For a partial history of Detroit's racialized urban renewal initiatives, especially

the demolishing of the African American Hastings Street/Paradise Valley neighborhood, see Suzanne E. Smith, *Dancing in the Street: Motown and the Cultural Politics of Detroit* (Cambridge, MA: Harvard University Press, 1999).

17. For a comprehensive account of Detroit's bankruptcy proceedings, including the Grand Bargain, see Nathan Bomey, *Detroit Resurrected: To Bankruptcy and Back* (New York: Norton, 2016).

18. Mark Stryker and John Gallagher, "DIA's Art Collection Could Face Sell-Off to Satisfy Detroit's Creditors," *Detroit Free Press*, May 24, 2013, accessed May 29, 2013, http://www.freep.com/article/20130523/NEWS01/305230154/DIA-Kevyn-Orr-Detroit-bankruptcy-art.

19. For data on average Detroit public sector pensions, see Steven Yaccino and Michael Cooper, "Cries of Betrayal as Detroit Plans to Cut Pensions," *New York Times*, July 21, 2013, accessed December 16, 2013, http://www.nytimes.com/2013/07/22/us/cries-of-betrayal-as-detroit-plans-to-cut-pensions.html?pagewanted=2&_r=0 Page.

   For examples of the opposition of the DIA collections to retired Detroit public workers' pensions, see Randy Kennedy, "The Agony of Suspense in Detroit," *New York Times*, October 3, 2013, C1+, especially C6; and Randy Kennedy, Monica Davey, and Steven Yaccino, "Foundations Aim to Save Pensions in Detroit Crisis," *New York Times*, January 14, 2014, A1+.

20. See Mark Brush, "What's More Valuable, 5% of the DIA Collection, or Detroiters' Pensions?," *Michigan Radio*, December 20, 2013, accessed December 20, 2013, http://michiganradio.org/post/whats-more-valuable-5-dia-collection-or-detroiters-pensions#stream/0.

21. Kennedy, "The Agony of Suspense," C6; Roberta Smith, "In Detroit, a Case of Selling Art and Selling Out," *New York Times*, September 10, 2013, C7. Compare this discourse about the place of art in the deindustrial city with one of the foundational advocacy texts for art in the industrial city: Ellen Gates Starr's "Art and Labor." Starr, Jane Addams's partner in the founding of the Hull House, a settlement house in Chicago, argued:

   > No civilized and happy people has ever been able to express itself without art. The prophet expands his "All great art is praise" into "The art of man is the expression of his rational and disciplined delight in the forms and laws of the creation of which he forms a part." . . . When life reaches a point at which it can furnish no more material for art, we cannot look to it for an artistic people. If in all the environment of a man's life, there is nothing which can inspire a true work of art, there is nothing to inspire a true love of it, could it be produced. The love of the beautiful grows by what it feeds on; and the food must be the common bread of life. That which makes the art-loving people, makes the artist also. Every nation which has left a great art record has lived an artistic life. (4)

   Ellen Gates Starr, "Art and Labor," Hull House Maps and Papers, 1895, accessed March 26, 2016, http://media.pfeiffer.edu/lridener/DSS/Addams/hh9.html.

22. Smith, "In Detroit."

23. Nathan Bomey and Matt Helms, "Detroit Pensioners Back Grand Bargain in Bankruptcy Vote," *Detroit Free Press*, July 22, 2014, accessed July 22, 2014, http://www.freep.com/article/20140721/NEWS01/307210176/Detroit-bankruptcy-pension-grand-bargain-vote. Details of the Grand Bargain in Alan Pyke, "Everything You Need to Know about Detroit's Bankruptcy Settlement," *Think Progress*, November 8, 2014, accessed November 6, 2015, http://thinkprogress.org/economy/2014/11/08/3590576/detroit-bankruptcy-conclusion-numbers/.

24. Stephanie Condon, "Gov. Rick Snyder: Government Bailout Is the Wrong Answer for Detroit," *CBS News*, July 21, 2013, accessed July 21, 2013, http://www.cbsnews.com/

news/gov-rick-snyder-government-bailout-is-the-wrong-answer-for-detroit/; Chris Isadore and Poppy Harlow, "Detroit Gets $195 Million Closer to Salvation," *CNN Money*, June 20, 2014, accessed June 20, 2014, http://money.cnn.com/2014/06/20/news/economy/detroit-bankruptcy-state-aid/.

25. Randy Kennedy, "'Grand Bargain' Saves the Detroit Institute of Arts," *New York Times*, November 7, 2014, accessed November 7, 2014, http://www.nytimes.com/2014/11/08/arts/design/grand-bargain-saves-the-detroit-institute-of-arts.html?_r=0.

26. As Thomas Sugrue notes, "In 2005, [then mayor Kwame] Kilpatrick approved the largest municipal pension restructuring in the United States to date. A 'veritable army' of financial professionals from the nation's top investment banks and insurance companies put together a $1.44 billion deal to fund the city's pension obligations using innovative but complex and highly risky derivatives and credit default swaps." Though the deal was highly praised as sound, it collapsed, as did similar risky financialized arrangements, during the run-up to the Great Recession. Thomas Sugrue, "Preface to the Princeton Classics Edition," in *The Origins of the Urban Crisis: Race and Inequality in Postwar Detroit* (Princeton, NJ: Princeton University Press, 2014), xx.

27. Sharon Zukin, *Loft Living: Culture and Capital in Urban Change* (Baltimore: Johns Hopkins University Press, 1982), 190–91 (emphasis in the original).

28. Ibid., 117.

29. For a description of the communities, see Aaron Shkuda, *The Lofts of SoHo: Gentrification, Art, and Industry in New York, 1950–1980* (Chicago: University of Chicago Press, 2016). The remaining performing artist–owned SoHo loft building that is both a residence and a performance venue is 537 Broadway, site of WeisAcres. The building was once owned by postmodern dance pioneer Simone Forti, who worked with current owner Cathy Weis to ensure that it stayed "in the dance family." In 2015, as the New York City luxury real estate market was heating up, Weis stated that she got multiple calls from realtors every week making multi-million-dollar offers. Personal conversation with Cathy Weis, November 17, 2015.

30. Florida's definition of creative class is "economic" though not "Marxian": "The Creative Class consists of people who add economic value through their creativity. It thus includes a great many knowledge workers, symbolic analysts and professional and technical workers, but emphasizes their true role in the economy." These workers' "property—which stems from their creative capacity—is an intangible because it is literally in their heads." Richard Florida, *The Rise of the Creative Class: And How It's Transforming Work, Leisure, Community and Everyday Life* (New York: Basic Books, 2002), 68. For one of the most trenchant critiques of Florida's thesis, see Mark J. Stern and Susan C. Seifert, *From Creative Economy to Creative Society* (Philadelphia: Reinvestment Fund, 2005), also available from *Grantmakers in the Arts Reader* 19, no. 3 (Fall 2008), accessed September 15, 2015, http://www.giarts.org/reader-19-3.

31. Mason Riddle, "On the Fringe: Interview with Richard Florida," *Public Art Review* 20.1, issue 39 (emphasis added), accessed April 5, 2016, http://www.creativeclass.com/rfc-gdb/articles/Interview%20with%20Richard%20Florida.pdf.

32. Florida makes this explicit when he writes, "I strongly believe that the key to improving the lot of underpaid, under-employed, and disadvantaged people lies not in social welfare programs or low-end make-work jobs, nor in somehow bringing back the factory jobs of the past, but rather in tapping their innate creativity, paying them appropriately for it, and integrating them fully into the Creative Economy." Florida, *Rise of the Creative Class*, 10.

33. Quoted in Martha Rosler, "Culture Class: Art, Creativity, Urbanism, Part II," *e-flux* 23, no. 3 (2011), accessed February 1, 2015, http://www.e-flux.com/journal/culture-class-art-creativity-urbanism-part-ii/.

34. On African American artist Theaster Gates's work to transform Chicago's South Side, see Carol Becker, Lisa Yun Lee, and Achim Borchardt-Hume, *Theaster Gates* (London: Phaidon, 2015); Kristin Juarez, "Theaster Gates Transports Time and Place," *International Review of African American Art* 24, no. 3 (2013): 2–6; and K. Reinhardt, "Theaster Gates's Dorchester Project in Chicago," *Journal of Urban History* 41, no. 2 (March 2015): 193–206. On African American artist Rick Lowe's Project Row Houses in Houston's predominantly black Third Ward, see Grant H. Kester, *The One and the Many: Contemporary Collaborative Art in a Global Context* (Durham, NC: Duke University Press, 2011), 214–22.

35. "New Museum Announces Ideas City Detroit Program: Public Conference April 30," New Museum—Ideas City, March 22, 2016, accessed March 22, 2016, http://us1.campaignarchive1.com/?u=c6bf7cce2a64f8749424edd72&id=da521d4944.

36. Michigan Council for the Arts and Cultural Affairs, accessed April 7, 2016, http://www.michiganbusiness.org/community/council-arts-cultural-affairs/. The council's "regranting agencies" to which artists must apply are likewise not located in Detroit. The "Detroit Metro Region" office has two locations, neither in the city. One is located in Mt. Clemens in Macomb County, twenty-six miles away; the other, which would serve Wayne County, is in Lansing, the state capital, ninety miles away.

37. See Wayne County [MI] Departments, accessed April 7, 2016, http://www.waynecounty.com/departments.htm.

38. As of this writing, there is no new official City Master Plan for Detroit. In February 2015, Mayor Duggan hired Maurice Cox as the city's new director of planning; Cox is best known for his work in post-Katrina New Orleans. Cox will oversee the development of a new plan, a process likely to take several years. See Tom Walsh, "Can Duggan Change History of Failed Master Plans?," *Detroit Free Press*, February 26, 2015, accessed January 13, 2016, http://www.freep.com/story/money/business/columnists/tom-walsh/2015/02/26/can-duggan-change-history-failed-master-plans/24087915/. The city has digital interface, "Current Master Plan Future General Land Use," adopted in 2009 and last updated/amended on November 25, 2014. See "Current Master Plan Future General Land Use," accessed April 15, 2017, https://data.detroitmi.gov/Property-Parcels/Current-Master-Plan-Future-General-Land-Use/89q2-aduf/data.

39. Louis Aguilar, "Red Wings Arena Cost at $627M, Could Go Higher," *Detroit News*, November 5, 2015, accessed January 30, 2016, http://www.detroitnews.com/story/business/2015/11/04/report-cost-new-red-wings-arena-rises/75146516/. For details on the arena's funding, see Bill Shea, "On Cost, Financing of Wings Arena: Here Are the Answers," *Crain's Detroit Business*, September 21, 2014/updated September 22, 2014, accessed January 30, 2016, http://www.crainsdetroit.com/article/20140921/NEWS/309219990/on-cost-financing-of-wings-arena-here-are-answers. The city sold the land for the arena to the Red Wings' owners, the Ilitch family, best known for Little Caesar's Pizza, for one dollar. Joe Guillen, "Red Wings' New Stadium Land Transfer Approved by City Council," *USA Today*, February 4, 2014, accessed January 30, 2016, http://www.usatoday.com/story/sports/nhl/wings/2014/02/04/detroit-red-wings-new-arena-land-transfer-approved/5211635/. For details on the M-1 Trolley, see Louis Aguilar, "M-1 Rail Helps Get Woodward Developments Rolling," *Detroit News*, June 22, 2015, accessed January 30, 2016, http://www.detroitnews.com/story/news/local/detroit-city/2015/06/21/rail/29084473/.

40. Matt Helms, "Detroit's New Planning Director: Dream Big," *Detroit Free Press*, July 4, 2015, accessed September 5, 2015, http://www.freep.com/story/news/local/michigan/detroit/2015/07/03/maurice-cox-detroitplanningdirector/29682221/http://www.freep.com/story/news/local/michigan/detroit/2015/07/03/maurice-cox-detroit-planning-director/29682221/.

41. See, for example, Melena Ryzik, "For Detroit Artists, Almost Anything Goes," *New York Times*, July 15, 2015, accessed November 18, 2015, http://www.nytimes.com/2015/07/16/arts/design/for-detroit-artists-almost-anything-goes.html.

42. Duany, "The Pink Zone."

43. Shikha Dalmia, "Bankrupt Detroit Doles Out Corporate Subsidies," *BloombergView*, January 22, 2014, accessed December 12, 2015, http://www.bloombergview.com/articles/2014-01-22/detroit-hopes-corporate-subsidies-work-this-time.

44. Colin Moynihan, "Born in Brooklyn, Now Making a Motown Move," *New York Times*, December 7, 2014, accessed January 4, 2016, http://www.nytimes.com/2014/12/08/arts/galapagos-art-space-will-make-detroit-its-home.html?_r=0.

45. Galapagos Art Space—The 2016 Detroit Biennial (emphasis in the original), accessed February 26, 2016, http://www.galapagosdetroit.com/2106-detroit-biennial/.

46. Moynihan, "Born in Brooklyn."

47. http://www.galapagosdetroit.com/anewmodelforfundingthearts/. Accessed February 26, 2016.

48. Robert Elmes quoted in Kirk Pinho, "Galapagos Art Space's Building Near Corktown for Sale for $6.25 Million," *Crain's Detroit Business*, January 7, 2016, accessed January 7, 2016.http://www.crainsdetroit.com/article/20160107/BLOG016/160109866/galapagos-art-spaces-building-near-corktown-for-sale-for-6-25-million.

49. Ibid.

50. John Gallagher, "Galapagos Selling Corktown Building, Answers Critics," *Detroit Free Press*, January 8, 2016, accessed January 9, 2016, http://www.freep.com/story/money/business/michigan/2016/01/08/detroit-brooklyn-galapagos-corktown/78519904/. In a sign of just how volatile Galapagos's real estate experiment in Detroit is proving to be, Elmes later withdrew the sale, now intending to turn the building into rental space. See John Gallagher, "Galapagos Team Keeping Building Near Corktown after All," *Detroit Free Press*, May 17, 2016, accessed June 2, 2016, http://www.freep.com/story/money/business/michigan/2016/05/17/detroit-corktown-galapagos-elmes/84484464/.

51. Galapagos Art Space—The 2016 Detroit Biennial. The current website does not include "2016," the original intended year of the Biennial, in its text, though the date persists in the url. Instead, the site now reads "Stay tuned." http://www.galapagosdetroit.com/2106-detroit-biennial/, accessed April 15, 2017.

52. Hyperlink in Galapagos Art Space—The 2016 Detroit Biennial, http://www.galapagosdetroit.com/2106-detroit-biennial/ to http://kunsthallegalapagos.com/. accessed May 7, 2016.

53. "Galapagos Goes Detroit," *Box Blog*, December 10, 2014, accessed January 12, 2015, http://blog.dylanbox.com/detroit/2014/12/10/galapagos-goes-detroit.html.

54. See pp. 27–30 in the full Detroit Works Project, *Detroit Future City: 2012 Detroit Strategic Framework Plan*, 2nd printing (May 2013), accessed September 5, 2015, http://detroitfuturecity.com/wpcontent/uploads/2014/12/DFC_Full_2nd.pdf, and p. 26 in the *Executive Summary*, 2nd ed., http://detroitfuturecity.com/wpcontent/uploads/2014/02/DFC_ExecutiveSummary_2ndEd.pdf), accessed September 1, 2015.

55. "Mayor Duggan's Development Chief Says Detroit Future City Is His Bible," *Deadline Detroit*, February 12, 2014, accessed January 13, 2016, http://www.deadlinedetroit.com/articles/8331/mayor_duggan_s_development_chief_says_the_detroit_future_city_plan_is_his_bible#.

56. Maurice Cox, "Detroit 101 Lecture Series: Urbanism and Design," Princeton University, March 2, 2016.

57. The notorious history of Michigan's emergency manager law contributes powerfully to Detroiters' suspicion of systemic disenfranchisement. While an emergency manager law, Public Act 72, had been on the books in the state since 1990, it was rarely used until

white Republican governor Rick Snyder took office in 2011. Snyder signed an enhanced version of the existing law, Public Act 4, which was subsequently rejected by Michigan voters. A new bill was signed into law (PA 436) shortly thereafter, reinstating the emergency manager; this new bill included the provision that the public could not repeal it. Snyder appointed emergency managers to run predominantly African American cities in the state, including Detroit, Flint, Benton Harbor, and Pontiac. For a summary of this history, see Josh Hakala, "How Did We Get Here? A Look Back at Michigan's Emergency Manager Law," *Michigan Radio*, accessed April 28, 2016, http://michiganradio.org/post/how-did-we-get-here-look-back-michigans-emergency-manager-law#stream/0.

58. *2012 Detroit Strategic Framework Plan*, 2nd printing (May 2013), 1, accessed September 5, 2015, http://detroitfuturecity.com/wpcontent/uploads/2014/12/DFC_Full_2nd.pdf.

59. For examples of art figured as public amenity in the *2012 Detroit Strategic Framework Plan*, see p. 514; as artisanal production space, p. 520; as facilitating dialogue, pp. 703, 737, 741.

60. For an example, see ibid., 459.

61. Ibid., 486, 511.

62. Ibid., 523.

63. Red Bull House of Art, accessed April 7, 2016, http://www.redbullhouseofart.com.

64. Jamie Peck, "Austerity Urbanism: American Cities under Extreme Economy," *City* 16, no. 6 (2012): 629.

65. Ibid., 636. For discussion of former mayor Bing's plan to shrink the city see p. 637.

66. L. Owen Kirkpatrick, "Urban Triage, City Systems, and the Remnants of Community: Some 'Sticky' Complications in the Greening of Detroit," *Journal of Urban History* 4, no. 2 (2015): 261–78.

67. Alex P. Kellogg, "Detroit's Smaller Reality," *Wall Street Journal*, February 27, 2010, accessed April 2, 2016, http://www.wsj.com/articles/SB10001424052748703503804575083781073108438.

68. N. Millington and T. Pedroni quoted in Jason Hackworth, "Rightsizing as Spatial Austerity in the American Rust Belt," *Environment and Planning A* 47, no. 4 (2015): 768.

69. Cox, "Detroit 101 Lecture Series."

70. Elena Herrada quoted in Anna Clark, "Can Urban Planning Rescue Detroit? The Hopes, Fears, and Possibilities of the Detroit Future City Plan," *Next City*, July 1, 2013, accessed April 13, 2016, https://nextcity.org/features/view/can-urban-planning-rescue-detroit.

71. Daniel Clement and Miguel Kanai, "Detroit Future City: How Pervasive Neoliberal Urbanism Exacerbates Racialized Spatial Injustice," *American Behavioral Scientist* 59, no. 3 (2015): 381.

72. "The Heidelberg Project," *RoadsideAmerica.com*, accessed February 1, 2016, http://www.roadsideamerica.com/story/21166.

73. Mike Kelley, "*Mobile Homestead* Brochure," Museum of Contemporary Art Detroit, n.d., n.p.

74. Shannon Jackson, "Just-in-Time: Performance and the Aesthetics of Precarity," *TDR: The Drama Review* 56, no. 4 (Winter 2012): 10.

75. The Heidelberg Project, accessed February 1, 2016, http://www.heidelberg.org/; Kelley, "*Mobile Homestead* Brochure," n.p. My analysis of Kelley's *Mobile Homestead* benefited greatly from Stacy Wolf, "Mike Kelley's *Day Is Done* and Community Musical Theatre," PS1 MoMA, invited lecture, December 15, 2013.

76. Bertolt Brecht, "Short Description of a New Technique of Acting," in *Brecht on Theatre*, ed. and trans. John Willett (New York: Hill and Wang, 1964), 139.

77. Terry Eagleton, "Brecht and Rhetoric," *New Literary History* 16, no. 3 (1985): 634.

78. *Brecht on Theatre*, 109; John Willett, *The Theatre of Bertolt Brecht: A Study from Eight Aspects* (London: Methuen, 1967), 173 (emphasis added).

79. The DIA and MOCAD are a half mile apart and form the base of the triangle. The apex is the *Heidelberg Project*, virtually equidistant from both the DIA and MOCAD and seemingly a world away from the activity and bustle of Midtown.

80. While a full accounting of the *Detroit Industry* murals exceeds the focus of this chapter, it is important to note here that Rivera actively inserted racial, ethnic, and gender diversity into his iconography as a critique of US industrialization's actual racism and sexism. For a full accounting of the murals, and of Rivera's time in Detroit, see Linda Banks Downs, *Diego Rivera: The Detroit Industry Murals* (New York: Norton and the Detroit Institute of Arts, 1999), and Mark Rosenthal, *Diego Rivera and Frida Kahlo in Detroit* (Detroit: Detroit Institute of Arts, 2015).

81. Downs, *Diego Rivera*, 21.

82. Ibid., 31.

83. Ibid., 23.

84. Jerry Herron, "Detroit: Disaster Deferred, Disaster in Progress," *South Atlantic Quarterly* 106, no. 4 (Fall, 2007): 680.

85. Brent D. Ryan, *Design after Decline* (Philadelphia: University of Pennsylvania Press, 2012), 69.

86. The *Heidelberg Project* and *Mobile Homestead* are not the only works that create gestic homes in Detroit, but they are the most enduring. Two other examples are Gregory Holm and Matthew Radune's *Ice House Detroit* (2009–10) and Osman Khan's complex and compelling "Come Hell or High Water," installed at MOCAD in 2013. For a discussion of *Ice House Detroit*, see Apel, *Beautiful Terrible Ruins*, 101–4. For an analysis of "Come Hell or High Water," see Judith Hamera, "Domestic(-ated) Desires, Tanked City," *TDR: The Drama Review* 58, no. 4 (Winter 2014): 12–22. For a gestic account of home in Lafayette Park, an integrated midcentury modern development designed by Mies van der Rohe, see Danielle Aubert, Lana Cavar, and Natasha Chandani, eds., *Thanks for the View, Mr. Mies: Lafayette Park, Detroit* (New York: Metropolis Books, 2012).

87. Paula Chakravartty and Denise Ferreira da Silva, "Accumulation, Dispossession, and Debt: The Racial Logic of Global Capitalism—An Introduction," *American Quarterly* 24, no. 3 (2012): 362.

88. David Graeber, "The Very Idea of Consumption: Desire, Phantasms, and the Aesthetics of Destruction from Medieval Times to the Present," in *Possibilities: Essays on Hierarchy, Rebellion, and Desire* (Oakland, CA: AK Press, 2007), 63.

89. For a detailed analysis of how Detroiters coped with this civic abandonment, see Kimberley Kinder, *DIY Detroit: Making Do in a City without Services* (Minneapolis: University of Minnesota Press, 2016).

90. J. C. Reindl, "Why Detroit's Lights Went Out," *USA Today*, November 17, 2013, accessed November 17, 2013, http://www.usatoday.com/story/news/nation/2013/11/17/detroit-finances-dark-streetlights/3622205/.

91. "Late Trash Pickup Makes for a Dirtier Detroit," *CBS Detroit*, November 11, 2012, accessed February 3, 2016, http://detroit.cbslocal.com/2012/11/28/late-trash-pick-up-makes-for-dirtier-detroit/.

92. "In Detroit, EMS Response Times Must Improve," *Detroit News*, September 5, 2014, accessed September 5, 2014, http://www.detroitnews.com/story/opinion/editorials/2014/09/25/detroit-ems-response-times/16221893/. According to the editorial, the national standard for EMS response to 911 calls is eight minutes.

93. See George Will's notorious characterization of Detroit as having a "culture problem." *This Week with George Stephanopoulos*, ABC News, July 28, 2013.

94. Chafets, *Devil's Night*, 5 (emphasis in the original).

95. Critical geographer David Harvey defines accumulation by dispossession as appropriation without investment in production. David Harvey, *Spaces of Global*

Capitalism: Towards a Theory of Uneven Geographical Development (London: Verso, 2006), 93.

96. Joel Kurth and Christine MacDonald, "Special Report: Detroit Braces for a Flood of Tax Foreclosures," *Detroit News*, July 1, 2015, accessed January 21, 2016, http://www.detroitnews.com/story/news/special-reports/2015/07/01/detroit-braces-flood-tax-foreclosures/29589915/.

97. Michele Oberholtzer, "Buying Detroit, Why a Not-So-Public Auction Could Devastate City Homeowners," *Occupy.com*, October 5, 2015, accessed January 21, 2016, http://www.occupy.com/article/buying-detroit-why-not-so-public-auction-could-devastate-city-homeowners.

98. Cheryl Harris in Rose Hackman, "One-Fifth of Detroit's Population Could Lose Their Homes," *Atlantic*, October 22, 2014; updated October 24, 2014, accessed November 30, 2014, http://www.theatlantic.com/business/archive/2014/10/one-fifth-of-detroits-population-could-lose-their-homes/381694/.

99. Holly Fournier, "Man Charged in Fatal Foreclosure Showdown in Detroit," *Detroit News*, December 1, 2014, accessed February 5, 2016, http://www.detroitnews.com/story/news/local/wayne-county/2014/12/01/rosedale-shooting/19731541/.

100. See Detroit Eviction Defense, http://detroitevictiondefense.org/index.php, accessed April 17, 2016. In addition to demonstrations, activists mounted a wide range of successful operations to help residents stay in their foreclosed homes. For example, Princeton University 2015 Dalai Lama fellow Marc Maxey created "A Citizens Guide to Real Estate Investment Detroit" to educate residents facing foreclosure about their options and offer an alternative to eviction. http://www.detroitcitizensguide.com/#detroit, accessed May 2, 2016.

101. "Building Detroit: Neighbors Wanted," accessed April 17, 2016, http://www.building-detroit.org/.

102. Les Christie, "Top 10 U.S. Cities for Chinese Homebuyers," *CNN Money*, December 4, 2013, accessed September 5, 2015, http://money.cnn.com/2013/12/04/real_estate/chinese-homebuyers/index.html.

103. Christine MacDonald, "Land Bank to Sell Properties to Occupants for $1,000," *Detroit News*, October 20, 2015, accessed October 20, 2015, http://www.detroitnews.com/story/news/local/detroit-city/2015/10/20/detroit-land-bank-sell-properties-occupants/74292160/.

104. Attorney Alice Jennings in "NAACP Legal Defense Fund: Detroit Water Service Shutoffs Are Discriminatory," *CBS Detroit*, July 21, 2014, accessed September 1, 2015, http://detroit.cbslocal.com/2014/07/21/naacp-detroit-water-service-shutoffs-are-racially-motivated/.

105. Matt Helms and Joe Guillen, "Judge Says No to Detroit Water Shutoff Moratorium," *Detroit Free Press*, September 29, 2014, accessed February 8, 2016, http://www.freep.com/story/news/local/detroit-bankruptcy/2014/09/29/water-shutoff-moratorium/16451483/.

106. Michelle Miller, "Detroit Water Shut-Offs Bring Scrutiny of the UN," *CBS News*, October 20, 2014, accessed October 20, 2014, http://www.cbsnews.com/news/detroit-water-shut-offs-brings-u-n-scrutiny/.

107. Joel Kurth, "Detroit Unlikely to Forgive Water Debts of Poor," *Detroit News*, December 15, 2015, accessed December 15, 2015, http://www.detroitnews.com/story/news/local/detroit-city/2015/12/15/detroit-unlikely-forgive-water-debts-poor/77371414/.

108. Christine Ferretti, "Up to 25K Face Water Shut-Offs in Detroit," *Detroit News*, May 5, 2015, accessed November 8, 2015, http://www.detroitnews.com/story/news/local/detroit-city/2015/05/04/water-shut-notices-go-detroit-may/26891145/.

109. Anna Clark, "Going without Water in Detroit," *New York Times*, July 3, 2014, accessed November 8, 2015, http://www.nytimes.com/2014/07/04/opinion/going-without-water-in-detroit.html.

110. Rose Hackman, "What Happens When Detroit Shuts Off the Water of 100,000 People," *Atlantic*, July 14, 2014, accessed February 5, 2016, http://www.theatlantic.com/business/archive/2014/07/what-happens-when-detroit-shuts-off-the-water-of-100000-people/374548/.

111. Mary M. Chapman, "Detroit Shuts Off Water to Residents but Not to Businesses Who Owe Millions," *Daily Beast*, July 26, 2014, accessed February 3, 2016, http://www.thedailybeast.com/articles/2014/07/26/detroit-shuts-off-water-to-residents-but-not-to-businesses-who-owe-millions.html.

112. "In Detroit, City-Backed Water Shut-Offs 'Contrary to Human Rights,' Say UN Experts," United Nations News Centre, October 20, 2014, accessed October 20, 2014, http://www.un.org/apps/news/story.asp?NewsID=49127#.VrI02igmbww.

113. "Superhero" from Tim Alberta, "Is Dan Gilbert Detroit's New Superhero?" *National Journal* in partnership with the *Atlantic*, February 27, 2014, accessed April 17, 2016, http://www.theatlantic.com/business/archive/2014/02/is-dan-gilbert-detroits-new-superhero/425742/; "Monopoly man" from Ian Thibodeau, "With over $1.6 billion Invested in Downtown Detroit, What Does Dan Gilbert Own?," *MLive.com*, February 20, 2015, accessed February 4, 2016, http://www.mlive.com/business/detroit/index.ssf/2015/02/with_over_16_billion_invested.html. See also Ian Thibodeau, "Dan Gilbert's Bedrock Tops 80 Properties Acquired in Downtown Detroit," *MLive.com*, January 6, 2016, accessed February 4, 2016, http://www.mlive.com/business/detroit/index.ssf/2016/01/dan_gilberts_bedrock_moves_top.html#incart_story_package.

114. Christine MacDonald and Joel Kurth, "Gilbert, Quicken Loans Entwined in Detroit Blight," *Detroit News*, July 1, 2015, accessed February 4, 2016, http://www.detroitnews.com/story/news/special-reports/2015/07/01/quicken-loans-blight-dilemma/29537285/.

115. US Department of Justice Office of Public Affairs, "United States Files Lawsuit Alleging That Quicken Loans Improperly Originated and Underwrote Federal Housing Administration-Insured Mortgage Loans," *Justice News*, April 23, 2015, accessed February 4, 2016, http://www.justice.gov/opa/pr/united-states-files-lawsuit-alleging-quicken-loans-improperly-originated-and-underwrote.

116. Julie Cresswell, "The New Mortgage Machine: Quicken Loans Faces Scrutiny, Like Big Banks Before It, and Its Feisty C.E.O. Is Firing Back," *New York Times*, January 22, 2017, BU 1+.

117. Anna Clark, "The Threat to Detroit's Rebound Isn't Crime or the Economy, It's the Mortgage Industry," *Next City*, December 7, 2015, accessed December 13, 2015, https://nextcity.org/features/view/detroit-bankruptcy-revival-crime-economy-mortgage-loans-redlining.

118. The *Heidelberg Project*'s proliferation of clocks and times parallels the number of its iterations. The work is evolving and changing, thus descriptions are contingent: inevitably a function of the specific times in which components were observed. Though I have visited the work routinely since 1987, the descriptions in this section come from the period covered in this chapter, 2011 to 2016, reflecting my visits on May 2, 2011; June 25 and 26, 2013; March 7, 2014; June 16, 2014; June 10 and 11, 2015; and November 2, 2015. Contact information for the *Heidelberg Project* is 1005 Parker, Unit #1, Detroit, MI 48214; phone: 313-458-8414; information@heidelberg.org.

119. My discussion of the *Heidelberg Project* here is neither a comprehensive history nor a comprehensive critical reading. Rather, I focus on selected examples of the

work's many *gestic* elements. For more on the project as a whole, see *Connecting the Dots: Tyree Guyton's Heidelberg Project* (Detroit: Wayne State University Press, 2007); Marion Elizabeth Jackson, *Tyree Guyton* (Detroit: Founders Society Detroit Institute of Arts, 1990); Wendy S. Walters, "Turning the Neighborhood Inside Out: Imagining a New Detroit in Tyree Guyton's Heidelberg Project," *TDR: The Drama Review* 45, no. 4 (Winter 2001): 64–93; and the documentary film *Come unto Me: The Faces of Tyree Guyton*, dir. Nicole Cattell (New York: Naked Eye Productions, 1999).

120. Walters, "Turning the Neighborhood Inside Out," 64.

121. For more on "demolition means progress," see Andrew R. Highsmith's analysis of the "redevelopment" of Flint, Detroit's deindustrial neighbor with a similar history on a smaller scale: *Demolition Means Progress* (Chicago: University of Chicago Press, 2015). Jerry Herron addressed Detroit's drive for demolition in *AfterCulture: Detroit and the Humiliation of History* (Detroit: Wayne State University Press, 1993), 138.

122. For a concise description of the razing of Paradise Valley, see the Detroit Historical Society, "Paradise Valley," in *Encyclopedia of Detroit*, accessed April 11, 2016, http://detroithistorical.org/learn/encyclopedia-of-detroit/paradise-valley. For reference to resentments of the demolition, see Smith, *Dancing in the Street*, 35.

123. See, for example, Robin Boyle and Peter Eisinger, "The U.S. Empowerment Zone Program: The Evolution of a National Urban Program and the Failure of Local Implementation in Detroit, Michigan," presentation, European Urban Research Association Conference, Copenhagen, 2001, accessed December 13, 2015, http://www.sbi.dk/eura/workshops/papers/workshop5/boyle.htm.
See also Puls quoted in Walters, "Turning the Neighborhood Inside Out."

124. Loveland Technologies, "Parcel Data and Property Ownership in Detroit, Wayne County, Michigan: McDougall Hunt," n.d., accessed April 11, 2016, https://makeloveland.com/us/mi/wayne/detroit/mcdougall-hunt#.

125. https://nyc.makeloveland.com//assessment/mi/wayne/detroit/mcdougall-hunt#, accessed April 11, 2016.

126. Property sale prices from Zillow, accessed June 2, 2016, http://www.zillow.com/homes/for_sale/Detroit-MI 48207/79062_rid/any_days/featured_sort/42.369293,-82.970939,42.336182,83.025871_rect/13_zm/.

127. The *Heidelberg Project* has been credited with refuting images of Detroit as blank slate/wilderness at least since 1999. See David M. Sheridan, "Making Sense of Detroit," *Michigan Quarterly Review* 38, no. 4 (1999): 346.

128. For a history of neighbors' resistance to the *Heidelberg Project*, see Walters, "Turning the Neighborhood Inside Out." Now there are, quite simply, far fewer neighbors left to take issue with the project.

129. D. Soyini Madison, "Foreword," in *Black Performance Theory*, ed. Thomas F. DeFrantz and Anita Gonzalez (Durham, NC: Duke University Press, 2014), viii.

130. Dance scholar Brenda Dixon Gottschild coined the term "invisibilized" to describe the diminution and outright denial of Africanist aesthetics and contributions by African American artists to classical, modern, and postmodern dance. See Gottschild, *Digging the Africanist Presence in American Performance: Dance and Other Contexts* (Westport, CT: Praeger, 1998), 2.

131. Bryant Keith Alexander, *The Performative Sustainability of Race: Reflections on Black Culture and the Politics of Identity* (New York: Peter Lang, 2012), 53.

132. Guyton was born in 1955.

133. See George Hunter, "Detroit Police Diversity Issues Predate National Debate," *Detroit News*, March 8, 2015, accessed April 18, 2016, http://www.detroitnews.com/story/news/local/wayne-county/2015/03/07/detroit-police-department-diversity/

24570427/; Detroit Historical Society, "Detroit Police Department," in *Encyclopedia of Detroit*, accessed April 18, 2016, http://detroithistorical.org/learn/encyclopedia-of-detroit/detroit-police-department; "Discuss Detroit: S.T.R.E.S.S. Memories," accessed April 18, 2016, http://www.atdetroit.net/forum/messages/62684/67830.html?1142292447.

134. *Urban Dictionary*, accessed April 18, 2016, http://www.urbandictionary.com/define.php?term=the+hood.

135. Finley, "Where Are the Black People?"

136. Walters, "Turning the Neighborhood Inside Out," 65.

137. Environmental studies theorist Rob Nixon defines "slow violence" as "a violence that occurs gradually and out of sight, a violence of delayed destruction that is dispersed across time and space, an attritional violence that is typically not viewed as violence at all." See Rob Nixon, *Slow Violence and the Environmentalism of the Poor* (Cambridge, MA: Harvard University Press, 2011), 2.

138. Rebecca Schneider, *Performing Remains: Art and War in Times of Theatrical Reenactment* (New York: Routledge, 2011), 174 (emphasis in the original).

139. Louis Aguilar, "City Defends Whole Foods Tax Break," *Detroit News*, July 29, 2011, ProQuest Newsstand.

140. Holland Cotter, "Mike Kelley, Influential American Artist, Dies at 57," *New York Times*, February 1, 2012, accessed April 29, 2016, http://www.nytimes.com/2012/02/02/arts/design/mike-kelley-influential-american-artist-dies-at-57.html?_r=0.

141. Nicole Rupersburg, "Mike Kelley's Last Homecoming," *Model D Media*, May 14, 2013, accessed April 13, 2015, http://www.modeldmedia.com/features/mikekelley513.aspx.

142. David Marsh, "Mike Kelley and Detroit," in *Mike Kelley: Catholic Tastes*, exhibition catalog, ed. Elizabeth Sussman (New York: Whitney Museum of American Art, 1993), 39.

143. Kelley describes this work, *Blackout*, in the context of other Detroit projects in "*Blackout* (2001)," *Mike Kelley: Minor Histories: Statements, Conversations, Proposals*, ed. John C. Welchman. (Cambridge, MA: MIT Press, 2004), 156–62. He also exhibited photographs of the Detroit area amusement park, Boblo Island, and the city's Belle Isle Aquarium (*Mike Kelley: Minor Histories*, 119–21).

144. Mike Kelley, "Mobile Homestead," artist's statement (Detroit: Museum of Contemporary Art Detroit, 2011), accessed April 29, 2016, http://www.mocadetroit.org/Mobile-HomesteadEssay.html.

145. Community programs in *Mobile Homestead* are supported by the Robert Rauschenberg Foundation.

146. Kelley shot three films of *Mobile Homestead*: one documenting its drive down Michigan Avenue to Westland, another documenting the return, and a third the dedication ceremony in which the work blew a tire and was not movable. The films included interviews with a wide range of residents. Because the films are not widely available, are no longer screened at MOCAD, and thus are not a publicly Detroit-based element of the work, I do not discuss them here.

147. Kelley, "Mobile Homestead."

148. Museum of Contemporary Art Detroit, "About: Mobile Homestead," n.d., accessed June 13, 2013, http://www.mocadetroit.org/Mobile-Homestead.html.

149. Kelley was explicit about the reversal of white flight as a dimension of the project. See Kelley, "Mobile Homestead." For a discussion of the suburban home and racial dynamics of the deindustrial, see Dianne Harris, *Little White Houses: How the Postwar Home Constructed Race in America* (Minneapolis: University of Minnesota Press, 2013).

150. Marsha Miro quoted in Lucy Li, "Mike Kelley's Mobile Homestead Arrives in Detroit," *Whitewall Magazine*, June 11, 2013, accessed May 1, 2016. http://www.whitewallmag.com/art/mike-kelleys-mobile-homestead-arrives-in-detroit.

151. Kelley, "Mobile Homestead."

152. Jerry Herron, "Motor City Breakdown: Detroit in Literature and Film," *Design Observer*, April 23, 2013, accessed June 1, 2013, http://places.designobserver.com/feature/motor-city-breakdown-detroit-in-literature-and-film/37840/.

153. While white former Detroiters are notorious for racialized(-ist) cathexes of former family homes, as Ze'ev Chafets describes in *Devil's Night* (5), the area's African American residents also feel the pull of these residences. See Mark Binelli's account of Marsha Cusic, including her explicit racial reading of Detroit's white gentrification in *Detroit City Is the Place to Be* (New York: Metropolitan/Holt, 2012), 283–85.

154. Property sale prices from Zillow, http://www.zillow.com/detroit-mi-48201/, accessed June 2, 2016.

155. Karen Bouffard, "Census Bureau: Detroit Is Poorest Big City in U.S.," *Detroit News*, September 17, 2015, accessed April 30, 2016, http://www.detroitnews.com/story/news/local/michigan/2015/09/16/census-us-uninsured-drops-income-stagnates/32499231/.

156. Louis Aguilar and Christine MacDonald, "Detroit's White Population Up after Decades of Decline," *Detroit News*, September 17, 2015, accessed April 30, 2016. http://www.detroitnews.com/story/news/local/detroit-city/2015/09/17/detroit-white-population-rises-census-shows/72371118/.

157. Rupersburg, "Mike Kelley's Last Homecoming."

158. Of course, not everyone has complied with this mandate to "keep out." Trying to secure unauthorized access to the lower levels of *Mobile Homestead* is a recurring project of local explorers and adventurers.

159. To be completely accurate, *Mobile Homestead* is fenced off from a parking lot that separates it from the street. Thanks to Maranatha Teferi, who, during our class visit to MOCAD, explicitly questioned the fence given the rhetoric of "community" used to describe its function.

160. Even Thomas Sugrue does this, returning to and commenting on the state of his grandparents' former home, though certainly not without august critical self-positioning. See Sugrue, *Origins of the Urban Crisis*, xxiii.

161. Miro quoted in Li, "Mike Kelley's Mobile Homestead Arrives in Detroit."

162. Carol J. Greenhouse, "Introduction," in *Ethnographies of Neoliberalism*, ed. Carol J. Greenhouse (Philadelphia: University of Pennsylvania Press, 2010), 9.

163. Ibid.

164. Kelley, "Mobile Homestead."

165. Kelley was describing a self-consciously "insipid" junior high school entry in a Veterans of Foreign Wars patriotic poster contest. His collaboratively produced entry won. See Welchman, *Mike Kelley*, 41.

166. In an oral history constructed from interviews with those who knew Kelley, Detroit-based journalist Nicole Rupersburg described *Mobile Homestead* as the artist's "most unabashedly sentimental, sincere work." See Rupersburg, "Mike Kelley's Last Homecoming."

CODA

1. Jeff Sharlet, "Bully Pulpit: Donald Trump, American Preacher," *New York Times Magazine*, April 14, 2016, 43.

2. Ibid., 42.

3. Anne Case and Angus Deaton, "Rising Morbidity and Mortality in Midlife among Non-Hispanic Americans in the 21st Century," *Proceedings of the National Academy of Sciences* 112, no. 49 (December 8, 2015), accessed June 2, 2016, http://www.pnas.org/content/112/49/15078.full#corresp-1.

4. Ibid.

5. David H. Autor, David Dorn, and Gordon H. Hanson, "The China Syndrome: Local Labor Market Effects of Import Competition in the United States," *American Economic Review* 103, no. 6 (2013): 2159.

6. Joseph Stiglitz quoted in Eduardo Porter, "Moving on from Farm and Factory," *New York Times*, April 27, 2016, B1+.

7. George Will, *This Week with George Stephanopoulos*, ABC News, aired July 28, 2013.

8. Kevin D. Williamson, "Chaos in the Family, Chaos in the State: The White Working Class's Dysfunction," *National Review*, March 28, 2016 (emphasis in the original), accessed May 3, 2016, http://www.nationalreview.com/article/432876/donald-trump-white-working-class-dysfunction-real-opportunity-needed-not-trump.

9. "Wages of Whiteness" from David Roedinger's *The Wages of Whiteness: Race and the Making of the American Working Class*, new ed. (New York: Verso, 2007); "possessive investment in whiteness" from George Lipsitz, *The Possessive Investment in Whiteness: How White People Profit from Identity Politics* (Philadelphia: Temple University Press, 1998).

10. Robert Kagan, "Order from Chaos: This Is How Fascism Comes to America," Brookings Institution, May 22, 2016, accessed May 23, 2016, http://www.brookings.edu/blogs/order-from-chaos/posts/2016/05/22-trump-fascism-in-america-kagan.

11. Svetlana Boym, "Nostalgia and Its Discontents," *Hedgehog Review* 9, no. 2 (Summer 2007): 7–18.

12. Ibid., 10.

13. James O'Toole and Others, "Work in America," Report of a Special Task Force to the Secretary of Health, Education, and Welfare (Washington, DC: Department of Health, Education, and Welfare, 1972), x.

14. Ibid., 25.

15. Ibid., 44.

16. Ibid., 100, 98.

17. See, for example, Allan Sheahen, "America Needs a Basic Income Guarantee," *The Hill*, August 21, 2013, accessed May 4, 2013, http://thehill.com/blogs/congress-blog/economy-a-budget/317887-america-needs-a-basic-income-guarantee; Noah Gordon, "The Conservative Case for a Guaranteed Basic Income," *Atlantic*, August 6, 2014, accessed September 4, 2014, http://www.theatlantic.com/politics/archive/2014/08/why-arent-reformicons-pushing-a-guaranteed-basic-income/375600/; S. M., "A Government-Guaranteed Basic Income: The Cheque Is in the Mail," Democracy in America—American Politics, *Economist Blog*, November 19, 2013, accessed May 4, 2014, http://www.economist.com/blogs/democracyinamerica/2013/11/government-guaranteed-basic-income.

18. In "Diamonds from Sierra Leone (Remix)," lyrics by Kanye West, *Late Registration*, producers Devo Springsteen, John Brion, and Kanye West, Roc-a-Fella Records (2005).

19. Michael Jackson's Museum News, accessed June 12, 2016, http://www.michaeljacksons-museum.com/news/.

20. Christin Nance Lazerus, "Six Years after Michael Jackson's Death, Gary's Jackson Street on the Upswing," *Chicago Tribune*, June 25, 2015, accessed June 12, 2016, http://my.chicagotribune.com/#section/-1/article/p2p-83860837/.

21. Michael Kimmelman, "The Lights Are On in Detroit," *New York Times*, January 11, 2017, C1.

22. Mark Stryker, "The End, and a New Beginning, for Detroit's Iconic Heidelberg Project," *Detroit Free Press*, August 14, 2016, accessed August 14, 2016. http://www.freep.com/story/entertainment/arts/2016/08/14/heidelberg-project-guyton-dismantle/88626738/.

23. Maurice Cox, meeting with Princeton course "The Arts of Urban Transition," November 1, 2016.

24. Detroit Narrative Agency/Allied Media Projects, accessed June 12, 2016. https://www. alliedmedia.org/dna.

25. Eric Lott, *Love and Theft: Blackface Minstrelsy and the American Working Class* (New York: Oxford University Press, 1993), 238.

REFERENCES

Acocella, Joan. "Walking on the Moon." *New Yorker*, July 27, 2009. http://www.newyorker.com/magazine/2009/07/27/walking-on-the-moon.

Adorno, Theodor W., and Max Horkheimer. *Dialectic of Enlightenment*. Translated by John Cumming. London: Verso, 1997.

Ager, Susan. "Tough, Cheap, and Real: Detroit Is Cool Again." *National Geographic*. Accessed February 29, 2016. http://www.nationalgeographic.com/taking-back-detroit/see-detroit.html.

Aguilar, Louis. "City Defends Whole Foods Tax Break." *Detroit News*, July 29, 2011. ProQuest Newsstand.

———. "M-1 Rail Helps Get Woodward Developments Rolling." *Detroit News*, June 22, 2015. http://www.detroitnews.com/story/news/local/detroit-city/2015/06/21/rail/29084473/.

———. "Red Wings Arena Cost $627M, Could Go Higher." *Detroit News*, November 5, 2015. http://www.detroitnews.com/story/business/2015/11/04/report-cost-new-red-wings-arena-rises/75146516/.

Aguilar, Louis, and Christine MacDonald. "Detroit's White Population Up after Decades of Decline." *Detroit News*, September 17, 2015. http://www.detroitnews.com/story/news/local/detroit-city/2015/09/17/detroit-white-population-rises-census-shows/72371118/.

Aitken, Rob. *Performing Capital: Toward a Cultural Economy of Popular and Global Finance*. New York: Macmillan, 2007.

Alberta, Tim. "Is Dan Gilbert Detroit's New Superhero?" *Atlantic*, February 27, 2014. http://www.theatlantic.com/business/archive/2014/02/is-dan-gilbert-detroits-new-superhero/425742/.

Alexander, Bryant Keith. *The Performative Sustainability of Race: Reflections on Black Culture and the Politics of Identity*. New York: Peter Lang, 2012.

Alexander, Jeffrey C. "The Celebrity-Icon." *Cultural Sociology* 4, no. 3 (November 1, 2010): 323–36.

Amin, Ash. "Post-Fordism: Models, Fantasies, and Phantoms of Transition." In *The Post-Fordist Reader*, edited by Ash Amin, 1–40. Oxford: Blackwell, 1994.

Andersen, H. C. (Hans Christian). "Text of 'The Red Shoes.'" In *Andersen's Fairy Tales*. 2013. http://www.gutenberg.org/ebooks/1597?msg=welcome_stranger#link2H_4_0018.

Anderson, Patrick. *So Much Wasted: Hunger, Performance, and the Morbidity of Resistance*. Durham, NC: Duke University Press, 2010.

Apel, Dora. *Beautiful Terrible Ruins: Detroit and the Anxiety of Decline*. New Brunswick, NJ: Rutgers University Press, 2015.

Apter, Emily. "Acting Out Orientalism: Sapphic Theatricality in Turn-of-the-Century Paris." In *Performance and Cultural Politics*, edited by Elin Diamond, 15–34. New York: Routledge, 1996.

Associated Press. "Jackson's Finances Probed." *Topeka Capital Journal/CJ Online.com*, May 4, 2005. http://cjonline.com/stories/050405/pag_jackson.shtml.

Aubert, Danielle, Lana Cavar, and Natasha Chandani, eds. *Thanks for the View, Mr. Mies: Lafayette Park, Detroit*. New York: Metropolis Books, 2012.

Auerbach, Eric. *Mimesis: The Representation of Reality in Western Literature*. Translated by Willard R. Trask. 50th anniversary edition. Princeton, NJ: Princeton University Press, 1953.

Austin, Dan, and Sean Doerr. *Lost Detroit: Stories behind the Motor City's Majestic Ruins*. Charleston, SC: History Press, 2010.

Autor, David H., David Dorn, and Gordon H. Hanson. "The China Syndrome: Local Labor Market Effects of Import Competition in the United States." *American Economic Review* 103, no. 6 (2013): 2121–168.

Awkward, Michael. *Negotiating Difference: Race, Gender, and the Politics of Positionality*. Chicago: University of Chicago Press, 1995.

Bacevich, Andrew J. "Going for Broke: He Told Us to Go Shopping. Now the Bill Is Due." *Washington Post*, October 5, 2008. http://www.washingtonpost.com/wp-dyn/content/article/2008/10/03/AR2008100301977.html.

Bamford, Kiff. *Lyotard and the Figural in Performance, Art, and Writing*. London: Continuum International, 2012.

Banet-Weiser, Sarah. "Branding the Crisis." In *Aftermath: The Cultures of Economic Crisis*, edited by Manuel Castells, Joao Caraça, and Gustavo Cardoso, 107–31. Oxford: Oxford University Press, 2012.

Baptist, Edward E. *The Half Has Never Been Told: Slavery and the Making of American Capitalism*. New York: Basic Books, 2014.

Bates, Beth Tompkins. *The Making of Black Detroit in the Age of Henry Ford*. Chapel Hill: University of North Carolina Press, 2012.

Bauman, Zygmunt. *Consuming Life*. Cambridge: Polity, 2007.

———. "Industrialism, Consumerism, and Power." In *The Consumption Reader*, edited by David B. Clarke, Marcus A. Doel, and Kate M. L. Housiaux, 54–61. London: Routledge, 2003.

———. *Society under Siege*. London: Polity, 2002.

Becker, Carol, Lisa Yun Lee, and Achim Borchardt-Hume. *Theaster Gates*. London: Phaidon, 2015.

Bell, Daniel. *The Coming of Post-industrial Society: A Venture in Social Forecasting*. New York: Basic Books, 1999.

Bell, Rudolph M. *Holy Anorexia*. Chicago: University of Chicago Press, 1985.

Bench, Harmony. "Monstrous Belonging: Performing 'Thriller' after 9/11." In *The Oxford Handbook of Dance and the Popular Screen*, edited by Melissa Blanco Borelli, 393–411. New York: Oxford University Press, 2014.

Bennett, Jane. "The Moraline Drift." In *The Politics of Moralizing*, edited by Jane Bennett and Michael J. Shapiro, 11–26. New York: Routledge, 2002.

Berlant, Lauren. *Cruel Optimism*. Durham, NC: Duke University Press, 2011.

Bernstein, Robin. *Racial Innocence: Performing American Childhood from Slavery to Civil Rights*. New York: New York University Press, 2011.

Beyers, Tim. "America's Drunk on Credit." *Motley Fool*, August 9, 2006. http://www.fool.com/personal-finance/general/2006/08/09/americas-drunk-on-credit.aspx.

Binelli, Mark. *Detroit City Is the Place to Be: The Afterlife of an American Metropolis*. New York: Metropolitan–Henry Holt, 2012.

Blake, John. "Return of the Welfare Queen." *CNNPolitics.com*, January 23, 2012. http://www.cnn.com/2012/01/23/politics/weflare-queen/.

Blau, Herbert. *The Audience*. Baltimore: Johns Hopkins University Press, 1990.

Bluestone, Barry, and Bennett Harrison. *The Deindustrialization of America: Plant Closings, Community Abandonment, and the Dismantling of Basic Industry*. New York: Basic Books, 1982.

Blyth, Mark. *Austerity: The History of a Dangerous Idea*. New York: Oxford University Press, 2013.

Bomey, Nathan. *Detroit Resurrected: To Bankruptcy and Back*. New York: Norton, 2016.

——. "Disastrous Kilpatrick Debt Deal May Have Been Illegal, but the City May Settle Anyway." *Detroit Free Press*, September 25, 2013. http://archive.freep.com/article/20130925/NEWS01/309250023/Detroit-swaps-legality-pension-Kevyn-Orr-Chapter-9-bankruptcy-debt.

Bomey, Nathan, and Matt Helms. "Detroit Pensioners Back Grand Bargain in Bankruptcy Vote." *Detroit Free Press*, July 22, 2014. http://www.freep.com/article/20140721/NEWS01/307210176/Detroit-bankruptcy-pension-grand-bargain-vote.

Bouffard, Karen. "Census Bureau: Detroit Is Poorest Big City in U.S." *Detroit News*, September 17, 2015. http://www.detroitnews.com/story/news/local/michigan/2015/09/16/census-us-uninsured-drops-income-stagnates/32499231/.

Bourdieu, Pierre. *Distinction: A Social Critique of the Judgement of Taste*. Translated by Richard Nice. Cambridge, MA: Harvard University Press, 1984.

Bowles, Hamish. "The Hamish Files: Detroit by Design." *Vogue*, December 14, 2014.

Boyd, Herb. "Harlem Week: Lackluster Reviews Don't Dismay Director of 'Motown the Musical.'" *New York Daily News*, August 6, 2012. http://www.nydailynews.com/new-york/uptown/harlem-week-lackluster-reviews-don-dismay-director-motown-musical-article-1.1417402.

Boyle, Kevin. *Arc of Justice: A Saga of Race, Civil Rights, and Murder in the Jazz Age*. New York: Henry Holt, 2004.

Boyle, Robin, and Peter Eisinger. "The U.S. Empowerment Zone Program: The Evolution of a National Urban Program and the Failure of Local Implementation in Detroit, Michigan." Presentation, European Urban Research Association Conference, Copenhagen, 2001. http://www.sbi.dk/eura/workshops/papers/workshop5/boyle.htm.

Boym, Svetlana. "Nostalgia and Its Discontents." *Hedgehog Review* 9, no. 2 (Summer 2007): 7–18.

Bramall, Rebecca. *The Cultural Politics of Austerity: Past and Present in Austere Times*. Basingstoke: Palgrave Macmillan, 2013.

Brandstetter, Gabriele. "The Virtuoso's Stage: A Theatrical Topos." *Theatre Research International* 32, no. 3 (July 2007): 178–95.

Braun, Stuart. "Danielle de Picciotto: 'Detroit Is the New Berlin.'" *DW.com*, November 11, 2013. http://www.dw.com/en/danielle-de-picciotto-detroit-is-the-new-berlin/a-17241866.

Brecht, Bertolt. "Short Description of a New Technique of Acting." In *Brecht on Theatre*, edited and translated by John Willett, 136–47. New York: Hill and Wang, 1964.

Broder, John M. "Witness Says Jackson Had 'Cash Flow Crisis.'" *New York Times*, May 4, 2005. http://www.nytimes.com/2005/05/04/national/04jackson.html?pagewanted=print&position=.

Brooks, Peter. *The Melodramatic Imagination: Balzac, Henry James, Melodrama, and the Mode of Excess*. New Haven, CT: Yale University Press, 1976.

Brown, Jayna. *Babylon Girls: Black Women Performers and the Shaping of the Modern*. Durham, NC: Duke University Press, 2008.

——. "From the Point of View of the Pavement: A Geopolitics of Black Dance." In *Big Ears: Listening for Gender in Jazz Studies*, edited by Nichole T. Rustin and Sherrie Tucker, 157–79. Durham, NC: Duke University Press, 2008.

Brown, Wendy. *Edgework: Critical Essays on Knowledge and Politics*. Princeton, NJ: Princeton University Press, 2005.

Brush, Mark. "What's More Valuable, 5% of the DIA Collection, or Detroiters' Pensions?" *Michigan Radio*, December 20, 2013. http://michiganradio.org/post/whats-more-valuable-5-dia-collection-or-detroiters-pensions#stream/0.

"Building Detroit: Neighbors Wanted." Accessed April 17, 2016. http://www.buildingdetroit.org/.

Butler, Judith. *Bodies That Matter: On the Discursive Limits of Sex.* New York: Routledge, 1993.

Carlson, Marvin. *The Haunted Stage: Theatre as Memory Machine.* Ann Arbor: University of Michigan Press, 2002.

Carolyn Murphy's Detroit. *Harper's Bazaar*, October 2014, 236.

Case, Anne, and Angus Deaton. "Rising Morbidity and Mortality Midlife among White Non-Hispanic Americans in the 21st Century." *Proceedings of the National Academy of Sciences* 112, no. 49 (December 8, 2015). http://www.pnas.org/content/112/49/15078.full#corresp-1.

Catanese, Brandi Wilkins. *The Problem of the Color[blind]: Racial Transgressions and the Politics of Black Performance.* Ann Arbor: University of Michigan Press, 2011.

Cattell, Nicole. *Come unto Me: The Faces of Tyree Guyton.* Naked Eye Productions, 1999.

Chafets, Ze'ev. *Devil's Night and Other True Tales of Detroit.* New York: Vintage, 1990.

Chakravartty, Paula, and Denise Ferreira da Silva. "Accumulation, Dispossession, and Debt: The Racial Logic of Global Capitalism—An Introduction." *American Quarterly* 64, no. 3 (September 2012): 361–85.

Chapman, Mary M. "Detroit Shuts Off Water to Residents but Not to Businesses Who Owe Millions." *Daily Beast,* July 26, 2014. http://www.thedailybeast.com/articles/2014/07/26/detroit-shuts-off-water-to-residents-but-not-to-businesses-who-owe-millions.html.

Cheng, Anne Anlin. *The Melancholy of Race: Psychoanalysis, Assimilation, and Hidden Grief.* New York: Oxford University Press, 2001.

Christie, Deborah, and Sarah Juliet Lauro. *Better Off Dead: The Evolution of the Zombie as Post-Human.* New York: Fordham University Press, 2011.

Christie, Les. "Top 10 U.S. Cities for Chinese Homebuyers." *CNN Money*, December 4, 2013. http://money.cnn.com/2013/12/04/real_estate/chinese-homebuyers/index.html.

"City Faces Negro Housing Problem: Southern Clergyman Declares 25,000 Live in One Restricted Area." *Detroit Free Press*, March 12, 1917. ProQuest Historical Newspapers.

Clark, Anna. "Can Urban Planning Rescue Detroit? The Hopes, Fears, and Possibilities of the Detroit Future City Plan." *Next City*, July 1, 2013. https://nextcity.org/features/view/can-urban-planning-rescue-detroit.

———. "Going without Water in Detroit." *New York Times*, July 3, 2014. http://www.nytimes.com/2014/07/04/opinion/going-without-water-in-detroit.html.

———. "The Threat to Detroit's Rebound Isn't Crime or the Economy, It's the Mortgage Industry." *Next City*, December 7, 2015. https://nextcity.org/features/view/detroit-bankruptcy-revival-crime-economy-mortgage-loans-redlining.

Clark, B. "The Riot." In *Anti-Negro Riots in the North 1863*, 23–24. New York: Arno Press and the New York Times, 1969.

Clark, Kenneth B. "A Conversation with James Baldwin." In *Conversations with James Baldwin*, edited by Fred L. Standley and Louis H. Pratt, 38–45. Jackson: University Press of Mississippi, 1989.

Clarke, David B., Marcus A. Doel, and Kate M. L. Housiaux. "General Introduction." In *The Consumption Reader*, edited by David B. Clarke, Marcus A. Doel, and Kate M. L. Housiaux, 1–24. London: Routledge, 2003.

Clay, Andreana. "Working Day and Night: Black Masculinity and the King of Pop." *Journal of Popular Music Studies* 23, no. 1 (2011): 3–18. doi:10.1111/j.1533-1598.2010.01261.x.

Clemens, Paul. *Punching Out: One Year in a Closing Auto Plant.* New York: Doubleday, 2011.

Clement, Daniel, and Miguel Kanai. "Detroit Future City: How Pervasive Neoliberal Urbanism Exacerbates Racialized Spatial Injustice." *American Behavioral Scientist* 59, no. 3 (2015): 369–85.

"Cleveland: At Least We're Not Detroit." *FreshBrewedTees.com*. Accessed October 28, 2013. http://www.freshbrewedtees.com/tees/cleveland-at-least-we-re-not-detroit.html.

Cochran, Terry. *Twilight of the Literary: Figures of Thought in the Age of Print*. Cambridge, MA: Harvard University Press, 2001.

Comaroff, Jean, and John L. Comaroff. "Alien-Nation: Zombies, Immigrants, and Millennial Capitalism." *South Atlantic Quarterly* 101, no. 4 (Fall 2002): 779–805.

———. "Millennial Capitalism: First Thoughts on a Second Coming." In *Millennial Capitalism and the Culture of Neoliberalism*, edited by Jean Comaroff and John L. Comaroff, 1–56. Durham, NC: Duke University Press, 2001.

Condon, Stephanie. "Gov. Rick Snyder: Government Bailout Is the Wrong Answer for Detroit." *CBS News*, July 21, 2013. http://www.cbsnews.com/news/gov-rick-snyder-government-bailout-is-the-wrong-answer-for-detroit/.

Conlin, Jennifer. "Choices Tables: In Detroit Revitalizing Taste by Taste." *New York Times*, October 8, 2014. http://www.nytimes.com/2014/10/12/travel/in-detroit-revitalizing-taste-by-taste.html?_r=0.

Connecting the Dots: Tyree Guyton's Heidelberg Project. Detroit: Wayne State University Press, 2007.

Conquergood, Dwight. *Cultural Struggles: Performance, Ethnography, Praxis*. Edited by E. Patrick Johnson. Ann Arbor: University of Michigan Press, 2013.

———. "Performing as a Moral Act: Ethical Dimensions of the Ethnography of Performance." *Literature in Performance* 5, no. 2 (1985): 1–13.

Cotter, Holland. "Mike Kelley, Influential American Artist, Dies at 57." *New York Times*, February 1, 2012. http://www.nytimes.com/2012/02/02/arts/design/mike-kelley-influential-american-artist-dies-at-57.html?_r=0.

Cowie, Jefferson. *Stayin' Alive: The 1970s and the Last Days of the Working Class*. New York: New Press, 2010.

Cowie, Jefferson R., and Lauren Boehm. "Dead Man's Town: 'Born in the U.S.A.,' Social History, and Working-Class Identity." *American Quarterly* 58, no. 2 (2006): 353–78. doi:10.1353/aq.2006.0040.

Cowie, Jefferson R., and Joseph Heathcott, eds. *Beyond the Ruins: The Meanings of Deindustrialization*. Ithaca, NY: Cornell University Press, 2003.

Cox, Maurice. Presentation at the Detroit 101 Lecture Series "Urbanism and Design" Princeton University, March 2, 2016.

Crawford, Krysten. "Michael Jackson to Lose Beatles Catalog?" *CNN Money*, May 5, 2005. http://money.cnn.com/2005/05/05/news/newsmakers/jackson_loan/index.htm?cnn=yes.

Crosthwaite, Paul, Peter Knight, and Nicky Marsh, eds. *Show Me the Money: The Image of Finance, 1700 to the Present*. Manchester: Manchester University Press, 2014.

Cullen, Jim. *Born in the U.S.A.: Bruce Springsteen and the American Tradition*. New York: HarperCollins, 1997.

Dalmia, Shikha. "Bankrupt Detroit Doles Out Corporate Subsidies." *BloombergView*, January 22, 2014. http://www.bloombergview.com/articles/2014-01-22/detroit-hopes-corporate-subsidies-work-this-time.

D'Amour, Lisa. *Detroit*. New York: Faber and Faber, 2011.

Davey, Monica. "Financial Crisis Just a Symptom of Detroit's Woes." *New York Times*, July 8, 2013.

"De-." *Oxford English Dictionary Online.* Accessed January 7, 2016. http://www.oed.com. ezproxy.princeton.edu/view/Entry/47600?rskey=jnBXAt&result=3&isAdvanced=false#eid.

Debord, Guy. *The Society of Spectacle.* Translated by Donald Nicholson-Smith. New York: Zone, 1995.

DeFrantz, Thomas F. "The Black Beat Made Visible: Hip Hop Dance and Body Power." In *Of the Presence of the Body: Essays on Dance and Performance Theory*, edited by André Lepecki, 64–81. Middletown, CT: Wesleyan University Press, 2004.

———. "Hip-Hop in Hollywood: Encounter, Community, Resistance." In *The Oxford Handbook of Dance and the Popular Screen*, edited by Melissa Blanco Borelli, 113–31. New York: Oxford University Press, 2014.

———. "Performing the Breaks: Notes on African American Aesthetic Structures." *Theater* 40, no. 1 (January 2010): 31–37. doi:10.1215/01610775-2009-017.

Detroit Historical Society. "Arsenal of Democracy." In *Encyclopedia of Detroit*. Accessed February 14, 2016. http://detroithistorical.org/learn/encyclopedia-of-detroit/arsenal-democracy.

———. "Detroit Police Department." In *Encyclopedia of Detroit*. Accessed April 18, 2016. http://detroithistorical.org/learn/encyclopedia-of-detroit/detroit-police-department.

———. "Paradise Valley." In *Encyclopedia of Detroit*. Accessed April 11, 2016. http://detroithistorical.org/learn/encyclopedia-of-detroit/paradise-valley.

Detroit Works Project. *Detroit Future City – 2012 Detroit Strategic Framework Plan.* http://detroitfuturecity.com/wpcontent/uploads/2014/12/DFC_Full_2nd.pdf.

Detroit Works Project. *Executive Summary*, 2nd ed. Accessed September 1, 2015. http://detroitfuturecity.com/wpcontent/uploads/2014/02/DFC_ExecutiveSummary_2ndEd.pdf.

"Devil's Night." *Wikipedia.* Accessed September 16, 2013. http://en.wikipedia.org/wiki/Devil's_Night.

Diamond, Elin. "Introduction." In *Performance and Cultural Politics*, edited by Elin Diamond, 1–12. London: Routledge, 1996.

Dickstein, Morris. *Dancing in the Dark: A Cultural History of the Great Depression.* New York: Norton, 2009.

Diggs Colbert, Soyica. *The African American Theatrical Body: Reception, Performance, and the Stage.* Cambridge: Cambridge University Press, 2011.

di Leonardo, Micaela. "Deindustrialization as a Folk Model." *Urban Anthropology and Studies of Cultural Systems and World Economic Development* 14, nos. 1–3 (1985): 237–57.

———. *Exotics at Home.* Chicago: University of Chicago Press, 1998.

Dinerstein, Joel. *Swinging the Machine: Modernity, Technology, and Africa American Culture between the Two World Wars.* Amherst: University of Massachusetts Press, 2003.

"Discuss Detroit: S.T.R.E.S.S. Memories." Accessed April 18, 2016. http://www.atdetroit.net/forum/messages/62684/67830.html?1142292447.

Ditzian, Eric. "Michael Jackson's Groundbreaking Career by the Numbers." *MTV.com News*, June 26, 2009. http://www.mtv.com/news/1614815/michael-jacksons-groundbreaking-career-by-the-numbers/.

Dolan, Jill. *The Feminist Spectator in Action: Feminist Criticism for the Stage and Screen.* Basingstoke: Palgrave Macmillan, 2013.

Doray, Bernard. *From Taylorism to Fordism: A Rational Madness.* Translated by D. Macey. London: Free Association Books, 1988.

Dore, Ronald. "Financialization of the Global Economy." *Industrial and Corporate Change* 17, no. 6 (2008): 1097–112.

Downs, Linda Banks. *Diego Rivera: The Detroit Industry Murals.* New York: Norton and the Detroit Institute of Arts, 1999.

Duany, Andres. "The Pink Zone: Why Detroit Is the New Berlin." *Fortune*, January 30, 2014. http://fortune.com/2014/01/30/the-pink-zone-why-detroit-is-the-new-brooklyn/.

Dudley, Kathryn Marie. *The End of the Line: Lost Jobs, New Lives in Postindustrial America.* Chicago: University of Chicago Press, 1997.

Duke, Alan. "Kenny Ortega Brings Tearful Testimony to Michael Jackson Death Trial." *CNN Entertainment*, July 11, 2013. http://www.cnn.com/2013/07/10/showbiz/jackson-death-trial/.

———. "Lawsuit Evidence: Michael Jackson Lost Dance Moves in Last Days." *CNN Entertainment*, June 16, 2013. http://www.cnn.com/2013/06/14/showbiz/jackson-death-trial/index.html.

Dziemianowicz, Joe. "Theatre Review: Detroit." *New York Daily News*, September 18, 2012. http://www.nydailynews.com/entertainment/music-arts/theater-review-detroit-article-1.1162183.

Eagleton, Terry. "Brecht and Rhetoric." *New Literary History* 16, no. 3 (1985): 633–38.

Edensor, Tim. *Industrial Ruins: Space, Aesthetics, and Materiality.* Oxford: Berg, 2005.

Edsall, Thomas B. "The Politics of Austerity." *New York Times*, November 5, 2011. http://campaignstops.blogs.nytimes.com/2011/11/05/the-politics-of-austerity/?_r=0.

Egan, Paul. "Testimony, Emails Shed Light on Right-to-Work Turmoil." *Detroit Free Press*, October 30, 2014. http://www.freep.com/story/news/politics/2014/10/30/lawsuit-sheds-light-michigan-capitol-turmoil-right-work/18157739/.

Ellison, Ralph. *Invisible Man.* New York: Knopf Doubleday, 2010.

Etheridge, Eric. "Rick Santelli: Tea Party Time." *New York Times "Opinionator" Blog*, February 20, 2009. http://opinionator.blogs.nytimes.com/2009/02/20/rick-santelli-tea-party-time/?_r=0.

Exhibit 307–2 [AEGL 000137453]. "Jackson V AEG Live Trial Exhibits." *TeamMichaelJackson.com*. Accessed July 11, 2015. http://www.teammichaeljackson.com/archives/8832.

Exhibit 311-1 [9, Faye, 1/3/13]. "Jackson V AEG Live Trial Exhibits." *TeamMichaelJackson.com*. Accessed July 11, 2015. http://www.teammichaeljackson.com/archives/8832

Exhibit 330-1 [10, Faye, 1/3/13]. "Jackson V AEG Live Trial Exhibits." *TeamMichaelJackson.com*. Accessed July 11, 2015. http://www.teammichaeljackson.com/archives/8832.

"Fact Sheet: America's Ownership Society: Expanding Opportunities." George W. Bush White House Archives, August 9, 2004. http://georgewbush-whitehouse.archives.gov/news/releases/2004/08/20040809-9.html.

Fast, Susan. *Dangerous (33 1/3).* New York: Bloomsbury, 2014.

———. "Difference That Exceeded Understanding: Remembering Michael Jackson (1958–2009)." *Popular Music and Society* 33, no. 2 (May 2010): 259–66.

Fast, Susan, and Stan Hawkins, eds. "Special Issue on Michael Jackson: Musical Subjectivities." Special issue, *Popular Music and Society* 35, no. 2 (May 2012): 145–319.

Faulkner, William. *Absalom, Absalom!* New York: Vintage, 1972.

Ferretti, Christine. "Up to 25K Face Water Shut-Offs in Detroit." *Detroit News*, May 5, 2015. http://www.detroitnews.com/story/news/local/detroit-city/2015/05/04/water-shut-notices-go-detroit-may/26891145/.

Ferriero, David R. "How to Be a 'Smooth Criminal.'" *The National Archives AOTUS Blog:* April 1, 2011. https://aotus.blogs.archives.gov/2011/04/01/how-to-be-a-smooth-criminal/.

Fey, Tina. *Bossypants.* New York: Little, Brown, 2011.

"Figure, Noun." *Oxford English Dictionary.* Accessed July 15, 2014. http://www.oed.com.ezproxy.princeton.edu/view/Entry/70079?rskey=9UiSVH&result=1&isAdvanced=false#eid.

"Figure, Verb." *Oxford English Dictionary,.* December 20, 2015. http://www.oed.com.ezproxy.princeton.edu/view/Entry/70080?rskey=zUNIYv&result=2&isAdvanced=false#eid.

Fine, Lisa M. *The Story of Reo Joe: Work, Kin, and Community in Autotown, USA*. Philadelphia: Temple University Press, 2004.

Fine, Sidney. *Violence in the Model City*. Ann Arbor: University of Michigan Press, 1989.

Finley, Nolan. "Where Are the Black People?" *Detroit News*, December 15, 2014. http://www.detroitnews.com/story/opinion/columnists/nolan-finley/2014/12/14/black-people/20322377/.

Fletcher, Angus. *Allegory: The Theory of a Symbolic Mode*. Ithaca, NY: Cornell University Press, 1964.

Flint, Jerry. "Meany Asks More Protectionism to Stop Loss of Jobs to Imports." *New York Times*, December 9, 1977. The New York Times (1851–2007). ProQuest Historical Newspapers.

Florida, Richard. *The Rise of the Creative Class: And How It's Transforming Work, Leisure, Community and Everyday Life*. New York: Basic Books, 2002.

Foley, Aaron. "Apple Shot a Commercial in Detroit; It's Great but Also Sucks." August 13, 2014. http://detroit.jalopnik.com/apple-shot-a-commercial-in-detroit-its-great-but-also-1620773281.

Ford, Henry. *My Life and Work (1922)*. Project Gutenberg, 2005. Accessed April 30, 2014. http://www.gutenberg.org/cache/epub/7213/pg7213-images.html.

"Ford River Rouge Factory Tour—Art of Manufacturing Theater." *The Henry Ford*. Accessed July 31, 2013. http://www.thehenryford.org/rouge/theater.aspx.

Forsyth, Randall W. "Chicago Is Not Detroit." *Barron's*, November 21, 2013. http://online.barrons.com/article/SB50001424053111904253404579205921128206510.html.

Foucault, Michel. *Discipline and Punish: The Birth of the Prison*. New York: Vintage, 1991.

Foulkes, Julia L. "Dancing in the Streets: The Arts in Postwar Cities—Introduction." *Journal of Urban History* 41, no. 6 (November 2015): 955–61.

Foulkes, Julia L., and Aaron Shkuda. "Dancing in the Streets: The Arts in Postwar U.S. Cities." Special Section, *Journal of Urban History* 41, no. 6 (November 2015): 955–1072.

Fournier, Holly. "Man Charged in Fatal Foreclosure Showdown in Detroit." *Detroit News*, December 1, 2014. http://www.detroitnews.com/story/news/local/wayne-county/2014/12/01/rosedale-shooting/19731541/.

Franko, Mark. "Dance and the Political: States of Exception." *Dance Research Journal* 38, nos. 1–2 (Summer–Winter 2006): 3–18.

———. *The Work of Dance: Labor, Movement, and Identity in the 1930s*. Middletown, CT: Wesleyan University Press, 2002.

Friedman, Milton. "The Social Responsibility of Business Is to Increase Its Profits." *New York Times Magazine*, September 13, 1970, 32–33, 122–24.

Friedman, Roger. "Jacko Pawned $2 Million Watch to Raise Dough; Banker Claims: 'I've Kept Him Alive.'" *FoxNews.com*, April 19, 2002. http://www.foxnews.com/story/2002/04/19/jacko-pawned-2-million-watch-to-raise-dough-banker-claims-ive-kept-him-alive.html.

Fuchs, Cynthia J. "Michael Jackson's Penis." In *Cruising the Performative*, edited by Sue-Ellen Case, Phillip Brett, and Susan Leigh Foster, 13–33. Bloomington: Indiana University Press, 1995.

Fuoss, Kirk. *Striking Performance/Performance Strikes*. Jackson: University of Mississippi Press, 1997.

"Galapagos Art Space—The 2016 Detroit Biennial." Accessed February 26, 2016. http://www.galapagosdetroit.com/2106-detroit-biennial/.

"Galapagos Goes Detroit." *Box Blog*, December 10, 2014. http://blog.dylanbox.com/detroit/2014/12/10/galapagos-goes-detroit.html.

Gallagher, John. "Galapagos Selling Corktown Building, Answers Critics." *Detroit Free Press*, January 8, 2016. http://www.freep.com/story/money/business/michigan/2016/01/08/detroit-brooklyn-galapagos-corktown/78519904/.

———. "Galapagos Team Keeping Building Near Corktown after All." *Detroit Free Press*, May 17, 2016. http://www.freep.com/story/money/business/michigan/2016/05/17/detroit-corktown-galapagos-elmes/84484464/.

Galster, George C. *Driving Detroit: The Quest for Respect in the Motor City*. Philadelphia: University of Pennsylvania Press, 2012.

Gardner, Sally. "The Dancer, the Choreographer and Modern Dance Scholarship: A Critical Reading." *Dance Research* 25, no. 1 (2007): 35–53.

Gates Starr, Ellen. "Art and Labor." Hull House Maps and Papers, 1895. Accessed March 26, 2016. http://media.pfeiffer.edu/lridener/DSS/Addams/hh9.html.

Gibb, Barry, Maurice Gibb, and Robin Gibb. *Stayin' Alive*. 1977.

Gill, Rosalind, and Andy Pratt. "In the Social Factory? Immaterial Labour, Precariousness and Cultural Work." *Theory, Culture & Society* 25, nos. 7–8 (2008): 1–30.

Glenn, Susan A. *Female Spectacle: The Theatrical Roots of Modern Feminism*. Cambridge, MA: Harvard University Press, 2000.

Gordon, Avery F. *Ghostly Matters: Haunting and the Sociological Imagination*. Minneapolis: University of Minnesota Press, 1997.

Gordon, Noah. "The Conservative Case for a Guaranteed Basic Income." *Atlantic*, August 6, 2014. Accessed September 4, 2014, http://www.theatlantic.com/politics/archive/2014/08/why-arent-reformicons-pushing-a-guaranteed-basic-income/375600/

Gottschild, Brenda Dixon. *Digging the Africanist Presence in American Performance: Dance and Other Contexts*. Westport, CT: Praeger, 1998.

Graeber, David. *Possibilities: Essays on Hierarchy, Rebellion, and Desire*. Oakland, CA: AK Press, 2007.

Graff, Ellen. *Stepping Left: Dance and Politics in New York City, 1928–1942*. Durham, NC: Duke University Press, 1997.

Greenberg, Stanley B. *Middle Class Dreams: The Politics and Power of the New American Majority*. Rev. ed. New Haven, CT: Yale University Press, 2006.

Greenburg, Zack O'Malley. *Michael Jackson, Inc.: The Rise, Fall, and Rebirth of a Billion-Dollar Empire*. New York: Atria/Simon and Schuster, 2014.

Greenhouse, Carol J. "Introduction." In *Ethnographies of Neoliberalism*, edited by Carol J. Greenhouse, 1–10. Philadelphia: University of Pennsylvania Press, 2010.

Greenhouse, Steven. "LTV Problems Stir Concerns on Survival of Steel Industry." *New York Times*, July 28, 1986. Accessed April 22, 2015. http://www.nytimes.com/1986/07/28/business/ltv-problems-stir-concerns-on-survival-of-steel-industry.html?pagewanted=all.

Greer, Edward. *Big Steel: Black Politics and Corporate Power in Gary, Indiana*. New York: Monthly Review Press, 1979.

Grossberg, Lawrence. "Postmodernity and Affect: All Dressed Up with No Place to Go." *Communication* 10 (1988): 271–93.

Guillen, Joe. "Detroit Red Wings' New Stadium Land Transfer Approved by City Council." *USA Today*, February 4, 2014. Accessed January 30, 2016. http://www.usatoday.com/story/sports/nhl/wings/2014/02/04/detroit-red-wings-new-arena-land-transfer-approved/5211635/.

Gundersen, Edna. "Jackson's Freedom Isn't Free." *USA Today*, June 14, 2005. Accessed July 16, 2015. http://usatoday30.usatoday.com/life/people/2005-06-13-jackson-finances_x.htm.

Guzman-Sanchez, Thomas. *Underground Dance Masters: Final History of a Forgotten Era*. Santa Barbara, CA: Praeger, 2012.

Hackman, Rose. "What Happens When Detroit Shuts Off the Water of 100,000 People." *Atlantic*, July 14, 2014. http://www.theatlantic.com/business/archive/2014/07/what-happens-when-detroit-shuts-off-the-water-of-100000-people/374548/.

———. "One- Fifth of Detroit's Population Could Lose Their Homes." Atlantic, October 22, 2014. http:// www.theatlantic.com/ business/ archive/ 2014/ 10/ one- fifth- of- detroits- population- could- lose- their- homes/ 381694/.

Hackworth, Jason. "Rightsizing as Spatial Austerity in the American Rust Belt." *Environment and Planning A* 47, no. 4 (2015): 766–82.

Haiven, Max. *Cultures of Financialization: Fictitious Capital in Popular Culture and Everyday Life*. Basingstoke: Palgrave Macmillan, 2014.

Hakala, Josh. "How Did We Get Here? A Look Back at Michigan's Emergency Manager Law." *Michigan Radio*. Accessed April 28, 2016. http://michiganradio.org/post/how-did-we-get-here-look-back-michigans-emergency-manager-law#stream/0.

Hamera, Judith. *Dancing Communities: Performance, Difference, and Connection in the Global City*. Basingstoke: Palgrave Macmillan, 2007.

———. "Domestic(-ated) Desires, Tanked City." *TDR: The Drama Review* 58, no. 4 (Winter 2014): 12–22.

———. "Regions of Likeness: The Poetry of Jorie Graham, Dance, and Citational Solidarity." *Text and Performance Quarterly* 25, no. 1 (January 2005): 15–27.

Hamer, Jennifer. *Abandoned in the Heartland: Work, Family, and Living in East St. Louis*. Berkeley: University of California Press, 2011.

Haraway, Donna. *Modest_Witness@Second_Millennium.Femaleman©_Meets_OncoMouseTM: Feminism and Technoscience*. New York: Routledge, 1997.

Hardt, Michael. "Affective Labor." *boundary 2* 26 (1999): 89–100.

Harney, Stefano, and Fred Moten. *The Undercommons: Fugitive Planning and Black Study*. Brooklyn: Minor Compositions, 2013.

Hartigan, John, Jr. *Racial Situations: Class Predicaments of Whiteness in Detroit*. Princeton, NJ: Princeton University Press, 1999.

Harvest of the Years. Ford Motor Company, Dearborn, MI, 1939.

Harvey, David. *Spaces of Global Capitalism: Towards a Theory of Uneven Geographical Development*. London: Verso, 2006.

———. *Spaces of Hope*. Berkeley: University of California Press, 2000.

"The Heidelberg Project." *RoadsideAmerica.com*. Accessed February 1, 2016. http://www.roadsideamerica.com/story/21166.

Helms, Matt. "Detroit's New Planning Director: Dream Big." *Detroit Free Press*, July 4, 2015. http://www.freep.com/story/news/local/michigan/detroit/2015/07/03/maurice-cox-detroitplanningdirector/29682221/http://www.freep.com/story/news/local/michigan/detroit/2015/07/03/maurice-cox-detroit-planning-director/29682221/.

Helms, Matt, and Joe Guillen. "Judge Says No to Detroit Water Shutoff Moratorium." *Detroit Free Press*, September 29, 2014. http://www.freep.com/story/news/local/detroit-bankruptcy/2014/09/29/water-shutoff-moratorium/16451483/.

Herron, Jerry. *AfterCulture: Detroit and the Humiliation of History*. Detroit: Wayne State University Press, 1993.

———. "Detroit: Disaster Deferred, Disaster in Progress." *South Atlantic Quarterly* 106, no. 4 (Fall 2007): 663–82.

———. "Motor City Breakdown: Detroit in Literature and Film." *Places*, April, 2013. https://placesjournal.org/article/motor-city-breakdown/.

Hewitt, Andrew. *Social Choreography: Ideology as Performance in Dance and Everyday Movement*. Durham, NC: Duke University Press, 2005.

High, Steven. "Beyond Aesthetics: Visibility and Invisibility in the Aftermath of Deindustrialization." *International Labor and Working-Class History* 84 (Fall 2013): 140–53.

———. *Industrial Sunset: The Making of North America's Rust Belt, 1969–1984.* Toronto: University of Toronto Press, 2003.

High, Steven, and David Lewis. *Corporate Wasteland: The Landscape and Memory of Deindustrialization.* Ithaca, NY: Cornell University Press, 2007.

Highsmith, Andrew R. *Demolition Means Progress.* Chicago: University of Chicago Press, 2015.

Higton, Mike. *Christ, Providence and History: Hans Frei's Public Theology.* London: Continuum/ T&T Clark, 2004.

Hinds, Julie. "Rush Limbaugh Prompts Republishing of Detroit Book 'Devil's Night.'" *Detroit Free Press,* August 24, 2013. http://www.freep.com/article/20130824/ENT03/ 308240026/Devil's%20Night%20Chafets%20Rush%20Limbaugh.

Hitchens, Peter. "From Motown to Ghost Town: How the Once Mighty Detroit Is Headed Down the Road to Ruin." *Daily Mail,* July 9, 2011. http://www.dailymail.co.uk/news/ article-2012971/From-Motown-Ghost-town-How-mighty-Detroit-heading-long-slow-road-ruin.html.

Hodges, Michael H. "How Detroit Got Its Groove Back." In *Canvas Detroit,* edited by Julie Pincus and Nichole Christian, 8–11. Detroit: Wayne State University Press, 2014.

Hoerr, John. *And the Wolf Finally Came: The Decline and Fall of the American Steel Industry.* Pittsburgh: University of Pittsburgh Press, 1988.

"The Hood." *Urban Dictionary,* April 18, 2016. http://www.urbandictionary.com/define. php?term=the+hood.

hooks, bell. "Homeplace (a site of resistance)." In *The Woman That I Am,* edited by D. Soyini Madison, 448–53. New York: St. Martin's, 1994.

Hudson, Michael W. *The Monster: How a Gang of Predatory Lenders and Wall Street Bankers Fleeced America.* New York: St. Martin's/Griffin, 2011.

Hughes, Amy E. *Spectacles of Reform: Theater and Activism in Nineteenth-Century America.* Ann Arbor: University of Michigan Press, 2012.

Hunter, George. "Detroit Police Diversity Issues Predate National Debate." *Detroit News,* March 8, 2015. http://www.detroitnews.com/story/news/local/wayne-county/2015/03/07/ detroit-police-department-diversity/24570427/.

Hutera, Donald. "Detroit: State of the Nation." *Theatre News Online,* n.d. http://www.theater-newsonline.com/LondonTheatreReviews/STATEOFTHENATION.cfm.

"In Detroit, EMS Response Times Must Improve." *Detroit News,* September 5, 2014. http:// www.detroitnews.com/story/opinion/editorials/2014/09/25/detroit-ems-response-times/16221893/.

Isadore, Chris, and Poppy Harlow. "Detroit Gets $195 Million Closer to Salvation." *CNN Money,* June 20, 2014. http://money.cnn.com/2014/06/20/news/economy/detroit-bankruptcy-state-aid/.

Isherwood, Charles. "Desperately Trying to Stay Stuck in the Middle." *New York Times,* September 18, 2012. http://theater.nytimes.com/2012/09/19/theater/reviews/ detroit-with-amy-ryan-and-david-schwimmer.html?_r=0.

———. "Down in the Basement, Family Tensions Stir." *New York Times,* March 12, 2013. http://theater.nytimes.com/2013/03/13/theater/reviews/detroit-67-at-the-public-theater.html?pagewanted=all.

———. "Hey, Diana, Smokey, Stevie: You're on Broadway!" *New York Times,* April 14, 2013. http://theater.nytimes.com/2013/04/15/theater/reviews/motown-the-musical-berry-gordys-story.html?pagewanted=all&_r=0.

Jackman, Michael. "Is Detroit the New LA?" *Metro Times,* January 28, 2015. http://www. metrotimes.com/Blogs/archives/2015/01/28/is-detroit-the-new-la.

"Jackson 5 Returns Home in Mayor Hatcher Benefit." *Jet*, February 18, 1971.

Jackson, Marion Elizabeth. *Tyree Guyton*. Detroit: Founders Society Detroit Institute of Arts, 1990.

Jackson, Michael. *Moonwalk*. New York: Crown Archetype, 2009.

———. *Smooth Criminal. Moonwalker*, standard version. Warner Bros. Entertainment, 2010.

———. *This Is It*. SONY/Columbia Pictures, 2009.

———. "Thriller." *Number Ones*. New York: Epic Music Video, 2003.

Jackson, Shannon. "Just-in-Time: Performance and the Aesthetics of Precarity." *TDR: The Drama Review* 56, no. 4 (Winter 2012): 10–31.

The Jackson Five. *Goin Places*. Epic Records and Philadelphia International Records, 1977.

Jefferson, Margo. *On Michael Jackson*. New York: Vintage Books, 2006.

Jessop, Bob. "Post-Fordism and the State." In *The Post-Fordist Reader*, edited by Ash Amin, 251–79. Oxford: Blackwell, 1994.

Johnson, Allan. "ABC on Top with King of Pop Special." *Chicago Tribune*, February 8, 2003. http://articles.chicagotribune.com/2003-02-08/news/0302080284_1_nielsen-ratings-viewers-living-with-michael-jackson.

Johnson, E. Patrick. *Appropriating Blackness: Performance and the Politics of Authenticity*. Durham, NC: Duke University Press, 2003.

Jones, Tamara. "Culkin Shared Jackson's Bed but Says He Wasn't Molested." *Washington Post*, May 12, 2005. http://www.washingtonpost.com/wp-dyn/content/article/2005/05/11/AR2005051102197.html.

Joseph, Miranda. *Debt to Society: Accounting for Life under Capitalism*. Minneapolis: University of Minnesota Press, 2014.

jruss. "The 1943 Detroit Riot." *jruss's Blog*. Walter P. Reuther Library, Wayne State University. June 12, 2012. http://reuther.wayne.edu/node/8738.

Juarez, Kristin. "Theaster Gates Transports Time and Place." *International Review of African American Art* 24, no. 3 (June 2013): 2–6.

Kafka, Franz. "A Hunger Artist." In *The Penal Colony: Stories and Short Pieces*. Translated by Willa Muir and Edwin Muir, 231–77. New York: Schocken, 1961.

Kagan, Robert. "Order from Chaos: This Is How Fascism Comes to America." Brookings Institution, May 22, 2016. http://www.brookings.edu/blogs/order-from-chaos/posts/2016/05/22-trump-fascism-in-america-kagan.

Keller, Bill. "New York Is Not Detroit. But . . ." *New York Times*, July 21, 2013. http://www.nytimes.com/2013/07/22/opinion/keller-new-york-is-not-detroit-but.html.

Kelley, Mike. "*Blackout* (2001)." In *Mike Kelley: Minor Histories: Statements, Conversations, Proposals*, edited by John C. Welchman, 156–62. Cambridge, MA: MIT Press, 2004.

Kelley, Mike. "'Mobile Homestead,' Artist's Statement." Detroit: Museum of Contemporary Art Detroit, 2011. http://www.mocadetroit.org/Mobile-HomesteadEssay.html.

Kelley, Robin D. G. *Race Rebels: Culture, Politics, and the Black Working Class*. New York: Free Press, 1996.

Kellogg, Alex P. "Detroit's Smaller Reality." *Wall Street Journal*, February 27, 2010. http://www.wsj.com/articles/SB10001424052748703503804575083781073108438.

Kennedy, Randy. "The Agony of Suspense in Detroit." *New York Times*, October 3, 2013.

———. "'Grand Bargain' Saves the Detroit Institute of Arts." *New York Times*, November 7, 2014. http://www.nytimes.com/2014/11/08/arts/design/grand-bargain-saves-the-detroit-institute-of-arts.html?_r=0.

Kennedy, Randy, Monica Davey, and Steven Yaccino. "Foundations Aim to Save Pensions in Detroit Crisis." *New York Times*, January 14, 2014.

Kennedy, Shawn G. "Orville L. Hubbard of Dearborn; Ex-Mayor a Foe of Integration." *New York Times*, December 17, 1982. http://www.nytimes.com/1982/12/17/obituaries/orville-l-hubbard-of-dearborn-ex-mayor-a-foe-of-integration.html.

Kester, Grant H. *The One and the Many: Contemporary Collaborative Art in a Global Context.* Durham, NC: Duke University Press, 2011.

Kimmelman, Michael. "The Lights Are On in Detroit." *New York Times,* January 11, 2017.

Kinder, Kimberley. *DIY Detroit: Making Do in a City without Services.* Minneapolis: University of Minnesota Press, 2016.

King, Jason. "Don't Stop Till You Get Enough: Presence, Spectacle, and Good Feeling in *Michael Jackson's This Is It.*" In *Black Performance Theory,* edited by Thomas F. DeFrantz and Anita Gonzalez, 184–203. Durham, NC: Duke University Press, 2014.

Kinney, Rebecca J. *Beautiful Wasteland: The Rise of Detroit as America's Postindustrial Frontier.* Minneapolis: University of Minnesota Press, 2016.

Kirkpatrick, L. Owen. "Urban Triage, City Systems, and the Remnants of Community: Some 'Sticky' Complications in the Greening of Detroit." *Journal of Urban History* 4, no. 2 (2015): 261–78.

Kisselgoff, Anna. "Stage: The Dancing Feet of Michael Jackson." *New York Times,* March 6, 1988. http://www.nytimes.com/1988/03/06/arts/stage-the-dancing-feet-of-michael-jackson.html.

K'Meyer, Tracy E., and Joy L. Hart. *I Saw It Coming: Worker Narratives of Plant Closing and Job Loss.* Basingstoke: Palgrave, 2011.

Koehn, Josh. "San Jose Is Not Detroit." *San Jose Inside,* October 2, 2013. http://www.sanjoseinside.com/news/entries/10_2_13_san_jose_detroit_xavier_campos_new_york_times.

"Kozlowski, Tyco Face More Questions." *CNN Money,* August 7, 2002. http://money.cnn.com/2002/08/07/news/companies/tyco_kozlowski/.

Kraut, Anthea. "'Stealing Steps' and Signature Moves: Embodied Theories of Dance as Intellectual Property." *Theatre Journal* 62, no. 2 (2010): 173–89. doi:10.1353/tj.0.0357.

Kurth, Joel. "Detroit Unlikely to Forgive Water Debts of Poor." *Detroit News,* December 15, 2015. http://www.detroitnews.com/story/news/local/detroit-city/2015/12/15/detroit-unlikely-forgive-water-debts-poor/77371414/.

Kutscher, Ronald E., and Valerie A. Personick. "Deindustrialization and the Shift to Services." *Monthly Labor Review,* June 1986, 3–13.

Kuttner, Robert. *Debtors' Prison: The Politics of Austerity versus Possibility.* New York: Vintage, 2015.

Langley, Paul. *The Everyday Life of Global Finance: Saving and Borrowing in Anglo-America.* New York: Oxford University Press, 2008.

La Berge, Leigh Claire. *Scandals and Abstractions: Financial Fiction of the Long 1980s.* New York: Oxford University Press, 2015.

"Late Trash Pickup Makes for a Dirtier Detroit." *CBS Detroit.* November 11, 2012. Accessed February 3, 2016. http://detroit.cbslocal.com/2012/11/28/late-trash-pick-up-makes-for-dirtier-detroit/.

Latzman Moon, Elaine. *Untold Tales, Unsung Heroes: An Oral History of Detroit's African American Community, 1918–1967.* Detroit: Wayne State University Press, 1993.

Lauro, Sarah Juliet, and Karen Embry. "A Zombie Manifesto: The Nonhuman Condition in the Era of Advanced Capitalism." *boundary 2* 35, no. 1 (2008): 85–108.

Lazerus, Christin Nance. "Six Years after Michael Jackson's Death, Gary's Jackson Street on the Upswing." *Chicago Tribune,* June 25, 2015. http://my.chicagotribune.com/#section/-1/article/p2p-83860837/.

Lazzarato, Maurizio. "Immaterial Labor." In *Radical Thought in Italy: A Potential Politics,* edited by Paolo Virno and Michael Hardy, 133–47. Minneapolis: University of Minnesota Press, 1996.

LeDuff, Charlie. *Detroit: An American Autopsy.* New York: Penguin, 2013.

Lee, Blair. "At Least Baltimore Is Not Detroit." *Gazette.net: Maryland Community News Online,* September 27, 2013. http://www.gazette.net/article/20130927/OPINION/130929269/-1/why-baltimore-is-not-detroit&template=gazette.

Leong, Melissa. "Spending Problem? Blame It on Your Brain." *Financial Post*, January 23, 2013. http://business.financialpost.com/personal-finance/retirement/rrsp/is-your-brain-high-on-spending-trick-it-into-saving.

Lepecki, André. *Exhausting Dance: Performance and the Politics of Movement*. New York: Routledge, 2006.

Lévy, Bernard-Henri. "The Three Stations of the Cross in Michael Jackson's Calvary." *Huffington Post*, August 1, 2009. http://www.huffingtonpost.com/bernardhenri-levy/the-three-stations-of-the_b_224224.html.

Levy, Jonathan. *Freaks of Fortune: The Emerging World of Capitalism and Risk in America*. Cambridge, MA: Harvard University Press, 2012.

Li, Lucy. "Mike Kelley's Mobile Homestead Arrives in Detroit." *Whitewall Magazine*, June 11, 2013. http://www.whitewallmag.com/art/mike-kelleys-mobile-homestead-arrives-in-detroit.

"Lindsay Lohan Money: Actress' Earnings and Debts in 2012." *Huffington Post*, December 12, 2012. http://www.huffingtonpost.com/2012/12/17/lindsay-lohan-money-actress-earnings-debts-2012_n_2317617.html.

Linkon, Sherry Lee, and John Russo. *Steeltown USA: Work and Memory in Youngstown*. Lawrence: University Press of Kansas, 2002.

Lipsitz, George. *The Possessive Investment in Whiteness: How White People Profit from Identity Politics*. Philadelphia: Temple University Press, 1998.

Lipton, Eric, and Stephen Labaton. "The Reckoning: Deregulator Looks Back, Unswayed." *New York Times*, November 16, 2008. http://www.nytimes.com/2008/11/17/business/economy/17gramm.html?pagewanted=all&_r=0.

Lloyd, Richard. *Neo-Bohemia: Art and Commerce in the Postindustrial City*. New York: Routledge, 2006.

Lott, Eric. *Love and Theft: Blackface Minstrelsy and the American Working Class*. New York: Oxford University Press, 1993.

Loveland Technologies. "Parcel Data and Property Ownership in Detroit, Wayne County, Michigan: McDougall Hunt." Accessed June 16, 2016. https://makeloveland.com/us/mi/wayne/detroit/mcdougall-hunt.

Lueck, Thomas J. "Record Industry Is Attacked by Top Star." *New York Times*, July 7, 2002. http://www.nytimes.com/2002/07/07/nyregion/record-industry-is-attacked-by-a-top-star.html.

Lyotard, Jean-François. *Discourse, Figure*. Translated by Antony Hudek and Mary Lydon. Minneapolis: University of Minnesota Press, 2011.

MacDonald, Christine. "Gilbert, Quicken Loans Entwined in Detroit Blight." *Detroit News*, July 1, 2015. http://www.detroitnews.com/story/news/special-reports/2015/07/01/quicken-loans-blight-dilemma/29537285/.

MacDonald, Christine. "Land Bank to Sell Properties to Occupants for $1,000." *Detroit News*, October 20, 2015. http://www.detroitnews.com/story/news/local/detroit-city/2015/10/20/detroit-land-bank-sell-properties-occupants/74292160/.

MacDonald, Christine, and Joel Kurth. "Special Report: Detroit Braces for a Flood of Tax Foreclosures." *Detroit News*, July 1, 2015. http://www.detroitnews.com/story/news/special-reports/2015/07/01/detroit-braces-flood-tax-foreclosures/29589915/.

MacIntosh, Jeane. "Jacko Got Off-Tracko, Rev. Al Says." *New York Post*, July 8, 2002. http://nypost.com/2002/07/08/jacko-got-off-tracko-rev-al-says/.

Madison, D. Soyini. "Foreword." In *Black Performance Theory*, edited by Thomas F. DeFrantz and Anita Gonzalez, vii–ix. Durham, NC: Duke University Press, 2014.

Mahmud, Tayyab. "Debt and Discipline." *American Quarterly* 64, no. 3 (September 2012): 469–94.

Malone, Jacqui. *Steppin' on the Blues: The Visible Rhythms of African American Dance*. Urbana: University of Illinois Press, 1996.

Manning, Harriet. *Michael Jackson and the Blackface Mask*. Surrey: Ashgate, 2013.

Manning, Susan. *Modern Dance, Negro Dance: Race in Motion*. Minneapolis: University of Minnesota Press, 2004.

Markeljevic, Ines. "Thriller Dance Script." Thrill the World, 2010. http://www.thrilltheworld.com/.

Marsh, David. "Mike Kelley and Detroit." In *Mike Kelley: Catholic Tastes*, exhibition catalog, edited by Elizabeth Sussman, 39–42. New York: Whitney Museum of American Art, 1993.

Martin, Randy. *Financialization of Daily Life*. Philadelphia: Temple University Press, 2002.

———. "A Precarious Dance, a Derivative Sociality." *TDR: The Drama Review* 56, no. 4 (Winter 2012): 62–77.

Maxey, Marc. "A Citizens Guide to Real Estate Investment Detroit." Accessed May 2, 2016. http://www.detroitcitizensguide.com/#detroit.

"Mayor Duggan's Development Chief Says Detroit Future City Is His Bible." *Deadline Detroit*, February 12, 2014. http://www.deadlinedetroit.com/articles/8331/mayor_duggan_s_development_chief_says_the_detroit_future_city_plan_is_his_bible#.VpZoLygmbww.

McCarren, Felicia M. *Dancing Machines: Choreographies of the Age of Mechanical Reproduction*. Stanford, CA: Stanford University Press, 2003.

McConachie, Bruce A. *Melodramatic Formations: American Theatre and Society, 1820–1870*. Iowa City: University of Iowa Press, 1992.

McDonald, Matthew, and Stephen Wearing. *Social Psychology and Theories of Consumer Culture*. London: Routledge, 2013.

McKenzie, Jon. *Perform or Else*. New York: Routledge, 2001.

Mercer, Kobena. "Monster Metaphors: Notes on Michael Jackson's Thriller." *Screen* 27, no. 1 (February 1986): 26–43.

Meredith, Robyn. "5 Days in 1967 Still Shake Detroit." *New York Times*, July 23, 1997. http://www.nytimes.com/1997/07/23/us/5-days-in-1967-still-shake-detroit.html?pagewanted=all.

Merle, Renae. "Minorities Hit Harder by Foreclosure Crisis." *Washington Post*, June 19, 2010. http://www.washingtonpost.com/wp-dyn/content/article/2010/06/18/AR2010061802885.html.

Mescher, Richard. "Timely Filing of Patent Applications: Lessons Learned from Michael Jackson and Smooth Criminal." *Technology Law Source*, December 31, 2013. http://www.technologylawsource.com/2013/12/articles/intellectual-property-1/timely-filing-patent-applications-lessons-learned-from-michael-jackson-and-smooth-criminal/.

Mesereau, Thomas. *Larry King Live*, June 14, 2006. *CNN.com Transcripts*. http://www.cnn.com/TRANSCRIPTS/0506/14/lkl.01.html.

Meyer, Stephen III. *The Five Dollar Day: Labor Management and Social Control in the Ford Motor Company*. Albany, NY: SUNY Press, 1981.

"Michael Jackson." Dance Heritage Coalition. Accessed May 14, 2015. http://www.dance-heritage.org/jackson.html.

"Michael Jackson Died Deeply in Debt." *Billboard*, June 26, 2009. http://www.billboard.com/articles/news/268276/michael-jackson-died-deeply-in-debt.

"Michael Jackson May Face a Cash Crunch." *CNN/People*, July 29, 2009. http://edition.cnn.com/2002/SHOWBIZ/Music/07/29/cel.jackson/.

"Michael Jackson—Six Years after Death Estate Generated $2 Billion." *TMZ.com*, June 25, 2015. http://www.tmz.com/2015/06/25/michael-jackson-6-years-death-anniversary-estate-money-billion-kids-children/.

"Michael Jackson's Meeting with the Gipper." *CNN Political Ticker*, June 26, 2009. http://politicalticker.blogs.cnn.com/2009/06/26/when-jackson-met-reagan/.

"Michael Jackson's Museum News." N.d. Accessed June 12, 2016. http://www.michaeljacksonsmuseum.com/news/.

Miller, Kiri. *Playing Along*. New York: Oxford University Press, 2012.

Miller, Michelle. "Detroit Water Shut-Offs Bring Scrutiny of the UN." *CBS News*, October 20, 2014. http://www.cbsnews.com/news/detroit-water-shut-offs-brings-u-n-scrutiny/.

Moore, Andrew. *Detroit Disassembled*. Akron, OH: Damiani/Akron Art Museum, 2010.

Moore, Heidi N. "John Thain's $35,000 'Commode on Legs' Outrage." *Wall Street Journal*, January 23, 2009. http://blogs.wsj.com/deals/2009/01/23/deal-journal-explainer-the-35000-commode-outrage/.

———. "Was Wall Street Drunk, Stupid, or Evil?" *Wall Street Journal*, July 23, 2008. http://blogs.wsj.com/deals/2008/07/23/was-wall-street-drunk-stupid-or-evil/.

Morisseau, Dominique. *Detroit '67*. London: Oberon Books, 2013.

Moten, Fred. "The Subprime and the Beautiful." *African Identities* 11, no. 2 (2013): 237–45.

Moten, Fred, and Stefano Harney. "Debt and Study." *e-flux Journal* 14 (March 2010). http://www.e-flux.com/journal/14/61305/debt-and-study/

Moy, Jon. "On Shinola, Detroit's Misguided White Night." *Four Pins*, March 26, 2014. http://fourpins.com/life/shinola-detroits-misguided-white-knight.

Moynihan, Colin. "Born in Brooklyn, Now Making a Motown Move." *New York Times*, December 7, 2014. http://www.nytimes.com/2014/12/08/arts/galapagos-art-space-will-make-detroit-its-home.html?_r=0.

M., S. "The Cheque Is in the Mail." *Economist Blog*, November 19, 2013. http://www.economist.com/blogs/democracyinamerica/2013/11/government-guaranteed-basic-income.

Mui, Ylan Q. "For Black Americans, Financial Damage from Subprime Implosion Is Likely to Last." *Washington Post*, July 8, 2012. https://www.washingtonpost.com/business/economy/for-black-americans-financial-damage-from-subprime-implosion-is-likely-to-last/2012/07/08/gJQAwNmzWW_story.html.

Mukherjee, Roopali. "Bling Fling: Commodity Consumption and the Politics of the 'Post-Racial.'" In *Critical Rhetorics of Race*, edited by Michael G. Lacy and Kent A. Ono, 178–94. New York: New York University Press, 2011.

Museum of Contemporary Art Detroit. "About: Mobile Homestead." *MOCADetroit.org*. Accessed June 13, 2013. http://www.mocadetroit.org/Mobile-Homestead.html.

"NAACP Legal Defense Fund: Detroit Water Service Shutoffs Are Discriminatory." *CBS Detroit*, July 21, 2014. http://detroit.cbslocal.com/2014/07/21/naacp-detroit-water-service-shutoffs-are-racially-motivated/.

Negri, Antonio. *Empire and Beyond*. Translated by Ed Emery. Cambridge: Polity, 2006.

Nelson, Bruce. *Divided We Stand: American Workers and the Struggle for Black Equality*. Princeton, NJ: Princeton University Press, 2001.

"New Industrial Era Is Marked by Ford's Shares to Laborers." *Detroit Free Press*, January 6, 1914, sec. 1+. ProQuest Historical Newspapers.

"New Museum Announces Ideas City Detroit Program: Public Conference April 30." *New Museum–Ideas City*, March 22, 2016. http://us1.campaignarchive1.com/?u=c6bf7cce2a64f8749424edd72&id=da521d4944.

Niebuhr, Reinhold. "Lessons of the Detroit Experience." *Christian Century* 82 (1965): 487–90

Nixon, Rob. *Slow Violence and the Environmentalism of the Poor*. Cambridge, MA: Harvard University Press, 2011.

"The Nixon-Presley Meeting 21 December 1970." National Security Archive, George Washington University. Accessed April 22, 2015. https://nsarchive.gwu.edu/nsa/elvis/elnix.html.

Noland, Carrie. *Agency and Embodiment.* Cambridge, MA: Harvard University Press, 2009.

Nyong'o, Tavia. "Have You Seen His Childhood? Song, Screen, and the Queer Culture of Childhood in Michael Jackson's Music." *Journal of Popular Music Studies* 23, no. 1 (2011): 40–57.

———. "The Scene of Occupation." *TDR: The Drama Review* 56, no. 4 (Winter 2012): 136–62.

"The Obama Plan to Rescue the Economy: Can We Afford It?" Transcript: *Face the Nation. CBS News,* March 9, 2009.

Oberholtzer, Michele. "Buying Detroit, Why a Not-So-Public Auction Could Devastate City Homeowners." *Occupy.com,* October 5, 2015. http://www.occupy.com/article/buying-detroit-why-not-so-public-auction-could-devastate-city-homeowners.

O'Brien, Timothy. "What Happened to the Fortune Michael Jackson Made?" *New York Times,* May 14, 2006. http://www.nytimes.com/2006/05/14/business/yourmoney/14michael.html?pagewanted=all&_r=1&.

O'Bryan, J. Duross. "Neverland Accounting." *Forbes,* July 2, 2009. http://www.forbes.com/2009/07/02/michael-jackson-bankruptcy-opinions-contributors-king-of-pop.html.

Oliete, Elena. "Michael, Are You Okay? You've Been Hit by a Smooth Criminal: Racism, Controversy, and Parody in the Video Clips 'Smooth Criminal' and 'You Rock My World.'" *Studies in Popular Culture* 29, no. 1 (October 2006): 57–76.

O'Toole, James, and Others. "Work in America." Report of a Special Task Force to the Secretary of Health, Education, and Welfare. Washington, DC: Department of Health, Education, and Welfare, 1972.

Pacheco, Patrick. "Playwright Lisa D'Amour on 'Detroit' and the Vultures of Mid-size American Decline." *BLOUINARTINFO International,* September 12, 2012. http://www.blouinartinfo.com/news/story/825086/playwright-lisa-damour-on-detroit-and-the-vultures-of-mid-size-american-decline.

Palley, Thomas I. "Financialization: What It Is and Why It Matters." Working Paper No. 525, Levy Economics Institute, Bard College, 2007.

Palmer, David. "Virtuosity as Rhetoric: Agency and Transformation in Paganini's Mastery of the Violin." *Quarterly Journal of Speech* 84, no. 3 (August 1998): 341–57.

Peck, Jamie. "Austerity Urbanism: American Cities under Extreme Economy." *City* 16, no. 6 (2012): 626–55.

Perillo, J. Lorenzo. "'If I Were Not in Prison, I Would Not Be Famous': Discipline, Choreography, and Mimicry in the Philippines." *Theatre Journal* 63, no. 4 (December 2011): 607–21.

Perry, Imani. *More Beautiful and More Terrible: The Embrace and Transcendence of Racial Inequality in the United States.* New York: New York University Press, 2011.

Peterson, Hayley. "Michael Jackson Owed $30 Million Annually in Interest Payments on the $500 Million in Debt He Accrued over Two Decades." *Daily Mail,* August 13, 2013. http://www.dailymail.co.uk/news/article-2391485/Michael-Jackson-paying-30MILLION-annually-just-payments-debt.html.

Phelan, Peggy. "'Just Want to Say': Performance and Literature, Jackson and Poirier." *PMLA* 125, no. 4 (2010): 942–47.

Phillips, Matt. "MarketBeat: Michael Jackson: Bank of America Got This Loan Off Its Books, but Should It Have?" *Wall Street Journal,* June 26, 2009. http://blogs.wsj.com/market-beat/2009/06/26/michael-jackson-bank-of-america-got-this-loan-off-its-books-but-should-it-have/.

Philipsen, Dirk. *The Little Big Number: How GDP Came to Rule the World and What to Do about It.* Princeton, NJ: Princeton University Press, 2015.

Pinho, Kirk. "Galapagos Art Space's Building Near Corktown for Sale for $6.25 Million." *Crain's Detroit Business,* January 7, 2016. http://www.crainsdetroit.com/article/20160107/BLOG016/160109866/galapagos-art-spaces-building-near-corktown-for-sale-for-6-25-million.

Pitts, Steven. "Organizing around Work in the Black Community: The Struggle against Bad Jobs Held by African Americans." In *Race and Labor Matters in the New U.S. Economy*, edited by Manning Marable, Immanuel Ness, and Joseph Wilson, 99–124. Lanham, MD: Rowman and Littlefield, 2006.

Pizzello, Chris. "Celebrity Bankruptcy: Mike Tyson, Donald Trump." *Los Angeles Times*, April 16, 2015. http://touch.latimes.com/#section/-1/gallery/p2p-77298571/?related=true.

Pollock, Della. "Performing Writing." In *The Ends of Performance*, edited by Peggy Phelan and J. Lane, 73–103. New York: New York University Press, 1998.

Pomerantz, Dorothy. "Michael Jackson Tops Forbes' List of Top-Earning Dead Celebrities, With $140 Million Haul." *Forbes*, October 15, 2014. http://www.forbes.com/sites/dorothypomerantz/2014/10/15/michael-jackson-tops-forbes-list-of-top-earning-dead-celebrities/.

Poon, Kina. "Remembering Michael Jackson." *Dance Magazine*, September 2009. http://www.dancemagazine.com/issues/September-2009/Remembering-Michael-Jackson.

Porter, Eduardo. "Moving on from Farm and Factory." *New York Times*, April 27, 2016.

Porter, Tony. *Globalization and Finance*. Cambridge: Polity, 2005.

Prechel, Harland. "Steel and the State: Industry Politics and Business Policy Formation, 1940–1989." *American Sociological Review* 55 (1990): 648–68.

Pugh, Megan. *America Dancing: From the Cakewalk to the Moonwalk*. New Haven, CT: Yale University Press, 2015.

Pulley, Brett. "Michael Jackson's Ups and Downs." *Forbes*, November 21, 2003. http://www.forbes.com/2003/11/21/cz_1121jackson.html.

Pyke, Alan. "Everything You Need to Know about Detroit's Bankruptcy Settlement." *Think Progress*, November 8, 2014. http://thinkprogress.org/economy/2014/11/08/3590576/detroit-bankruptcy-conclusion-numbers/.

Rabinbach, Anson. *The Human Motor: Energy, Fatigue, and the Origins of Modernity*. New York: Basic Books, 1990.

Ragosti, Sonya, Tallese D. Johnson, Elizabeth M. Hoeffel, and Malcolm P. Drewery, Jr. "The Black Population: 2010." 2010 Census Briefs, September 2011. http://www.census.gov/prod/cen2010/briefs/c2010br-06.pdf.

Ranciere, Jacques. *The Flesh of Words: The Politics of Writing*. Translated by Charlotte Mandel. Stanford, CA: Stanford University Press, 2004.

Raphael, Timothy. *The President Electric: Ronald Reagan and the Politics of Performance*. Ann Arbor: University of Michigan Press, 2009.

Rawlins, J. W. "Letter to the Editor: Detroit Has Problem in Housing Conditions." *Detroit Free Press*, June 23, 1917. ProQuest Historical Newspapers.

Reason, Matthew, and Dee Reynolds. "Kinesthesia, Empathy, and Related Pleasures: An Inquiry into Audience Experiences of Watching Dance." *Dance Research Journal* 42, no. 2 (2010): 49–75.

Reed, Adolph. "Reinventing the Working Class." *New Labor Forum* 13, no. 3 (Fall 2004). doi:10.1080/748900131.

Reindl, J. C. "Why Detroit's Lights Went Out." *USA Today*, November 17, 2013. http://www.usatoday.com/story/news/nation/2013/11/17/detroit-finances-dark-streetlights/3622205/.

Reinhardt, K. "Theaster Gates's Dorchester Project in Chicago." *Journal of Urban History* 41, no. 2 (March 2015): 193–206.

Reyes Taubman, Julia. *Detroit: 138 Square Miles*. Detroit: Museum of Contemporary Art Detroit, 2011.

Riddle, Mason. "On the Fringe: Interview with Richard Florida." *Public Art Review* 20.1, no. 39. Accessed April 5, 2016. http://www.creativeclass.com/rfcgdb/articles/Interview%20 with%20Richard%20Florida.pdf.

Roach, Joseph. *Cities of the Dead: Circum-Atlantic Performance*. New York: Columbia University Press, 1996.

Roberts, Tamara, and Brandi Wilkins Catanese, eds. Special issue, *Journal of Popular Music Studies* 23, no. 1 (May 2011): 1–143.

Robertson, Aaron. "The Future Was Already Here: Detroit's Afrofuturist Enclaves." *Metro Times*, August 10, 2016. Accessed August 12, 2016, http://www.metrotimes.com/detroit/the-future-was-already-here-detroits-afrofuturist-enclaves/Content?oid=2459448.

Rodowick, D. N. *Reading the Figural, Or, Philosophy after the New Media*. Durham, NC: Duke University Press, 2001.

Roediger, David R. *The Wages of Whiteness: Race and the Making of the American Working Class*. Revised and expanded edition. London: Verso, 2007.

Rogers, Thomas. "The Life and Death of a 'Cool' City." *New Republic*, September 12, 2014. https://newrepublic.com/article/119394/new-berlin-rise-and-fall-cool-cities.

Rosenthal, Mark. *Diego Rivera and Frida Kahlo in Detroit*. Detroit: Detroit Institute of Arts, 2015.

Rose, Tricia. "A Style Nobody Can Deal With: Politics, Style, and the Postindustrial City in Hip Hop." In *Microphone Fiends: Youth Music and Youth Culture*, edited by Andrew Ross and Tricia Rose, 71–88. New York: Routledge, 1994.

Rosler, Martha. "Culture Class: Art, Creativity, Urbanism, Part II." *e-flux* 23, no. 3 (2011). http://www.e-flux.com/journal/culture-class-art-creativity-urbanism-part-ii/.

Rottenberg, Josh. "Michael Jackson's Movie Ambitions Included 3-D Film of 'Thriller,' 'Red Shoes' Remake." *Entertainment Weekly*, October 30, 2009. http://www.ew.com/article/2009/10/30/michael-jackson-movie-ambitious.

Rowthorn, Robert, and Ramana Ramaswamy. "Deindustrializaiton—Its Causes and Implications." *Economic Issues*, no. 10. Washington, DC: International Monetary Fund, 1997.

Rupersburg, Nicole. "Mike Kelley's Last Homecoming." *Model D Media*, May 14, 2013. http://www.modeldmedia.com/features/mikekelley513.aspx.

Ryan, Brent D. *Design after Decline: How America Rebuilds Shrinking Cities*. Philadelphia: University of Pennsylvania Press, 2012.

Ryzik, Melena. "For Detroit Artists, Almost Anything Goes." *New York Times*, July 15, 2015. http://www.nytimes.com/2015/07/16/arts/design/for-detroit-artists-almost-anything-goes.html.

Salpukas, Agis. "U.S. Steel Earnings in 3d Quarter Fell 75.9% to $27 Million." *New York Times (1923-Current File)*. October 26, 1977. The New York Times (1851–2007). ProQuest Historical Newspapers.

Samson, Jim. *Virtuosity and the Musical Work: The Transcendental Studies of Liszt*. Cambridge: Cambridge University Press, 2003.

Savigliano, Marta. "Worlding Dance and Dancing Out There in the World." In *Worlding Dance*, edited by Susan Leigh Foster, 163–90. Basingstoke: Palgrave Macmillan, 2011.

Savran, David. *Highbrow/Lowdown: Theater, Jazz, and the Making of the New Middle Class*. Ann Arbor: University of Michigan Press, 2009.

Schechner, Richard. *Between Theater and Anthropology*. Philadelphia: University of Pennsylvania Press, 1985.

Schneider, Rebecca. *Performing Remains: Art and War in Times of Theatrical Reenactment*. New York: Routledge, 2011.

Schui, Florian. *Austerity: The Great Failure*. New Haven, CT: Yale University Press, 2014.

See, Sarita. "Gambling with Debt: Lessons from the Illiterate." *American Quarterly* 64, no. 3 (September 2012): 495–514.

Sharlet, Jeff. "Bully Pulpit: Donald Trump, American Preacher." *New York Times Magazine*, April 17, 2016.

Shaw, Len G. "Detroit's New Housing Problem." *Detroit Free Press*, June 3, 1917, sec. E1. ProQuest Historical Newspapers.

Shea, Bill. "On Cost, Financing of Wings Arena: Here Are the Answers." *Crain's Detroit Business*, September 21, 2014. http://www.crainsdetroit.com/article/20140921/NEWS/309219990/on-cost-financing-of-wings-arena-here-are-answers.

Sheridan, David M. "Making Sense of Detroit." *Michigan Quarterly Review* 38, no. 4 (1999). http://quod.lib.umich.edu/cgi/t/text/text-idx?cc=mqr;c=mqr;c=mqrarchive;idno=act2080.0038.301;rgn=main;view=text;xc=1;g=mqrg.

Shimpach, Shawn. "Realty Reality: HGTV and the Subprime Crisis." *American Quarterly* 64, no. 3 (September 2012): 515–42.

Shkuda, Aaron. *The Lofts of SoHo: Gentrification, Art, and Industry in New York, 1950–1980.* Chicago: University of Chicago Press, 2016.

Silva, Jennifer M. *Coming Up Short: Working-Class Adulthood in an Age of Uncertainty.* New York: Oxford University Press, 2013.

Singer, Ben. *Melodrama and Modernity: Early Sensational Cinema and Its Contexts.* New York: Columbia University Press, 2001.

Skocpol, Theda, and Vanessa Williamson. *The Tea Party and the Remaking of Republican Conservatism.* New York: Oxford University Press, 2012.

Smardz Frost, Karolyn. *I've Got a Home in Glory Land: A Lost Tale of the Underground Railroad.* New York: Farrar, Straus and Giroux, 2007.

Smit, Christopher R., ed. *Michael Jackson: Grasping the Spectacle.* Surrey: Ashgate, 2012.

Smith, Ethan, and Kate Kelley. "Michael Jackson's Other Battle: Staving Off Financial Disaster." *Wall Street Journal*, June 8, 2005. http://www.wsj.com/news/articles/SB111819644592353818?mg=reno64-wsj.

Smith, Roberta. "In Detroit, a Case of Selling Art and Selling Out." *New York Times*, September 10, 2013.

Smith, Suzanne E. *Dancing in the Street: Motown and the Cultural Politics of Detroit.* Cambridge, MA: Harvard University Press, 1999.

Smith, William H. "The Drunkard; Or, The Fallen Saved; A Moral Domestic Drama in Five Acts: The Acting Edition, No. 136 (New York: WM Taylor and Co. 1850)." In *Uncle Tom's Cabin,* dir. Stephen Railton, Act I, Scene 1; Act III Scene 1. Institute for Advanced Technology in the Humanities, Electronic Text Center, University of Virginia, 2002. http://utc.iath.virginia.edu/sentimnt/snplwhsal1t.html.

Snow, Richard. "Henry Ford's Experiment to Build a Better Worker." *Wall Street Journal*, May 9, 2013. http://online.wsj.com/article/SB10001424127887324059704578471112978065632.html.

Soloski, Alexis. "Detroit '67: Get Ready." *Village Voice*, March 13, 2013. http://www.village-voice.com/2013-03-13/theater/detroit-67-get-ready/full/.

Soriano, Cesar G. "Michael Jackson Announces 10-Concert Comeback." *USA Today*, March 5, 2009. http://usatoday30.usatoday.com/life/music/news/2009-03-05-jackson-comeback_N.htm.

Stanley, Alessandra. "Television Review; A Neverland World of Michael Jackson." *New York Times*, February 6, 2003. http://www.nytimes.com/2003/02/06/arts/television-review-a-neverland-world-of-michael-jackson.html.

Stanton, Cathy. *The Lowell Experiment: Public History in a Postindustrial City.* Amherst: University of Massachusetts Press, 2006.

Stein, Judith. *Pivotal Decade: How the United States Traded Factories for Finance in the Seventies.* New Haven, CT: Yale University Press, 2010.

———. *Running Steel, Running America: Race, Economic Policy and the Decline of Liberalism.* Chapel Hill: University of North Carolina Press, 1998.

Stern, Mark J., and Susan C. Seifert. "From Creative Economy to Creative Society." *Grantmakers in the Arts Reader* 19, no. 3 (Fall 2008). http://www.giarts.org/reader-19-3.

Sternheimer, Karen. *Celebrity Culture and the American Dream: Stardom and Social Mobility.* New York: Routledge, 2011.

Stewart, Kathleen. *Ordinary Affects.* Durham, NC: Duke University Press, 2007.

Stiglitz, Joseph. "Moral Bankruptcy." *Mother Jones*, February 2010. http://www.motherjones.com/politics/2010/01/joseph-stiglitz-wall-street-morals.

Stolberg, Sheryl Gay. "A Private, Blunter Bush Declares, 'Wall Street Got Drunk.'" *New York Times*, July 23, 2008. http://www.nytimes.com/2008/07/23/washington/23bush.html?_r=0.

Stone, Chad. "Austerity Prolongs the Pain." *U.S. News & World Report*, September 5, 2014. http://www.usnews.com/opinion/economic-intelligence/2014/09/05/recession-austerity-spending-cuts-have-had-lasting-impact-on-jobs.

Stryker, Mark. "The End, and a New Beginning, for Detroit's Iconic Heidelberg Project." *Detroit Free Press*, August 14, 2016. http://www.freep.com/story/entertainment/arts/2016/08/14/heidelberg-project-guyton-dismantle/88626738/.

Stryker, Mark, and John Gallagher. "DIA's Art Collection Could Face Sell-Off to Satisfy Detroit's Creditors." *Detroit Free Press*, May 24, 2013. http://www.freep.com/article/20130523/NEWS01/305230154/DIA-Kevyn-Orr-Detroit-bankruptcy-art.

Sugrue, Thomas. *The Origins of the Urban Crisis: Race and Inequality in Postwar Detroit.* Princeton, NJ: Princeton University Press, 2014.

Szalai, Jennifer. "First Words: The Tough Love of 'Austerity.'" *New York Times Magazine*, August 4, 2015.

Talen, Bill. *What Should I Do If Reverend Billy Is in My Store?* New York: New Press, 2003.

Taraborrelli, J. Randy. *Michael Jackson: The Magic and the Madness.* Basingstoke: Palgrave Macmillan, 2004.

———. *Michael Jackson: The Magic, the Madness, the Whole Story 1958–2009.* New York: Hachette, 2009.

Tarr, David G. "The Steel Crisis in the United States and the European Community: Causes and Adjustments." In *Issues in US-EC Trade Relations*, edited by Robert E. Baldwin, Carl Hamilton, and André Sapir, 173–98. Conference Report (National Bureau of Economic Research). Chicago: University of Chicago Press, 1988.

Terkel, Studs. *Working.* New York: HarperCollins, 1975.

"Text: President Bush Addresses the Nation." *Washington Post*, September 20, 2007. http://www.washingtonpost.com/wp-srv/nation/specials/attacked/transcripts/bushaddress_092001.html.

Thibodeau, Ian. "Dan Gilbert's Bedrock Tops 80 Properties Acquired in Downtown Detroit." *MLive.com*, January 6, 2016. http://www.mlive.com/business/detroit/index.ssf/2016/01/dan_gilberts_bedrock_moves_top.html#incart_story_package.

———. "With over $1.6 Billion Invested in Downtown Detroit, What Does Dan Gilbert Own?" *MLive.com*, February 20, 2015. http://www.mlive.com/business/detroit/index.ssf/2015/02/with_over_16_billion_invested.html.

Thomas, Richard W. *Life for Us Is What We Make It: Building Black Community in Detroit, 1915–1945.* Bloomington: Indiana University Press, 1992.

Toossi, Mitra. "Consumer Spending: An Engine for U.S. Job Growth." *Monthly Labor Review*, November 2002, 12–22.

Tsing, Anna Lowenhaupt. *Friction: An Ethnography of Global Connection.* Princeton, NJ: Princeton University Press, 2005.

Turbow, Will, Elizabeth A. Cloyd, and David C. Allen. "Northwest Indiana Pushes for Economic Development." *Indiana Business*, January 1986. ProQuest US Newsstream.

Turner, Victor. *From Ritual to Theatre: The Human Seriousness of Play.* New York: PAJ Publications, 1982.

Ubel, Peter A. *Free Market Madness: Why Human Nature Is at Odds with Economics.* Cambridge, MA: Harvard Business Review Press, 2009.

United Nations News Centre. "In Detroit, City-Backed Water Shut-Offs 'Contrary to Human Rights,' Say UN Experts." October 20, 2014. http://www.un.org/apps/news/story. asp?NewsID=49127#.VrI02igmbww.

US Bureau of Labor Statistics. "Detroit Area Economic Summary." April 30, 2014. www.bls. gov/regions/midwest/summary/blssummary_detroit.pdf.

US Census Bureau. "Figure 13.1: Unemployment Rate, by Race and Hispanic Origin: 1980–1998." Labor Force, Employment, and Earnings, May 1, 2015. *Statistical Abstracts of the United States* (1999). https://www.census.gov/prod/99pubs/99statab/sec13.pdf.

———. "Table 23. Michigan—Race and Hispanic Origin for Selected Large Cities and Other Places: Earliest Census to 1990." July 15, 2005. http://www.census.gov/population/ www/documentation/twps0076/MItab.pdf.

"U.S. Certifies 2,500 Steel Workers for Special Unemployment Help." *New York Times (1923-Current file)* 21 Sep. 1977, sec. Business and Finance. ProQuest Historical Newspapers.

US Congressional Budget Office. "The Effects of Import Quotas on the Steel Industry: A CBO Study." Washington, DC: Congressional Budget Office, July, 1984.

———. "Industrial Policy Debate." December 1983. Accessed May 1, 2015. https://www.cbo. gov/sites/default/files/98th-congress-1983-1984/reports/doc29a-entire.pdf.

US Department of Justice, Office of Public Affairs. "United States Files Lawsuit Alleging That Quicken Loans Improperly Originated and Underwrote Federal Housing Administration-Insured Mortgage Loans." *Justice News*, April 23, 2015. http://www. justice.gov/opa/pr/united-states-files-lawsuit-alleging-quicken-loans-improperly-originated-and-underwrote.

US Department of Labor. "Labor Force Statistics from Current Population Survey: Unemployment Rate." Accessed May 16, 2015. http://data.bls.gov/timeseries/ LNU04000000?years_option=all_years&periods_option=specific_ periods&periods=Annual+Data.

US House of Representatives, Committee on the Budget. "The Path to Prosperity: Restoring America's Promise." *Fiscal Year 2012 Budget Resolution*, April 5, 2011.

Van der Zwan, Natascha. "Making Sense of Financialization." *Socioeconomic Review* 21, no. 1 (2014): 99–129.

Vineyard, Jennifer. "Michael Jackson Shocks Al Sharpton by Calling Tommy Mottola Racist." *MTV.com News.* Accessed January 10, 2015. http://www.mtv.com/news/1455976/ michael-jackson-shocks-al-sharpton-by-calling-tommy-mottola-a-racist/.

Virno, Paulo. *A Grammar of the Multitude.* Los Angeles: Semiotext(e), 2004.

———. *Multitude: Between Innovation and Negation.* Translated by Isabella Bertoletti, James Cascaito, and Andrea Casson. Los Angeles: Semiotext(e), 2008.

Vogel, Joseph. *Man in the Music: The Creative Life and Work of Michael Jackson.* New York: Sterling, 2011.

Walser, Robert. "Popular Music Analysis: Ten Apothegms and Four Instances." In *Analyzing Popular Music*, edited by Allan F. Moore, 16–38. New York: Cambridge University Press, 2003.

Walsh, Tom. "Can Duggan Change History of Failed Master Plans?" *Detroit Free Press*, February 26, 2015. http://www.freep.com/story/money/business/columnists/tom-walsh/ 2015/02/26/can-duggan-change-history-failed-master-plans/24087915/.

Walters, Wendy S. "Turning the Neighborhood Inside Out: Imagining a New Detroit in Tyree Guyton's Heidelberg Project." *TDR: The Drama Review* 45, no. 4 (Winter 2001): 64–93.

White, Hayden. *Figural Realism: Studies in the Mimesis Effect*. Baltimore: Johns Hopkins University Press, 1999.

Wickstrom, Maurya. *Performing Consumers: Global Capital and Its Theatrical Seductions*. New York: Routledge, 2006.

Wilkerson, Isabel. *The Warmth of Other Suns: The Epic Story of America's Great Migration*. New York: Random House, 2010.

Willett, John. *The Theatre of Bertolt Brecht: A Study from Eight Aspects*. London: Methuen, 1967.

Williams, Jeremy. *Images of America: Detroit—The Black Bottom Community*. Charleston, SC: Arcadia, 2009.

Williams, Linda. "Melodrama Revised." In *Reconfiguring American Film Genres: History and Theory*, edited by Nick Browne, 42–88. Berkeley: University of California Press, 1998.

———. *Playing the Race Card: Melodramas of Black and White from Uncle Tom to O. J. Simpson*. Princeton, NJ: Princeton University Press, 2001.

Williamson, Kevin D. "Chaos in the Family, Chaos in the State: The White Working Class's Dysfunction." *National Review*, March 28, 2016. http://www.nationalreview.com/article/432876/donald-trump-white-working-class-dysfunction-real-opportunity-needed-not-trump.

Williams, Raymond. *The Long Revolution*. Peterborough, ON: Broadview Encore Editions, 2001.

———. *Marxism and Literature*. Oxford: Oxford University Press, 1997.

———. *Problems in Materialism and Culture: Selected Essays*. New York: Verso, 1980.

Winnicott, D. W. *Playing and Reality*. New York: Tavistock, 1971.

Wolf, Stacy. *A Problem Like Maria: Gender and Sexuality in the American Musical*. Ann Arbor: University of Michigan Press, 2002.

Woosley, Ben. "Credit Card Industry and Personal Debt Statistics (2005 and Prior)." *Credit Card News*, September 13, 2007. http://www.creditcards.com/credit-card-news/credit-card-statistics-2005-prior-1276.php.

"Word of the Year." Merriam-Webster, Inc. December 20, 2010. http://www.merriam-webster.com/word-of-the-year/2010-word-of-the-year.htm.

"Workers Must Live Decently." *Detroit Free Press*, April 18, 1914, sec. 1+. ProQuest Historical Newspapers.

Wren, Anne, ed. *The Political Economy of Service Transition*. New York: Oxford University Press, 2013.

Wright, Nathan. "Portraits of the Stars: What They May Look Like in the Year 2000." *Ebony*, August 1985.

Yaccino, Steven, and Michael Cooper. "Cries of Betrayal as Detroit Plans to Cut Pensions." *New York Times*, July 21, 2013. http://www.nytimes.com/2013/07/22/us/cries-of-betrayal-as-detroit-plans-to-cut-pensions.html?pagewanted=2&_r=0 Page.

Zukin, Sharon. *Loft Living: Culture and Capital in Urban Change*. Baltimore: Johns Hopkins University Press, 1982.

INDEX

Note: Bold page numbers refer to figures

financialization (*cont.*)
  figures of African Americans and, 16–17,
    63, 70, 87, 154, 190
  ideal subject of, 56, 74, 77, 83–84, 102
  irrationality of, 56, 61, 67, 70, 77–79,
    85, 187
  as melodrama, 60–63, 80–84, 90, 147
  Michael Jackson as figure of, 2, 15, 16,
    54–102, 147, 194
  moralization in, 55, 62, 78–87, 95–96,
    219n122
  neoliberalism and, 58–59, 74, 79, 83, 87,
    90, 92, 219n129, 220n136
  operations of, 6, 54, 58–59, 68, 74,
    86–87, 95–96
  race and, 12, 16–17, 56, 62–63, 70, 77,
    80–81, 87–90, 95, 154, 169–70, 186–90
  representations of, 2, 4, 12, 14–16, 15, 16,
    54–102, 147, 194
  role in Detroit, 109, 147–48, 150, 154–55,
    162, 169–70, 186–87, 233n26
  See also credit bubble; debt
Finley, Nolan, 145
fiscal innocence, 89–90
Forbes Magazine, 77
Ford, Henry, xiii, 11, 155, 182, 184, 225n28
  Five Dollar Day, 73, 124, 129, 228n97
  racially gendered decency bargain, 117–18,
    124–44, 185
  "rescue" of Inkster, 117–18, 124,
    225n28, 226n43
  See also Fordism
Ford Hunger March Massacre, 164, 226n43
Fordism, 23, 50, 111, 122, 126, 179,
    185, 207n50
  definition, 11
  Detroit and, 2, 16, 170
  "good life," 8, 43, 172
  human motor in, 43–45
  labor-management compact and, 4, 10
  racially gendered, 29–30
  subjectivity, 25–27, 127
  See also Fordist bargain; post-Fordism
Fordist bargain, 8, 166, 170, 172
  decency and, 125–29
  in *Detroit*, 18, 128, 137–39, 228n104
  in *Detroit '67*, 18, 132
  labor-management compact, 4, 137
  in *Motown the Musical*, 18, 128
  private home and, 126–30

  racial and gendered decency and, 117–18,
    124–44, 185
  whiteness and, 124–44, 129–31, 135
  See also industrial-affective bargain
Ford Motor Company (FMC), 171, 181,
    200n6, 225n34
  Art of Manufacturing Theater,
    116–17, 225n38
  Five Dollar Day, 73, 124, 129, 228n97
  Hunger March Massacre, 164, 226n43
  Motown modeled after, 2, 39–40, 46,
    116, 122
  Racial and gendered decency bargain,
    117–18, 124–44, 185
  River Rouge plant, 116–17, 164,
    225n38, 226n43
  Sociological Department, 117, 124–27,
    133, 136
  Wayne Assembly Plant, 40
  See also Fordism
Forti, Simone, 233n29
Fortress Investment Group, 85
Fossil, 145
Foucault, Michel, 58
Foulkes, Julia L., 146
Four Tops, 109
  "Reach Out, I'll Be There," 112
Franko, Mark, 205n23
free trade
  criticisms of, 42, 190
  US steel industry and, 23
Friedman, Milton, 193, 219n129

Gagosian, Larry, 181
Galapagos Art Space, 185, 235n51
  Kunsthalle Galapagos, 156
  local response to, 156
  move to Detroit, 154
  as real estate venture, 155, 235n50
  See also Detroit Biennial
Gardner, Sally, 36
Gary, IN, 49, 56, 197
  mayors, 5, 47
  Michael Jackson's childhood in, xiv, 2, 21,
    23, 32, 39, 42, 46, 93, 96, 194–**95**
  Neverland and, 21, 24, 44, 50, 55, 58
  steel industry contraction effects, 7,
    11, 42, 96
Gates, Theaster, 151
  ArtHouse: A Social Kitchen, 194

racial integration, 29–30, 47, 50, 130, 133, 229n115

racial segregation, xiii, 5, 29–30, 118, 127, 129–31, 134–35, 139–42, 169–71, 212n126, 226n53, 242n153. *See also* redlining

racism, xii–xiv, 6, 18, 29, 40, 105, 111, 121, 133, 153, 178, 181, 196, 228n104
  austerity and, 95–96
  challenges to, 15, 33, 39, 47, 50, 122, 132, 170
  color-blindness and, 63, 146–48, 152, 187
  consumption and, 17, 76
  Detroit housing and, 30, 118, 123, 127, 129–31, 134–35, 139–42, 169–71, 226n53, 242n153
  Detroit police and, 112–13, 118, 133–34, 140–41, 144, 164, 178
  dismissals of African American unemployment and, 30, 47, 95
  figurations of Detroit as blank slate and, 148, 152
  financialization and, 63, 78, 81, 83, 90
  Henry Ford and, 117–18, 127–39
  industrialization and, 7–8, 11, 30, 46, 47, 129–30, 142, 196–97, 209n86, 237n80
  kunst-washing and, 157–61
  in music industry, 44, 64–65, 109, 131
  racist violence in *Detroit '67*, 111–13, 122, 133–34, 140–41, 143–44, 229n115
  Reagan administration and, xi, 5, 30
  steel industry and, 7, 46–47
  subprime loan crisis and, 5, 17, 63, 81, 87–88, 90–91, 192
  Trump presidential campaign and, 189–93
  unions and, 46–47, 209n86
  water shutoffs, 168
  welfare queen figure, 5, 23, 87–88, 95, 189, 221n145
  See also blackface minstrelsy; redlining; slavery

Racism in the Music Industry Summit, 64

Rainer, Yvonne, 35

Rawls, Lou
  All Things in Time, 176

Ray, Ola, 37–38, 49

Reagan, Nancy, 21–**22**, 25
  "Just Say No" campaign, 23

Reagan, Ronald, xi, 5–6, 42, 47, 58, 87, 95, 189, 204n10

visit with Michael Jackson, 17, **22**–23, 53, 204n4

Reagan Democrats, xi, xi–xii, 5, 8, 30, 189

Red Bull House of Art (Detroit, MI), 158

redlining, 18, 169–70. *See also* racial segregation

"The Red Shoes," 53
  as austerity figure, 17, 93, 97, 99
  as melodrama, 17, 93–94
  Michael Jackson's interest in, 93
  parallels with Michael Jackson's life, 17, 98–100, 102, 221n165
  plot summary, 92–93

Reed, Adolph, 30

Regis Galerie (Las Vegas, NV), 17, 69, 71, 74

"Report on Work" (1972), 192–93

Republican Budget Resolution of 2012, 102

Republican Party, xi, 11, 95–96, 102, 115, 149, 189–90, 193, 221n145, 222n177, 235n57

re-siting/re-citing, 18, 35
  definition, 119
  haunting and, 122–39
  performativity and, 107
  theater and, 115, 118–40, 144

"restorative nostalgia" (Boym), 192

Reverend Billy (Bill Talen), 72

Rhodes, Steven, 168

Richard, Gabriel, 148

right-to-work laws, 11

Rihanna, 194

Rivera, Diego
  Detroit Industry murals, 146, 162–64, 230n7, 237n80

Roach, Joseph, 119, 141, 218n81, 226n51

Rock Ventures, 154

Rodowick, D. N., 14

Roediger, David, 8, 209n86

Romanticism, 15, 28, 31, 34, 38, 99

Romero, George
  Dawn of the Dead, 49

Roosevelt, Franklin, 140, 199n2

Rose, Tricia, 26–27

Ross, Diana, 109–10, 128

Rupersburg, Nicole, 242n166

Rust Belt, 5–6, 11, 23, 27, 29–30, 55, 119, 191

Ryan, Amy, **108**

Sacco and Vanzetti funerals, 164

Santa Barbara County, CA, 62, 66, 80–81, 87

Santelli, Rick, 87

Michael Jackson's mental state during rehearsals for, 101
Michael Jackson's pleasure in, 97, 100
rehearsals, 17, 93, 97, 99, 101
Thriller, 23, 53–56, 72, 83, 102, 190, 213n147
dancing in, xiv, 2, 17, 26, 36–37, 45, 47–51, 97, 212n133
LP in *Heidelberg Project*, 14, **177**
mis en scène of, 47, 49
Tiller, John, 211n110
transitional object, 24–25, 205n18
transitional subject, 17, 32, 47–48, 54–55, 91
celebrities and, 24–25
Travolta, John, 7
Trudeau, Gary, 204n10
Trump, Donald, 57, 196, 214n14
"birtherism" of, 189
nostalgia in appeal of, 191–92
race(-ism) in presidential campaign of, 189–93, 197
as "strongman", 191
use of "law and order", 191
Tsing, Anna Lowenhaupt, 59–60
Turner, Victor, 225n28
Tyco, 71, 82
Tyson, Mike, 57, 214n14

UBS, 63
Uncle Tom's Cabin, 61–63, 81, 89
United Auto Workers, xiii, 11
United Nations, 168
United Steelworkers of America, 42, 47
US Steel, 40, 42, 54
USX, 42. *See also* US Steel

van Eikels, Kai, 204n15
Village Voice, 112
Virno, Paolo, 10–11, 31–32, 207n50, 207n52, 207n53, 207n55, 213n152
virtuosity, 110, 207n54
alienation and identification in, 33–34
Michael Jackson and, 17, 23–27, 30–45, 48–51, 54–56, 70, 74, 91, 99, 101, 193–94, 207n52, 213n152
in "normal" sense, 31–32
as plot, 34
in popular performance, 26, 27, 31–35
post-Fordism and, 31, 204n15, 231n9

as relational, 17, 31–32, 207n53, 207n55
as virtuous labor, 30–39, 51, 211n112
Vogue, 145

Walker, Denise Jordan, 21
Wallace, George, xiii, 30
Wall Street Journal, 54, 214n5
Walser, Robert, 34
Walters, Wendy S., 171, 176, 179
War on Drugs, 22–23
War on Poverty, 118
Wayne County, MI, 152, 166–67, 234n36
Wayne State University, xi, xiii, 153, 181
WDET-FM, xi, xiii
Weis, Cathy, 233n29
welfare queen figure, 5, 23, 87–88, 95, 189, 221n145
West, Kanye, 194
White, Hayden, 13–14
whiteness, 23, 40, 87, 136, 172, 224n27, 235n57
austerity and, 95
consumption and, 76
dance and, 43–44, 46, 50, 211n112
deindustrialization and, xii, 7–8, 26, 29–30, 41, 63, 113, 117, 128, 140–42, 186, 189–92
Detroit population, xiii, 5–8, 13, 109, 112–13, 117, 119, 123, 128–30, 132–35, 139–42, 145, 147, 161, 166, 178–79, 181, 183, 185–86, 189, 196–97, 199n3, 225n40, 228n97, 242n153
in Detroit redevelopment, 145, 147, 157, 186–87
Detroit residential segregation and, xiii, 5, 29–30, 118, 127, 129–31, 133–35, 139–42, 169–71, 212n126, 226n53, 242n153
Fordist bargain and, 124–44, 129–31, 135
in industrial era, 8, 41, 44, 46–48, 63, 120, 127–30, 133–35, 209n86
Michael Jackson and, 24, 26, 32, 44, 46, 50, 58, 64–65, 72, 81
in *Mobile Homestead*, 183–85
Motown and, 113, 123
presumptive spectatorship and, 117, 138
Reagan Democrats, xi–ii, 5, 8, 30, 189
in *Saturday Night Fever*, 27–29, 206n35
in theater casting, 107, 109, 112
Trump presidential campaign and, 189–93
white childhood, 89
white flight, 6, 119, 166, 183, 187, 241n149